The Predatory Sea

EARLY AMERICAN STUDIES

Series editors: Kathleen M. Brown, Roquinaldo
Ferreira, Emma Hart, and Daniel K. Richter

Exploring neglected aspects of our colonial, revolutionary, and early
national history and culture, Early American Studies reinterprets
familiar themes and events in fresh ways. Interdisciplinary
in character, and with a special emphasis on the period from
about 1600 to 1850, the series is published in partnership
with the McNeil Center for Early American Studies.

A complete list of books in the series is available from the publisher.

The Predatory Sea

Human Trafficking and Captivity in the
Seventeenth-Century Caribbean

Casey Schmitt

PENN

UNIVERSITY OF PENNSYLVANIA PRESS

PHILADELPHIA

Publication of this book was supported by a grant from the
Hull Memorial Publication Fund of Cornell University.

Published by
University of Pennsylvania Press
Philadelphia, Pennsylvania 19104-4112
www.pennpress.org

Printed in the United States of America on acid-free paper
10 9 8 7 6 5 4 3 2 1

A Cataloging-in-Publication record is
available from the Library of Congress.

Hardback ISBN 978-1-5128-2814-6
Ebook ISBN 978-1-5128-2815-3

To Ben, for everything, always

Only when we focus on what ordinary people are actually doing, rather than on what they should be doing, can we see the broader picture of reality.

—Epeli Hauʻofa, "Our Sea of Islands"

CONTENTS

PREFACE

This book emerged, after many false starts, from a simple research question. If the Spanish had engaged in slavery in the Americas for over a century before the English and French established their own colonies, did that influence how and why the English and French adopted slavery in the Caribbean? Put another way, did slavery as it existed in the Spanish Caribbean shape how it would evolve in neighboring English and French colonial societies? In attempting to answer that question over a decade of research, however, I encountered a surprising dissonance between what I read in the archives, especially in Spain's colonial archives, and what I had expected to find based on the standard account of English and French colonial development in the Caribbean. As I struggled to reconcile these increasingly divergent portraits of the century between 1570 and 1670, I became convinced of the need to prioritize Spanish archival and secondary sources as a way to write a different history of the English and French Caribbean. This book is the result of that conviction. What follows is my attempt to understand a century of Caribbean history from the perspectives of the people whose testimonies I encountered in the Spanish colonial archives.

As I tried to reconcile the portrait of the early Caribbean that emerged from Spanish sources, I confronted a secondary literature on English and French Caribbean colonization that tended to be written with specific objectives. With important exceptions, the history of the sixteenth- and seventeenth-century Caribbean is dominated by studies of the eighteenth-century sugar plantation complex.[1] That scholarly emphasis is not without reason. The widespread adoption of slave-based sugar plantation agriculture transformed the Caribbean in the eighteenth century, turning islands like Jamaica, Barbados, Martinique, and Saint-Domingue into the wealthiest colonies of the British and French empires. By the mid-eighteenth century, Jamaica went from being a relatively neglected outpost of the Spanish Caribbean to the home of Britain's most impressive naval squadron and the source of wealth for the empire's most influential subjects. It was also a charnel house, where the industrial

production of sugar killed enslaved Africans and their descendants at appalling rates. Like Saint-Domingue, the wealth derived by white elites in Jamaica
came from a horrifyingly efficient system of labor transportation in the form
of the transatlantic slave trade and the will of imperial elites to protect and
foster this system of naked exploitation.[2] The wealth produced through the
violence of racialized plantation slavery in the eighteenth-century Caribbean
fueled empires, their subjects, and growing capitalist industries in Europe.[3]
Sugar transformed the Caribbean along with the wider Atlantic world and, as
a result, much of the scholarship on the seventeenth-century Caribbean has
sought to explain the origins of that eighteenth-century world.[4]

When I began the research that became the core of this book, the historiographic tendency to treat earlier centuries as a prelude to the eighteenth
century influenced what I expected to find in the archives. Even my original
research question was shaped by a desire to explain the social and legal origins of the societies of the eighteenth-century Caribbean. I expected to find
evidence of the process by which English and French colonists learned how
to exploit enslaved labor by mimicking preexisting Spanish and Portuguese
models in the Caribbean and Brazil.[5] I also expected to find evidence of legal
borrowing through which the English and French created legal statutes and
codes to reinforce racialized slavery by drawing on Spanish precedents.[6] And
I assumed that islands such as Barbados, Jamaica, or Saint-Domingue would
provide the most archival evidence since race-based plantation agriculture
assumed its most productive and brutal form in those spaces.

None of those expectations or assumptions bore themselves out when
I began to work in Spain's colonial archives. I did not encounter a process
whereby the English and French gradually turned to slavery as a result of
the rise of plantation agriculture. Rather, I found evidence of an immediate
engagement on the part of ship captains, mariners, and merchants with slavery that predated English and French colonization in the Caribbean. Nor
did the geographic concerns of Spanish sources seem to fit what I expected.
Islands that tend not to garner much attention in the secondary literature—
largely because they failed to become wealth-producing behemoths in the
eighteenth century—appeared again and again in Spanish sources. Places
like St. Christopher, Tortuga, and Providencia preoccupied Spanish officials
and seemed to be important islands for sixteenth- and seventeenth-century
English and French sailors, ship captains, and, eventually, metropolitan officials interested in investing in colonies. Archival sources that failed to add
up to my expectations convinced me of the need to start with what those

sources were actually describing rather than what I had assumed that I would find in them.

And one thing kept coming up in the Spanish archival sources that I read. Throughout the letters and reports from the sixteenth- and seventeenth-century Spanish Caribbean, I encountered testimonies that centered on experiences of captivity and human trafficking. Those testimonies came from both captives and their captors. African and Indigenous inhabitants of the Spanish Caribbean, free and enslaved, attested to being seized from ships or during raids on coastal communities, port towns, or inland settlements. Their captors, often multinational companies of European traffickers, transported them away from their communities of belonging in order to profit from selling them into slavery elsewhere. Prior to the 1620s, those captives were often sold into slavery in commercially underserved parts of the Spanish Caribbean. After the 1620s, English, French, and Dutch colonies became common destinations.

Some people liberated themselves from captivity through marronage or, in the aqueous geography of the Caribbean, by escaping to neighboring islands through maritime marronage. Self-liberated captives who escaped to Spanish Caribbean islands testified before officials on those islands about their experiences, providing a rich archival record of captivity over this century of Caribbean history. Captors, too, left archival traces of their activities when the Spanish took the occasional prisoner following thwarted raids or attempts at trade. Under interrogation, traffickers described the nature of what I began to think of as slaving practices involving captive-taking and human trafficking that looked very different from the transatlantic slave trade and plantation complex of the eighteenth century.[7] Testimonies that at first seemed extraordinary and incongruent with the secondary literature began to look appallingly unremarkable the more I read in the Spanish colonial archives. That realization served as the spark for this book.

Spain's colonial archives are not the usual repository for historians of the English or French Caribbean. But, when read alongside English and French sources, Spanish archival documents and the scholarship produced by historians of the Spanish Caribbean revealed a deeply entangled sixteenth- and seventeenth-century Caribbean world in which subjects of different monarchs, Africans and their descendants, and Indigenous populations interacted, conducted business, formed alliances, fought, raided, and enslaved one another. Taken in the aggregate, those interactions were formative for English and French colonial development in the Caribbean during the seventeenth century. That experience shaped where and how those colonies—and the subsequent trade in enslaved people throughout the greater Caribbean—developed over a century of Caribbean history.

The Caribbean was a complex, dynamic world defined by unfreedom well before the eighteenth century. That said, this is not a book that seeks to narrate a pre-history or explain the origins of that eighteenth-century world. Rather, the focus here is on the experiences and perspectives of people whose lives traversed the greater Caribbean by choice or coercion between 1570 and 1670. It is, in other words, a book about the historical strategies of specific people—captors and their captives—in the context of a particular moment. Opportunism, marginality, and vulnerability shaped the choices of individual actors across this century of Caribbean history. To be sure, the consequences of those choices would influence the development of the eighteenth-century Caribbean. But that fact should not distract us from the experiences of a wide variety of people who were far more than predecessors to their eighteenth-century descendants. Centering the slaving strategies of captors and the responses of their captives reveals a world too often overshadowed by what would come next.

The Predatory Sea

Introduction

For a book about French and English slaving and colonization in the Caribbean, it seems appropriate to begin with Pierre Bélain d'Esnambuc, the man whom scholars describe as the father of the French Caribbean for his role in establishing the first Crown-sanctioned French colony in the region on the island of St. Christopher in 1627.[1] But rather than telling the more familiar story of his role as royal governor, I begin with the less well-known maritime activities that led to d'Esnambuc's position as royal governor of an island divided between the French and the English.[2] Doing so underscores a deeply entangled Caribbean world centered around captivity and human trafficking that predated either French or English colonization and that would continue to influence those colonies and the greater Caribbean throughout the seventeenth century.

In 1619, d'Esnambuc departed Le Havre in northern France as the captain of the *Marquise* with merchant financing and a commission to raid in Atlantic territories claimed by either Spain or Portugal.[3] He sailed to the Caribbean where he formed a company with an English and a Dutch ship and began raiding the shipping lanes and coastal communities of the Spanish Main near Cartagena de Indias. By late 1620, d'Esnambuc's multinational company of traffickers sailed to a tiny island called Caymito, located off the western tip of Hispaniola. They careened their vessels and restocked their supplies of food and water. Among the multinational sailors who labored to build huts, construct a forge, cut firewood, and sew canvas sails were an unspecified number of people of African descent whom d'Esnambuc and his companions had taken captive during the course of their raids along the Spanish Main.

At Caymito, d'Esnambuc and his companions also engaged in trade with the autonomous Maroon communities and Iberian settlers who lived just across the water along the Tiburon Peninsula of western Hispaniola. Central to those trade relations were the captives of African descent, who would

Map 1. Caymito and western Hispaniola

have found themselves trafficked into slavery at Hispaniola or elsewhere had a Spanish fleet not discovered d'Esnambuc's encampment at Caymito in January 1621. During the ensuing battle, the Spanish destroyed the English ship and took possession of the Dutch ship. Only the *Marquise* escaped the bay at Caymito. Rather than being sold into slavery in the Greater Antilles, the captives of African descent returned to Cartagena de Indias and its environs with the Spanish fleet. Meanwhile, d'Esnambuc and his crew escaped to the volcanic island chain of the Lesser Antilles in the eastern Caribbean, where European traffickers had long conducted a brisk trade with the Indigenous inhabitants of those islands, the Kalinago. It was in the Lesser Antilles that d'Esnambuc encountered a nascent English settlement on St. Christopher, which encouraged his transition from a career in trafficking to one as a colonizer on behalf of the French Crown.

While the story of d'Esnambuc as a ship captain involved in captive-taking and human trafficking in the western Caribbean is less familiar than his better-known career as a royal governor, it also reveals a Caribbean world shaped by practices of raiding and captive-taking that ensnared a wide variety of people. As the example of d'Esnambuc makes clear, these practices of captive-taking and human trafficking became deeply embedded in the earliest English and French colonies in the Caribbean, influencing the location and development of those subsequent colonies. And tracing the activities of individuals like d'Esnambuc also reveals glimpses into the lived experiences of captives who were forcibly dislocated by moments of violence. Before I turn to some of the conclusions drawn from these questions and their historiographic stakes, let me elaborate on d'Esnambuc's career as a trafficker and his role as royal governor. Doing so reveals the connections between captive-taking, human trafficking, and colonization that are central to the arguments presented in this book.

We left d'Esnambuc escaping from Caymito to the volcanic island chain of the Lesser Antilles in the eastern Caribbean.[4] Once there, he entered a crowded maritime scene, as French, English, and Dutch traffickers anchored at the island homelands of the Kalinago, who traded with Europeans for iron tools and weapons.[5] In exchange, Kalinago populations allowed traffickers to dwell temporarily on their islands and provided them with foodstuffs and tobacco.[6] Captivity and slaving practices were also central to these networks of intercultural trade. The Kalinago conducted raids against Spanish territories, especially Puerto Rico, where they took captives of European, African, and Indigenous descent.[7] Some captives found themselves incorporated into Kalinago societies while others were sold to European ship captains who turned a profit by ransoming them back to Spanish Caribbean territories.[8]

The trade in tobacco, however, drew the colonizing ambitions of merchant financiers in England and, in 1623, an Englishman named Thomas Warner arrived at the island of St. Christopher after fleeing a failed attempt to colonize Guiana.[9] The Kalinago offered the Englishmen housing and refreshment, as they had innumerable European sailors over the preceding half century, assuming as they did so that the Englishmen would leave as soon as their vessels were careened and water casks filled. But the Englishmen did not leave, nor could they dispossess the Kalinago alone. So, when d'Esnambuc and his crew arrived at St. Christopher, ostensibly to trade with the Kalinago, Warner permitted the French to settle alongside the English colony in exchange for an alliance of mutual defense against the Kalinago and neighboring Spanish colonies. The combined English and French forces defeated the Kalinago on St. Christopher and dispossessed them of the island. Some Kalinago survivors of the attack fled to neighboring islands controlled by Kalinago in the Lesser Antilles while others were enslaved by the English and French on St. Christopher.[10]

From there slaving played an immediate role in the development of the island colony. Ships of all nations called on early St. Christopher, and the enslaved population grew quickly as traffickers sold captives of African and Indigenous descent into slavery on the island.[11] By 1627, Warner and d'Esnambuc signed a treaty that contained provisions to control the mobility of enslaved and indentured people around the island. Those treaty provisions represented the first legal system referencing slavery in either the French or the English Caribbean, and they happened both long before the island transitioned to sugar plantation agriculture and before the island's population reached an enslaved majority.[12] The rapid adoption of slavery on St. Christopher reflected the fact that the French and English had experience with slavery through the efforts of men like d'Esnambuc to traffic captives into slavery in the Spanish Caribbean. Captivity and slaving practices shaped where and how the first non-Spanish colony developed in the Caribbean and became a part of life on that island colony from the very beginning.

Creating a Predatory Sea

The history sketched above situates early French and English colonization within an entangled, multicultural matrix of relationships and practices that developed over the half century leading up to the 1620s and that pivoted around captivity and slavery. Entangled history provides a methodology for understanding the sixteenth- and seventeenth-century Caribbean as an interconnected space of porous borders and dynamic intercultural interactions. At its most basic, entangled history, or *histoire croisée*, examines the multiple points of overlap, intersection, or crossover between different societies.[13] In histories of the Atlantic world, entangled history provides a framework for analyzing points of intersection between different empires and their subjects. As historian Eliga Gould has argued, such an approach casts the British Atlantic world as a periphery of the Spanish where relations between the two empires were "fundamentally asymmetric" because Spain was "the senior and historically preeminent" power.[14] From an Atlantic perspective, entangled history approaches reveal the ways in which Spain's cultural, economic, and political primacy in the Americas shaped how non-Iberians defined and enacted their own empires.[15]

Iberian precedents in the Atlantic world, then, shaped the activities of the English, French, and Dutch in the sixteenth- and seventeenth-century

Caribbean and created opportunities for English, French, and Dutch ship captains and merchants to engage in trade throughout the Spanish Caribbean. Access to captives who could be sold into slavery proved essential for traffickers who sought to establish trade relations, which Spain considered contraband, with Spanish Caribbean residents. For their part, Spanish Caribbean residents established informal trade relations with northern Europeans as a pragmatic way to access the markets of the Atlantic world. Geography mattered in terms of how those trade relations functioned. Larger and better-served ports were more vulnerable to raiding by northern European traffickers, while smaller and underserved ports were more receptive to informal trade with non-Iberian ship captains. By the mid-sixteenth century, for example, men like d'Esnambuc and his multinational company raided coastal communities and shipping near Cartagena de Indias in order to seize captives whom they trafficked into slavery in the commercially underserved western half of Hispaniola. It becomes clear that, through these practices of raiding and trafficking, English, French, and Dutch colonial and commercial activities in the Caribbean were deeply entangled with Iberian practices from the very beginning.

But entanglements in the Atlantic world went deeper than just those between imperial planners in Europe or between their subjects in the Americas.[16] So, while one approach to entangled history emphasizes imperial entanglements, scholars also use entangled history to decenter empires and to stress the importance of cross-cultural interactions. As scholars Marcy Norton and Ralph Bauer argue, entangled histories of the Atlantic world offer a way to trace "the agentive capacities" of a wide variety of people, many of whom "have traditionally been ignored as a result of both Eurocentric historiographic paradigms and the nature of the sources" available to historians.[17] If one model of entangled history traces how European elites imagined and enacted empire as a competitive and comparative process from the top down, an alternative model begins with the entanglements of a multiethnic assortment of people whose quotidian interactions shaped colonial and imperial development from the bottom up. As this approach suggests, European imperial planners could not enact their imperial ambitions in the Atlantic world as if extra-European spaces were blank slates. Europeans encountered powerful polities in the Americas and Atlantic Africa, which forced them to respond to political ecologies beyond their control and to negotiate relations of power with Indigenous and African peoples.[18]

Resistance to colonialism and enslavement on the part of Indigenous and African peoples created spaces outside of Spanish claims to authority in the sixteenth- and seventeenth-century Caribbean. Traffickers—ever keen on new markets but operating on the margins of European trade in the Caribbean and wider Atlantic world—established cross-cultural networks of trade and dependency with populations outside of Spanish authority as early as the mid-sixteenth century.[19] As the case of d'Esnambuc illustrates, traffickers found trade partners among both Maroon communities in the Greater Antilles and Kalinago populations in the Lesser Antilles. If the commercial and political structure of Iberian empires in the Atlantic world influenced the nature of French, English, and Dutch activities, in other words, so too did Spanish relations with Indigenous and African peoples in the sixteenth- and seventeenth-century Caribbean. Cross-cultural entanglements explain where and how France and England established their first colony in the Caribbean.

Cross-cultural relations were not static over the century of Caribbean history covered in this book. Dynamics on the ground shifted in response to local, regional, and Atlantic-wide changes, making some people more or less vulnerable to captivity and human trafficking at different moments. Susceptibility to captivity over this period depended on multiple factors. Because a market for enslaved people of African and Indigenous descent existed in the Spanish Caribbean and in subsequent English and French colonies, vulnerability often came down to race. Racially stigmatized people could be and were trafficked into slavery in colonial societies where racialized slavery was already in practice. But race was not the only factor that contributed to an individual's vulnerability to captivity.

Before the establishment of English, French, or Dutch colonies in the Caribbean, traffickers depended on regional allies for safe anchorages and access to supplies like food, wood, and water. The populations that welcomed traffickers, such as the Kalinago or Maroon communities throughout the Greater Antilles, were of Indigenous or African descent, but only rarely did traffickers risk seizing captives from among their allies in the decades before the establishment of non-Iberian colonies in the Caribbean. People of African and Indigenous descent also held corporate, religious, or martial statuses in Spanish Caribbean societies, which meant that if traffickers attempted to sell individuals close to where they had been taken captive, those individuals could and did appeal to local Spanish authorities to intervene.[20] Successful slaving ventures required seizing captives at a physical remove from the places where traffickers either anchored their vessels or conducted business. Traffickers often targeted free and enslaved people of African and Indigenous descent from places like Cartagena de Indias or the Yucatán Peninsula, for example, in order to traffic them into slavery in smaller ports throughout the Spanish Caribbean where their status was not locally recognized.

Dynamics shifted dramatically with the establishment of English and French colonies in the Caribbean beginning in the 1620s, and regional practices of captive-taking accelerated with the breakdown of the Iberian Union and the end of the Portuguese monopoly on the transatlantic slave trade in 1640. With access to safe anchorages and new markets at English and French colonies, traffickers targeted a wide variety of people, including European sailors and soldiers who were trafficked into informal servitude throughout the 1630s and 1640s. Over those same decades, conflict between Spain and Portugal disrupted the transatlantic slave trade to Spanish America. Traffickers engaged in widespread raiding, even against former allies, to make a profit from the anarchic state of the transatlantic and intra-Caribbean slave trades. By the 1660s, European efforts to reform, commercialize, and formalize the transatlantic and intra-Caribbean slave trades meant that, increasingly, slave status was equated with Blackness across the Caribbean, creating unique vulnerabilities for people of African descent, including legally free people, who were taken captive and trafficked into slavery away from their communities of belonging.[21] Race and vulnerability to captivity were clearly linked, but untangling the varied manifestations of that vulnerability reveals how the dynamics of this predatory sea shifted and changed over a century of Caribbean history.

Experiences in a Predatory Sea

In reconstructing this world, Spanish colonial archives provide a much fuller picture of the decades leading up to and directly following English and French colonization in the Caribbean. Sources related to the Caribbean in the English and French archives prior to the 1660s are notoriously thin. Civil and political upheaval in both England and France alongside the diffuse nature of colonization for both nations in the first half of the seventeenth century means that far better archival sources exist, respectively, after the English Restoration in 1660 and after the enactment of French imperial reforms by Jean-Baptiste Colbert in 1665. At the same time, the entanglement of subjects of different monarchs, Africans and their descendants, and Indigenous populations on the ground in the Caribbean is reflected in the archival sources produced during the sixteenth and seventeenth centuries. I relied on what I call an entangled archival methodology for this book, using Spain's colonial archives along with the scholarship of historians of the Spanish Caribbean to fill in the gaps in the English and French archives to understand this critical century of Caribbean history. Ample sources within Spain's colonial archives attest to French and English slaving and colonizing activities in the Caribbean as well as the importance of practices of raiding and captive-taking to that colonial development.

More importantly than sources that attest to the activities of northern Europeans across this century of violence, the Spanish archives also contain the testimonies of individuals who experienced captivity and unfreedom in the Caribbean. Sources from the perspective of African or Indigenous people who experienced unfreedom in the early seventeenth-century Anglo- or Franco-Caribbean are nonexistent in the archives of either England or France. Rather, scholars tend to read the documentation left by English and French slaveholders and slave traders against the grain in order to think about the lived experiences of slavery in the early English and French Caribbean. Historians have employed critical fabulation to write about the experiences of the enslaved, using a deep knowledge of sources and historical context to surmount silences in the archives.[22] Other scholars engage more critically with the politics of the archive of slavery and its racialized construction in terms of what can and cannot be known about the lives and experiences of the enslaved. Archival silences, according to Marisa J. Fuentes, should force historians to meditate on the power and loss represented by those archives.[23] At the same time, not all archives are silent in the same way. This book adds to growing research in non-English archives as a way to access the testimonies and experiences of enslaved people, drawing on the myriad voices in the Spanish archives of individuals who articulated experiences of mobility, vulnerability, community, and notions of freedom across a century of Caribbean violence.[24]

The Spanish colonial archives provide a unique source base for histories of slaving and slavery in the sixteenth- and seventeenth-century English and French Caribbean.[25] Within the letters and reports produced by Spanish Caribbean officials are thousands of manuscript pages containing testimonies from self-liberated captives who fled to Spanish Caribbean spaces as well as the depositions of a wide variety of English, Irish, French, and Dutch sailors who had been caught by Spanish authorities.[26] These testimonies provide surprisingly rich details about captives and their captors, especially compared to the English or French sources. They also differ in important ways from the ledgers, financial statements, court cases, and plantation documents that scholars have so skillfully mined in order to write histories of slavery in the eighteenth-century Caribbean. Slavery—whether as an economic system, legal institution, or lived experience—was not the reason why the testimonies central to this book were compiled or delivered to Spain. Rather, care went into the process of recording and preserving the testimonies of captives and their captors because of the entangled nature of Atlantic-wide geopolitics and imperial competition. The experiences of captives and their captors were written down for the information that those individuals provided about Spain's European rivals in the Caribbean. For this reason, Spanish officials recorded what captives observed from their moment of captivity to their act of self-liberation. They recorded details about where an individual was from, how and when they had entered the Caribbean, how long they had been in Caribbean waters, what other islands or ports they had been to, and what they had witnessed along the way. These eyewitness accounts of the development of non-Iberian Caribbean colonies are exceedingly rare in English- and French-language archives and, when they do exist, were penned by elites. The testimonies in the Spanish archives provide snapshots of how this world of vulnerability and violence shaped English and French slaving and colonization in the Caribbean.

The testimonies central to this book provide rare glimpses into a critical century of Caribbean history when extant English and French archival sources are thin, but they also have limitations, especially in terms of whose experiences were recorded. People appear in these sources when voluntary or forced mobility ensnared them in wider geopolitics, which means that the archival sources that I draw upon here prioritize the experiences of individuals whose lives crossed and recrossed imperial and aqueous spaces. That mobility tended to be gendered, with far more testimonies from men than women appearing in the Spanish sources, especially before the 1650s and 1660s. Childcare responsibilities and women's unique vulnerability to sexual and other kinds of violence undoubtedly limited the number of women who chose to liberate themselves from slavery through maritime journeys.[27] At the same time, near constant warfare during the sixteenth and seventeenth centuries meant that forced mobility and dislocation were not entirely uncommon experiences for a wide variety of people. Reading across the archival record has allowed me to trace some instances of generational violence and dislocation as warfare and imperial competition unsettled Caribbean islands multiple times. In the end, I argue that the archival sources analyzed here reveal more than they conceal about the experiences of captives and their captors, and the wider slaving practices that shaped their lives.

The scholarship of historians working on the Spanish Caribbean also proved indispensable to fully understand the world that northern European traffickers navigated. This has meant interloping in a historiography on the Spanish Caribbean that I hope this book will make more visible to scholars working in the English and French Caribbean. The work of historians Jennifer Wolff and Elsa Gelpí Baíz for Puerto Rico, Juan José Ponce Vazquéz, Marc Eagle, and Lissette Acosta Corniel for Hispaniola, and David Wheat, Bethany Aram, and María Cristina Navarrette Peláez for a wider view of trade and slavery in the sixteenth- and seventeenth-century Spanish Caribbean proved especially critical.[28] Working across languages and archives depends on rich historiographies in order to draw connections across geographic regions.

Entangled history as a methodological and archival approach to the sixteenth- and seventeenth-century Caribbean provides a critical reappraisal of a century of English and French Caribbean history. Two key interventions presented in this book relate to the nature of early English and French Caribbean colonization and the adoption of race-based slavery in those subsequent colonies. Scholars have tended to analyze the process of English and French colonization from the perspective of a single empire, often emphasizing the development of a single island at the expense of inter-island and regional connections. This book builds on recent scholarship that explicitly deemphasizes English and French imperial perspectives in favor of portraying the Caribbean as an interconnected space defined by entanglements between Europeans, Africans, and Indigenous populations.[29] This approach offers a view of Caribbean colonization from the bottom up, built not as a result of imperial planning but rather from a diffuse array of petty financial decisions made by a multiethnic assortment of people.[30] Traffickers like d'Esnambuc occupied and integrated Caribbean spaces into networks of cross-cultural trade centered around captivity and slavery decades before their respective monarchs issued licenses for the establishment of official colonies. As this book shows, the earliest English and French island colonies in the Caribbean developed because of those islands' place in networks of captive-taking and human trafficking, which predated the imperial plans of officials in either England or France.

The archival sources and methodology of this book also invite a reappraisal of the history of slavery in the English and French Atlantics. Slavery as a social or legal institution did not exist in either England or France when subjects of those crowns began establishing colonies in the Caribbean. The lack of a metropolitan model from which English or French colonists could draw raises the question of why and how those colonists adopted racialized slavery in American colonies. In the standard telling, the English and French exploited a wide variety of indentured and enslaved labor during the early seventeenth century without an explicit, codified understanding of slavery as a racialized or hereditary institution. According to that logic, it was the rise of sugar plantation agriculture in the 1640s and 1650s that led to a dramatic increase in the number of enslaved Africans in the English and French Caribbean. The demographic changes that accompanied sugar production created a corresponding need for English and French colonial officials to define chattel slavery legally and to construct a racist logic that justified the brutal exploitation of Africans and their descendants.[31] Put simply, this historiographic debate rests on the assumption that English and French colonists needed to learn how to be slaveholders and that they did so in order to take advantage of the opportunities presented by plantation agriculture after mid-century. A critical reading of Spanish archival sources from the sixteenth and seventeenth centuries, however, reveals that English and French ship captains, mariners, and colonial governors had experience with slaving and slavery from their entanglements in the Spanish Caribbean. Practices of slavery were embedded legally, economically, and socially in the English and French Caribbean from the very beginning.

This book uses the term "trafficker" to describe the individuals who profited by taking people captive and trafficking them into slavery between 1570 and 1670. I use the term provocatively and capaciously in order to highlight the subtle ways in which the terminology we employ as historians has the power to illuminate or underscore the racialized violence at the center of maritime predation in this period. The threat of violence hung over all commercial exchanges between subjects of different monarchs in the sixteenth- and seventeenth-century Atlantic world. Thwarted commercial ventures could, and often did, end in forced trade or outright plundering. While historians have recognized this slippage between trade and warfare, English, French, and Dutch merchants and ship captains developed a particular form of belligerent trade in the late sixteenth- and early seventeenth-century Caribbean that depended on captive-taking and human trafficking.[32] The violent nature of this trade was shaped, in part, by economic and social conditions in the Spanish Caribbean. Spanish Caribbean residents demanded access to enslaved people in order to exploit their labor or to display them as visible markers of their socioeconomic status, but the ability to purchase enslaved Africans via the transatlantic slave trade was limited in the Spanish Caribbean ports that were not directly served by Iberian commercial networks.

For northern European merchants, as Gregory O'Malley argues, this made having access to enslaved captives "the next best thing to coin" for establishing informal and, from the perspective of the Spanish Crown, illegal trade relations with Spanish Caribbean communities.[33] This particular combination of factors incentivized raiding, captive-taking, and human trafficking. Centering the experiences of captives reveals the dislocating violence at the center of sixteenth- and seventeenth-century smuggling.

The traffickers in this book tend to be treated in the historiography as pirates or smugglers. An analysis that accounts for the economy of captive slavery and human trafficking over a century of Caribbean history calls for a different set of terms. The raids conducted by d'Esnambuc's company at Caymito and countless others, I argue, reflect a specific kind of maritime violence that developed over the course of the sixteenth century and that would have profound implications for colonial development and the elaboration of the intra-Caribbean slave trade into the seventeenth century. Ship captains, like d'Esnambuc in 1620, received merchant-syndicate financing for their ventures and were expected to make a profit for the individuals who had invested in their voyages.[34] In a process known in the sixteenth and seventeenth centuries as "making a voyage," privately funded ship captains and their crews engaged in a wide variety of activities to recuperate investments and bring home a profit. Making a voyage by carrying hides, indigo, ginger, sugar, dyewoods, and tobacco from the Caribbean to European markets was facilitated through the establishment of predictable commercial connections with Spanish Caribbean residents, who likewise relied on northern European traffickers for access to Atlantic markets.

While this might seem like straightforward smuggling or piracy, establishing technically illicit trade in one part of the Caribbean often depended on taking people of African and Indigenous descent, both free and enslaved, captive from other parts of the Spanish Caribbean. The ship captains at Caymito, for example, used maritime raids in one part of Spain's Caribbean territories in order to traffic captives into another. The northern European ship captains and sailors analyzed here were not exclusively slave traders, smugglers, merchants, pirates, or corsairs but opportunistic individuals engaged in a wide variety of improvisational activities that contemporary Europeans referred to as "traffique."[35] As this book shows, making a voyage through trafficking in the sixteenth- and seventeenth-century Caribbean often involved trafficking human captives in exchange for goods that could be transported back to European markets. Individuals involved in that specific form of raiding and belligerent trade in captives are referred to here as traffickers.

The use of "traffickers" calls deliberate attention to the frustrating slipperiness surrounding the myriad terms used to describe maritime predation in the early modern Atlantic world. Those terms fall along a spectrum of legality based on whether mariners had the support of a European monarch (corsairs and privateers), or if they lacked that support (buccaneers and pirates). For this study, framing maritime predation around European interpretations of their legality presents several problems. First, piracy was not a lifelong profession in most cases. Individual mariners and ship captains, like d'Esnambuc, could engage in occasional acts of piracy without being considered *hostes humani generis*, or "enemies of all humankind."[36] The latter definition of piratical acts at sea comes from Roman jurisprudence in which Rome sought to undergird their expanding territorial empire by labeling as criminals those who challenged their claims to sovereignty over distant aqueous spaces.[37] In the early modern Atlantic world, European monarchs echoed this Roman understanding of piracy for those mariners who acted against their interests. Crucially, however, competing European monarchs, colonial officials, and even trading communities on the peripheries of empires often supported these so-called enemies of all humankind. As historian Kevin McDonald argues, this view of pirates as *hostes humani generis* has become "one of the most enduring legal fictions of all time."[38] Terminology that describes the behavior of mariners depending on the legality of their actions lacks precision, in other words, because one person's pirate was another person's privateer, corsair, or smuggler. More importantly, that terminology reinforces European claims to territorial and oceanic sovereignty—claims that were actively and continuously contested by Indigenous inhabitants, Africans and their descendants, and competing European powers throughout the early modern Americas. Adopting the terminology used by empires to describe maritime predation replicates and adds rhetorical weight to European claims to territorial sovereignty even when a wide range of individuals resisted and contested those claims on the ground.

There is a more fundamental reason why I use the term "trafficker" in this book, and it reflects the power of language to shape our perspectives, often in unintentional ways. The issues surrounding the use of European jurisdictional terminology to describe maritime predation, after all, become clearer when certain acts of seaborne violence are viewed from the perspective of its victims. The captives of African descent in the Dutch hulk at Caymito, in other words, would not have thought of their captors through the language of corsairs, buccaneers, sea beggars, or privateers. To the people taken captive in late 1620 and early 1621, this multinational group of maritime predators were, quite simply, their captors. The myriad labels used to describe seaborne predators reflect the common definition of piracy—the act of engaging in theft at sea. But, even if racially marginalized individuals were often treated *as if* they were property and plunder in the early modern era, the language employed by scholars should avoid conflating people with inanimate goods seized through acts of maritime theft. A focus on what maritime predators were actually doing over a century of Caribbean violence reveals the centrality of captive-taking and human trafficking. The use of the term "traffickers" underscores the nature of this violent slaving economy and describes the actions of maritime predators rather than their juridical status within the realm of European geopolitics. It is not a perfect solution. Traffickers, of course, also engaged in property theft that did not involve human captives depending on the voyage. As I argue throughout the book, however, captive-taking and human trafficking were central to the activities of sailors and ship captains who sought to make a voyage between 1570 and 1670. The deliberate use of "traffickers" underscores the deeply intertwined histories of piracy, slavery, colonialism, and imperialism in a way that prioritizes the perspectives of the captive people caught up in this predatory sea.

Chapter Outline

This book opens with a view of slaving practices in the Caribbean during the second half of the sixteenth century. Building on the work of scholars such as Tessa Murphy, Ernesto Mercado-Montero, Carolyn Arena, and Erin Woodruff Stone, Chapter 1 emphasizes the role of Indigenous polities in shaping how Europeans encountered the Caribbean.[39] These relations proved formative to subsequent efforts at colonization and colonial development, despite the tendency in the historiography of the Caribbean to downplay those entanglements. Scholarship that seeks to explain early colonization as a prelude to the rise of the plantation complex tends to gloss over Indigenous Caribbean history, for example, portraying Indigenous peoples as disappearing in order to make room for sugar and slavery.[40] Where Indigenous polities do appear is as the first generation of enslaved Caribbean laborers who, as a result of war, disease, and overwork during the sixteenth century, suffered a demographic catastrophe that scholars argue explains the European decision to switch to the importation of enslaved African labor.[41] Many Indigenous populations, especially in the Greater Antilles, did suffer enslavement and appalling demographic decline during the sixteenth century. As recent scholarship has shown, however, other Indigenous populations, such as the Kalinago of the Lesser Antilles, retained their territorial sovereignty and influenced European colonization over the course of the sixteenth, seventeenth, and eighteenth centuries.[42]

Kalinago populations maintained their autonomy in the eastern Caribbean, but that autonomy depended on trade with Europeans for iron implements. Cross-cultural trade with European mariners undergirded Kalinago power in the eastern Caribbean, with captive-taking and human trafficking central to those commercial relationships. The Kalinago conducted raids against places like Puerto Rico in order to take captives, many of whom cultivated foodstuffs and tobacco for their Kalinago captors. For their part, European traffickers anchored at Kalinago-dominated islands in the Lesser Antilles to barter for tobacco, food, and, sometimes, the captives held by their Kalinago trade partners. The purchasing of European and African captives seized by the Kalinago allowed traffickers to ransom those captives back to places like Puerto Rico, providing a unique means for traffickers to make a voyage. Not all informal trade in the Spanish Caribbean depended on cross-cultural ransoming. Spanish Caribbean residents in smaller markets, where demand and prices were high, often traded openly with traffickers, especially for enslaved Africans seized from Portuguese transatlantic slave ships. Rather than commercially isolated, as Chapter 1 demonstrates, Spanish Caribbean residents in smaller markets sat at the nexus of dynamic, albeit often violent, cross-cultural trade networks.

The improvisational methods used by traffickers to make a voyage meant that they relied on regional allies, especially the Kalinago, for safe anchorages and access to supplies. Chapter 2 traces how one of those anchorages, the island of St. Christopher, emerged as the first Crown-sanctioned English and French colony in the Caribbean. Historians tend to analyze the colonization of St. Christopher through the lens of the Atlantic-wide tobacco boom, arguing that Thomas Warner selected the island as a colony for tobacco cultivation because it was "quiet," "distant from Spanish control," and "removed as far as possible from contact with Spanish and Indigenous population centers."[43] Demand for tobacco was the catalyst behind merchant financiers dispatching colonists to the greater Caribbean, but understanding why English elites were interested in supporting colonies does not explain where a successful colony finally developed or how it survived. The Kalinago of St. Christopher treated the English colonists under Warner as they had the innumerable northern European mariners who temporarily dwelled on their island to conduct trade, repair their ships, and rendezvous with other traffickers. By the time it became clear to the Kalinago that the Englishmen intended to stay, hundreds of English settlers had arrived at the island. Even still, Warner defended his nascent colony from Kalinago reprisals—who threatened the English from powerful population centers throughout the Lesser Antillean chain—only through an alliance with d'Esnambuc and the French. As a joint English and French colony, traffickers continued to call on St. Christopher, linking the island to slaving practices from the beginning. Rather than peripheral to the wider Caribbean, St. Christopher remained as central to regional, violent trade as it had been under the Kalinago.

The Kalinago were not the only allies that traffickers had in the greater Caribbean. Maroon communities in the Greater Antilles also established commercial ties with European mariners in order to maintain their hard-won freedom and autonomy during the late sixteenth and early seventeenth centuries.[44] Much like St. Christopher, however, these relationships would be disrupted by commodity demand in Europe and the establishment of northern European colonies in the western Caribbean. Chapter 3 traces how traffickers had used places like Caymito and neighboring Tortuga to engage in trade with residents in western Hispaniola since the late sixteenth century, often trading for dyewood that fetched high prices in European markets. The exchange of captives and manufactured goods for dyewood in the western Caribbean drew ships to the region, but it also attracted the attention of elites in the Caribbean and Europe.

When a Spanish assault on Nevis drove off that island's English governor, Anthony Hilton, in 1629, he and the English survivors fled to Tortuga, where a multinational settlement of mariners had been engaged in robust trade for nearly seventy years. Hilton received the financial backing of the puritan Providence Island Company, which demanded a monopoly on all the dyewood traded from the island but granted ships of all nations permission to transport dyewood on their behalf.[45] Without the need to rely on regional allies and with a new market for the sale of captives, traffickers engaged in increased raiding and captive-taking throughout the western Caribbean in the 1630s and 1640s, including against their former Maroon allies in western Hispaniola.

Histories of non-Iberian European colonization of the Caribbean often emphasize inter-imperial competition in the early history of those colonies. Like chess pieces, island colonies from this perspective were gained and lost over a tumultuous half century of Atlantic-wide competition that culminated with the English invasion of Spanish Jamaica in 1655.[46] Chapter 4 recenters the experiences of captives, building on recent work that seeks to understand the human consequences of inter-imperial competition and territorial contestation between the 1620s and the 1660s.[47] This recentering focuses on the experiences of individuals in order to illuminate the socially disruptive effects of this half century for those who were vulnerable to captivity and commodification. At forty-two years old in 1646, for example, Catalina Angola had obtained her freedom along with that of her three children from the father of her children, a Spanish presidio captain, on the island of Providencia. Catalina had previously been enslaved to the English on Providence Island before the Spanish invaded and expelled the English in 1641. She was among the people of African descent seized from either intra-Caribbean slave ships or a coastal community near Cartagena de Indias and trafficked into slavery among the English on Providence Island during the 1630s. The violent, non-linear nature of her trajectory into slavery did not prevent Catalina Angola from forming a life for herself and her children, the youngest of whom was a boy, Salvador Francisco, named after his father.

Their domestic security would not last. By 1666, a Jamaican-sponsored expedition attacked the Spanish presidio on Providencia and raided the island for captives. Among the captives of African descent carried back to Jamaica and trafficked into slavery was Catalina's son. Although a legally free man in his community of belonging, Salvador Francisco de la Peña experienced the effects of racialized anonymity and commodification that defined the experiences of many people of African and Indigenous descent during moments of inter-imperial contestation.[48] For Catalina, her small family, and many others like them, Providencia under the Spanish was not a chess piece in a game of inter-imperial competition but a home where diasporic community formation, family, and freedom had, briefly, been possible.

The final two chapters of the book conclude with European efforts to reform the transatlantic and intra-Caribbean slave trades in the 1660s and the consequences of those reform efforts on traffickers and the people they took captive. Officials in Spain responded to the increasingly chaotic nature of the transatlantic and intra-Caribbean slave trades in 1662 by issuing a new monopoly slave-trading contract, called an asiento, to a pair of merchants from Genoa named Domingo Grillo and Ambrosio Lomelín. The new asiento for the slave trade to Spanish America differed in important ways from previous contracts. Rather than conduct the transatlantic slave trade themselves, Grillo and Lomelín negotiated for permission to purchase enslaved Africans at English, French, or Dutch islands in the Caribbean and transship those enslaved peopled to specific Spanish American port cities. As Chapter 5 shows, however, Grillo and Lomelín did not invent this trade. Rather, I argue that their contract formalized preexisting and informal practices of human trafficking that had been formed over the previous half century. Plans for the new intra-Caribbean slave trade, however, confronted a Caribbean world accustomed to raiding, captive-taking, and informal trade. As the monopoly slave-trading companies of England and the Dutch Republic negotiated with the Genoese merchants to secure a position as supplier of enslaved Africans, raiding and informal human trafficking continued. Rather than reform, the Grillo and Lomelín asiento sparked regional and Atlantic-wide commercial competition that made the Caribbean an even more volatile place for many people of African and Indigenous descent vulnerable to captivity and trafficking.

Some people taken captive and trafficked into slavery liberated themselves from captivity, but by the 1660s, the creation of the new asiento complicated their efforts to obtain freedom in Spanish Caribbean territories. Chapter 6 shows how free people of African descent who were taken captive and trafficked into slavery across imperial borders, in particular, encountered a Spanish Atlantic that was profoundly shaped by the efforts of the 1660s to reform the transatlantic and intra-Caribbean slave trades. Their experiences add important context to a growing body of scholarship on the movement of people of African descent across imperial borders in the seventeenth and eighteenth centuries. During the 1660s, Spanish officials in the Caribbean responded to the arrival of self-liberated Africans and their descendants by establishing a sanctuary policy in which enslaved people who escaped to Spanish America from any English, French, or Dutch Caribbean colony and sought baptism in the Catholic Church were granted their freedom. As scholars have argued, by the late seventeenth century, the Spanish sanctuary policy provided important avenues for freedom for enslaved people who could get to Spanish territories in the Americas.[49]

For captives of African descent who had been considered legally free in Spanish America before their captivity by northern European traffickers, however, the Spanish sanctuary policy did not necessarily mean returning to their communities of belonging. Rather, the creation of the new asiento complicated their claims to free status, especially since representatives of the asiento wielded immense judicial power in order to prevent smuggling and interloping on their trade monopoly. A focus on captives' encounters with Spanish Caribbean authorities in the 1660s reveals the vulnerability of people of African descent, enslaved and free, in a Caribbean world that by mid-century increasingly equated African maritime mobility with slavery. This book reframes the imperial reforms of the 1660s and 1670s by examining them, not just as the foundations for the dramatic increase in the transatlantic slave trade to the Caribbean, but as a legacy of long-standing regional practices of captive-taking and human trafficking. The conclusion explores the consequences of these arguments for our understanding of the early history of race and slavery in the English and French Caribbean and Atlantic worlds.

CHAPTER 1

"A Sea of Islands"

Cross-Cultural Trade and Captive Slavery

In the summer of 1579, three ships anchored briefly at a small island called Mona off the western coast of Puerto Rico. All three ships held captives who anxiously awaited their fates while their captors, a pair of French ship captains, planned their next move. For the 190 women, men, and children chained belowdecks on the two French ships, the respite at Mona brought urgently needed food and water after they survived the horrors of the Middle Passage. The Indigenous inhabitants of that island cultivated specific foods, such as lemons, to alleviate sicknesses caused by monotonous, nutritionally deficient shipboard diets. For the captives on the third ship, however, this moment was potentially less cathartic. One of those captives—the twenty-nine-year-old Spanish governor of Puerto Rico, Francisco de Obando y Mexía—likely observed the French ships refit at Mona with particular outrage. The French had seized the ship carrying Obando and his entourage between Puerto Rico and Hispaniola before diverting it to Mona. As a captive, Obando would have watched helplessly as the inhabitants of Mona and the French ship captains bartered within miles of Puerto Rico's shores.

For the French captains, the abduction of such high-status Spanish captives was a stroke of luck that they leveraged in order to force the sale of the African captives. As ransom for their governor, Puerto Rico's residents purchased the enslaved Africans shackled on the French ships for nearly 1,500 pounds of sugar, 4,000 cattle hides, an unspecified quantity of pearls, and other items of value, including a silver cross.[1] Obando, who had been recuperating his health in Hispaniola before his captivity, died shortly after his release, while the 190 African captives from the Senegambian region of West Africa found themselves either dispersed into slavery across Puerto

Rico or transshipped and sold again through the informal intra-Caribbean slave trade.

The abduction and death of the governor of Puerto Rico make this moment particularly dramatic, but a close reading of these events reveals surprisingly quotidian aspects of informal trade and practices of making a voyage in the mid-sixteenth-century Caribbean. For one, this was not the first time that one of the two French captains had trafficked Africans into slavery in Puerto Rico. Three years earlier one of those Frenchmen, Jean Hacquet, sold an unspecified number of Africans into slavery in Guadianilla (near present-day Guayanilla) on the south-central coast of Puerto Rico. On that voyage, the residents of Guadianilla had traded willingly with Hacquet, who sailed away from Puerto Rico with hides and produce worth 50,000 *livres*.[2] On both of his voyages, Hacquet relied on Indigenous populations in the Caribbean for access to safe anchorages, food, wood, and fresh water. That the Indigenous inhabitants of Mona produced the exact kinds of foodstuffs most commonly used to refresh sailors and captives after an Atlantic crossing suggests the regularity with which ships anchored at their small island. Clearly, Hacquet was not alone in using Mona during voyages of captive-taking and human trafficking in the Spanish Caribbean over the second half of the sixteenth century. The fact that Mona's Indigenous population traded with Hacquet and his companion on Hacquet's second voyage, even when they arrived with Obando as a prisoner, underscores the level of impunity that the inhabitants of Mona enjoyed in their commercial relations with foreign ship captains.

Northern European traffickers like Hacquet used a variety of routes and strategies in order to profit from the dynamic, regional economies of the Greater Antilles. Recent scholarship on the economic vitality of the wider Spanish Caribbean helps frame the allure of areas like Puerto Rico for northern European traffickers and challenges an older tendency to describe much of the sixteenth-century Spanish Caribbean as peripheral or commercially isolated. That isolation is frequently attributed to the development of Spain's official fleet system, known as the *Carrera de Indias*. The biannual fleet system sailed in armed convoy in order to protect Spanish merchant shipping from attacks by Spain's European rivals. The convoy departed Seville and divided in the Caribbean, with half of the fleet conducting trade at Cartagena and Portobelo, while the other half served the viceroyalty of New Spain through the port of Veracruz. At the conclusion of the annual trade fairs that accompanied the arrival of the Carrera de Indias in those ports, both halves of the convoy wintered at Havana before sailing back to Spain via the Bahamian

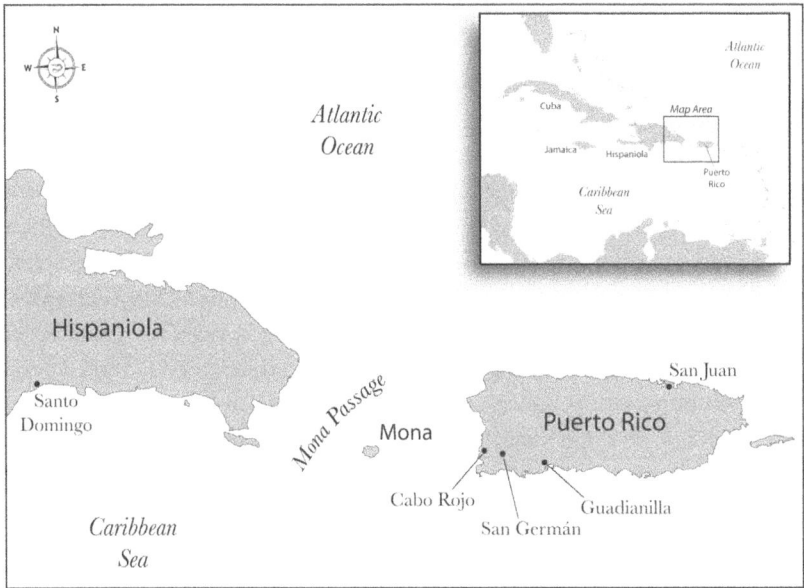

Map 2. The Mona Passage and Puerto Rico

Channel.[3] While less vulnerable to capture, the armed fleet system disadvantaged Spanish Caribbean ports on the peripheries of official trade, where shipping costs for licensed trade ran excessively high.[4] Ports on the edges of the Carrera de Indias suffered from a consistent lack of access to licensed trade that should have debilitated their economic development.

By centering informal trade, however, recent scholarship has revealed the dense commercial networks that connected the Spanish Caribbean to markets throughout the Atlantic world. Rather than being commercially isolated, places like Puerto Rico sat at the nexus of intra-Caribbean and transatlantic trade networks. As historian Jennifer Wolff has recently shown, although few registered ships out of Seville anchored at Puerto Rico over the second half of the sixteenth century, the island served as an important entrepôt for informal trade. Portuguese merchants, in particular, integrated Puerto Rico into trade networks spanning the southern Atlantic from West and West Central Africa to Brazil. For many of those merchants, Puerto Rico provided an opportunity to sell enslaved African captives without paying taxes. This informal trade functioned in a variety of ways, including Portuguese ship captains claiming that distress at sea forced them to anchor at San Juan, where they sold enslaved Africans to cover the cost of ship repair and supplies. Others sold captives in Puerto Rico covertly before sailing to the destination listed on their licenses. To explain the disparity in the number of enslaved Africans on board their ships when they arrived at their intended destination, they claimed that the captives whom they had sold in Puerto Rico had died at sea.[5] Nor was San Juan alone in serving as an entrepôt for this informal trade. Hispaniola and Jamaica also provided Portuguese merchants with commercial opportunities at the edges of legality.[6] According to historian Marc Eagle, these "unofficial nexuses for human cargoes" participated in a burgeoning intra-Caribbean slave trade as local merchants transshipped enslaved Africans to other markets in the region.[7] Rather than being peripheral backwaters, places like Puerto Rico were deeply connected to transatlantic and intra-Caribbean trade networks over the second half of the sixteenth century.

Informal trade supported local economies in the Spanish Caribbean, but not all population centers in the Greater Antilles received the same benefits from Luso-Atlantic trade networks. Disparity in access to trade across the islands of the Greater Antilles created commercial opportunities for northern European traffickers like Hacquet. Over the second half of the sixteenth century, more densely populated areas tended to attract Portuguese merchant and transatlantic slave ships, often at the expense of smaller ports and towns. The population and economy of Puerto Rico, for example, centered around San Juan. At the same time, notoriously difficult roads across the island left residents on the island's southern and western coasts less connected to San Juan's commercial networks. According to historian Elsa Gelpí Baíz, the relative commercial isolation of places like Guadianilla or San Germán in southern and western Puerto Rico created a different social ethic surrounding trade with northern European interlopers.[8] Traffickers like Hacquet, in other words, found local residents in smaller, less saturated ports throughout the Spanish Caribbean often more willing to engage in illicit trade with Spain's European competitors. Sea lanes dense with merchant vessels, including ships transporting enslaved Africans, also attracted northern European traffickers willing to engage in maritime raiding and captive-taking in order to make their voyages. Crucial to the efforts of traffickers were small islands and their inhabitants.

Hacquet and others like him encountered a sea of small islands in the late sixteenth-century Caribbean. That statement seems obvious, yet to view Caribbean geography from the perspective of late sixteenth-century European traffickers reveals the outsized, and often overlooked, importance of small islands. As historian Epeli Hau'ofa has argued for the Pacific, viewing maritime geography from the perspectives of how ordinary people navigated archipelagoes reveals "'a sea of islands' rather than . . . 'islands in the sea.'"[9] The latter description denotes isolated spots of land separate from the wider maritime world, while the former forces a recognition of connections, interdependence, and expansiveness. Caribbean history has tended toward the latter. With notable exceptions, histories of the region focus on the development of specific island colonies in relative isolation from the wider sea surrounding them.[10] Histories of Caribbean islands tend to begin with European colonization, with the unfortunate consequence of excluding from those histories the innumerable small Caribbean islands that either never gained the colonizing attention of Europeans or failed altogether as colonies.[11] Crucially, however, northern European traffickers incorporated many of those small islands into voyages of violent raiding and human trafficking over the second half of the sixteenth century.

The two voyages of Jean Hacquet during the second half of the sixteenth century frame this chapter. Centering his routes, strategies, and trade partners reveals two important aspects about how this informal, and often violent, trade functioned. First, Hacquet's experiences with Puerto Rico reveal the importance of smaller, less saturated Spanish Caribbean ports for northern European traffickers. The cattle ranches and farms that dotted the southern and western coasts of Puerto Rico funneled hides and other produce into places like San Germán, in turn drawing northern European traffickers. Local residents often engaged in that trade willingly and, when they did not, traffickers used violence to force trade. Crucially, the voyages of men like Hacquet to the Caribbean year after year created knowledge of safe anchorages throughout the region where traffickers refitted their ships, replenished their supplies, and shared information about commercial opportunities with one another. From the Indigenous inhabitants of Mona to the autonomous Kalinago of the Lesser Antilles, northern European traffickers forged alliances based on cross-cultural trade with Indigenous populations throughout the Caribbean. Intermediaries of African descent also facilitated informal trade between traffickers and Spanish Caribbean residents. At the same time, violence permeated the strategies of men like Hacquet. While his second voyage involved the seizure of a ship transporting Puerto Rico's governor, others like him targeted ships that bore enslaved Africans. Tracing the experiences and trajectories of people of African descent caught up in these networks of violent, informal trade sheds light on the centrality of captivity and human trafficking to these practices of informal, cross-cultural trade in the sixteenth-century Caribbean. By the early seventeenth century, the routes and practices forged by traffick- ers like Hacquet would shape the locations, economies, and societies of the first Crown-sanctioned English and French colonies in the Caribbean. Under- standing the development of those spaces requires delving into the world that preceded them.

Making a Voyage: Atlantic Africa

In the sixteenth century, northern European traffickers like Hacquet engaged in a wide range of activities—often in the same voyage—from acts of piracy to privateering, slaving, trading, salvaging, raiding, and smuggling. The sizes and types of these ventures varied widely, with less well funded ventures setting out in smaller ships with fewer guns—precluding direct assaults on Spanish American port cities, for example, and encouraging less belligerent trade. Often, ships under a hundred tons traveled alone or in pairs to smuggle with local Spanish Caribbean residents. Motivating the actions of traffickers above all was the need to recoup and augment the merchant capital invested in equipping their ships. Referred to as "making a voyage," financial success helped traffickers build a reputation that made attracting funding for future voyages that much easier.[12] Between the 1550s and the 1610s, for example, merchants in the French city of Rouen sponsored hundreds of smaller voy- ages to the West Indies for the cured hides that fed that city's growing leather industry.[13] Traffickers found access to hides in the Greater Antilles easier when they trafficked captive people of African and Indigenous descent in exchange, which meant that many of the French captains commissioned to smuggle in the Caribbean sailed first to West or West Central Africa where they obtained enslaved Africans through various means, from purchase to seizing women, men, and children through violent raids on Portuguese ships and coastal factories.

The first of Hacquet's voyages to Puerto Rico began when he was equipped out of Honfleur on the seventy-ton *Sallamandre* in November 1575. Like many French ship captains during the second half of the sixteenth century, Hac- quet's license listed him as sailing from France to "la côte de Serlione" and the "Indes de Pérou"—geographic destinations left vague enough for Hacquet to improvise in order to make his voyage once at sea.[14] He joined many French and English shipmasters who purchased or seized human captives along the West African coast from Senegal to Gambia in order to trade in Spanish America.[15] In Sierra Leone during the mid-sixteenth century, a Mane invasion of Zape communities drew slave ships to that region, where slavers purchased Zape war captives, along with captives taken during conflicts between the subsequent and competing Mane states.[16] If Hacquet stuck to his itinerary, the captives that his crew loaded into the cramped and terrifying hold of the *Sallamandre* would have been people caught in the middle of ongoing Mane-Zape warfare. Nor would Hacquet have been alone—from 1571 through 1595, French slavers from the port of Le Havre alone recorded 123 voyages to Sierra Leone.[17] If purchasing enslaved Africans proved difficult, traffickers turned to raiding Portuguese factories and ships for African captives.

As the captain of a single vessel, Hacquet likely acquired enslaved Africans in Senegambia through barter rather than violence. Many of his contemporaries, however, opted for the latter. In 1566, for example, a French fleet consisting of four vessels attacked the Portuguese fort on the island of Arguin off the coast of North Africa. During the raiding that followed, the French seized an unspecified number of captives described as "Muslims, men and women, and Blacks."[18] The island of Arguin served as the first African *feitoria*, or factory, established by the Portuguese to siphon off the trans-Saharan trade in gold dust and enslaved people to the Mediterranean world. The latter proved by far more profitable. By the mid-fifteenth century, the Portuguese used Arguin to conduct a regular slave trade between North Africa and Iberia, which reached its peak by the 1520s and 1530s, when approximately two thousand enslaved women, men, and children passed through the fort annually. By the time of the French attack, some of those captives found themselves transported to Spanish Caribbean markets as well.[19] As an entrepôt in the Mediterranean and burgeoning transatlantic slave trade, the French understood the value of raiding Arguin. For the captives, some of whom might have been free Zenaga who served as intermediaries between Portuguese merchants and inland Sudanese markets, the French raid resulted in their forced transportation across the Atlantic and into slavery.[20] French raids against Portuguese factories and ships proved common enough that Portuguese transatlantic slave ship captains received instructions to load enslaved Africans on board their ships as quickly as possible to avoid attacks.[21] Despite demands from the Portuguese merchant community for better defense of trade in Atlantic Africa, factories and shipping lanes remained vulnerable to raids throughout the second half of the century.[22]

Cross-Cultural Trade in the Lesser Antilles

Using the trade winds, the Lesser Antilles offered the first chance for the captives and crew of the *Sallamandre* to access fresh food and water after the Atlantic crossing.[23] They arrived in the island homelands of the Kalinago at an opportune time. Relations between the Spanish and Kalinago had turned increasingly hostile by the second half of the sixteenth century, creating demand among Kalinago populations in the Lesser Antilles for an alternative source of European ironware such as knives, hooks, hatchets, saws, nails, sickles, and hoes. Spanish fleets had anchored in the Lesser Antilles since the earliest years of colonization, bartering with the Kalinago for food, wood, and water. During the first few decades of the sixteenth century, however, Spanish slave-raiding in the Lesser Antilles and a failed attempt to colonize Guadeloupe in 1525 had soured relations between the Spanish and Kalinago.[24] By mid-century, Kalinago war parties engaged in seasonal raiding of Spanish colonies like Trinidad and Puerto Rico, seizing captives of Spanish and African descent and burning settlements to the ground.

The escalation of tensions with the Spanish meant that the Kalinago welcomed trade with northern European traffickers like Hacquet. In 1585, for example, Francis Drake described how the Kalinago on Dominica "treated us very kindely," even as they held "a Spaniard or twaine prisoner."[25] Over a decade later, one French observer explained that "every year a large quantity of ships arrive" to trade in the Lesser Antilles.[26] The influx of iron tools that resulted from this trade helped Kalinago canoe builders work more efficiently, providing the floating armadas that, in turn, raided places like the towns along the southern coast of Puerto Rico.[27] Traffickers, too, benefited from access to safe anchorages, information, food, wood, and water in the islands of the Lesser Antilles, which became unofficial entrepôts for northern European vessels seeking to make a voyage in the Spanish Caribbean by the second half of the sixteenth century.

Of primary importance for vessels like that of Hacquet was food and water. The standard practice in western Europe for equipping maritime ventures was to provide a ship with six months' worth of provisions, even when vessels needed to provide food for captives from Atlantic Africa or when they stayed in Caribbean waters far beyond six months.[28] The Kalinago's desire to obtain European ironware coincided, in other words, with the need of northern European sailors to augment their meager food rations, helping create practices of cross-cultural trade on the islands of the Lesser Antilles.

The foodstuffs produced by Kalinago women, in particular, fueled traffickers' extended stays in the Caribbean. According to one French observer, Europeans traded "principally for cassava, which is the bread of the Indies."[29] For mariners, cassava provided a nutritious equivalent to ship biscuit because it could be stored on board for long periods of time without going bad. However, producing cassava bread from the root of *Manihot esculenta* took skill and experience. According to Gonzalo Fernández de Oviedo y Valdés, although cassava was "the ordinary bread of . . . the islands," Kalinago women first had to soak, drain, and dry it to expunge the deadly prussic acid from the raw form.[30] The result was bread that Robert Harcourt likened to "our Oaten cakes in England . . . very excellent" and served about "a finger thicke."[31] Traffickers throughout the sixteenth and early seventeenth centuries depended on Kalinago women in the Lesser Antilles to convert the deadly root into edible and durable cassava bread.[32] For the enslaved Africans held on ships like that of Hacquet, Kalinago-produced foodstuffs provided potentially life-saving nutrition after the deprivations of the Middle Passage.

For Hacquet, a stop in the Lesser Antilles also gave him a chance to glean valuable information about markets or the locations of Spanish fleets from fellow traffickers or Kalinago trade partners. Northern Europeans sought "hides, sugar and *cassia fistula*" from trade partners in "Puerto Rico, Española, Jamaica, [or] Cuba." Successful ventures meant that traffickers needed the latest information on where exactly they could find Spanish Caribbean residents who would be willing to trade.[33] Traffickers also confronted various dangers, such as episodic Spanish armadas patrolling coastlines or changes in local politics that led to the prosecution of informal trade where it was formerly permitted, which meant that they needed to gather whatever intelligence they could before attempting trade.[34] To facilitate their commerce and avoid dangers, shipmasters exchanged vital intelligence with one another while refitting in places like the Lesser Antilles. Sometimes information was shared between captains and crews while ships anchored alongside one another loading supplies. In other moments, northern European ship captains left covert messages for their counterparts. In Barbuda, for example, Spanish observers reported that northern European ship captains hid sea snail shells in trees with notes inside in order to communicate essential information about regional trade and potential dangers.[35] Between the opportunity to refresh his vessel and obtain information, the Lesser Antilles provided a useful anchorage for Hacquet and the *Sallamandre* after the Atlantic crossing.

While Hacquet likely just bartered for food, wood, and water, other northern European traffickers found additional opportunities to make their voyage through cross-cultural trade with the Kalinago. The French fleet that had raided Arguin in 1566, for example, found the Kalinago of Dominica offering more than foodstuffs. Prior to the arrival of that French fleet, a Kalinago war party from Dominica had raided neighboring Puerto Rico. According to one Spanish report, the Kalinago that attacked the southern coast in 1566 had seized "all of the Spaniards and Blacks that they could" before setting fire to haciendas and returning to the Lesser Antilles with captives of African and European descent.[36] When the French fleet from Arguin arrived at Dominica, they used the opportunity to barter European ironware and other goods with the Kalinago in exchange for the Puerto Rican captives. For the French, those Puerto Rican captives gave them a pretext for anchoring at the neighboring Spanish island. Once at San Juan, the French ransomed the individuals who had been seized by the Kalinago back to their families and communities, using the opportunity to sell the captives from Arguin into slavery. Redeemed from captivity among the Kalinago on Dominica, in other words, the Puerto Rican captives facilitated the sale of the Arguin captives through an opportunistic form of ransom.[37] It was a strategy that Hacquet, too, adopted during his second voyage to traffic in Puerto Rico thirteen years later.

In addition to supplies and information, traffickers like Hacquet found opportunities for predation in the Lesser Antilles during the second half of the sixteenth century. Portuguese transatlantic slave ships also refreshed at islands like Dominica, which meant that some northern European traffickers haunted the waters around the Lesser Antilles seeking prey, with often extreme consequences for African survivors of the Middle Passage.[38] After refreshing his ship's water casks and food supplies at Dominica in April 1592, for example, Captain William King and the crew of the heavily armed *Salomon* encountered a hundred-ton, Portuguese transatlantic slave ship, likely also intending to use Dominica to refresh their water supplies. Instead, King and his crew seized the vessel, along with the 270 captive women, men, and children who were shackled belowdecks. King set a course for Puerto Rico, ostensibly to arrange for the sale of the captive Africans.[39] Rather than a direct voyage to Puerto Rico, however, the Africans seized by King bore captive witness to continued acts of maritime violence. Near the harbor of San Juan, King first "gave chase" to a frigate that escaped and then seized a seventy-ton English vessel smuggling wine from the Canary Islands to Puerto Rican residents with the African captives still belowdecks in King's ship.[40] Without enough food for the captive Africans, King abandoned most of them—survivors of the Middle Passage and a violent maritime confrontation at Dominica—on a foreign, hostile coastline in western Puerto Rico.

A lack of food led to the desertion by traffickers of many African women, men, and children who arrived weakened and terrified after the deprivations of the Atlantic crossing. A year before King's seizure of a Portuguese transatlantic slave ship, French traffickers seized a slave ship near Angola. They took half of the enslaved Africans and the Portuguese mariners as captives and sailed for the Caribbean, but a lack of food forced them to abandon eleven of the Angolan captives near Santiago de Cuba, where residents of the island found them half starved and in possession of only an axe and a flint for survival. Their discovery led to their sale into slavery at public auction in Santiago de Cuba.[41] These cases also underscore the importance of the trade in foodstuffs with the Kalinago for both northern European traffickers but, especially, for the enslaved Africans whom they seized and trafficked. For the fifteen enslaved Africans who remained with King, their extended captivity continued. For his part, King likely kept fifteen people captive because his ships could afford provisions for the smaller number of captives and he knew that Spanish residents in the western Caribbean would be willing to purchase a few enslaved Africans at a time, since this could be done more covertly. After the *Salomon* set sail for Hispaniola, no further archival records point to the eventual fate of those fifteen Africans.[47] Their experiences of maritime violence and repeated dislocations, after surviving the Middle Passage, illuminate the experiences of countless others caught up in Caribbean maritime predation during the late sixteenth century.

Hacquet and the crew of the *Sallamandre* sailed to the Lesser Antilles in 1575 because they knew what they would find there. With Zape war captives chained belowdecks, Hacquet first sought out trade among the Kalinago for invaluable supplies of food, wood, and water but also for information about trade opportunities in the Spanish Caribbean. The cassava produced by Kalinago women helped the Zape war captives on board the *Sallamandre* avoid abandonment and starvation on unfamiliar shores in the Caribbean. At the same time, the shipboard confinement of the Zape captives remained perilous as northern European traffickers like William King predated in the waters around the Lesser Antilles. Nor would their sale into slavery necessarily be quick. As the *Sallamandre* sailed for the southern coast of nearby Puerto Rico, Hacquet might have wondered about whether or not he would find purchasers for the people belowdecks. For the Zape war captives, the illicit nature of their sale into slavery risked prolonged shipboard confinement and hunger as supplies ran low while Hacquet sought out buyers. Uncertainty and trepidation no doubt loomed over everyone on board the *Sallamandre* as the Lesser Antilles receded in the distance.

"Fulfillment of Their Burden": Informal Trade at Puerto Rico, 1575

As the *Sallamandre* approached the southern coast of Puerto Rico in 1575, Hacquet might have fired the ship's cannons to alert coastal residents of his intentions to trade. For Puerto Rican residents outside of the orbit of San Juan, Hacquet's approach would not have been all that unusual since traffickers like Hacquet routinely connected them to wider Atlantic markets and carried away their island produce. By the second half of the sixteenth century, Puerto Rico served as an unofficial entrepôt for multiple forms of trade across the island, most of which was considered illegal by imperial officials. On the one hand, Portuguese transatlantic slave ship captains frequented San Juan to sell enslaved Africans without paying taxes on their sale. These ships, known as *arribadas forzosas* or "forced arrivals," claimed distress as a pretext for sailing to ports not listed on their license. They also carried a wide variety of trade goods in addition to enslaved Africans and accounted for nearly 40 percent of Atlantic traffic to Puerto Rico by the 1580s.[43]

On the other hand, population centers at a remove from San Juan relied increasingly on trade with northern European traffickers like Hacquet. Nor was Puerto Rico an exception within the Greater Antilles. Rural denizens of northern and western Hispaniola also developed strong commercial ties with northern Europeans, while the urban center of Santo Domingo emerged as an entrepôt for Portuguese arribadas. On both islands, however, residents lacked consistent ways to transport island produce to European markets. Portuguese transatlantic slave ships called at Puerto Rico, Hispaniola, and even Jamaica, on their way to other port cities in Spanish America, but they tended not to pass by those islands on their return voyages to Europe.[44] The hides, sugar, and, eventually, ginger that accumulated in commercially underserved parts of the Spanish Caribbean therefore provided opportunities for traffickers like Hacquet to make their voyages. If Hacquet approached the southern coast of Puerto Rico by firing the ship's cannons, he would have been following a well-worn script that had long orchestrated informal trade between northern Europeans and rural Spanish Caribbean residents.

Informal trade in the sixteenth-century Spanish Caribbean followed predictable patterns that gave structure and coherence to otherwise illicit commercial interactions.[45] Traffickers left Europe in late winter or early spring, as soon as the ice thawed in northern European ports, in order to avoid as much of the Atlantic hurricane season as possible on their return trip. The predictability of traffickers' arrival in parts of the Caribbean also gave their Spanish Caribbean trade partners time to prepare the cattle hides that drove informal trade in the region.[46] Writing in 1577, a Spanish notary in Santo Domingo named Jerónimo de Torres composed a detailed account of the flourishing informal trade conducted by traffickers like Hacquet throughout the Spanish Caribbean. As Torres explained, northern European traffickers annually brought "a great quantity of goods" to exchange for "hides, tallow, sugar and other products." The notary described how, "in order to facilitate commerce, the inhabitants [of La Yaguana in western Hispaniola] construct houses next to the ports, in which they stockpile the majority of their products until the [foreign] ships arrive."[47] This extensive trade could not occur without some scheduling. Producing and stockpiling perishable tropical produce depended on the predictable arrival of northern European traffickers, whose voyages were likewise timed to the seasonality of frozen European harbors and Atlantic hurricanes.

Northern Europeans like Hacquet gained access to markets in the Spanish Caribbean through the trafficking of enslaved people and through smuggling European manufactured goods, especially high-quality textiles and wine. According to Torres, northern European traffickers "brought many slaves and many fine cloths . . . and many linens and merchandise [such as] soap and wax."[48] That said, the prices, measured in cattle hides, that were paid for enslaved people compared with manufactured goods would have incentivized human trafficking for northern European ship captains and merchants who sought to make a voyage. According to Torres, enslaved captives brought between fifty and sixty hides per person.[49] Not only were African captives more valuable to traffickers than manufactured goods, but demand for enslaved individuals among Spanish Caribbean residents in the Greater Antilles meant that northern European ship captains and merchants found willing trade partners despite the illicit nature of the trade. As Torres described, purchasing enslaved captives from traffickers represented a "great luxury" that few Spanish Caribbean residents of the Greater Antilles turned down.[50] Northern European merchants and ship captains who had captives to traffic found ready trade partners throughout the Caribbean, and they often sailed to multiple ports—a kind of coastal foraging—to traffic captives into slavery.[51] As Torres described, traffickers ranged across the Spanish Caribbean to make a voyage or, in his words, in order to seek "the fulfillment of their burden."[52]

As was the case with William King, not all northern European traffickers purchased or seized captive women, men, and children in Atlantic Africa before entering the Caribbean. While King and many others raided Portuguese transatlantic slave ships in the Caribbean for captives, other traffickers targeted coastal populations and local shipping. The coastal regions of the Spanish Main—present-day Venezuela and Colombia—provided northern European traffickers with opportunities to raid towns, villages, and ports for captives of African descent who could be sold into slavery elsewhere. As will be seen in subsequent chapters, among the individuals caught up in this raiding and trafficking were people who were considered legally free in their communities of belonging. Captives seized from along the Spanish Main found themselves forcibly transported to smaller markets throughout the Greater Antilles where they were trafficked into slavery. According to Torres, for "each slave picked up, as a stolen good," along the Spanish Main, traffickers "receive[d] between forty or fifty hides" in places like western Hispaniola or southern Puerto Rico.[53]

Tensions undoubtably ran high during these commercial relations since not all trade was conducted peacefully. If denied trade, traffickers could, and sometimes did, resort to violence by holding residents for ransom or threatening to burn homes and villages if local residents did not supply them with trade goods, money, or food.[54] Perhaps because trade could so quickly descend into violence, some traffickers and Spanish Caribbean residents created bonds of trust with local residents, including through the use of Catholic ritual. According to the archbishop of Santo Domingo in 1594, residents of the western portion of the island traded extensively with "English and French heretics." That trade involved socializing between Catholics and Protestants, including eating and drinking together.[55] Some northern European ship captains who arrived year after year cultivated even deeper ties with residents of western Hispaniola. As the archbishop lamented, "in some ports they name the heretics as godparents to their children when they are baptized."[56] Protestant participation in Catholic baptismal ceremonies strengthened the social and commercial ties traffickers forged and facilitated trans-confessional

trade in a moment when religious violence between Catholics and Protestants raged in Europe.[57]

The extent of Hacquet's personal connections in southern Puerto Rico are
unclear from surviving archival sources. As the *Sallamandre* approached Guadianilla, Hacquet might have signaled through cannon fire to coastal residents
that he had arrived to trade. Or perhaps, if he had personal connections on the
island, he sent a sloop to shore under the cover of darkness to alert colleagues
in Puerto Rico of his arrival. A misstep at the point of establishing trade with
Spanish Caribbean residents could have been financially disastrous for Hacquet and the crew of the *Sallamandre*. In 1583, for example, another French
ship called the *Dragon* arrived low on provisions and with African captives
chained belowdecks in the town of Coamo in south-central Puerto Rico.
The ship's captain, Jean Bourdon, sent a French Dominican priest ashore to
arrange for the sale of twelve Africans in order to purchase foodstuffs. Perhaps
Bourdon assumed that a priest could facilitate technically illicit trade more
easily among the Catholic population of south-central Puerto Rico.

The ploy failed and Spanish authorities arrested the Dominican priest,
seized the twelve African captives, and sold them at public auction.[58] The
fact that the French captain had relied on a priest, who proved an ineffec-
tive intermediary, indicates that he lacked personal connections in Puerto
Rico to facilitate informal trade. Failure, however, did not deter Bourdon. By
January of the next year, the French ship captain began outfitting the *Dragon*
for another venture to the Spanish Caribbean with a wide variety of textiles,
including shirts, caps, handkerchiefs, canvas doublets, and bulk fabric.[59]
The success of Hacquet's venture, therefore, might have come from previous
experience and commercial ties on the island. Perhaps Hacquet arrived at
the kind of trade fair described by Torres, or perhaps he was anticipated by
commercial partners who prepared the trade goods in advance of his arrival
in southern Puerto Rico. Either way, in the end Hacquet and the crew of the
Sallamandre sold an unspecified number of Zape war captives into slavery in
Puerto Rico for hides and produce worth 50,000 livres.[60]

From there, however, Hacquet's luck ran out and his strategies shifted. On
the homeward voyage, somewhere between Puerto Rico and Normandy, the
Sallamandre encountered the 150-ton *Dauphin*, commanded by Edmond de
Sahures. Making a voyage created competition between ship captains, even
those of the same religious or national background, and that competition
permeated their efforts to obtain and traffic captives with myriad forms of
violence. Outmanned and outgunned, Hacquet could do little but watch the

Dauphin sail away with the Puerto Rican hides and produce taken off his ship, which Sahures later sold in Cherbourg and Honfleur.[61] In the belligerent trade of the sixteenth century, privately funded vessels technically flying the same flag often treated one another as targets for raiding. Undeterred, and perhaps learning a thing about easy money, Hacquet returned to Normandy where, at Le Havre, sponsors equipped the *Sallamandre* for raiding.[62] By May 1576, Hacquet and his crew seized the *Foudre*, a richly laden ship returning to Rouen from the West Indies.[63] And, by the summer of 1579, Hacquet and the *Sallamandre* were back in the Caribbean with 190 enslaved African captives.[64] This time Hacquet sailed in a company with another ship but, unlike his earlier voyage, he anchored at a small island off of Puerto Rico's western coast, called Mona. Like the Kalinago homelands of the Lesser Antilles, Mona also offered northern European traffickers allies, a safe anchorage, and access to food and fresh water. The Indigenous inhabitants of Mona, moreover, served as intermediaries in a robust informal trade with residents of western Puerto Rico. It was perhaps that fact, as much as access to safe anchorage and supplies, that drew Hacquet and many others like him to the small island over the second half of the sixteenth century.[65]

Indigenous Intermediaries: Mona and Informal Trade

Geography and history conspired to make Mona an important anchorage for northern European traffickers. Geographically, the small island sat at a crossroads in the Mona Passage, which provided ships anchored there with access to both Puerto Rico and the western Caribbean. From Mona, prevailing west-northwest winds through the Mona Passage allowed northern European traffickers to skirt the northern coast of Hispaniola, avoiding potential encounters with Spanish galleons at Santo Domingo.[66] At the western tip of Hispaniola, traffickers tacked south, either anchoring at Tortuga off the northwestern coast of Hispaniola or sailing farther south to islets like Caymito off the Tiburon Peninsula of western Hispaniola.[67] At each anchorage, traffickers establish networks of trade with local inhabitants—Indigenous, African, and European—who were living on the edges of Spain's licensed commercial system. Dependence on certain winds and currents for safe passage gave small islands outsized influence on the routes and customs developed by traffickers. Crucially, the island of Mona also emerged as an important entrepôt because of the Indigenous population on the island—a population whose history producing foodstuffs for Puerto Rico allowed them to establish mutually beneficial trade relations with northern European traffickers by the second half of the sixteenth century.

Hacquet undoubtedly knew of the reputation of the island's Indigenous population, who descended from peoples taken captive and enslaved by the Spanish.[68] Beginning in the early sixteenth century, Spanish slavers transported Indigenous captives to Mona where they were tasked with producing foodstuffs like cassava bread to feed Puerto Rico's growing population. Described as a *granjería*, or breadbasket, Mona exported an estimated one hundred tons of cassava bread to Puerto Rico in the 1510s alone.[69] The foodstuffs produced on the island also allowed the Spanish to use it as a collection and reshipment point for the intra-Caribbean Indigenous slave trade during the first few decades of the sixteenth century. By mid-century, the descendants of the first enslaved Indigenous people had added European livestock to the cultivation of cassava and operated farmland in San Germán, Sabana Grande, and Hormigueros in Puerto Rico as well.[70] By the time Hacquet anchored at Mona in 1579, Spanish laws had prohibited the Indigenous slave trade for nearly forty years, and Mona had transformed into an entrepôt for a different kind of trade, albeit one still tied to slavery and human trafficking.

At the center of Mona's commercial networks in the 1570s was the island's leader, a cacique named Diego Ramírez. Although it is tempting to imagine the cross-cultural trade conducted at Mona as simple bartering of trinkets in exchange for food, archival evidence points to much more sophisticated and lucrative commercial exchanges. Ramírez and the Indigenous population of Mona served as intermediaries in a thriving informal trade and the goods that passed through the island connected it and neighboring Puerto Rico with global, Atlantic, and intra-Caribbean trade circuits. On the Indigenous side, the trade did start with food. Ramírez and his companions at Mona cultivated specific foodstuffs that would appeal to European crews in the middle of extended sea voyages, including oranges to alleviate scurvy and cassava for a Caribbean version of ship biscuit.[71] Trade involved goods as quotidian as canvas for sails and as exotic as pepper or, in one case, a ring set with an emerald from the Indian Ocean. Fabric of varying qualities and types also proved especially popular with Mona's inhabitants, who traded it with residents of western Puerto Rico and with the captains and crews of passing ships.[72] Ramírez and his companions also participated in the slave trade, trafficking any captive Africans sold to them to trade partners in Puerto Rico. In some cases, Ramírez even relied on enslaved intermediaries in Puerto Rico to conduct informal trade on his behalf.[73]

Traffickers anchored at Mona for trade and foodstuffs, which proved essential for continuing their voyages into the western Caribbean. Much like the Kalinago homelands in the Lesser Antilles, traffickers used the respite at Mona to refit their vessels, remaining among Ramírez and the Indigenous populations for weeks at a time. Hacquet might have anchored at Mona with the intention of making a voyage much like that of another French trafficker, a man English observers called Monsieur de Barbotière. In 1593, Barbotière used cannon fire to signal to the Indigenous inhabitants of Mona as he approached the island. By the time he anchored, Ramírez and some of his companions would have met the French ship with foodstuffs and other trade goods. Over eighteen days, Barbotière and his crew refit their vessel in the company of Ramírez and the Indigenous population of Mona before using the prevailing winds of the Mona Passage to sail to western Hispaniola. As will be seen in the third chapter, Barbotière likely traded with intermediaries of African descent in western Hispaniola, either enslaved or members of autonomous Maroon communities in the region.[74] According to an English captain who encountered Barbotière in Mona and western Hispaniola, the French captain used some of the foodstuffs and other goods that he had purchased from Ramírez and the Indigenous inhabitants of Mona to trade for "hides which he had taken by traffike" in western Hispaniola.[75] Traffickers, in this sense, made their voyages by connecting markets between Mona and the western Caribbean and through a reliance on Indigenous and African intermediaries and trade partners. For his part, Hacquet may well have intended a similar trajectory to that of Barbotière.

Traffickers also anchored at Mona for information, much as they did with the Kalinago homelands of the Lesser Antilles. The consequences of sailing uninformed could be dire, both financially and physically. Northern European traffickers sailed with merchant syndicate financing that needed to be repaid when vessels completed their voyages. Despite the tendency to view all non-Iberian ships in the Caribbean in the second half of the sixteenth century through the lens of well-funded ventures like that of the Elizabethan privateer Francis Drake, the experiences of men like Barbotière and Hacquet were far more common. And debt undergirded their Caribbean activities. Six years prior to Hacquet's second voyage, for example, a French ship captain named Pierre Feron purchased a 110-ton ship named *La Louise* along with a smaller boat and ample maritime supplies like anchors and cordage for the not inconsiderable sum of 3,142 livres.[76] Traffickers often brought a smaller ship, like a sloop, in order to sail along rugged coastlines and coves to engage in informal trade.[77] Licensed for trade to the Barbary Coast, which might have involved preying upon Portuguese transatlantic slave ships, Feron nonetheless appeared anchored at the island of Mona along with another French ship from Dieppe. The two captains sailed together for the western Caribbean, no doubt to make a voyage and repay their debts by bartering for cattle hides, sugar, and ginger along the way.[78]

Trade at Mona facilitated the coastal foraging necessary for Feron and his companion to recoup the merchant financing invested in their voyages, while the Mona Passage allowed them to avoid Spanish galleons that periodically patrolled the waters near Santo Domingo. Armed confrontations with Spanish vessels could prove fatal for the smaller vessels preferred by traffickers. In 1586, for example, Captain Guillaume Malherbe of the *Tigre* attempted to return to Europe with nearly 90,000 livres' worth of goods from trade in the Caribbean when he encountered Spanish galleons. After an armed confrontation the *Tigre* sank, taking with it the lives of Malherbe and nearly eighty other sailors along with the financial hopes of the merchants invested in the voyage.[79] Information and safe anchorages clearly proved essential to making a voyage in this moment of predatory Caribbean trade.

Perhaps Hacquet learned about commercial opportunities in Hispaniola during his time refitting the *Sallamandre* at Mona. Hacquet likely would have found a market in Hispaniola, but another opportunity presented itself in the channel between Puerto Rico and Hispaniola.[80] In a lone ship sailing back to Puerto Rico was that island's governor, Francisco de Obando, who had been in Santo Domingo recovering from a "grave illness."[81] Hacquet and his crew seized the ship, taking the governor and his traveling companions as captives. The capture of Puerto Rico's governor and his entourage created an opportunity for Hacquet to use *rescate* to make his voyage, ransoming Obando for the sale of the 190 enslaved captives still on board the *Sallamandre*.[82] The strain was too much for the Spanish governor, who died shortly after his release from captivity.[83] In the end, for the second time in less than five years, Hacquet and the crew of the *Sallamandre* set a course for Normandy with a hold full of Puerto Rican hides and produce.

Placing the two voyages of Hacquet into a wider context illuminates the entangled nature of trading, raiding, and captive-taking for traffickers who sought to make a voyage during the second half of the sixteenth century.

Alongside the actions of his contemporaries, Hacquet's two voyages appear less exceptional and more embedded in a regional economy. Crucially, understanding the quotidian nature of this violent informal economy forces us to grapple with what this all meant for captives caught up in raids and trafficked into slavery illicitly. One of the 190 enslaved Africans shackled belowdecks on Hacquet's ship at Mona in 1579, a woman who would be baptized with the name Catalina, experienced the violent, nonlinear nature of the transatlantic and intra-Caribbean slave trades for people seized and trafficked by men like Hacquet during the second half of the sixteenth century. To trace her experiences in this moment, we must return to the deck of the *Sallamandre* as residents of Puerto Rico bartered with Hacquet in order to purchase Catalina and her shipmates.

Rescate and Sale in Puerto Rico

Catalina and her shipmates might have caught a glimpse of the erstwhile governor of Puerto Rico and his companions on the island of Mona. Enslaved to a landowner and wealthy *vecino* of western Puerto Rico after her time at Mona, Catalina likely eventually learned about the nefarious way in which she had been sold into slavery when the man who claimed ownership over her became the center of an investigation into informal trade in Puerto Rico. For that brief moment when Catalina and her shipmates shared their status as captives with Obando and other elite residents of Puerto Rico at Mona, it is unclear if the Senegambians would have known why their French captors held Spanish captives as well. For Hacquet and the French crew of the *Sallamandre*, Obando and his entourage provided an opportunity to make their voyage through a practice known as *rescate*.

Defined as "rescue," the practice of rescate developed over centuries of Christian-Muslim warfare in the Mediterranean world and evolved alongside practices of slaveholding in the Caribbean. The use of captives to facilitate trade was long-standing in both the Mediterranean and Caribbean worlds. In fact, as scholars Kaiser Wolfgang and Guillaume Calafat have argued, in the Mediterranean, "trading captives allowed merchants and ship captains to establish commerce with political and religious enemies."[84] By the sixteenth century, Spanish merchants in the Caribbean used rescate to describe the purchase of Indigenous captives from their Indigenous captors. Rescate, in this sense, implied a religious rescue or redemption—the Indigenous captives, according to the Spanish, had been rescued from so-called idolatry by virtue of having been purchased from Indigenous captors and sold into slavery among Catholics.[85] On the other hand, rescate also referred to trade with foreigners. Often, rescate implied some kind of violence or force. Northern European interlopers on Spain's commercial monopoly in the Caribbean, according to officials on the ground, threatened violence if Spanish Caribbean officials did not permit trade or, as was the case with Hacquet, used ransom to force trade. Threat facilitated commerce and, eventually, rescate was used to describe any trade with non-Iberian merchants, forced or not, that was considered illicit by Spanish metropolitan officials.[86]

Hacquet was not alone in using the ransom of captives to facilitate trade. The French fleet from Arguin, discussed above, provides another example of how northern European traffickers leveraged captives in order to make a voyage. Just as a trans-confessional trade in the Mediterranean flourished through practices of captive-taking and redemption, the French fleet sold the captives from Arguin through the ransoming of Puerto Rican prisoners from Dominica. It should hardly be surprising that European traffickers carried a modified version of this practice to the Spanish Caribbean in order to facilitate informal trade. In 1556, for example, a crew of French traffickers raided the hacienda of the mayor of San Germán, taking the mayor and a notary as captives in the process. According to Spanish reports, the traffickers kept the two men for a number of days before they ransomed them in exchange for "meat and some things to eat."[87] Just as the French crew from Arguin ransomed captives purchased from the Kalinago, rescate provided traffickers with a method for engaging in trade across imperial borders in the sixteenth-century Caribbean. By the middle of the seventeenth century, as will be seen in later chapters, this practice transformed into using prisoners of the Caribbean's many inter-imperial wars to engage in informal trade through rescate. And, while the redemption of San Germán's mayor and notary allegedly only yielded foodstuffs, Hacquet would use the practice to engage in a more extensive and lucrative trade.

As was clear from his first voyage to Puerto Rico, Hacquet did not need elite Spanish captives in order to traffic people like Catalina and her shipmates into slavery. Residents of southern and western Puerto Rico engaged in widespread, informal trade with northern European traffickers throughout the second half of the sixteenth century. Some of that trade involved local residents allowing northern European ships to anchor along the coast for extended periods of time. Even Richard Grenville, captain of the *Tiger* that transported ill-fated English colonists to Roanoke in 1585, anchored at Las Boquillas in southern Puerto Rico. Over the weeks that Grenville and the English spent there, English artist John White made several paintings depicting their temporary encampment and the flora and fauna of the island.[88] For traffickers like Hacquet, moreover, the cattle ranchers of western Puerto Rico made for ready commercial partners. Herds of longhorn cattle ranged wild in areas such as San Germán, Guayama, and Ceiba, out of reach of imperial officials in San Juan. Ranchers employed mounted hunters, who used half-moon–shaped blades called *jarretas* to take down cattle. Their hides, tallow, and meat provided the lifeblood of informal trade in western Puerto Rico over the second half of the sixteenth century.[89] While Hacquet did not need elite Spanish captives to make his voyage, the fortuitous encounter with the ship transporting Puerto Rico's governor would provide him with more lucrative trade with elites from San Juan.

In the end, Catalina and her shipmates were sold across the island. Since Puerto Rico served as an entrepôt in the resale of enslaved Africans, it is likely that many of Catalina's shipmates would be sold again and transshipped across the Spanish Caribbean.[90] According to reports produced during an investigation into this moment of informal trade, "almost all of the *vecinos* were guilty" of trading openly with Hacquet. Some Spanish residents even did business on the deck of the *Sallamandre*, for "the hides and sugars they had."[91] Residents in western Puerto Rico purchased Senegambian captives from Hacquet, including the man who first purchased Catalina.[92] Elites in San Juan also responded to the ransom demands of Hacquet through the negotiations of an island resident named Juan Dias de Santana, who set the price for the healthy, adult shipmates of Catalina at forty *arrobas* of sugar each and arranged for the transportation of sugar and hides to the western port of Vargas to purchase captives for residents of San Juan.[93] Even the religious elite of San Juan got involved. The bishop of Puerto Rico, Diego de Salamanca, purchased twelve of Catalina's shipmates in exchange for a quantity of pearls and a silver cross.[94] Some residents sent intermediaries to conduct business with Hacquet. The man who purchased Catalina, a royal official in San Germán named Pedro Méndez de los Ríos, sent another resident to purchase her on his behalf off of the deck of the *Sallamandre*.[95] Catalina found herself enslaved on the expansive cattle ranch of Méndez de los Ríos near Cabo Rojo in western Puerto Rico.[96] Within a decade of her original sale, Catalina gave birth to a mixed-race child.[97] Perhaps Catalina's child indicated that she labored in a domestic setting and used whatever intimacies that space provided to create affective ties that might have improved her situation.[98] Perhaps her pregnancy resulted from sexual violence. Perhaps, too, she shared her bondage in Cabo Rojo with other Senegambian captives from the *Sallamandre*.

During her enslavement, Catalina might also have labored in the production of ginger—a crop that would bring more men like Hacquet to traffic captives into slavery in western and southern Puerto Rico. In 1582, Spanish residents in Puerto Rico began the commercial cultivation of ginger. At the same moment, Spanish officials on the island began the construction of fortifications that required increasing amounts of labor to build and maintain. The confluence of these two events led to the rapid increase in the importation of enslaved Africans, 75 percent of whom arrived through technically illicit channels in the late sixteenth century.[99]

The production of ginger contributed to the informal slave trade, especially with northern European traffickers like Hacquet, for several reasons. First, demand for ginger proved highest in northern Europe, especially England and the Netherlands where the root proved an essential ingredient in humoral medicinal treatments for inhabitants of cold, wet climates. Second, the production season for ginger meant that producers in the Spanish Caribbean often missed the Spanish fleet system. Ginger was cultivated in the Caribbean beginning in January but needed a period to dry before it could be shipped. Spanish Caribbean residents who risked shipping ginger through licit channels in the March fleet system often ended up with a rotten shipment by the time it arrived in Spain. Perhaps more importantly, however, ginger shipped best packed in cattle hides. As historian Bethany Aram notes, the entwined nature of these commodities—cattle hides and ginger—brought greater numbers of northern European traffickers to places like southern and western Puerto Rico in the late sixteenth century. Those same traffickers, in turn, brought additional African captives who labored in the production of hides, ginger, and, eventually, sugar.[100] The growing number of northern European traffickers in the Spanish Caribbean in the next century would facilitate English and French colonization.

Captivity and Trafficking from a Kalinago Perspective

Not all northern European traffickers treated their regional allies well, with some leaving violence and distrust in their wake. Concluding this chapter requires thinking about these moments from the perspective of some of those

allies. Specifically, the experiences of the Kalinago reveal the sometimes brutal nature of cross-cultural trade in the late sixteenth century. By the 1620s,
when the Kalinago would host the first permanent English colonists in the
Caribbean, they had spent a century defending their island homelands from
encroachment. That defense relied on cross-cultural trade with northern
European traffickers, who sometimes betrayed their hosts in order to make
their voyage. In the winter of 1581, for example, a Kalinago war party aimed
their large *canáoas*, or canoes, for the island they called Ouboüémoin. Generations of war parties just like theirs had embarked on the same journey to
raid the island that their Taíno enemies had called Borriken. The new occu-
pants called it Puerto Rico, and the hundreds of Kalinago warriors who sailed
there that winter carried a special vendetta against the *sihuiyábonum*, or
Spanish, who lived there. Guiding the war party were Kalinago who had been
purchased as slaves by Spanish residents of San Germán before they escaped
by building canáoas out of view of the Spanish. Their escape proved fatal for
the residents of San Germán.[101]

When their self-liberated kin returned, the normal feasting and drinking that preceded Kalinago raids might have been rushed.[102] Not all of the
Kalinago who had been sold into slavery had escaped, and the war party
sought both revenge and liberation of their kin who remained as slaves on
Ouboüémoin. Once on shore, the Kalinago waged a campaign of "fire and
blood" against San Germán.[103] Spanish observers reported that the Kalinago
burned San Germán to the ground and attacked each of the haciendas that
held Kalinago as slaves, liberating their kin and seizing European and African captives before slaughtering livestock and setting fire to the remaining
buildings. Spanish reports would describe San Germán as "depopulated" in
the wake of this and subsequent Kalinago raids over the next decade.[104]

The war party in 1581 redeemed their kin from slavery and punished the
Spanish who had purchased them. Seeking revenge against the men who had
taken their kin captive in the first place, however, would be more complicated. Before they had betrayed their Kalinago hosts, those French sailors
had been allies and trade partners who provided the tools and weapons that
undergirded Kalinago power in the eastern Caribbean. Turning these trade
partners away risked cutting the Kalinago off from the strategic metal and
manufactured goods that their trade partners brought. Nor could the Kalinago raid the settlements of the men who had deceived their kin and trafficked
them into slavery in Puerto Rico. The French had no permanent settlements
in the region. Instead, they used Kalinago islands to obtain food, wood, and

water and to repair their ships. For the Kalinago war party that returned to the Lesser Antilles with their liberated kin and a number of new captives, therefore, the victory might have rung hollow. They had not punished the men who had made captives of their kin. In the future, however, they would know to be more cautious during trade with northern Europeans and would remain on the lookout for those who they called *acamátêti likia*, translated as "pirates who put Kalinago in irons and take them away."[105]

The phrase acamátêti likia distinguished between European trade partners and so-called pirates who took captives and trafficked them into slavery. By the middle of the seventeenth century, the category of human traffickers had become such a standard part of the Kalinago's daily vocabulary that it was recorded by the Dominican missionary and linguist Raymond Breton in his 1665 French-Kalinago dictionary. The example of European traffickers seizing Kalinago trade partners and selling them into slavery in Puerto Rico in the 1580s would clearly not be a singular occurrence. Crucially, the linguistic need on the part of the Kalinago to separate trade partners from potential pirates reveals a central tension that underpinned almost all cross-cultural trade in the sixteenth- and seventeenth-century Caribbean—the potential for violence as a result of a trade that centered around captive slavery.

For the Kalinago warriors who returned from the 1581 raid on Puerto Rico, their continued alliance with northern Europeans likely seemed a mixed blessing. The craftsmen who labored on the fleets of canáoa worked faster as a result of the tools that Europeans brought. The Kalinago also had a new outlet for the captives that they seized during their raids. At the same time, among their European trade partners were "the pirates who put Kalinago in irons and take them away." The Kalinago were aware of the centrality of captive-taking and human trafficking to their northern European trade partners—they, too, profited from the European obsession with captive slavery. Perhaps for this reason, the Kalinago accepted the risk that trade with northern Europeans might bring acamátêti likia into their communities. Through the end of the sixteenth century, Kalinago power in the eastern Caribbean meant that they could punish anyone who purchased their kin as slaves. As the coming decades would show, however, the Kalinago did not anticipate that the success of their European trade partners in making their voyages would encourage the arrival of a very different kind of northern European, this one less concerned with temporarily dwelling in Kalinago-dominated spaces and more with claiming those spaces as their own. The routes and practices developed by traffickers and the alliances they formed with the Kalinago would facilitate English and French colonization in ways that permanently shifted the balance of power in the eastern Caribbean.

Traffickers, too, encountered a different world by the first decades of the seventeenth century. By this time informal trade had become an ingrained part of the economic, social, and political lives of many Spanish Caribbean residents.[106] Navigating the greater Caribbean in search of trade opportunities, however, was risky for European ships and sailors. Sailing was a dangerous activity in the sixteenth century. Contrary winds might delay a voyage, leading to dwindling food and water supplies, or storms might damage the ship. Even if a voyage went well, traffickers faced confrontations with Spanish galleons tasked with defending Caribbean sea lanes. Political changes as well, such as the appointment of a new governor, could lead to the prosecution of informal trade where it had formerly been permitted. Responding to these dangers required that northern European merchants and ship captains establish safe anchorages throughout the Caribbean for the purpose of refitting their vessels and exchanging information.

As traffickers anchored at the same spaces year after year, they developed commercial connections with local inhabitants across the greater Caribbean, from the Kalinago of the Lesser Antilles to the mixed-race cattle ranchers of southern Puerto Rico and western Hispaniola, and the Indigenous inhabitants of Mona. These regional allies provided vital food, shelter, and information to northern European traffickers. By the opening decades of the seventeenth century, however, the anchorages used by traffickers over the previous half century came to the attention of colonizing interests in Europe. The establishment of official colonies in the Lesser Antilles beginning in the 1620s would have profound implications for traffickers, their trade partners, and people of African and Indigenous descent vulnerable to captivity and human trafficking.

CHAPTER 2

"Betwixt Ye Two Rivers"

Human Trafficking and Colonization

The Kalinago of the Lesser Antilles continued to act as brokers of intercultural trade with northern European traffickers into the first two decades of the seventeenth century. Their European trade partners brought prestige goods like glass beads and mirrors as well as essential iron implements like nails, needles, knives, hoes, axes, and saws.[1] In turn, the Kalinago continued to provide food, wood, water, and safe anchorage as they had over the previous half century. For all that remained the same, however, Kalinago populations in the Lesser Antilles witnessed subtle changes over the first decade of the seventeenth century. Notably, the northern Europeans who anchored at their islands desired even more *itámanle*, or tobacco. The Kalinago had introduced tobacco consumption to European- and African-descended sailors in the sixteenth century, but now their trade partners loaded more tobacco than seemed necessary for the smoking or snuffing needs of the men on their ships.[2] For the *oüábou*, or captains, of Kalinago populations on islands throughout the Lesser Antilles this was not necessarily a problem—demand for tobacco brought ships, and ships brought the iron tools that made their lives easier. During the early 1620s, the oüábou of the island of Liamuiga, a man named Tegreman, facilitated trade in tobacco and food with numerous groups of northern European traffickers in exchange for the goods they brought. He did not anticipate that European demand for tobacco or the arrival of a group of twenty-six Englishmen in 1624 served as harbingers of profound changes on the horizon. Unlike the traffickers who had come before them, the Englishmen whom Tegreman settled in houses "betwixt ye two rivers" next to the *táboüi*, or communal men's house, would not leave once their ships were repaired and the men rested.[3] Instead, those Englishmen meant to stay.

The experiences of a Canary Islander named Simón Martines offer another window into cross-cultural trade and nascent settlements in the Lesser Antilles in 1624. That year, Martines had labored on a Jamaican ship ferrying trade goods to Santiago de Cuba when a crew of French traffickers attacked it. The traffickers took Martines and an unnamed boy captive and forced them to work on their ship over the next eleven months as it sailed from the western Caribbean to multiple locations in the Lesser Antilles. Once in the Lesser Antilles, the French ship passed islands and waterways bustling with northern European traffickers. Between Dominica and Martinique, Martines witnessed English, French, and Dutch traffickers forming what he described as "a flotilla of corsairs" that acted in concert with one another, traded with the Kalinago for tobacco and food, cultivated their own tobacco, and cut dyewood.[4] Among the ship captains of that "flotilla" was Pierre Bélain d'Esnambuc who, four years earlier, had escaped a nearly fatal encounter with Spanish galleons at the small island of Caymito off the southwestern tip of Hispaniola. By the fall of 1624, Martines met d'Esnambuc at Martinique where the Norman ship captain was trading with the Kalinago and exchanging information with a multinational company of ships captains. Within two years, d'Esnambuc transitioned from trafficking to become the governor of the first Crown-sanctioned, permanent French colony in the Caribbean. Established alongside the original twenty-six Englishmen whom Tegreman settled near the communal men's house on Liamuiga, the French and English colonization of an island that Europeans called St. Christopher disrupted practices of cross-cultural trade that traffickers had forged with the Kalinago over the previous century.

Centering the experiences of individuals like Tegreman or Simón Martines recasts the history of early European colonization in the Lesser Antilles. Rather than an inevitable outcome of northern Europeans' desire to secure Caribbean territory to meet the growing European demand for tobacco, the colonization of St. Christopher emerges as a contingent process embedded in the networks of cross-cultural trade and widespread raiding that traffickers had established over the previous half century. The twenty-six Englishmen who settled on Liamuiga, under the command of Thomas Warner, arrived in January 1624 after fleeing Roger North's failed attempt at colonizing Guiana.[5] According to historians, Warner learned of St. Christopher when he was in Guiana, and he selected the island for an English colony because it was "quiet," "distant from Spanish control," and "removed as far as possible from contact with the Spanish and Indian populations centers."[6] All were important qualities for colonists who sought to cultivate tobacco without fear of

Spanish and Indigenous reprisals, but those descriptions are oddly discordant with the perspectives of individuals like Tegreman or Martines. As oüábou of the Kalinago population of Liamuiga, Tegreman permitted Warner and his twenty-six companions to occupy dwellings among his people as part of long-standing networks of cross-cultural trade established by northern European traffickers, not as permanent colonists but as temporary trade partners. Traffickers frequented Kalinago-dominated islands not because they were isolated spaces but precisely because of the proximity of the Lesser Antilles to the Spanish Caribbean. Martines's description of a "flotilla of corsairs" who traded with the Kalinago, refreshed their vessels, and used islands like St. Christopher as a base for raiding and trafficking in the Spanish Caribbean would fit more comfortably alongside the Caribbean world that Tegreman had known from decades of experience. From the perspectives of both men, St. Christopher was neither quiet nor isolated when Warner and the English colonists arrived.

The same dynamics that made St. Christopher a useful base for traffickers—alliances with the Kalinago and integration into a regional economy of raiding and trafficking—made it an appealing location for colonization. Crucially, those dynamics explain the survival of Warner and his twenty-six men when they first arrived, and trafficking networks continued to shape colonial development after Warner and d'Esnambuc became governors. Northern European traffickers involved in raiding Iberian ships, coastal communities, and small vessels continued to use St. Christopher to careen their vessels, purchase food, and exchange information after 1624. At the same time, traffickers found Kalinago-dominated islands in the Lesser Antilles less receptive to cross-cultural trade in the aftermath of the violence surrounding the colonial dispossession of Tegreman and his people from Liamuiga. As a result, traffickers became more reliant on St. Christopher as a maritime base in the Caribbean, and their activities shaped the development of St. Christopher in important ways, especially in terms of the adoption of slavery by colonists on the island. Commercial ties with traffickers created an early commitment to slavery among St. Christopher's inhabitants, who proved more than willing to purchase people taken captive through regional raiding. Beginning in 1627, the governors of St. Christopher negotiated a series of treaties meant to control the island's growing population of unfree people. These treaties reflect the commitment of island residents to slavery and represent the earliest iterations of laws related to slavery in either the English or French Caribbean, the contours of which were shaped not by legal precedent in Europe but, rather, by a vernacular understanding of slavery developed by traffickers over the half century before colonization. Beginning with patterns of cross-cultural trade established with the Kalinago in the Lesser Antilles, traffickers influenced the development of St. Christopher from a maritime base to an island colony embedded in networks of informal trade and human trafficking.

Trade and Dwelling Among the Kalinago

By the late sixteenth century, the Kalinago had established their power in the eastern Caribbean by defending their islands from Spanish slaving expeditions and by launching successful raids of their own against neighboring Puerto Rico. This détente made islands like St. Christopher, Martinique, and Dominica ideal locations for northern European traffickers to provision and refit their vessels during long Caribbean cruises necessary for making their voyages. Traffickers often spent extended periods of time among the Kalinago of the Lesser Antilles, living in the sorts of onshore dwellings that Tegreman provided for Warner or that Martines witnessed in Martinique. For traffickers, this ability to dwell temporarily on Kalinago islands provided them with more than just foodstuffs. Crucially, traffickers used these anchorages to perform the essential labor of careening and caulking their vessels. In the warm, tropical waters of the Caribbean, careening and caulking the hulls of ships had to be performed every two to four months because of the prevalence of the teredo worm, a mollusk that could eat through the hulls of ships.[7] This laborious task involved half exposing the hull in order to scrape or burn off marine animals, fungus, and barnacles. Seams and splits would be stuffed with tarred oakum before sailors covered the entire hull with pitch and, if it was available, a second coat of quicklime—a toxic, white paste that deterred mollusks—in a process known as caulking. Sailors found many of the natural ingredients essential for careening throughout the Caribbean, but islands in the Lesser Antilles provided an especially abundant supply of natural pitch for caulking and whelks, the shells of which sailors cooked down to produce quicklime.[8] This process left crews immobile and vulnerable, making safe anchorages in the Lesser Antilles essential for traffickers. For their part, the Kalinago profited from these extended stays by providing shelter, food, and, increasingly, tobacco in exchange for European trade goods.[9]

European demand for tobacco in the late sixteenth and early seventeenth centuries had consequences for the world that traffickers navigated and the networks of trade they developed. By the 1590s, the Kalinago faced competition in attracting northern European traffickers, especially from the nascent tobacco plantations on the Spanish island of Trinidad, where traffickers also found safe anchorages and access to trade. The English, French, and Dutch vessels that navigated the Orinoco River as groups of northern Europeans attempted colonization along its basin passed Spanish Trinidad, located at the mouth of the Orinoco River delta. Under the command of Rodrigo Manuel Nunes Lobo, a Portuguese man who maintained widespread commercial connections with Portuguese, English, and French merchant communities, Trinidad emerged as a popular rendezvous for traffickers and merchants of all nationalities during the late sixteenth and early seventeenth centuries. Much like the informal trade fairs of Hispaniola, the tobacco trade out of Trinidad was seasonal and often involved traffickers anchored at Trinidad or the nearby island of Margarita for two to three months at a time. The tobacco trade reached huge proportions, and by 1611, nearly one million pounds of tobacco from Trinidad and eastern Venezuela arrived annually in London alone.[10] Recognizing the growing importance of tobacco to regional networks of trade, Kalinago populations throughout the Lesser Antilles also began to cultivate more of the weed for their northern European trade partners. For captives to labor in their tobacco fields, the Kalinago raided surrounding Spanish Caribbean populations and, occasionally, even Portuguese transatlantic slave ships.[11] Growing demand for tobacco in Europe alongside regional competition to supply it meant that small-scale merchants and shipowners throughout Europe regularly sent ships to the Caribbean to make their voyage by returning with the sweet-scented tobacco for European markets.[12] Tobacco, in other words, joined hides and ginger as a commodity that drove informal trade in the greater Caribbean.

The growing tobacco trade in the eastern Caribbean peaked in the 1610s before Spanish policies and English politics made the trade less attractive to investors. By 1606, the Spanish Council of the Indies responded to widespread informal trade in the greater Caribbean by instituting a ten-year ban on the cultivation of tobacco.[13] The policy met with mixed success, especially in parts of Spain's Caribbean territories that received little by way of legal trade. More successful were occasional acts of violence against northern Europeans caught interloping in Spanish territory, such as the capture of twenty-seven sailors off of the English ships the *Ulysses* and the *Primrose* at Trinidad in 1608. Despite the claims of the English sailors from those ships that they paid a ransom of 20,000 ducats for the release of their companions, Spanish authorities in Trinidad ordered the men hung as pirates and interlopers.[14] For English merchants, violence and the ban on tobacco cultivation cooled investment in small-scale smuggling voyages at the same time that James I negotiated a peace with Spain. In the Treaty of London, signed in 1604, James I disavowed any Englishmen who used violence against subjects of the Spanish Crown in the Americas while also declaring that English subjects had the right to colonize any American territory not actively settled by a European monarch—ignoring completely the sovereign Indigenous polities in those spaces.[15] For English merchants, the threat of violence by Spanish officials in the Caribbean coupled with the risk of criminal proceedings in England incentivized the investment in colonization schemes in the early seventeenth century.[16] Traffickers, of course, continued to receive merchant financing for their voyages throughout the 1610s and 1620s, but they increasingly shared Caribbean waters with vessels of Englishmen charged with establishing colonies in the region. For those would-be colonists, practices of intercultural trade that traffickers had established over the previous half century created circumstances in which Indigenous populations like the Kalinago initially welcomed them on the assumption that their occupation of Kalinago spaces would be temporary.

Testimony from the ill-fated voyage of John Nicholl to Guiana in 1605 sheds light on how intercultural trade and communication with the Kalinago was supposed to function—if only because the interactions of Nicholl and his compatriots with the Kalinago of St. Lucia went so disastrously wrong.[17] Nicholl and the sixty-seven other Englishmen on board the *Olive Branch* were colonists sent by Oliphe Leigh to join the nascent English settlement that his brother, Charles Leigh, had established at Wiapoco, along the modern-day Oyapock River. The captain of the *Olive Branch*, however, overshot Guiana and spent weeks "plying to and again" along the coast before hunger and thirst forced them to land at St. Lucia. As Nicholl explained, "we had no sooner anchored, but the [Kalinago] came in their Periagos or Boats aboard us with great store of Tobacco, Plantains, Potatoes, Pines, Sugar Canes, and diverse other fruits, with Hens, Chickens, Turtles & Iguanas." The next day the English went ashore and the oüábou of the Kalinago on St. Lucia, a man named Antonio, settled the English in "five or seven houses planted by a pleasant fresh water river" for the price of a "Hatchet."[18] Welcoming a European vessel with food and providing its crew with housing next to a source of fresh water, all at a preset price, highlights the regularity with which Antonio and the Kalinago of St. Lucia engaged in cross-cultural trade with Europeans.[19]

Map 3. Orinoco and the Windward Islands

For Antonio and the Kalinago of St. Lucia, these transactions with Nicholl and his crew likely seemed normal, and they undoubtedly expected the English to begin refitting their vessel, as European mariners had done innumerable times over the previous half century. Traffickers had frequented the region since the mid-sixteenth century to harass the pearl fisheries of Margarita and, later, to engage in widespread informal trade for tobacco with

Trinidad.[20] In fact, relations between the English and Kalinago only soured when, after the *Olive Branch* sailed away from St. Lucia, the bulk of the English remained behind and started fortifying their settlement—clearly signaling to Antonio and the other Kalinago on the island that the newcomers intended on staying. The Kalinago attacked the English settlement and the few English survivors fled to the Spanish mainland. As this example highlights, the Kalinago welcomed trade, even when it brought Europeans onto their shores for extended periods, but they refused to allow permanent occupation.

From Dwelling to Colonizing

As hubs of information, safe anchorages, and trade, the Lesser Antilles played a prominent role in early seventeenth-century colonization from efforts to settle Guiana to the establishment of Jamestown.[21] It was, then, no coincidence that parts of the Lesser Antilles became the locations of England's and France's first Caribbean colonies and not at all because those islands were considered the periphery of the Spanish empire. Rather, the proximity of the Lesser Antilles to Spanish Caribbean settlements and the autonomy of those islands' Kalinago inhabitants drew northern European traffickers to the region, many of whom had experience with similar trade relations with Indigenous populations in Guiana and Brazil. Traffickers made certain spaces in the Lesser Antilles useful to their designs—engaging in everything from trade with the Kalinago to using captive labor to cut logwood and cultivate tobacco. These crews, in a sense, colonized without claiming sovereignty over islands in the Lesser Antilles. They dwelled in the region during their sojourns, year after year, integrating places like St. Christopher and Martinique into a regional and transatlantic economy decades before monarchs in England or France granted commissions for the colonization of the region.

Simón Martines, the hapless mariner who opened this chapter, witnessed firsthand how northern European traffickers dwelled temporarily in the Lesser Antilles in order to engage in raiding and informal trade throughout the Caribbean.[22] After capturing the sixty-ton Spanish ship in the waters between Jamaica and Cuba, Martines's French captor, a man named Pantel, set sail for the Lesser Antilles. At Martinique, Pantel reunited with a cohort of traffickers, among them Pierre Bélain d'Esnambuc, and several Dutch and English captains, who were refitting, exchanging information, trading with the Kalinago, and harvesting tropical staples. The largest of the seven ships

Martines described was a Dutch vessel at 150 tons, while the smallest was an eighty-ton English ship. The Dutch shipmaster had sailed from Europe with four other ships, one of which sank during a naval skirmish off the coast of Puerto Rico, and another went down near Havana. The English captain left Martinique in order to cruise for prizes along Tierra Firme, with the goal of sailing from there to Havana, while several of the French shipmasters had recently been cruising around St. Vincent and were loading wood, water, and foodstuffs like cassava for a voyage to Jamaica and Cuba. The process of refitting their vessels provided these traffickers with a venue in which they could exchange information, form partnerships, and share strategies across linguistic and ethnic boundaries.[23]

In order to harvest tropical staples, some northern European traffickers stayed for extended periods in the Lesser Antilles. For example, Martines and the French crew spent nearly four months at Martinique, where Pantel considered Martines's labor on land as valuable as it was at sea. According to Martines, he found himself forced "to work with the Indians" in addition to loading fustic, a yellow dyewood, onto the ship. The Kalinago welcomed trade with the new arrivals, to whom "they gave cassava."[24] And, although Martines omitted a description of them in his testimony, the Europeans would have lived in rudimentary dwellings on shore in Martinique—either constructed by the crew or rented from their Kalinago hosts.[25] The ubiquity of these sorts of temporary dwellings can help explain inaccurate Spanish Caribbean reports regarding the presence of French colonies decades before the French Crown sanctioned colonial expansion in the region. In 1586, for example, Spanish officials in Santo Domingo warned the Crown that "the French have settled on Dominica."[26] That island, however, would not be formally claimed by the Compagnie des Îles de l'Amérique for almost another fifty years. Even as late as 1675, an English report described Dominica as inhabited entirely by Kalinago.[27] The reports of a French "settlement" on Dominica in 1586 were, in all likelihood, the temporary dwellings of the sort Pantel and his crew occupied in Martinique during their four-month stay. Nor were Martinique and Dominica the only islands of the Lesser Antilles where the Kalinago hosted northern European traffickers on a regular basis.

Like their counterparts in Martinique and Dominica, the Kalinago of St. Christopher also provided northern European traffickers with food and temporary shelter in exchange for European manufactured goods. According to a Dutch sailor named Jan Petre, the Kalinago of St. Christopher welcomed him and the other twenty-seven crew members of the Dutch ship that he served on when they arrived from Amsterdam around 1625. Petre and his cohort spent fifteen days at the island where they refitted their ship after the Atlantic crossing and purchased cassava and other supplies from the Kalinago. For their part, according to Petre, the Kalinago sought knives and axes "and other things used to cut wood" from the traffickers.[28] Those tools eased the labor of Kalinago craftsmen, especially the individuals responsible for felling trees and hollowing out the trunks to make the large *canáoa*, or dugout canoes, that connected Kalinago populations throughout the Lesser Antilles.[29] The Dutch captain of Petre's ship knew to bring trade goods sought after by the Kalinago, and he sailed away from St. Christopher with durable foodstuffs. Petre and his cohort left for Puerto Rico where they smuggled along the coast over the course of two days before being discovered by a Spanish patrol. With ample supplies of food, wood, and water, the Dutch traffickers fled Puerto Rico for the western Caribbean, seizing along the way a small Spanish ship transporting tobacco and a Portuguese frigate carrying wine to Santo Domingo. A failed smuggling run at Jamaica ended Petre and his companions' attempts to make their voyage, but their experiences highlight the importance and regularity of cross-cultural trade between northern European traffickers and the Kalinago of St. Christopher on the eve of English and French colonization in the region.[30]

For the early history of colonization in the Lesser Antilles, the longstanding Kalinago practice of renting houses or shelters to northern European traffickers, who dwelled on certain islands for extended periods of time, explains the survival of the first English colonists on the island of St. Christopher. As Martines reported, St. Christopher was "populated with Indians and . . . with them twenty-six English who have their houses . . . and cultivate tobacco."[31] In January 1624, six months prior to Martines's arrival, Thomas Warner, an Englishman who had fled from Roger North's failed colony in Guiana, received merchant financing in London in order to transport a small group of colonists to the island. And, by September 1625, Warner was also granted the first English commission to colonize in the Lesser Antilles. As a result, historians have long considered the arrival of those English settlers to St. Christopher as the beginning of English colonization in the Caribbean. And, from an institutional perspective, the settlement of St. Christopher in 1624 and subsequent granting of a colonial patent to Warner in 1625 did, in fact, make that island England's first Caribbean colony. But the tendency to begin the story of colonization in the Lesser Antilles in the 1620s or to treat Warner as being responsible for the "discovery of St. Christopher" obscures the role of preexisting cross-cultural practices in shaping how Warner and his English settlers were able to occupy the island in the first place.[32]

Making sense of the success of the English venture on St. Christopher requires thinking about Warner and the English settlers through the lens of the commercial etiquette developed by the Kalinago and northern European traffickers in the fifty years before 1624. To borrow from historian Michael Guasco, this analysis means thinking about the Caribbean "*as it was* rather than what it would become."[33] At the most basic level, this analysis explains why Warner—with a company of only fifteen settlers—could claim land and establish a permanent colony in Kalinago territory without the kind of bloodshed that met John Nicholl and his company at St. Lucia.[34] At least initially, Tegreman and the Kalinago on St. Christopher saw the English venture as another opportunity to trade with Europeans for a short term. In much the same way that the Kalinago on St. Lucia provided Nicholl and his crew with housing near a freshwater river, Warner "with licence of King Tegreman" received permission to settle "betwixt ye two rivers neare to ye Kings house." For Tegreman, providing European mariners with housing near access to fresh water was part of the quotidian trade relations that had allowed the Kalinago to maintain sovereignty in the Lesser Antilles over the previous century. Although often described as permission to establish a colony, Tegreman's "licence" should be read as granting Warner and his companions access to water, food, and shelter on the kind of temporary basis that long defined relations between traffickers and the Kalinago.[35]

The Kalinago welcomed European trade partners, but they welcomed them on their own terms—as allies who occupied designated spaces for limited periods of time. Tegreman also had every reason to believe that Warner's occupation would be temporary, no matter how obvious the colonizing intentions of the English might appear in hindsight. The Kalinago on St. Christopher had hosted northern European traffickers on what, to contemporary Spanish observers at least, appeared to be a regular basis from at least the 1610s.[36] Although Warner claimed the island was "unoccupied" in his bid to get a commission, for example, there were at least twenty-five or thirty traffickers dwelling among the Kalinago when he arrived.[37] Nor would the initial efforts of the English to plant tobacco have raised Tegreman's suspicions. Northern European traffickers sometimes engaged in longer-term resource exploitation of the sort Martines experienced for four months in Martinique.[38] The decision to provide Warner with temporary housing on the part of the Kalinago did not represent a "colonial bargain" in which "a degree of native political and cultural autonomy [was] exchange[d] for a grudging consent."[39] Rather, King Tegreman's decision to permit Warner and his company to dwell on the island fit within Kalinago economic and political strategies. When Warner sailed back to England in 1625 with a cargo of tobacco that he hoped would secure him a colonial commission and financial support to recruit more colonists, he likely did not understand fully how the survival of his initial party had depended on relations established between the Kalinago and European traffickers over the previous century. His return to the island a year later with three ships and over a hundred colonists, however, would permanently transform cross-cultural interactions in the Lesser Antilles.

Colonialism and Violence on St. Christopher

Untangling the early years of Crown-sanctioned settlement on St. Christopher remains a challenge with surviving archival documentation.[40] The majority of English and French manuscript sources about St. Christopher during the 1620s were written decades later and, usually, in the context of Anglo-French conflicts over territorial sovereignty on the shared island.[41] Basic facts, such as the chronology of French or English settlement, were often written with an eye toward establishing one empire's primacy in colonial claims-making. The colonial commissions of the subsequent English and French governors offer even less guidance. For example, Warner's commission claimed St. Christopher as "wholly vacant or inhabited only by savage people," despite the Frenchmen who were living on the island when Warner arrived. The commissions granted to d'Esnambuc and his fellow Norman ship captain, Urbain du Roissy, declared that the two had "after fifteen years searching for fertile lands . . . discovered the islands of St. Christopher and Barbade."[42] Perhaps unsurprisingly, then, historians are also conflicted about the early development of European settlements on the island.[43] But eyewitness testimonies from Spanish archives, such as that of Martines, can shed much-needed light on those early encounters on St. Christopher.

The popularity of St. Christopher as a waystation for traffickers, including several captains in Pantel's cohort, continued even after the arrival of Warner and the English settlers. Captain Pantel dropped anchor there in 1624 and interacted enough with the Kalinago and the English for Martines to be able to roughly estimate—almost accurately, it turned out—how many English settlers Warner had with him.[44] Maritime traffic, after all, had made

St. Christopher an attractive island for English colonization. Ill-supplied colonies made the survival of settlements perilous at best—a fact made pain-
fully obvious by other failed sixteenth-century English colonies.[45] Warner's
friendly attitude toward northern European traffickers like Pantel, therefore,
might have reflected his desire to integrate the island colony into networks of
raiding and informal trade. He certainly approved of their methods; on his
return voyage from receiving his colonial commission in London, equipped
with three ships and at least sixty enslaved Africans, Warner attempted to
raid the Spanish colony of Trinidad, but with no success.[46] In addition to
using coerced labor to produce tropical staples, Warner also likely envisioned
a future in which St. Christopher would continue to serve as a node in wider
networks of human trafficking, raiding, and informal trade.

Among the traffickers whom Martines encountered during his captivity
on Martinique, for example, was d'Esnambuc, the Norman ship captain and
petty nobleman who had extensive experience raiding and smuggling in the
Caribbean.[47] The early years of d'Esnambuc's maritime career, so euphemisti-
cally described in his commission as "fifteen years searching for fertile lands,"
were actually spent trafficking and raiding throughout the Atlantic world. In
1619, for example, d'Esnambuc received financial backing in Rouen to purchase or seize enslaved captives in West Africa and traffic them into Iberian
settlements in Brazil and the Caribbean, a voyage that ended disastrously at
the islet of Caymito in 1621.[48] Several years after that encounter, d'Esnambuc
was cruising near the island of Trinidad. Off the coast of Martinique, Martines claimed that d'Esnambuc and his crew were refitting in order to raid
the Spanish Main and sail from there to Jamaica and Cuba. During the brief
reunion with Captain Pantel, d'Esnambuc also would have learned about the
nascent English settlements on St. Christopher. That said, he might have been
familiar with Warner's colony already. According to the French Dominican
Jean-Baptiste Du Tertre, "by an admirable conduct of the Providence of God,"
d'Esnambuc and Warner arrived at St. Christopher at the same time.[49] Du
Tertre wrote in the 1640s in the midst of Anglo-French conflicts over control of the island, and historians therefore often dismiss his chronology and
place Warner on the island first. Considering the role of St. Christopher in
networks of trading and raiding, it is also possible that d'Esnambuc anchored
at St. Christopher alongside Warner in 1623 or 1624 in order to refit his vessel
and trade with the Kalinago before leaving to raid in the western Caribbean.

The arrival of over a hundred English colonists by 1626 exposed the mis-
understanding that had initially ensured amity between Warner and the

Kalinago on St. Christopher. However, determining the exact chronology of the island's deteriorating cross-cultural relations and subsequent bloodshed is difficult with available sources. English and French sources provide different narrations of the violence between colonists and Kalinago; Du Tertre claims that the English and French uncovered a Kalinago plot to destroy the fledgling settlements and joined together to massacre their Kalinago hosts, although he gives two different dates for when this occurred, while English sources from John Hilton to Captain John Smith describe several different attacks and counterattacks, each with imprecise chronology, and some involving just the English and others the English and the French together.[50] Fighting did break out on the island when it became clear to Tegreman that the new settlements were unlike the earlier temporary camps established by mariners, likely late in 1626, and the warfare ended badly for the Kalinago. While in 1624 Martines described the English as living alongside the Kalinago in relative peace, by 1628 witnesses reported that there were no longer any autonomous Kalinago inhabiting St. Christopher.[51]

Violence between the Kalinago and the northern Europeans had repercussions for the colonial development of St. Christopher and for traffickers throughout the Lesser Antilles. The Kalinago who survived the conflict regrouped on Kalinago-dominated islands like St. Lucia and Dominica, where they spread word of the perfidiousness of their former trade partners. Traffickers found themselves unwittingly embroiled in the conflict as a result. Passing through the Lesser Antilles shortly after 1626, a French sailor named Thomas Cordero bore witness to how dynamics between northern European traffickers and the Kalinago had changed. At St. Lucia, Cordero and his companions encountered seven northern European sailors being held captive on that island by the Kalinago, and as they approached Dominica, the Kalinago there fled upon the approach of the French ship. More ominous for settlers on St. Christopher were Cordero's reports of "six armed piraguas with ample water and foodstuffs" that, he assumed, were headed to exact revenge on the northern Europeans of St. Christopher. Perhaps simple revenge was the goal. More likely, however, the Kalinago embarked in their armed canáoa to liberate "their women and children" from slavery among the Europeans on the island.[52] The very real threat of retaliation by powerful Kalinago to the south, some of whom had survived violence on St. Christopher, created the conditions in which the English and French agreed to cohabitate on the island and to sign an alliance of mutual defense.[53] At the same time, the enslavement of Kalinago captives of war further committed the colony to the institution of slavery.

The establishment of a Crown-sanctioned colony diverged dramatically from the patterns of trade and semipermanent dwelling that defined northern European traffickers' use of St. Christopher. Colonial expansion under Warner and d'Esnambuc would come to represent territorial acquisition, political consolidation, and Indigenous dispossession. Dwelling, as traffickers understood and practiced it, prioritized movement, cultural fluidity, and trade within a borderless, multinational maritime world.[54] The latter created the infrastructure that facilitated the former, as northern European traffickers established practices and forged alliances with the Kalinago that allowed Warner to settle on St. Christopher in the first place. Despite the obvious differences between the two modes of operating in the region, however, the future of St. Christopher represented something of a hybrid between dwelling and colonizing. After a near-fatal encounter with a Spanish galleon between Jamaica and Cuba shortly after he departed from Martinique, d'Esnambuc and his crew limped back to St. Christopher. Rather than simply refit his vessel, d'Esnambuc threw his lot in with the English colonists and sought a French colonial commission and financial backing to establish a French settlement on the island. But colonization did not mean a complete departure from trafficking networks. The island remained a node for raiding and informal trade in ways that would greatly influence the society that developed there.

Multinational Settlement and Slavery on St. Christopher

The selection of St. Christopher as a site for settlement emerged from the island's preexisting role in regional networks of raiding and informal trade, and the activities of traffickers continued to influence colonial development on the island. The prior careers of d'Esnambuc and du Roissy familiarized them with informal trade, captive-taking, and slavery in a Caribbean context. They knew about the role played by St. Christopher in provisioning and refitting European ships involved in transatlantic and intra-Caribbean trade. After 1626, St. Christopher's three governors worked to co-opt the role of provisioning and regional trade previously occupied by the Kalinago, and, to that end, they welcomed ships of all nations that were involved in regional trafficking. Warner, d'Esnambuc, and du Roissy also signed a treaty in 1627 to lay out how they planned to protect and partition the island. Read closely, treaty articles designed to regulate trade, establish an international court, and control the movement of enslaved people underscore the future that St. Christopher's three governors imagined for the island colony. Rather than signal a transition from plundering to planting, practices of raiding and informal trade continued after the 1620s and shaped the ways in which colonialism on the island unfolded.

In the aftermath of warfare with the Kalinago, Warner, d'Esnambuc, and du Roissy proclaimed themselves "Governours Each in their quarter" since they had "togeather Conquered the island of St. Christophers from the [Kalinago]."[55] Territory in the southeast and northwest was claimed for France, where relatively flat land provided the French with arable soil. The English claimed the middle, where plantations spread along the north-central and south-central coasts, divided by high peaks in the center of the island. Harbors dotted the southern coast at Pointe de Sable in the west, Fort Charles in the center, and the Fort of Basseterre in the east. The division of the island gave English and French colonists access to harbors and land for planting. But traveling from one French settlement to the other required passing through English territory, while traveling by land from English settlements in the north to those in the south meant traversing French possessions. Governing an island split between colonists described as "people of such different dispositions" and having a geography that required constant interaction shaped the contours of the initial agreement to partition the island.[56] In 1627, Warner, d'Esnambuc, and du Roissy met to negotiate a treaty designed to regulate cohabitation, addressing everything from a defensive alliance to policing the movement of enslaved and indentured laborers.

The first of the treaty's ten articles addressed trafficking. Well aware of the island's role as a node in regional networks of informal trade and raiding, Warner, d'Esnambuc, and du Roissy stipulated that "Noe ship shall come to traffique in the Island but by permission of the sayd Governours."[57] Further, traffickers who received permission to trade had the prices of their merchandise set by the English and French governors of the island. Read alongside their colonial commissions, this first treaty article underscores how the island's three governors envisioned the role of trafficking and multinational trade and how that vision contradicted metropolitan plans for the region. The colonial commissions of Warner, d'Esnambuc, and du Roissy all granted the proprietors a monopoly on future profits from St. Christopher. James Hay, the Earl of Carlisle, financed the English colony and received a yearly pension from the Crown and all duties and customs paid on imports from St. Christopher for a period of ten years.[58] For the French, investors in the Compagnie des Îsles de l'Amérique financed colonization in exchange for a monopoly on the "traffic of money and goods to be collected and obtained from the said Islands" for the first twenty years of colonization.[59] The commissions, then, required trade with St. Christopher to be conducted through specific metropolitan ports where appropriate customs could be collected and remitted to the proprietors. On the ground, however, the first treaty laid out a system whereby Warner, d'Esnambuc, and du Roissy controlled trade in and out of the island, permitting ships to traffic with island residents in ways remarkably similar to the cross-cultural trade that had existed between the Kalinago and northern European traffickers prior to colonization.[60] Allowing ships to anchor at St. Christopher, refit their vessels, and purchase provisions provided island residents with trade goods and attracted ships that would transport the tobacco or other tropical staples produced on the island. Co-opting the economic niche established by the Kalinago prior to colonization allowed St. Christopher's three governors to ensure the constant arrival of trade goods and ship captains willing to transport island-produced tobacco back to Europe.

The three governors penned additional articles intended to facilitate trade and maintain peace on the island. First, the governors created a court system. Merchant communities throughout western Europe had long relied on international courts to settle commercial disputes between subjects of different monarchs. The purpose of these courts, which followed Roman civil law rather than English common law, was to litigate commercial disputes quickly so that merchants could continue their voyages.[61] Ships often transported goods that could spoil or rot, which meant that getting tied up in lengthy legal disputes risked financial ruin. Merchants also needed a court system that transcended the different legal heritages of England and continental Europe. The result were international courts based in Roman civil law that addressed commercial disputes quickly in western Europe. Warner, d'Esnambuc, and du Roissy replicated this model for disputes that might arise on St. Christopher. According to the treaty, "If there happen any difference quarrels or fighting," then "the delinquents shall be judged by the French and English." Individuals sentenced for criminal behavior would be sent "each in his quarter for execution of the sentence."[62] Justice, in other words, would be transparent, swift, and recognized as legitimate in multinational settlements and by their trade partners.

Warner, d'Esnambuc, and du Roissy went further in their efforts to address the particular concerns of governing an island shared by two nations—particularly two nations frequently at war on the other side of the

Atlantic. According to the treaty, St. Christopher's three governors pledged to maintain peace and neutrality on the island even if England and France declared war against one another in Europe.[63] The agreement between the three governors reversed the concept of "no peace beyond the line" that European officials had adopted to prevent violence in the Caribbean from leading to warfare in Europe. In 1559, France and Spain signed the Treaty of Cateau-Cambrésis, which declared that violence between subjects of different crowns west of the prime meridian and south of the Tropic of Cancer would not be subject to treaty law and therefore could not be used as a pretext for war in Europe. This imaginary line separating European treaty law from the Western Hemisphere is often referred to as the "Line of Amity."[64] Rather than see themselves as the potential cause of warfare in Europe, however, the three governors of St. Christopher recognized the threat posed by competition between European monarchs to their own Caribbean-based experiment in multinational settlement. Only if their respective monarchs expressly ordered them to attack one another would the governors break the island-wide alliance, and even then, they agreed to give each other warning before doing so. By 1629, English and French colonists fought one another over access to land regardless of the treaty, but the article underscores the desires of the island's three governors to maintain peace and facilitate commerce.[65]

The 1627 treaty also highlights how the commerce that the island's three governors sought to facilitate involved human trafficking. Slavery was embedded in the colonial development of St. Christopher from the very beginning—on Warner's first voyage back to the island with his colonial commission, he brought sixty enslaved Africans, and both the English and the French enslaved Kalinago war captives after 1626. But the creation of a legal framework for the institution of slavery on St. Christopher was distinct among early slave societies because traffickers brought their own understanding of slavery that had developed over decades of trafficking people throughout the Spanish Caribbean. Unlike other nascent English and French slaveholding societies, the treaty articles that laid out the policing of St. Christopher's enslaved population never defined the institution of slavery in terms of who could be enslaved and whether that status was perpetual and inheritable. In English colonies where historians argue that the "first" slave laws were passed, such as Massachusetts Bay in 1640, debates over the social and legal contours of slavery took on particular importance.[66] This was especially true for both English and French colonies, since they lacked a metropolitan legal framework from which to draw for the enslavement of other people.[67] But the English and French on

St. Christopher constructed a legal apparatus for slavery without the apparent need to define the institution. Traffickers like d'Esnambuc and du Roissy had extensive experience trafficking human beings in the Caribbean, providing them with a vernacular understanding of slavery as an institution that applied to captives of African and Indigenous descent.[68] They simply did not need to define it clearly in positive law to hold Kalinago war captives as slaves, for example. By 1627, slavery and the policing of enslaved mobility was laid out in the first treaty signed between St. Christopher's three governors because those men had long experience with the institution. Raiding and smuggling over the late sixteenth and early seventeenth centuries, in other words, created the conditions that facilitated a commitment to slavery in the first English and French colony in the Caribbean.

St. Christopher remained a central node in networks of traffickers after colonization, which yoked the early economy and society of the island to slavery much earlier and more fully than historians have recognized. In fact, the earliest system for policing the mobility of enslaved people in either the French or English Caribbean was established through the treaty signed by the three governors of St. Christopher in 1627. This is a story not often told in the wider history of slavery in the Caribbean. Scholars of the Anglo-Caribbean, for example, tend to emphasize Barbados as the first colony to develop into a slave society during the seventeenth century, partly due to the far better archival evidence for Barbados's population and partly because of that island's success cultivating sugar. Less attention has been paid to St. Christopher's role in the development of slavery, despite extensive anecdotal evidence about the trade in captive people to the island. By the 1630s, for example, Spanish officials in Puerto Rico reported on ships fitting out at St. Christopher for raids throughout the greater Caribbean and for slaving voyages directly to West Africa.[69] Evidence also points to traffickers from as far as New England ferrying St. Christopher–produced salt and tobacco back to Massachusetts in exchange for enslaved captives.[70] The informal nature of networks of human trafficking to early St. Christopher, however, frustrates attempts to quantify the trade or even the number of enslaved captives held there before mid-century.

Bound labor took on an immediate importance on St. Christopher.[71] Even without accurate census data, evidence for the growth of the island's enslaved population can be inferred from the rapid changes made to the treaty articles addressing the mobility of enslaved people on the shared island. According to the original 1627 treaty, colonists "shall restrayne men or Slaves in their plantations that shall not Belong to them" and "Keep them till such tyme as they shall have given Each other notice of the sayd men or Slaves."[72] But by 1637 this informal policing proved insufficient. According to the renegotiated treaty, if "any Servant or Slave shall run away from either Nation to the other" or be "conveyed or transported off the Island," then a fine of 10,000 pounds of tobacco would be levied against the "Nation" responsible.[73] This legislation, meant to control the movement of enslaved and indentured laborers, reflects the early and deep commitment of the English and French "nations" on St. Christopher to the exploitation of enslaved people. For an island colonized by two ship captains whose previous maritime careers involved human trafficking throughout the greater Caribbean, that commitment should hardly be surprising. The fact that the treaty article specifically mentioned enslaved people being transported off of the island underscores the continual arrival of traffickers to St. Christopher, embedding the island's economy in regional networks of trade and trafficking. For traffickers, non-Iberian colonies in the Lesser Antilles provided alternative means of making a voyage by the 1630s.

Colonies, Salt, and Making a Voyage

By the 1630s, northern European ship captains and their crews had various strategies for making a voyage—some of which remained unchanged from the second half of the sixteenth century, while others represented new adaptations to the presence of English, French, and Dutch colonies in the Caribbean. Traffickers, for example, continued to use St. Christopher after the island was colonized in much the same way as they had when cross-cultural trade on the island the Kalinago called Liamuiga had been dictated by them. They continued to anchor at the island in order to purchase food, exchange information, and form companies, especially during the salt boom that started in the 1630s on neighboring islands such as St. Martin or the Caicos. Despite the colonial presence on St. Christopher, traffickers even continued to practice forms of temporary dwelling in order to cultivate tobacco or exploit other resources before continuing their voyages. And from St. Christopher, traffickers also continued to engage in the same kinds of raiding, smuggling, and human trafficking that had defined the region since the late sixteenth century. The transatlantic carrying trade in support of new colonies, however, provided traffickers with new opportunities. Ship captains accepted commissions to transport colonists and supplies, for example, in order to turn to raiding and smuggling once their official trade was completed. And the presence of English and French colonists who employed the labor of European indentured servants also provided traffickers with markets for sailors seized as captives during maritime raids.[74] Traffickers incorporated new colonies into their practices of making a voyage in ways that influenced the development of colonies throughout the greater Caribbean.

Traffickers continued to raid Iberian shipping and settlements in the early seventeenth century, specifically targeting transatlantic slave ships, and many of them continued to refit their vessels at St. Christopher.[75] Warfare between the Kalinago and English and French colonists around 1626 had led to a deterioration of cross-cultural relations throughout the Lesser Antilles, which served to draw traffickers to St. Christopher, since many no longer found as warm a welcome on Kalinago-dominated islands. For traffickers, raids followed patterns that had been established over the previous half century, but the presence of English and French settlers in the Lesser Antilles opened additional markets for traffickers. According to the governor of Puerto Rico, Enrique Enríquez de Sotomayor, the presence of English and French colonies in the Lesser Antilles aggravated the persistent problem of maritime raids against transatlantic slave ships. He reported that his English and French neighbors on St. Christopher had "sent ships to Angola" to bring enslaved Africans back to the island and that those voyages were supplemented by raids on Iberian transatlantic slave ships. According to Enríquez, traffickers waited at St. Christopher to attack transatlantic slave ships on their route to Tierra Firme. As he wrote, "the slave trade will be made much more difficult" as a result of English and French settlements in the Lesser Antilles.[76] By 1628, the ships of at least twelve traffickers arrived at St. Christopher over a two-month period.[77] For the island's three governors, who envisioned St. Christopher serving as a regional entrepôt from the very beginning, the arrival of traffickers provided bound labor, European manufactured goods, and an outlet for their growing tobacco production.

The large number of ships that called at St. Christopher in the late 1620s sometimes forced ship captains to turn to older methods of making a voyage, such as temporarily dwelling on the island to harvest or cultivate tropical staples. A colonized St. Christopher provided northern European merchants and ship captains with a new source of tobacco in the Caribbean, as English and French settlers turned their attention to cultivating the crop almost immediately. The same year that Warner, d'Esnambuc, and du Roissy signed the first island-wide treaty, northern European merchants and ship captains began arriving to carry off the island's tobacco crop. The number of ship captains who arrived to transport tobacco, however, sometimes exceeded local supply in the late 1620s. In those cases, ship captains could either sail away empty-handed or blend their maritime labor with temporarily dwelling on the island. In 1627, for example, an English captain named Charles Saltonstall arrived at St. Christopher to trade for tobacco with island colonists. Unfortunately for Saltonstall, "some Hollanders" had arrived before him and "carried away with them all the Tobacco." Without access to tobacco through trade, Saltonstall resorted to the same kinds of longer-term resource exploitation that traffickers had engaged in during the era prior to colonization. The English captain "resolved there to stay, and imploye himself & his company in planting Tobacco, hoping thereby to make a voyage."[78] Saltonstall and his crew, in other words, transitioned to planting tobacco themselves when it became clear that there was none for purchase at St. Christopher. His choice echoes that of Martines's French captors, who had remained at Martinique for four months to cut and load dyewood. In much the same way, Saltonstall and his crew planted tobacco, and temporarily dwelled on St. Christopher, in order to make a voyage. His example blurs the line between colonists and seamen—the population of colonists on St. Christopher would have also included sailors who, like Saltonstall and his crew, moved in and out of planting depending on their circumstances.

Supporting colonial development through the transatlantic carrying trade helped ship captains in Europe finance voyages to the Caribbean. Once in the region and at the conclusion of official business, many then turned to older practices of raiding, captive-taking, and human trafficking. According to an English sailor from Bristol named John Johnson, ship captains sometimes kept their intentions of turning to raiding a secret, even from their crews. Johnson was employed on a ship called the *Saint Peter*, which delivered one hundred colonists and indentured servants to Barbados when the ship's captain, Eric Boll, ordered the crew to "make a turn for the Indies" rather than return to England. In Johnson's retelling of the events, the crew opposed this course of action. In response, Boll supposedly produced a "letter from the King that commanded everyone to obey him." From Barbados, the *Saint Peter* followed a path well worn by traffickers to the Venezuelan coast, along the Spanish Main, and north to Hispaniola. They careened the ship at either Tortuga or Caymito before sailing for the Bahama Channel, where they seized a Spanish frigate from Cuba that was loaded with wheat.

Unfortunately for Johnson, when Captain Boll sent a number of sailors from the *Saint Peter* to sail the frigate home, the Cuban crew rose up and retook the frigate, sailing the now-imprisoned English crew back to Havana. Johnson's testimony is full of holes—allegedly the English ship did not encounter a single ship or person after they left Barbados until the ill-fated attempt to seize the Cuban frigate—and his claims that Captain Boll forced the crew into raiding could have been spurious. Even if Johnson were lying, he chose an excuse that seemed plausible, undoubtedly because sometimes captains did use dishonesty and force with their crews.[79] Whether or not the crew knew ahead of time of Captain Boll's intentions, the voyage of the *Saint Peter* reveals how ship captains continued to make their voyages through raiding and smuggling, even after the establishment of northern European colonies in the Caribbean.

By the 1630s, another method for making a voyage involved loading and transporting salt back to Europe. Access to salt had become a pressing issue for the Netherlands by the late sixteenth century as their war against Spain cut them off from the abundant salt pans of the Iberian Peninsula. As historian Eric Sluiter has argued, the Spanish prohibition on Dutch trade in salt in Iberia pushed salt rakers into the Caribbean. By 1600, for example, between thirty and forty Dutch ships loaded salt at the abundant salt pans of the Punta de Araya, a peninsula off the coast of modern-day Venezuela. The routes that Dutch ships took to Araya carried them through the Lesser Antilles where, according to observations made by the governor of Puerto Rico, they all stopped at St. Christopher for food, wood, and water.[80] Traffickers who employed their crews raking salt at the Punta de Araya blended their activities with informal trade and raiding along the Spanish Main. By 1605 the Council of the Indies dispatched a Spanish fleet to Araya, where they took nine Dutch ships and executed the crews.[81] But Dutch, English, and French traffickers also found ample salt pans in the Virgin Islands and the Caicos. According to one report, the Caicos possessed "some salt pans so abundant" with large, white rocks of salt that they drew a constant traffic of ships.[82] The salt pans of St. Martin, located at the northern tip of the Lesser Antilles, also attracted numerous ships, and since St. Martin lacked sources of fresh water, the activities of salt rakers there depended on their ability to access fresh water at St. Christopher.[83]

The salt pans on St. Martin drew French, English, and Dutch traffickers where the captains exploited the labor of their crews and of captives of African and Indigenous descent in the arduous work of raking and loading salt.

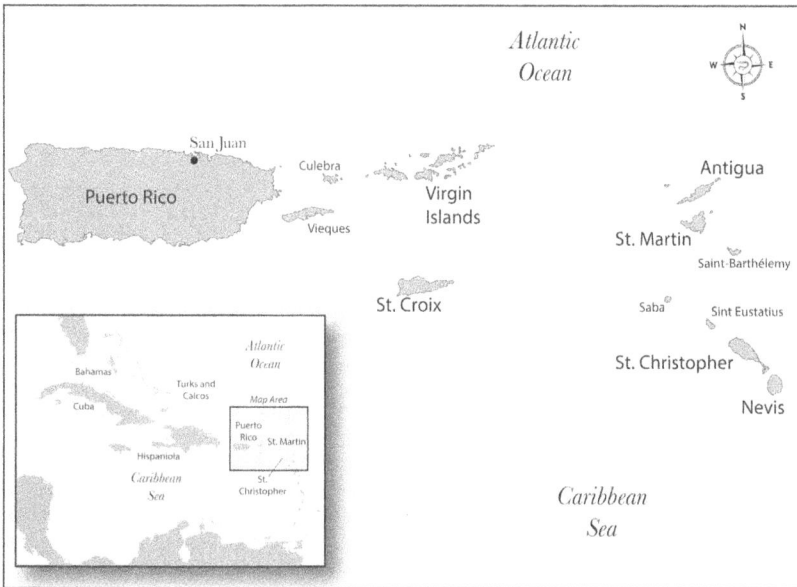

Map 4. St. Christopher, St. Martin, and Puerto Rico

Some contemporary estimates suggested that St. Martin's salt pans could fill four hundred boats a year, and according to one eyewitness, nearly fifty ships at a time loaded salt at the island in 1631.[84] Much as they had at Punta de Araya, many of the ship captains who called at St. Martin blended salt raking with other maritime activities, including raiding and captive-taking. Captives seized in places as far as Brazil or along the Spanish Main could be put to profitable labor by their captors at St. Martin and then trafficked into slavery in places like St. Christopher.[85] By 1633, at least forty enslaved people of African descent and an unspecified number of Indigenous captives from Brazil labored in the salt pans of St. Martin. With only one hundred European soldiers and mariners on the island, the enslaved captives comprised more than one-third of the total population on the eve of a Spanish assault on the island.[86] The dependence of salt rakers on food and fresh water from St. Christopher tied the Anglo-French island to multinational networks of trade and human trafficking. Warner, for example, described a "great concourse of ships" calling at the island in the 1630s. Those ships undoubtedly brought more to St. Christopher than European trade goods, and the presence of neighboring salt pans at St. Martin provided traffickers with additional means of making their voyages.

St. Christopher's role as a provisioning station for St. Martin continued even after the Spanish took brief possession of the island from 1633 until 1648. Reports from Puerto Rico about the ships of all nations loading salt at St. Martin convinced Spain's Council of the Indies to act, and in 1633, they ordered five ships from the annual transatlantic fleet to dislodge the Dutch and establish a Spanish fort. The governors of Puerto Rico and Santo Domingo received orders to send provisions to the garrison at St. Martin. Within months, however, the Spanish captain in charge of the garrison, Cebrián de Liçaraçu, complained that the island had nothing but brackish water and that his counterparts in Puerto Rico and Santo Domingo neglected to send provisions. One expedient available to Liçaraçu to feed the garrison in the early months of the occupation was ransoming Dutch, French, and English captives seized off of ships that continued to arrive at St. Martin to neighboring St. Christopher.

Ransoming prisoners for provisions quickly emerged as a method to cover informal trade between the two islands. That trade became so well established that when a new Spanish captain arrived at St. Martin in 1638—Liçaraçu's soldiers had mutinied and locked him in jail because he allegedly subjected them to hard labor without adequate provisions—Warner sent a letter to the new captain. In addition to bragging about the "great concourse of ships" at St. Christopher, Warner offered the new Spanish captain, Luis de Valdes, the same "good neighborliness" that he had maintained with Liçaraçu, namely, trade in "ships, boats, biscuit, cassava, meat, wine, and all types of clothing and shoes."[87] Rather than close off access to trade at St. Martin, the fifteen years of Spanish occupation provided new opportunities for traffickers and helped St. Christopher's merchant community establish trade networks with their Spanish neighbors.

Captives of other kinds also facilitated trade. Involvement in intra-island diplomatic activities such as prisoner of war exchanges provided traffickers who arrived at St. Christopher with access to Spanish Caribbean ports and, often, informal trade. And raiding Iberian shipping produced numerous prisoners. Between 1630 and 1632, for example, at least six Portuguese transatlantic slave ships were taken at sea. The crews of those ships and the African captives, who experienced this maritime violence after the horrors of the Middle Passage, ended up in northern European colonies like St. Christopher.[88] The captive crew members from seized ships offered opportunities for traffickers to engage in prisoner exchanges with neighboring Spanish Caribbean settlements. The case of a New Englander named Captain John Stone casts light on how trafficking, informal trade, and diplomacy knit together the northern Lesser Antilles. In 1632, Stone anchored at St. Christopher to refit his vessel and trade when he was asked by Warner to transport several Portuguese prisoners to neighboring Puerto Rico. Earlier, a Dutch navigator named David Pieterszoon de Vries had delivered those captive Portuguese sailors, and likely a number of African captives, to St. Christopher, reflecting the continued importance of raiding and human trafficking in the region. For Captain Stone, the Portuguese prisoners represented an opportunity.

Prisoner of war exchanges had allowed Spanish captains at St. Martin to establish trade ties with St. Christopher, and Stone used the same tactics to engage in informal trade in Puerto Rico. Stone is better known for his 1634 death at the hands of the Pequot and Niantic in retaliation for Stone's having seized Niantic captives near a Dutch trading post in New Netherland. His death, along with that of John Oldham two years later, was used as a catalyst for the Pequot War that ravaged New England between 1636 and 1638.[89] But, two years before his death, Stone was at St. Christopher loading Portuguese prisoners onto his ship. He understood the benefit of transporting prisoners to a Spanish Caribbean settlement and carried captives and trade goods to smuggle into Puerto Rico. De Vries, who reunited with Stone in New Netherland, reported that Stone considered himself "very well treated by the Spanish governor" of Puerto Rico.[90] Considering Stone's reputation as an unscrupulous "trader-adventurer" in New England and the regional precedent of using prisoner exchanges as a cover for informal trade, Stone's description of being well treated almost certainly alluded to being permitted to trade at Puerto Rico. Like traffickers had done in the Lesser Antilles for decades, Stone used St. Christopher to make a voyage through informal trade that, even into the 1630s, revolved around the seizure of human captives and informal trade networks with neighboring Spanish Caribbean settlements.

Maritime Mobility and Bound Labor

Early correspondence and interactions with neighboring Spanish settlements highlight how traffickers and the three governors of St. Christopher worked together to establish the island as an entrepôt in regional trade networks. It was no accident, as Warner wrote to his Spanish counterpart on St. Martin in 1636, that "a great concourse of ships" called at St. Christopher within a decade of colonization.[91] That "great concourse of ships" contributed to the rapid growth of the island's population of bound laborers and provided an outlet for island-grown products. The maritime traffic that facilitated regional trade, however, was not always beneficial for colonial development. For one, traffickers had many options for trade, both formal and informal. For some northern European ship captains, the prices and regulations set by St. Christopher's three governors proved too restrictive, and they turned instead to smuggling with Spanish Caribbean residents, hoping to make, in the words of one contemporary observer, "a quick fortune through free trade with foreigners."[92] Traffickers, after all, used St. Christopher as one of many different nodes throughout the greater Caribbean. And while the continual arrival of ships served colonial development, those ships also provided disgruntled colonists, indentured servants, and enslaved people with a means to seek freedom in Spanish-held territory or in the multinational settlements of the western Caribbean.

Over the course of the 1630s and 1640s, traffickers brought captives of African and Indigenous descent, goods seized in raids, and even small prize ships to sell at St. Christopher. In the early fall of 1637, for example, a Dutch trafficker called at the island with Indigenous captives and a prize ship seized from Portuguese Brazil. He arrived at a propitious time. The price of tobacco had crashed throughout the Atlantic by the mid-1630s, and the declining economic prospects of colonists on St. Christopher made some wish to leave the island, whether or not they received permission to do so from their respective governors. Among those who wanted to leave was an English planter who had spent the previous six years attempting to make a living on St. Christopher. By 1637, he opted instead to purchase the Brazilian prize ship from the Dutch along with a captive Indigenous boy, about fourteen or fifteen years old, whom he would traffic into slavery in neighboring Puerto Rico. Rather than petition for a license to depart St. Christopher, the English planter purchased the ship and the captive boy for three thousand pounds of tobacco and escaped in the dead of night with four other Englishmen.

Once at Puerto Rico, the Englishman testified to Governor Iñigo de la Mota Sarmiento that he wished to offer his services to the Spanish Crown and petitioned for a license to be sent to Spain. As he explained, he sought employment with the Spanish because he "had no intention of returning to his own country as a poor man."[93] As a signal of his goodwill toward the Spanish, the Englishman provided detailed information about St. Christopher's fortifications, armaments, and population. As will be seen in Chapter 4, disgruntled colonists who renounced their allegiances to struggling colonial projects provided the Spanish with invaluable information—information that

Spanish imperial officials often used to plan assaults on the settlements of their European competitors.

Indentured servants and enslaved people who lacked the means to purchase a ship nonetheless found ways off of St. Christopher. The constant traffic of ships loading food and water for laborers in the salt pans of St. Martin, for example, provided one means of escape. According to an Englishman who escaped servitude in St. Christopher with six others onboard an English ship loading salt at St. Martin, "every year French, Dutch, and English ships never fail to arrive [at St. Martin] to load salt." For the Englishmen, the regular arrival of European ships promised a means of escaping the Lesser Antilles altogether and, perhaps, returning to Europe.[94]

There was a gendered dimension to risking one's life at sea in order to escape unfreedom. In 1644, for example, a large group of refugees from St. Christopher arrived at St. Martin only to discover that the island was under the authority of the Spanish. Some of the group decided to continue their voyage to the western Caribbean where they planned to settle on the island of Tortuga. Four of the women remained on St. Martin, likely because they considered the voyage too dangerous or because they imagined life on St. Martin preferable to what they might find in Tortuga. One of the four women found work in the household of St. Martin's Spanish governor, and during her time there she bore him a child. While the circumstances surrounding her pregnancy are unclear from surviving archival documents, she and the other women who escaped with her chose domestic labor and servitude on St. Martin over the uncertainty of continuing to seek a new life at sea.[95]

If they survived the voyage, the companions of the four women who remained on St. Martin would have joined growing settlements in the western Caribbean formed, in part, by individuals who escaped unfreedom in the Lesser Antilles. Knowledge of the opportunities available in the western Caribbean spread through the networks of trade that traffickers maintained between places like St. Christopher and Tortuga. In the winter of 1632, for example, nine individuals washed up on the shore of Puerto Rico in a small vessel. The three Frenchmen, four Englishmen, and two Englishwomen were indentured servants who escaped from near Basseterre in one of the French portions of St. Christopher. When brought before the Spanish governor, one of the Frenchmen declared that hunger and desperation forced them to land at Puerto Rico. According to their testimonies, the group had sought freedom on the island of Tortuga because of the "very poor treatment" they received on St. Christopher. As they explained, they had heard of the "ample brazilwood" on Tortuga, which promised to provide the men in the group with economic opportunities away from the increasingly coercive plantation regime of St. Christopher.[96] Trafficking networks, in other words, presented a double-edged sword for the three governors of St. Christopher: they both maintained trade and communication, but information and maritime mobility hampered their ability to control the island's population of bound laborers. For their part, traffickers came to benefit from the multinational encampments being established in the western Caribbean as they expanded networks of raiding and captive-taking alongside official colonization.

Practices established by traffickers who sought to make a voyage during the late sixteenth and early seventeenth centuries shaped the development of the first Caribbean colony of England and France. Amicable relations with the Kalinago drew traffickers to certain islands of the Lesser Antilles. The Kalinago had carved out these islands as spaces of autonomy that led to the creation of mutually beneficial cross-cultural trade between the Kalinago, who sought European manufactured goods like iron axes, and northern European traffickers, who needed spaces in the Caribbean to refit their vessels, purchase foodstuffs, and share information. The testimonies of individuals like Simón Martines provide insight into how those cross-cultural relations functioned, while the disastrous voyage of John Nicholl and his company underscores what was at stake for northern Europeans in Kalinago spaces. Crucially, what the failed attempt by Nicholl to settle on St. Lucia reveals is the power of the Kalinago to set the terms of cross-cultural trade and effectively retaliate against Europeans who overstayed their welcome.

At the same time, the Kalinago expected northern Europeans to pass extended periods of time on their shores, temporarily dwelling in rented structures as they engaged in the arduous work of refitting their vessels or harvesting tropical staples like dyewoods. This context helps explain both why Warner, d'Esnambuc, and du Roissy selected Liamuiga for colonization and how the first English colonists survived before reinforcements arrived. Traffickers, like the soon-to-be governors of the French portions of St. Christopher, had developed trade ties with the Kalinago and recognized the importance of the island as a node in transatlantic and intra-Caribbean trade. The choice of co-opting the Kalinago's preexisting position as intermediaries in regional trade networks drew ships to the island even after official colonization, which helped the early English and French settlements on

St. Christopher avoid the dearth and suffering that accompanied early colonization in places that lacked those ties, such as Jamestown.

The predatory careers of d'Esnambuc and du Roissy along with the role that Liamuiga had played as a trafficking entrepôt prior to colonization shaped the way the colonies developed after the island's three governors received their colonial commissions. Two important characteristics emerge from a close reading of the treaty signed by d'Esnambuc, du Roissy, and Warner in 1627. First, the governors clearly envisioned St. Christopher continuing as an important rendezvous for traffickers. It is no coincidence that the first article of the treaty references explicitly ships arriving "to traffique" at the island and established protocols for the three governors to control that trade. The familiarity that d'Esnambuc and du Roissy had with Liamuiga's preexisting role in trafficking networks also accounts for the second characteristic of colonial society on the island—namely, an early commitment to slavery. Both d'Esnambuc and du Roissy had prior experience with captive-taking and human trafficking that shaped their expectations of the role that Indigenous and African captives would occupy on the island. There was, in other words, no need for the island's three governors to define in positive law an institution that they were already familiar with from years of trafficking captives into slavery throughout the Spanish Caribbean. As the island's three governors continued to welcome traffickers, the English and French settlements on St. Christopher emerged as multinational spaces defined by high degrees of maritime mobility and a large population of bound laborers.

As Simón Martines understood from his captivity between Jamaica and Santiago de Cuba, the activities of northern European traffickers were not confined to the Lesser Antilles. Smaller, less saturated ports in places like western and northern Hispaniola, Jamaica, and eastern Cuba also created opportunities for informal trade in the western Caribbean. Over the course of the late sixteenth and early seventeenth centuries, traffickers relied on a multiethnic assortment of trade partners to establish safe anchorages in the western Caribbean, from Spanish Caribbean residents to African Maroon communities and Indigenous nations such as the Yucatec Maya. As was the case in the Lesser Antilles, these anchorages allowed traffickers to spend extended periods of time raiding and trading in the western Caribbean. The nearly two years that Jan Petre spent on board the vessel of a Dutch trafficker in the waters of the western Caribbean in the 1620s would have been unimaginable without access to secure locations to refit the ship, load wood, water, and foodstuffs, and avoid being in open water during the worst of the Caribbean hurricane season.

Certain anchorages, such as the island of Tortuga off the coast of western Hispaniola, also attracted the colonizing attention of metropolitan planners and merchants in England and France. Violence, instability, and war, however, thwarted English and French attempts to create a regional, informal entrepôt on the model of St. Christopher in the western Caribbean during the 1620s and 1630s. For populations of African descent, especially Maroon communities in western Hispaniola, imperial and commercial competition in the western Caribbean during the early seventeenth century made them particularly vulnerable to captivity and human trafficking. As the next chapter shows, the same patterns of dwelling and informal trade that allowed Warner, d'Esnambuc, and du Roissy to establish themselves as governors of St. Christopher refracted in the western Caribbean, with grim consequences for populations of African and Indigenous descent in the region.

CHAPTER 3

"They Took Him to Sea"

Captivity and Violence Before Mid-Century

From a young age, captivity had forced Francisco da Costa to adapt rapidly to circumstances beyond his control. In 1638, when he was twelve or thirteen years old, French traffickers took Costa captive from a fishing boat in the Bay of All Saints off the coast of Brazil and forced him to serve on their ship. As a captive on the ship, he learned French and adapted to the norms and maritime labor routines of his captors. This linguistic and cultural fluency meant that when his captors trafficked him into slavery at Tortuga, an island located off the northwestern coast of Hispaniola, the governor of that island purchased the young French-speaking, Afro-descended fisherman from Brazil to work in his household.

Cultural and linguistic adaptability continued to serve Costa when he escaped the governor's household and fled into Tortuga's mountainous interior. There, Costa encountered two Indigenous men from the Yucatán Peninsula named Andrés and Marcos, who had also liberated themselves from slavery among the French. Together, the three men constructed a boat and navigated to the sparsely populated northwestern coast of Hispaniola. The trio spent nearly two months traversing the rugged interior of Hispaniola, communicating through a combination of sign language and Yucatec Maya, before encountering a Spanish village.[1] Their experiences underscore the vulnerability of people of African and Indigenous descent in the Caribbean and wider Atlantic world to captivity, dislocation, and slavery in the first half of the seventeenth century, but they also speak to the determination, ingenuity, and resilience of individuals like Costa, Andrés, and Marcos, who formed cross-cultural alliances in their bid to gain or regain their freedom.

During his brief enslavement to the French governor of Tortuga, Costa lived and worked in a multiethnic society shaped by maritime raiding and human trafficking. He likely encountered other captives from Brazil on Tortuga, of both African and Indigenous descent, alongside a wide variety of trafficked people from throughout the greater Caribbean, including numerous Yucatec Maya speakers like Andrés and Marcos. By the 1630s, French, English, Dutch, Irish, and Portuguese settlers occupied the island as well. Some had escaped poverty or indentured servitude in the Lesser Antilles, while others labored as servants on Tortuga. The island's inhabitants grew tobacco for export and foodstuffs to support the numerous ships of all nations that refit at Tortuga. Many of the men on the island made a living by dividing their time on land and at sea. A sailor from Normandy and former indentured servant on St. Christopher, for example, described his amphibious life on Tortuga in terms of seasonal periods of "growing tobacco and going to sea as a corsair."[2] The two activities were linked since maritime raids supported the commercial development on the island colony. Attacks on Spanish Caribbean settlements supplied Tortuga's residents with tools for plantation agriculture, including sugar production, as well as with captives forced to labor in the production of crops for export. The beans, cassava, and tobacco cultivated by captives like Costa, Andrés, and Marcos supported the traffickers who, in turn, brought more captive people to the island. By the late 1630s, Tortuga's position within practices of regional raiding and human trafficking created a population with an enslaved majority that depended on the regular arrival of ships of all nations for survival. It was a profitable, if unstable, foundation for a colony.

In many ways, what Costa experienced as a captive corresponds with how historians have understood the colonial development of Tortuga. Scholars argue that seventeenth-century Tortuga, settled by so-called "outcasts from several nations" who hunted feral cattle and engaged in maritime predation, was particularly "informal, lawless, and stateless."[3] After being taken captive as a boy and trafficked into slavery on the island, Costa's experiences seem to reaffirm this image of Tortuga. But the establishment of multinational settlements that were dependent on raiding and human trafficking was not unique to Tortuga during the first half of the seventeenth century. In fact, the scholarly emphasis on Tortuga as a uniquely lawless place obscures the ways in which multinational settlement, maritime raiding, and human trafficking were part of long-standing, regional practices that tied the island to other English, French, and Dutch territories in the Caribbean. Many of the people involved in claiming and settling Tortuga first gained experience in colonization projects in the Lesser Antilles. Like St. Christopher and St. Martin, for example, Tortuga by the 1630s was divided between European colonists of different nations who embraced the exploitation of enslaved and captive labor from the beginning. And like St. Christopher and St. Martin, maritime raiding provided European settlers on Tortuga with the means to establish themselves as planters. If Tortuga was lawless, in other words, it was not uniquely so among the island colonies of England, France, and the Netherlands in the early seventeenth century.

Centering Tortuga within networks of trading, raiding, and human trafficking reveals the impact of English, French, and Dutch colonization in the mid-century Caribbean on individuals like Costa, Andrés, and Marcos as well as the traffickers who had taken them captive. Crucially, the presence of northern European colonies in the region contributed to the vulnerability of populations of Africans and people of Indigenous descent in the greater Caribbean as trafficking networks that had formerly facilitated local alliances transitioned to meet the demand for bound labor and plantation implements. The process in the western Caribbean mirrored the events that had led to the dispossession of the Kalinago on St. Christopher and Anglo-French colonization of that island. As they had in the Lesser Antilles, northern European traffickers relied on safe anchorages and commercial allies in the western Caribbean to make their voyages, and by the 1610s, some of that trade was conducted with African Maroons and Indigenous populations. In exchange for cattle hides, dyewood, and foodstuffs, African and Indigenous commercial allies purchased clothing, iron tools, and sometimes even captives from a multinational assortment of traffickers. But much as the tobacco trade led to colonization and the unraveling of relations between traffickers and the Kalinago in the Lesser Antilles, the dyewood trade of the western Caribbean attracted the colonizing interests of the English Providence Island Company by the 1630s.

The establishment of two official English colonies in the western Caribbean, at Tortuga and the island of Providencia off of the coast of modern-day Nicaragua, led to increased raiding for captives throughout the western Caribbean, including against the Maroon communities who had formerly served as commercial partners for traffickers. As an official colony, Tortuga replicated aspects of St. Christopher's colonial society—it was also multinational, committed to slavery from the beginning, and dependent on maritime connections that made policing the movement of bound laborers difficult. These characteristics applied equally to the colony established on Providence

Island. Traffickers had used both islands as anchorages prior to colonization, and they continued to traffic captives to both places after the establishment of Crown-sanctioned colonies. The practices of traffickers, in other words, had an impact on the development of those colonies. Compared to the slow growth of the enslaved African population in colonial Virginia, for example, the immediate embrace of slavery resulted in the rapid increase in the enslaved populations in Tortuga and Providence Island.[4]

The growing density of trafficking networks across the Caribbean would also have a significant impact on populations of African and Indigenous descent. Crucially, an analysis of Tortuga that treats the island not as singular but, instead, as part of the Caribbean and wider Atlantic world provides context for the experiences of captives like Costa, Andrés, and Marcos. In order to make their voyages, northern European traffickers targeted people of African and Indigenous descent and trafficked them into slavery. The rapid development of English, French, and Dutch colonies during the middle decades of the seventeenth century led to increased raiding for captives throughout the Caribbean and wider Atlantic world, raids that netted numerous people whose experiences mirrored those of Costa, Andrés, and Marcos. The testimonies of Costa and others provide an important window onto raiding and human trafficking in this period from the perspectives of captives themselves. From their initial vulnerability to captivity, to their experiences of serial dislocation, and the ambiguity of freedom for those who escaped, captive testimonies allow for a reconstruction of the predatory, violent world of the greater Caribbean in the decades leading up to mid-century. Emphasizing the perspectives of captives reveals the process whereby networks of cross-cultural trade established by northern European traffickers with local allies, especially African and Indigenous communities, created opportunities for the colonizing ambitions of imperial planners in Europe. Cross-cultural trade and captive slavery were deeply entangled with colonization in the western Caribbean in the decades leading up to mid-century.

Traffickers and Maroons in Western Hispaniola

Prepared cattle hides attracted multinational traffickers to islands like Tortuga and Caymito as early as the mid-sixteenth century. Residents of Hispaniola rapidly increased the cattle populations across the island over the sixteenth century. Similarly to Puerto Rico, those cattle provided residents at a remove from official trade networks with the opportunity to engage in informal trade.[5] By the first decades of the sixteenth century, Spanish land-owners moved from corralling their cattle to a system of open grazing in the rugged, hilly interior of the island, known as the *montes*. Residents of His-paniola hunted the feral cattle using a spear mounted with a half-moon blade called a *jarretadera*. The multitudes of cattle on the island meant that anyone who slaughtered a cow could keep the meat as long as they brought the hide back to the Spanish landowner who claimed ownership over the dead ani-mal. In practice, as historian Gabriel de Avilez Rocha has shown, cattle herds in the *montes* provided a wide variety of individuals with the opportunity to profit off of an illicit trade in hides with passing English, French, Portuguese, or Dutch ships.[6] Access to the *montes* and trade with Spain's European com-petitors also created pathways for autonomy for the island's Maroon commu-nities who forged commercial ties with northern European traffickers during the second half of the sixteenth century.

Marronage on Hispaniola coincided with the earliest stages of coloniza-tion. In the 1510s, a Taíno cacique named Enrique abandoned Spanish colo-nial society with a group of fellow Taíno women and men, settling in the Bahoruco Mountains in the south-central portion of the island. For decades the Taíno population under Enrique remained autonomous of Spanish authority, occasionally raiding Spanish settlements and using the rugged ter-rain of the *montes* to remain hidden from Spanish patrols. Africans enslaved to the Spanish liberated themselves during the early sixteenth century, either joining Enrique's community or forming their own Maroon settlements. After continued harassment by Spanish patrols, Enrique signed a treaty with the Spanish in 1533 that guaranteed his community's independent status in exchange for Enrique's promise to return any people of African or Indige-nous descent who escaped coerced labor among the Spanish to join his set-tlement. Despite the treaty, self-liberated people of African and Indigenous descent had created a "sprawling constellation of autonomous communi-ties" in Hispaniola's *montes* over the sixteenth century that did not answer to either Enrique or the Spanish.[7]

When Spain's European competitors anchored at islands like Tortuga or Caymito after mid-century, they encountered numerous trade partners who brought cattle hides, salted meat, and other island produce to exchange for European manufactured goods and even captives. The voyage of a cohort of traffickers to western Hispaniola in 1610 sheds light on the nature of the trade between Maroon communities and Spain's European competitors.[8] Captive

Map 5. Hispaniola and eastern Cuba

slavery remained central to informal trade networks in western Hispaniola, even when traffickers' local trade partners were themselves self-liberated from slavery. In 1610 three ships, two English and one Dutch, arrived at Cabo de Tiburon, a narrow peninsula jutting off of the southwestern coast of Hispaniola. One of the ships fired a cannon, a common tactic used by traffickers to announce their arrival to trade partners. In response, seven or eight armed men from the Maroon community rode on horseback to the coast in order to ensure the friendly intentions of the new arrivals and to signal to the rest of the community that it was safe to approach the ships.

The Maroons conducted trade with the new arrivals for seventeen days, exchanging at least two hundred hides and a significant quantity of salted meat for the manufactured goods essential to their survival. For individuals from Senegambia among the Maroons of Cabo de Tiburon, the use of horses to raise cattle in order to trade their hides would have mirrored their experiences with cross-cultural trade in Atlantic Africa.[9] The community's ten women transformed the Rouen cloth, thread, and canvas that the Maroons purchased from those English and Dutch traffickers in 1610 into clothing, while the men would use the lances and knives to hunt cattle and wild pigs for sustenance and trade. The ten muskets, powder, and shot that they purchased from the traffickers underscored the precarity of the Maroons' hard-won autonomy in the face of armed Spanish soldiers who periodically patrolled the region.[10]

The English and Dutch traffickers also carried captives to western Hispaniola—twenty-three enslaved women and men who found themselves sold to the Maroons in exchange for hides and salted meat. The archival records of this transaction reveal nothing about those twenty-three individuals beyond their number and the fact that the English had seized them after a maritime raid on a Portuguese transatlantic slave ship.[11] Basic details—their names, ages, or genders—were not recorded. With that in mind, it is still worth pausing to consider the overlapping currents of warfare, slavery, and dislocation that thrust those twenty-three people into a new life among the Maroons of Cabo de Tiburon, even if the only way to approximate their experiences is through a broad survey of the Atlantic-wide context surrounding their multiple captivities.

The twenty-three captives might have entered slavery as a result of warfare in West Central Africa. Since the founding of Luanda in 1575, located just north of the Kwanza River along the coast, Portuguese colonial officials took a direct role in West Central African warfare and the slave trade. Two rival kingdoms, that of Kongo and Ndongo, vied for alliances with the Portuguese as their leaders sought territorial expansion and the consolidation of their rule. After sending several failed diplomatic and religious missions to the kingdom of Ndongo, by 1580 relations between the Portuguese and Ndongo fell apart and led to nearly half a century of open warfare in the region.[12] During the course of that warfare, the Portuguese relied on Imbangala mercenaries from south of the Kwanza River to raid Ndongo territory for the express purpose of seizing captives for the slave trade. As historian David Wheat has shown, the intensification of regional warfare in West Central Africa starting in the 1580s matched the increased arrival of enslaved Angolans in the Spanish Caribbean.[13]

Warfare continued in West Central Africa into the seventeenth century, when Njinga Mbandi, or Queen Njinga, took over the Ndongo throne. Although the Portuguese attempted to subdue Njinga, she evaded capture over the first few decades of the seventeenth century. The Dutch conquest of Luanda in 1641 provided Njinga with allies who helped her wage war against the Portuguese, although the Portuguese defeat of the Dutch in 1648 led Njinga to begin negotiating a treaty with Portugal's representatives, which she finalized in 1657.[14] The extensiveness of this regional warfare can be seen in the demographic shift of the transatlantic slave trade. Whereas previously the majority of enslaved Africans transported across the Atlantic came from the Senegambia and Upper Guinea, scholars refer to the transatlantic slave trade during the first four decades of the seventeenth century as an "Angolan wave" in which the majority of enslaved Africans who arrived in the Americas were West Central Africans.[15]

If this was the case for the twenty-three captives, they would have shared linguistic and cultural traits that stemmed from their regional background as well as the scars and traumatic memories of West Central African warfare. By the time they were sold to the Maroons of Cabo de Tiburon, they also shared the horrors of the Middle Passage and the experience of a violent maritime raid on their floating prison. Perhaps some of the captives forged networks of kinship while on board the ship that carried them across the Atlantic. If so, the English and Dutch attack on the transatlantic slave ship severed most of those precarious ties. Perhaps some of the twenty-three West Central Africans sold in western Hispaniola were family members or would have seen one another through the framework of kinship forged through their shipboard experiences together.[16] Those relationships might have provided some comfort to the twenty-three captives at Cabo de Tiburon.

If traffickers had not disrupted the transatlantic voyage of the Portuguese ship transporting the twenty-three captives, they would have been sold into slavery in Spanish America, likely Cartagena or Portobelo, where West Central Africans were quickly becoming the demographic majority of the enslaved population.[17] The twenty-three West Central Africans, in other words, might have lived and labored among people whose cultural and linguistic background matched their own.[18] They did not, at least not right away, but the Central African captives perhaps had more in common with the Maroons of Cabo de Tiburon than meets the eye. According to the testimony of a French sailor who lived among the Maroons for four years, the Afro-descended inhabitants of Cabo de Tiburon were "very *Ladinos*," a term that signaled their familiarity with Spanish language, religion, and culture.[19] The French sailor testified that the captain of the community was an older Zape man, although he neglected to share the captain's name. The ethnonym "Zape" was an umbrella term used by Iberians for a wide range of people from Sierra Leone in West Africa.

Between the 1550s and 1570s, an invasion of the kingdom of the Zape by refugees from the collapsing Mali empire, known as the Mane, led to a surge in slave exports from Sierra Leone. European slave traders purchased captives both from merchants at the Cape Verde Islands and from West African groups in Upper Guinea who maintained their autonomy from the Mane states, such as the Kokoli on the upper Nunez River.[20] The French sailor's description of the Maroon leader's age and background indicate that he entered slavery as a result of Mane-Zape warfare during the final decades of the sixteenth century. The demographics of the transatlantic slave trade leading up to 1600 point to many of the other Maroons being Zape as well. For the twenty-three West Central African captives sold in western Hispaniola, the West African background of the Maroons would have been foreign. At the same time, the Maroons' familiarity with Iberian culture might have facilitated a shared cultural intelligibility for the West Central Africans. Crucially, both the West African Maroons and the West Central African captives understood slavery as a status applied to cultural outsiders who were expected to labor and expand kinship groups, or who could be used to facilitate trade.[21]

With a population of only fifty people, the majority of whom were men, the Maroons of Cabo de Tiburon likely purchased the twenty-three West Central African captives to undergird their autonomous existence. Stable Maroon communities throughout the Americas relied on the presence of women. Maroon women bore the children who contributed to population maintenance and performed essential agricultural labor for the community. West Central African women also played significant roles in religious practices that maintained an equilibrium between the spiritual and the material worlds.[22] If the captives trafficked in 1610 included women, they would have been incorporated along gendered lines among the Maroons. Male captives would have been expected to contribute to the defense of the community and participate in hunting cattle and producing hides. Trade with northern European traffickers created spaces of autonomy in Hispaniola, and maintaining that autonomy involved trade in captive people. While the Maroons of Cabo de Tiburon established themselves at a remove from the Spanish in Santo Domingo, their community was nonetheless deeply entangled in European imperial competition and politics. Survival, sustenance, and profit flowed into Hispaniola's Maroon communities through trade with northern European traffickers.

Trade between Maroon communities and traffickers was about more than just commerce. Both groups faced existential threats and found in their cross-cultural alliance various ways to mitigate the dangers they confronted. As the example of the Maroons of Cabo de Tiburon makes clear, Maroons in western Hispaniola relied on traffickers for manufactured goods and captives

to strengthen their communities. The threats to Maroon autonomy and survival in this moment should not be understated, especially in the context of
the high demand for enslaved Africans throughout the Greater Antilles. A
case from Cabo de San Nicolás, located in the northwest portion of Hispaniola, highlights the myriad dangers Maroons faced as a result of economic
conditions in the Spanish Caribbean.

In 1606, a ship from neighboring Cuba carried Spanish soldiers to Cabo
de San Nicolás where they raided the Maroon community and seized all
thirty African and Afro-descended residents along with six or seven northern Europeans found trading among the Maroons. The Cuban soldiers carried the thirty women, men, and children first to Santiago de Cuba and then
Havana, where their sale into slavery netted between four and five thousand
ducados or nearly £1,600 sterling for their captors.[23] For his part, the governor
of Santo Domingo, Antonio Osorio y Villegas, denounced the Cuban soldiers
who, he wrote, "came to the land that I govern and took away from it prizes
that I had in my hands."[24] Rather than view the raid as beneficial in Hispaniola's ongoing efforts to conquer the Maroon communities in the northern and
western portions of the island, Osorio lamented the loss of the value of the
captives for Hispaniola's royal coffers. Competition between Cuba and Hispaniola for African captives, as this example highlights, added to the threats
that Maroons faced and compounded their need to secure access to firearms
and other weapons from European traffickers.

Traffickers also faced new commercial and physical dangers in the early
seventeenth century. Maroon communities had not been the only trade partners for northern European traffickers in Hispaniola—Spanish residents at a
remove from the commercial center of Santo Domingo had also maintained
extensive trade ties with northern European traffickers since the middle of
the sixteenth century. The notoriety of that trade, which included the equivalent of trade fairs between northern Europeans and their local trade partners,
drew the attention of imperial planners in Spain who approved of a dramatic
plan to depopulate towns and villages on the western and northern coasts of
the island in 1604. For officials in Santo Domingo the depopulations promised to funnel informal trade away from distant ports and coves on the island
and toward their orbit.[25] For many northern European traffickers who lacked
trade ties in the island's capital, the depopulations reduced the number of
trade partners available.[26] For sailors and ship captains, this threatened their
ability to make a voyage. Word had spread in Europe that trade was becoming harder to come by—in 1607, for example, three Dutch ships returned to

the Netherlands with mixed results after spending seventeen months trading in Hispaniola. The first of the three ships returned with 150 hides, while the second ship carried sixty back to Europe. The voyage of the third ship was a complete disaster for the investors and the crew alike, returning with only five hides on board. According to a Dutch captain, this paltry cargo threatened the sailors' wages. He explained that "the merchants [in Europe] do not want to pay the salaries of the mariners who return without hides after all that time."[27] Sailors, and especially their families, would have felt the sting of lost wages from nearly two years of labor.

Perhaps the pain of hunger would have been slightly mitigated by the fact that those sailors returned at all. Traffickers relied on local residents, like the Maroon communities, for safe anchorages, food, and information about Spanish patrols, without which they risked capture and execution by Spanish soldiers. A small crew of six Dutch sailors, for example, landed at the Banda del Norte of Hispaniola in search of food and trade in 1607. Rather than allies, they encountered Spanish soldiers who took them prisoner and seized their vessel. After being interrogated under torture by officials in Santo Domingo, Governor Osorio declared them pirates and ordered the Dutch captain and three other sailors garroted. The two youngest Dutch crew members he condemned to serve on the galleys.[28] Failing to make a voyage threatened the wages of sailors and survival of their families, but going ashore uninformed in Spanish territory could be deadly. Information gleaned at safe anchorages like Tortuga or Caymito and from local allies in western Hispaniola, including Maroon communities, proved essential for traffickers who sought to make a voyage in the first decade of the seventeenth century.

Maroon communities created cross-cultural alliances and trade networks with northern European traffickers in order to defend their autonomy and remain at a remove from Spanish authorities. Access to trade goods, especially weapons, allowed Maroons to occupy territory far from Spanish population centers around Santo Domingo. Put simply, Maroons in western Hispaniola in the first decade of the seventeenth century did not have to remain close to Spanish towns or haciendas to access the supplies that were essential to their survival. Rather, they transformed Hispaniola's feral cattle and hogs into much-needed manufactured goods and weapons through trade with northern European traffickers. Beyond hides and food, Maroon communities provided traffickers with vital information about the presence of Spanish fleets or armed patrols in the region. The mutually beneficial nature of these relationships echoes the alliances discussed in Chapter 2 between the Kalinago

and northern European traffickers prior to the 1620s. In the case of the Lesser
Antilles, the Kalinago received European manufactured goods, like iron axes,
by providing traffickers with safe anchorages, foodstuffs, and information. In
both cases, traffickers dwelled for periods of time among their African and
Indigenous allies, strengthening the social and commercial ties that undergirded traffickers' ability to use certain anchorages in networks of raiding and
smuggling.

But, just as dwelling in the Lesser Antilles transitioned to colonization
in the 1620s, the popularity of Tortuga and western Hispaniola among traffickers also drew the attention of English and French settlers.[29] Colonization
and, more specifically, efforts to develop plantation agriculture on Tortuga
shattered the alliances forged between Afro-descended populations and
European traffickers in the western Caribbean. The catalyst for that rupture
occurred thousands of miles away from Tortuga's shores in the form of a textile revolution sweeping Europe. At the center of that revolution were the
dyewoods that traffickers brought back to Europe after voyages of raiding
and captive-taking in the Caribbean.

A Dyewood Interlude

A trade in dyewoods beginning in the late sixteenth century incited the transformation of Tortuga from a refuge for traffickers to a jointly held English
and French colony by the late 1620s. After all, the island had little else to recommend it as a permanent colony, especially in the wake of an Atlantic-wide
devaluation of tobacco beginning in the mid-1620s. Decades of traffickers
profiting from transporting dyewood from Tortuga and the western Caribbean, however, convinced English investors in the Providence Island Company to finance an official colony on Tortuga. Dyewood was a valuable export.
Europeans had long relied on organic plant and animal materials to produce
pigments for textiles, and beginning in the fifteenth century, new sources of
richer and longer-lasting dyes accompanied territorial expansion.[30] A dyewood trade in the western Caribbean formed one of the ways that traffickers
made a voyage, blending the cutting and loading of dyewoods with older practices of raiding and informal trade in the late sixteenth and early seventeenth
centuries. By the 1620s, European sailors, ship captains, colonists, and colonial
investors clearly understood the connection between dyewoods and profit,
which had sweeping consequences for the history of places like Tortuga.

European merchants engaged in the dyewood trade from the Americas beginning in the sixteenth century. Ships returning to Europe from the Americas needed heavy cargo to serve as ballast, and the cut logs from dyewoods turned hold space normally allotted to ballast into something far more lucrative for the transatlantic crossing back to Europe. To engage in the trade for dyewoods, Europeans relied on Indigenous knowledge and labor. Accessing dyewoods in Brazil, the Caribbean, or Central America depended on the ability of European merchants to establish trade alliances with Indigenous societies, many of whom performed the arduous labor of cutting the heavy timber and transporting the logs to coastal regions in exchange for European manufactured goods, especially iron blades. This was true of a type of dyewood called brazilwood, for example, which Indigenous Tupi communities in coastal Brazil harvested and sold to Portuguese and later French merchants.[31] Logwood, the heartwood of a tropical tree that flourished in the greater Caribbean, especially the Yucatán Peninsula, also emerged as an important transatlantic commodity because of Indigenous knowledge and labor.[32] Aztec and Mayan textile producers oxidized a dye produced from Central American logwood to create a rich black color—a color difficult for European textile manufacturers to reproduce with available organic materials and practices. The demand for logwood surged following the Spanish encounter with Mesoamerican techniques in the 1520s and 1530s.[33] The value of logwood in Europe, for example, meant that it was frequently listed among the commodities seized in maritime raids by Spain's European competitors. Cargoes of licit and illicit dyewood returned to Europe and were used in the workshops of the so-called *tailleurs de brésil* (Brazilian tailors) of Flanders and Bruges.[34]

Theft was not the only means through which northern European traffickers engaged in the dyewood trade, especially in regions beyond the direct control of Spain. Rather, they often adapted practices of temporary dwelling and resource exploitation to cut and load dyewood throughout the western Caribbean. Traffickers established some of the earliest anchorages for this kind of labor in the Yucatán Peninsula, which abounded with logwood and with locations that were geographically isolated from Spanish administrative oversight, such as Laguna de Términos in the Bay of Campeche, Cozumel Island, or near the small town of Bacalar.[35] According to the Governor of Yucatán in 1565, Luis de Céspedes y Oviedo, the region as a whole produced "such a quantity [of dyewood] that . . . they could load every year all of the caracks in the world."[36] Less than a decade later, reports about settlements of foreign dyewood cutters in the Yucatán circulated in Campeche. By 1573,

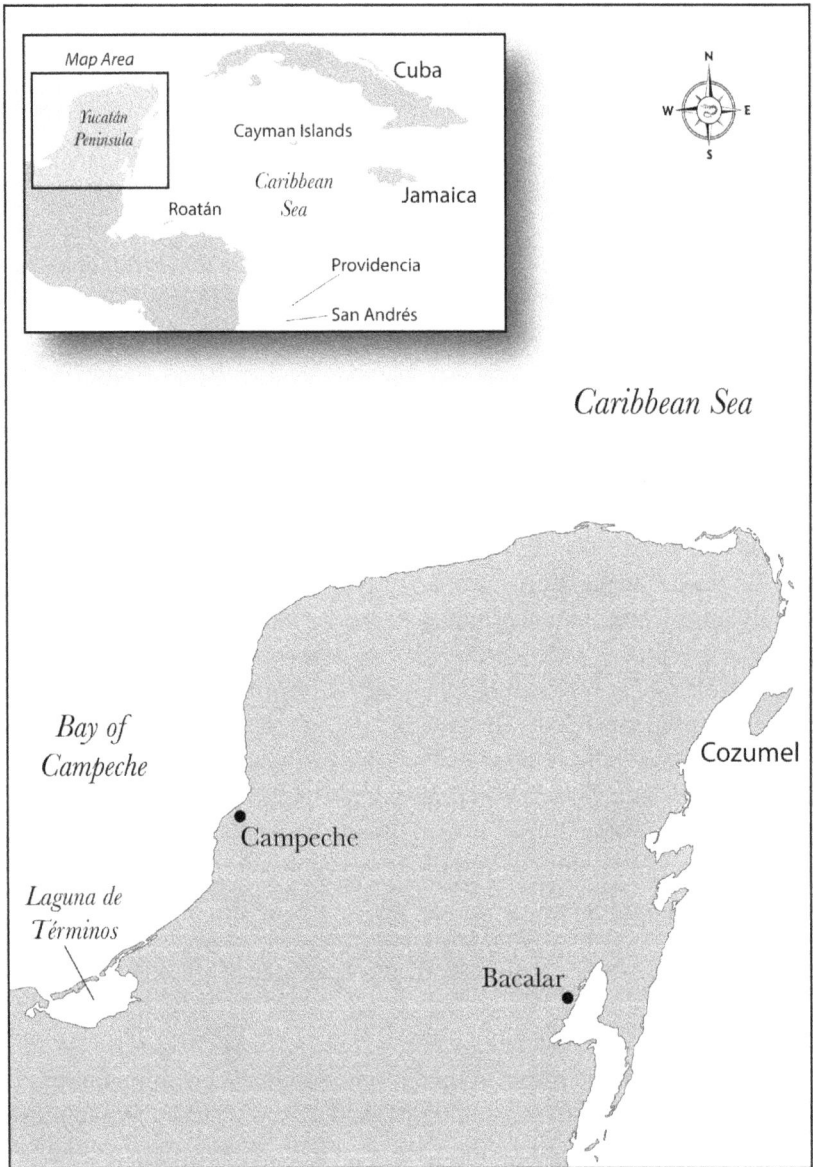

Map 6. Providencia and Campeche

Spanish officials reported on two different settlements, one at Bacalar and the other at Laguna de Términos, where traffickers cut dyewood and traded with local Maya populations.[37]

Relations between northern European traffickers and Maya populations in the Yucatán Peninsula ran the spectrum from peaceful cohabitation and trade to violent raiding and human trafficking. The Spanish had not reduced all of the Maya of the Yucatán Peninsula during early sixteenth-century *entradas* in the region, and the presence of autonomous Maya communities created opportunities for traffickers to establish alliances in the region. Those alliances sometimes involved joint military actions. As the governor of the Yucatán, Gerónimo de Quero, reported in 1634, a Dutch assault of Campeche that year had been successful because the Dutch received aid from local Maya populations. Maya near Bacalar also helped northern Europeans nearly a decade later.[38] But, as the captivity and trafficking experienced by Andrés and Marcos shows, not all of the cross-cultural encounters between Maya and northern Europeans were peaceful. Maya oral traditions about the "Way Kot" attest to these complicated cross-cultural relationships that developed over the course of the late sixteenth and seventeenth centuries. According to the French ethnographer Michel Boccara, the Way Kot was a *brujo*, or witch, who changed form and engaged in trade, including the trade in human beings. Stories of the Way Kot revolved around the slippage between good and bad, benefit and harm, in ways that echoed Maya experiences with northern European traffickers and dyewood cutters.[39] For all of the trade goods brought by northern European traffickers in exchange for dyewoods, Maya populations also encountered individuals who sought to seize and traffic them into slavery.

The dual activities of trading with or raiding among Maya populations in the Yucatán allowed northern European traffickers to make their voyages during a brief, and rare, interlude in European warfare during the first two decades of the seventeenth century. Exhausted after eighty years of war, Spain negotiated a treaty with England's James I in 1604 and a separate truce with the Dutch Republic in 1609. Peace threatened to foreclose many of the financial opportunities previously open to ship captains and sailors, especially for those who were unwilling to flout the law completely. Traffickers had used the previous half century of warfare as a pretext for raiding, and their merchant financiers in Europe had made creative use of letters of marque and letters of reprisal to defend their actions.[40] The brief peace did not end raiding entirely; northern European traffickers continued to raid Iberian shipping and Spanish Caribbean territories, but peace meant that they risked execution as pirates if caught by the Spanish in the Caribbean or being taken to court on their return to Europe.[41]

For some traffickers, dyewood offered a solution to the difficulties of making a voyage in a moment of peace. Throughout the 1610s, for example, when Spanish officials in Hispaniola captured and interrogated northern European sailors around Tortuga and western Hispaniola, many defended their presence in the region by describing their employment as cutting and loading dyewood.[42] No doubt many were, but as the example of English and Dutch trading networks with Maroon communities in western Hispaniola in 1610 makes clear, many traffickers continued older practices of raiding and informal trade as well. Dyewood cutting was one among many activities that traffickers were involved in, but it offered a vernacular legal strategy for sailors confronted with Spanish accusations of piracy. Traffickers' claims to Spanish authorities echoed wider European debates about the nature of sovereignty in the early seventeenth century. Northern European traffickers tacitly asserted that cutting dyewood in territory unsettled by the Spanish or among autonomous Indigenous or African communities broke no laws. Just as English, French, and Dutch jurists argued that Spain could not claim to possess territories that it did not effectively occupy, traffickers defended practices of raiding and smuggling in the 1610s by tying their activities to the trade in dyewood in territories beyond the effective authority of the Spanish Crown.[43] For their part, Spanish Caribbean officials rejected the arguments presented by captured European mariners and worked to suppress their activities.

Anchorages frequented by traffickers in the western Caribbean played a key role in the dyewood trade in the late sixteenth and early seventeenth centuries. Ships sailing to and from the Yucatán Peninsula anchored at islands like Caymito and Tortuga alongside Cabo de Tiburon in western Hispaniola. Further west, anchorages at the islands of San Andrés and Santa Catalina off the coast of modern-day Nicaragua and even the island of Roatán off the Honduran coast served northern European vessels as well.[44] Traffickers had established dwellings at each of these anchorages by the early seventeenth century. The best description of one of these anchorages comes from reports on Caymito, where the soon-to-be governor of St. Christopher, Pierre Bélain d'Esnambuc, and a multinational company of mariners had built shacks as well as a cooperage and a forge by the 1610s.

Described as a "peaceful habitation," the anchorage at Caymito had clearly been established to support the voyages of traffickers, who blended the dyewood trade with raiding and captive taking. The commander of a Spanish fleet who razed the settlement in late 1620, for example, seized 800 quintals of brazilwood and 30 quintals of logwood at Caymito. The different types of dyewoods at the small island underscore the ways that d'Esnambuc and his cohort blended cutting or trading for dyewood with raiding. Beyond the dyewood, the dwelling at Caymito boasted ample foodstuffs, tobacco, hides, ammunition, and nautical supplies including at least thirty ship anchors—materials essential for the maintenance of ships and their crews.[45] By the 1610s, raiding and the dyewood trade brought European traffickers to the western Caribbean, where they encountered increasingly well-established anchorages and, often, alliances with Indigenous and African trade partners. The lucrative trade in dyewoods that drew so many traffickers to the region, however, would soon also attract permanent colonists, with sweeping consequences for the former trade partners of traffickers in the region.

Migration from the Lesser Antilles to Tortuga

By the 1620s and 1630s, ship captains tasked with transporting supplies and people to the developing colonies in the Lesser Antilles often sailed west, making their voyages profitable through practices that had been established by traffickers over the previous decades. English and French captains hired to transport indentured servants and colonists to St. Christopher in the 1620s, for example, frequently sailed on to the western Caribbean to trade for dyewood, tobacco, and hides before returning to Europe. Some even raided, when necessary, along the way.[46] Other ship captains contracted directly with private residents in St. Christopher who sought transportation to the western Caribbean, often without the permission of colonial authorities.[47] For colonial authorities in places like St. Christopher, the "great concourse of ships" sailing to the western Caribbean carried away portions of the island's laboring population as well.[48] Indentured servants, enslaved people of African and Indigenous descent, and even frustrated colonists had heard rumors of opportunity in the western Caribbean through maritime networks, and many risked their lives to reach the anchorages established by traffickers over the previous half century. These unofficial anchorages would become the basis for official colonization by 1630 under the auspices of the Providence Island Company.

Both push and pull factors encouraged migration from the Lesser Antilles to the western Caribbean in the 1620s and 1630s. Rumors about the rich dyewood trade attracted people unhappy with their circumstances in the Lesser Antilles to places like Tortuga. A group of escaped indentured servants from St. Christopher testified in Puerto Rico, for example, that their goal had been to reach Tortuga because of the "great quantities of brazilwood" on that island. For the seven men and two women who had imagined an easier life cutting dyewood on Tortuga, their dreams were thwarted by contrary winds and a lack of water, which drove them to neighboring Puerto Rico. That they risked the voyage at all indicates that they had been familiar with the stories sailors told about ships laden with dyewood and about life in distant Tortuga and beyond the reach of colonial authorities. Nor were they alone. By the late 1620s, Spanish Caribbean officials learned about growing settlements throughout western Hispaniola, Tortuga, the Cayman Islands, Isla Vaca, and other anchorages where residents cut dyewood and cultivated beans, cassava, and tobacco for trade with passing vessels.[49]

Multiple push factors contributed to the unofficial migration to the western Caribbean, including political discord on St. Christopher, a Spanish invasion in 1629, and an Atlantic-wide crash in tobacco prices by the mid-1630s. Problems started in 1629, when English colonists on St. Christopher crossed into French land to plant. The timing of this English encroachment into French territory coincided with the end of the five-year term of the island's first indentured servants, underscoring the dim economic prospects for the poorest English residents. When they refused to voluntarily vacate the occupied French territory, the Compagnie de Saint Christophe in Paris dispatched six ships under the command of the Sieur de Cahuzac with three hundred soldiers and sailors from France to force the issue in June 1629.[50] Rumors had been circulating in metropolitan France of a planned Spanish invasion of St. Christopher, and after reducing the English to the territorial boundaries of the 1627 treaty, the ships were supposed to remain and reinforce the island's defenses.

The English conceded to the superior French force—some returned to their portion of the island while others simply left. But the French ships also abandoned the island. The lure of making a voyage through raiding and smuggling in the greater Caribbean enticed those French captains away at precisely the moment when they were needed most. Six months after the French ships departed St. Christopher, forty-nine Spanish sails commanded by Admiral Fadrique de Toledo arrived to dislodge the settlers.[51] The island's remaining population fled. Around four hundred people sheltered in the rugged interior of St. Christopher while the Spanish torched houses and fields across the island and in neighboring Nevis.[52] Most inhabitants of the two islands escaped by sea, sailing to St. Martin, Tortuga, and western Hispaniola.[53]

Among those who fled was a former ship captain and erstwhile governor of Nevis, Anthony Hilton, along with over a hundred colonists from that island. The group had prior experience with displacement. In 1626, Hilton and his company had established a plantation on the windward coast of St. Christopher, only to be driven off by Kalinago defending their territory against foreign encroachment. The company of settlers under Hilton then attempted to reestablish their plantation closer to Warner's original settlers, but in 1628, they abandoned St. Christopher altogether in favor of more autonomy on the neighboring island of Nevis. Fadrique de Toledo's attack a year later destroyed what they had built and exacerbated Hilton's already precarious finances. Unable to repay his creditor, London merchant Thomas Littleton, and faced with the prospects of rebuilding Nevis's ruined infrastructure, Hilton and his company instead left Nevis and sailed west to Tortuga.[54]

Rumors of opportunity on Tortuga had abounded in St. Christopher, and as a former ship captain, Hilton likely knew more than most about the trade opportunities that transected the western Caribbean. The company from Nevis joined nearly eighty French survivors from St. Christopher who had also fled to Tortuga, where each group established separate plantations, thereby recreating the quasi-autonomous "patchwork of discrete plantations" that the English and French had created on St. Christopher.[55] Hilton's gamble that settlement on Tortuga would offer access to maritime trade quickly paid off; according to a French observer, shortly after Hilton and his company arrived, a French trafficker named Brondel anchored at Tortuga. In exchange for dyewood, foodstuffs, and tobacco, Brondel sold an unspecified number of African-descended captives as slaves.[56] Much as they had on St. Christopher, traffickers played an early role in facilitating the development of a colony on Tortuga through trade in captive people.

Providence Island Company, Dyewood, and Colonization

Ship captains would soon have another reason to anchor at Tortuga. Fadrique de Toledo's assault on St. Christopher and Nevis convinced Hilton of the need to seek merchant financing in England for the expensive task of fortifying the island. He sought that support from the newly formed Providence Island Company, who received a request in May 1631 from "150 persons [who] have planted" on Tortuga, asking for "the protection and Assistance of this Company for the effecting of a Plantation."[57] The perpetually indebted company agreed to send ordinance and supplies to Tortuga, but they demanded in exchange that colonists pay them a 20 percent duty on all island produce.[58] While settlers in Tortuga grew tobacco and foodstuffs, members of the Providence Island Company expected to profit the most from the island's ample stands of dyewood trees. In the second condition for providing financial support, the Providence Island Company banned any dyewood cutting on the island by individuals without a license from the company, which would retain one-fifth of any profit made from the dyewood trade. Hilton agreed to the terms, and in June 1631, the company requested and received an extension of their charter to include Tortuga, which they renamed Association Island.[59]

There was just one problem with the company's dyewood plans: the English Crown had banned the importation of dyewoods to England since the late sixteenth century. Those bans stemmed from complaints that domestic textile workers misused the coloring derived from dyewoods, either producing fabrics that faded too quickly or damaging the cloth when they applied it.[60] The ban did not stop the company from pursuing their monopoly, but it did force them to accept the involvement of French and Dutch intermediaries. To work around the English ban, the Providence Island Company permitted non-English ships to transport cut dyewood from Tortuga and carry it to company agents in France and the Dutch Republic. Any Dutch or French ship was permitted to load dyewood at Tortuga for the company's profit, but the English ban meant that the company relied on Hilton to make sure that profits from this multinational dyewood trade ended up in company coffers. Instead, Hilton largely pocketed the proceeds and used the arrival of northern European traffickers to purchase captives.[61]

Many of the ships that called at Tortuga in the 1630s carried captives of African and Indigenous descent. Traffickers found a ready market at Tortuga for the captives they had seized during raids against Spanish Caribbean communities and shipping lanes. Those same captives often found themselves forced to cut the trees, strip them of their bark, and stack dyewood logs for transport. By 1633, for example, Hilton employed forty captives of African descent in dyewood cutting. Rather than attempt to ban the trade in human captives, members of the Providence Island Company responded to the state of affairs on the island by requesting that Hilton make twenty of those captive Africans the property of the company. He was instructed to send the profits of their labor back to England.[62]

Within three years, continual raiding in the Caribbean by ships that called on Tortuga led to a Spanish assault on the island colony. That act of violence ushered in even more violence against racially stigmatized communities in the Spanish Caribbean, as the Providence Island Company commissioned captains to raid neighboring Spanish territories and shipping lanes. Recognizing the importance of captive-taking to the maritime violence carried out by those captains, the company also instructed ship captains to sell captives of African descent taken as "prizes" into slavery in English colonies like St. Christopher or Virginia. The Spanish attack on Tortuga, in other words, provided the Providence Island Company with an opportunity to formalize preexisting practices of raiding, captive-taking, and human trafficking.

The profits were considerable. In 1636, the *Happie Return* sailed from England with instructions to form a company with Dutch ships, raid for captives, and sell them into slavery.[63] Within a year, Captain Newman of the *Happie Return* sold an unspecified number of captives of African descent in Virginia and New England, returning to England in 1638 with trade goods valuable enough that the company's share was £2,000.[64] According to historians Linda Heywood and John Thornton, between 1631 and 1639, ships commissioned by the Providence Island Company seized over three thousand African captives, most from West Central Africa, from Portuguese slave ships alone.[65] Traffickers responded to imperial competition in the 1630s and 1640s with intensified raiding and captive-taking, relying on islands like Tortuga for safe anchorages and as a market for captive people.

Captivity and Slavery in the Western Caribbean, 1630–1640

The colonization of Tortuga and Providence Island created an increasingly predatory environment in the greater Caribbean in the decades leading up to mid-century. As had been the case with northern European traffickers and the Kalinago in the Lesser Antilles in the 1620s, colonial outposts in the western Caribbean made traffickers less reliant on their former trade partners— African, Indigenous, or Iberian—for access to safe anchorages and trade. The growing number of English, French, and Dutch colonies throughout the greater Caribbean also created new markets for traffickers, who sold a wide variety of captive people into varying degrees of unfreedom, from African and Indigenous captives sold into slavery to European prisoners of war sold into servitude. Violence shaped the lived experiences of captives in the Caribbean and throughout the Atlantic world. According to scholars, environmental changes tied to a mini ice age beginning around 1640 caused instability throughout the wider Atlantic world as droughts, erratic weather, and crop failures from England to West Central Africa exacerbated increasing commercial and political competition throughout the Atlantic world.[66] While warfare disrupted English and French trade to their developing Caribbean colonies, it also provided the pretext for increased raiding and captive taking in the Caribbean. Raiding and captive-taking was even formalized by colonial officials in the Caribbean, with the French authorizing the legal sale in St. Christopher of Africans seized as captives in 1634 and Dutch authorities allowing the same at Curaçao in 1641.[67] For some West and West Central African survivors of the Middle Passage, similar forms of violence and instability that had led to their enslavement in Atlantic Africa continued in the waters of the Caribbean.

The English and French refugees from the Lesser Antilles who arrived at Tortuga late in 1629 carried expectations about how their new colony would develop. They sought to replicate the model of colonial development cut short by the Spanish attack on St. Christopher and Nevis, namely, the exploitation of enslaved African and Indigenous labor in the production of staple crops for export to Europe. For their part, traffickers proved more than willing to accommodate the increasing demand for bound labor. Non-Iberian colonies in the western Caribbean meant that traffickers no longer had to rely on regional allies for safe anchorages, information, and trade. The ability of traffickers to find safe anchorages in the colonies of Tortuga and Providence Island translated to increased violence, especially for communities of African and Indigenous descent. Raiding throughout the western Caribbean rapidly expanded the population of enslaved laborers on Tortuga and Providence Island with some reports suggesting that both islands reached a slave majority by mid-century.[68]

On Tortuga, nearly half of those enslaved captives were Yucatec Maya speakers who had been taken captive by their former trade partners and trafficked into slavery on the island. By the 1650s, slave raiding on the Yucatán Peninsula increased. The example of a French trafficker named Captain Marin highlights the regularity and seasonality of this raiding. As the Afro-Brazilian captive Francisco da Costa testified, "Captain Marin has at Tortuga a frigate of war and with her he sails every year to the coasts of Campeche and he kidnaps all of the Indians there . . . a great quantity of men and women and he sells them for tobacco or money" in Tortuga.[69] Captives seized from the Yucatán and trafficked into slavery in Tortuga faced dire circumstances: one witness on the island estimated that at least half of the Yucatec Maya captives died within several years of arrival due to mistreatment and hard labor.[70] Yucatec Maya speakers like Andrés and Marcos, whose experiences opened this chapter, entered slavery through trafficking networks like those elaborated by Captain Marin, and many died as a result. As the next chapter will discuss, many also escaped. Some, like Andrés and Marcos, fled to surrounding Spanish territories, while others joined growing Maroon communities in the rugged interior of Tortuga.

The presence of northern European colonies in the western Caribbean left traffickers less reliant on African or Iberian trade partners in Hispaniola as well. Rather than allies, by the 1640s many former trade partners became the targets of raids instead. Scattered archival evidence points to traffickers increasingly seizing both captives and plantation tools in Spanish towns and coastal settlements in order to meet the demand of colonists in Tortuga and elsewhere. Iberian settlements along the northern coast of Hispaniola, where traffickers had engaged in informal trade throughout the late sixteenth and early seventeenth centuries, became the scenes of increasingly more violent raids in the decades leading up to mid-century. In the early 1640s, for example, traffickers raided "a large *ingenio* for grinding sugar" on the northern coast of Hispaniola. According to reports, the traffickers seized "all the sugar that had been made, and even the coppers and slaves used to make it."[71] They took both the tools necessary to reconstruct a sugar mill on Tortuga and the enslaved people who had the knowledge and experience required to produce sugar from cane.[72] The raids yielded results in Tortuga. By the 1650s, Spanish officials reported that on Tortuga there was "a mill where they say sugar is made" worked by "at least 70 black slaves."[73] Colonial development in the western Caribbean contributed to the vulnerability of populations of African descent to captivity and displacement as trafficking networks that had formerly facilitated local alliances transitioned to meeting the demand for bound labor and plantation implements.

The ability of traffickers to access food, information, and safe anchorages in European colonies throughout the Caribbean contributed to the vulnerability of populations of African descent beyond Hispaniola as well. Iberian populations along the southern and eastern coasts of Cuba, for example, had served as frequent trade partners for traffickers in the late sixteenth and early seventeenth centuries. By the 1640s, these same coasts witnessed widespread raiding and captive-taking. The experiences of a young man named Miguel Matamba speak to the chaos of raiding and violence in this moment.[74]

Matamba labored as a slave on the *hato*, or cattle ranch, of a Havana resident named Diego de Sotolongo when three ships arrived on the coast. The traffickers, in this case predominantly French, raided the cattle ranches along the coast and seized Matamba and two others, a man named Luis Criollo and a young boy named Ventura Angola.

Raiding and violence would not have been new experiences for Matamba, whose name suggests that he was from the Kimbundu-speaking kingdom of Matamba. Perhaps he had witnessed the warfare between Portugal and Queen Njinga that led to the Ndongo queen seizing the kingdom of Matamba in the 1630s. He might have entered slavery as tribute given to the Portuguese by regional *sobados*, or political units, who had been defeated by Portugal and forced into the position of tribute-paying vassals.[75] Or, perhaps, he was a war captive seized when the Portuguese governor of Angola deployed Imbangala mercenaries to raid Matamba.[76] Imbangala warriors tended to absorb young men from the communities they raided, while enslaving women and children. If Miguel Matamba entered slavery as a result of an Imbangala raid, he might have been among the numerous children trafficked across the Atlantic as a result of increasingly violent West Central African warfare during the late sixteenth or early seventeenth centuries.[77] Warfare and slave raiding destabilized Miguel Matamba's West Central African homeland in the early decades of the seventeenth century, and that process of violent dislocation continued in the Caribbean as well.

Seized from their communities in eastern Cuba, Matamba and his companions found themselves forced to labor on their captors' vessels for nearly a year before he and Luis Criollo were trafficked into slavery in Tortuga. The young boy, Ventura Angola, was forced to remain with the traffickers, either to be sold elsewhere or to continue in a laboring capacity on their ships. For the boy, the loss of his West Central African companions undoubtedly compounded the terror and isolation he experienced as a maritime captive on ships involved in raiding. Although trafficked together, Matamba and Luis Criollo were sold to different people in Tortuga, severing whatever ties the two men developed during their captivity.[78] The captivity and violence experienced by Matamba and his companions at the hands of French traffickers was only one among many moments of dislocation and forced transportation in the mid-seventeenth century. The regularity of such violence, however, doubtless did little to mitigate their own feelings of fear, uncertainty, or loss.

For his part, Matamba formed a new community in slavery in Tortuga that facilitated his escape. The composition of that new community also sheds light on the extensive networks of raiding and captive-taking that fed the demand for enslaved labor among the newly planted colonists on the island. Three months into his enslavement, Matamba escaped in the night alongside a Yucatec Maya man, and two women and a man of African descent who had been taken captive in Campeche. The three men and two women opted to leave Tortuga, rather than join the island's growing Maroon communities. They seized a boat from along the beach and rowed themselves to Hispaniola where, like Costa, Andrés, and Marcos, they made their way to Spanish-held territory and testified to their experiences. As the next chapter will explore, the group's escape did not result in their freedom but rather the return of the two African men to those who claimed ownership over them and the Indigenous man and women to the confines of encomienda labor in the Yucatán Peninsula.

Perhaps, however, returning to the communities from which they had been taken was the group's goal, even if it meant a return to coerced labor. After all, they had another option when they devised their escape—join the Maroon communities in the rugged interior of Tortuga. That they chose to return to territory claimed by Spain perhaps indicates familial or social ties to which Matamba and his companions sought to return. As it turns out, Maroon autonomy in the interior of Tortuga would have been short-lived. As the next chapter will show, those self-liberated communities would face more dislocations when Spain responded to the ongoing depredations of traffickers by invading Tortuga not once but twice between 1635 and 1653.

Prisoners of the Thirty Years' War

If the establishment of plantations on Tortuga and Providence Island served as one among several factors that intensified raiding and captive-taking throughout the greater Caribbean in the decades leading up to mid-century, the other was war. The Thirty Years' War (1619–1648) contributed to the expansion of northern European colonizing activities in the Caribbean, which in turn created both new opportunities for seizing captives and additional markets for their sale. Warfare in Europe also made European prisoners of war vulnerable to being trafficked into conditions of unfreedom in the greater Caribbean. The experiences of a Basque soldier named Josef de Bergara highlight the consequences of war and colonization on the trade in human captives during this chaotic, violent moment.[79] Born in the town of

Oñate in the Basque province of Guipúzcoa, Bergara served in the Spanish theaters of Milan, Flanders, and Germany during the 1620s. After ten years of service, he petitioned for a license to return to Basque country, either to retire from the hard life of a soldier or possibly just to visit family before returning to the front lines. His fate, however, would be very different. Within days of departing Dunkirk, two Dutch ships attacked the frigate that carried him and other soldiers while enroute to San Sebastian.

During the sea battle, Dutch cannon fire demasted the frigate and the Dutch took the goods and soldiers off the ship. Rather than a short voyage to Basque country, Bergara found himself captive on a Dutch ship headed for the Lesser Antilles. They arrived at St. Christopher in May 1638, where Bergara and the other unspecified number of soldiers were sold, ostensibly as servants. Bergara did not mention in his subsequent testimony if his servitude had a term limit, but it hardly would have mattered. As a captive trafficked without a legally recognized contract or, especially, any means of enforcing the terms of his servitude he would have labored without a way to regain his autonomy.[80] As a prisoner of war and a captive, Bergara was trafficked into a form of unfreedom on St. Christopher at a moment of particularly high demand and low supply of indentured and enslaved labor in the Lesser Antilles. The same warfare that led to Bergara's captivity had also disrupted the transatlantic trade in indentured and enslaved people, a situation that would worsen during the 1640s.[81] According to New Englander John Winthrop, by the 1640s, "the warres in England kept servantes from comminge" to American colonies.[82] In the case of Bergara and his shipmates, however, the wars that disrupted trade produced a different source of coerced labor for colonists in the Lesser Antilles.

Bergara arrived during a tumultuous and difficult moment on St. Christopher, although the disorder that he encountered on the island would facilitate his escape a year later. Tobacco prices had crashed as colonists in the growing number of northern European colonies throughout the Atlantic world overproduced the crop. Increased production glutted the market.[83] Politically and economically, the turn in the Atlantic tobacco market strained relations on St. Christopher, which were already aggravated by political changes on the island. The death of the island's first French governor, Pierre Bélain d'Esnambuc, in 1636 had led to infighting between the deputy governor of the French quarter, René de Béthoulat de La Grange-Fromenteau, and the incoming governor-general of the French Antilles, Phillippe de Longvilliers de Poincy. Tensions grew so intense between the two that Poincy would send his former deputy governor back to France to face charges of treason in 1641.[84] The drop in tobacco prices hurt planters across the island. After dispatching his deputy governor, Poincy ordered a ban on the cultivation of tobacco in the French quarters of St. Christopher, ordering settlers to "only plant foodstuffs," according to what Bergara heard during his time on the island. His English counterpart, Thomas Warner, also faced resistance when he signed an agreement with Poincy to enact a similar ban on tobacco on the English portions of the island—an indication of how intertwined their networks of trade remained into the 1630s and 1640s—but neither governor succeeded in fully curbing tobacco cultivation.[85]

The fight over tobacco cultivation led some French and English colonists to experiment with indigo production. Producing indigo in the seventeenth century involved soaking the stems of the plant in large vats of fermented, decomposing liquid, which coerced laborers agitated with large paddles under the scorching tropical sun—labor that was, in other words, difficult and noisome.[86] Fortunately for Bergara, the Frenchman who claimed ownership over his labor opted to abandon the struggling colony of St. Christopher and try his luck in Tortuga. In March 1639, Bergara boarded a small ship with the other members of the Frenchman's household. En route, they landed at the southern coast of Puerto Rico to load more water and food. Once on shore in Spanish territory, Bergara fled to San Germán and testified about everything that had transpired. Years after his initial captivity in the waters of the English Channel, Bergara was finally able to make his way home.

The experiences of Bergara and his shipmates were not exceptional. That a pair of Dutch ship captains could traffic European captives into servitude in St. Christopher in the late 1630s exposes the extent to which Atlantic warfare and metropolitan neglect of Caribbean colonies shaped the lived experiences of a wide range of people. The testimony of another soldier, Raimundo Burgos, similarly reveals how traffickers used the disorder of the 1630s and 1640s to profit off of the labor of European captives, in this case on Tortuga. Burgos, an Irishman from the city of Galway, also started his career as a soldier under the employ of the Spanish king, fighting to suppress a rebellion in the northeastern Spanish province of Cataluña in 1640. After being captured by the French, Burgos was carried to a prison in Barcelona and later to France, where he was held for three years before being ransomed by a royalist English ship captain who fought on the side of Charles I at the start of the English Civil War. As the tides of the war turned in favor of Parliamentarians, the ship Burgos served on crossed the Atlantic and anchored at St. Christopher, where the English ship captain who had ransomed him in France died.[87] Burgos labored in the local coasting trade on the island for two years before a French trafficker took him captive and carried him to Tortuga. As Burgos later testified, he spent the year planting and curing tobacco for a French colonist on Tortuga before he escaped to Santo Domingo.[88] The forced servitude experienced by Bergara and Burgos underscores the permissive nature of labor markets in this chaotic, violent moment, as a wide range of people experienced captivity and forms of unfreedom in nascent Caribbean colonies.

Warfare and trade disruptions also exacerbated the vulnerability of people of African and Indigenous descent to captivity, enslavement, and serial dislocation throughout the greater Caribbean. Northern European traffickers continued to target transatlantic slave ships as they had over the previous half century, but renewed warfare opened easier, legal methods for trafficking those captives into slavery within the English and French colonies of the Lesser Antilles. With French entry into the Thirty Years' War in 1635, the Compagnie de Saint Christophe even authorized the introduction and sale in St. Christopher of any African captives seized from the Spanish by traffickers of all nations.[89] That authorization compounded experiences of violence and dislocation for African captives who had already survived captivity in Africa and the horrors of the Middle Passage. A Spanish pilot named Domingo de Fonseca testified to the heightened risk of passing through the Lesser Antilles, albeit from the privileged position of a pilot rather than an enslaved captive. In September 1638, the unnamed ship that Fonseca piloted arrived at Dominica to refresh the ship's wood and water stores to prepare for the voyage across the Caribbean to New Spain. At Dominica, however, Fonseca described the approach of "a large frigate of *pechelingues* [Flemish]" who "entered and robbed and carried" the slave ship back to St. Christopher.[90]

The sparse description from the perspective of the ship's pilot proves woefully inadequate for thinking about or imagining what this moment of maritime violence would have been like for the unspecified number of African captives shackled below decks. For what it lacks in depth, the pilot's testimony does hint at the frequency of this sort of maritime violence. As a prisoner on St. Christopher for three days, Fonseca allegedly heard the French boast that between all of the islands that France claimed in the Lesser Antilles there were more than ten thousand enslaved Africans "whom they had taken as prizes."[91] Fonseca's imprisonment among the French of St. Christopher was brief—he was ransomed back to Spanish territory as a pretext for informal trade, a practice described in Chapter 2. The African captives might have found themselves trafficked into slavery elsewhere or sold in St. Christopher while that island grappled with economic and political unrest. The archival traces of those captives end abruptly after their sale in St. Christopher.

Warfare and the growth of northern European settlements in the western Caribbean amplified raiding and captive-taking along the Spanish Main during the 1630s, as traffickers rushed to meet the demand for coerced labor in those nascent colonies. Crucially for captives of African descent, the violence and dislocation that they experienced at the hands of traffickers in the Caribbean echoed previous experiences of warfare and enslavement in places like Upper Guinea or West Central Africa. Crosscurrents of warfare throughout the Atlantic, both European and African, transected the lives of people trafficked into slavery in the decades leading up to mid-century. The captivity and trafficking of four African men to Providence Island in the early 1630s reveals the overlapping ways that warfare and captivity impacted the lives of Africans and their descendants in the greater Caribbean. The four men— Francisco Biafra, Juan Biafra, Geronimo Angola, and Damian Carabalí— worked as enslaved boatmen in Cartagena for a widow named Doña Mariana Clavijo. Tasked with transporting wine from Cartagena to the Magdalena River sometime in 1634, traffickers attacked their small vessel along the coast and took all four men to Providence Island where, according to the testimony of Francisco Biafra, the English governor, Philip Bell, purchased the men for "twenty-six libras of tobacco and a pig each."[92] The four men had experience as sailors, however, which they used to flee their captivity.

Within several months of their sale, they made plans with six European men who labored on the island in order to escape. The group stole Governor Bell's boat and made their way to Spanish territory near the San Juan River in modern-day Costa Rica. During their flight from Providence Island, tensions broke out between the men and one European was killed while an unnamed fifth African man died of natural causes. By the time the group was discovered at the mouth of the San Juan River by a passing ship, three of the remaining Europeans had fled, leaving only the four African men, an indentured servant from London, and a young Dutch servant to testify before Spanish authorities about their captivity and escape.[93] As will be seen in the next chapter, the maritime mobility of captives throughout the Caribbean provided Spanish authorities with strategic information that resulted in several invasions of Tortuga, Providence Island, and elsewhere.

The archival record of the four men taken captive near Cartagena and trafficked into Providence Island ends with their testimony before Spanish officials, who asked nothing about the details of their lives beyond who claimed ownership over them and the nature of their captivity at the hands of the English. All we have are their names and the fact that they had been enslaved in Atlantic Africa, sold in Cartagena, and taken captive by northern European traffickers in the Caribbean. The last names of the four men can help us imagine what the trajectories of their lives had been before they liberated themselves from captivity in Providence Island.[94] The last names of Francisco and Juan Biafra and that of Damian Carabalí mean that the three men were from Biafara in the Upper Guinea region in West Africa between the Casamance and Grande Rivers. Their homelands had been ravaged by raiding between the Bijagó, Biafada, and Banhun as these coastal groups sought captives to exchange for iron bars in the context of escalating violence precipitated by the slave trade.[95] Their experiences of warfare, captivity, and the Middle Passage would have echoed those of Geronimo Angola, whose provenance in West Central Africa undoubtedly made him intimately familiar with the chaos of warfare and human trafficking as well.

During the tumultuous middle of the seventeenth century, the violence that resulted in the multiple experiences of captivity of Biafra and his companions reverberated throughout the Atlantic world. Although exceptionally well-documented cases cannot stand in for the multitudes of experiences of people of African descent in this moment, the experiences of Biafra and his companions allow for a broad sketch of the currents of violence that brought captives to nascent northern European colonies throughout the greater Caribbean in the decades leading up to mid-century. Crucially, a wide variety of people experienced captivity and trafficking in this moment, from European prisoners of war to Yucatec Maya. The testimonies gathered by Spanish Caribbean officials from self-liberated captives like Biafra or Francisco da Costa, whose experiences opened this chapter, provide a vivid portrait of the networks of raiding and captive-taking that transected the Caribbean at mid-century and the multitudes of people who fell victim to regional violence and human trafficking. Those testimonies, as will be seen in the next chapter, also informed Spanish Caribbean officials about the state of their rivals' colonies—information that would be used to deadly effect during the first half of the seventeenth century.

When Francisco da Costa gave his testimony to Spanish officials in the late 1640s, the fate of the French colony from which he and his Yucatec Maya companions escaped was likely not foremost on his mind. He answered the officials' questions, forced to speak as best he could for Andrés and Marcos because the Audiencia of Santo Domingo lacked a Maya translator, while the notary scribbled down his responses.[96] He recounted his own captivity from a fishing vessel in Bahía and his experience of being sold into slavery to the French governor of Tortuga. He recounted everything he saw during his time on that island, including a description of the fortifications and an estimation of the number of men capable of bearing arms—information of vital importance to the Spanish officials who questioned him. But Costa also testified to his legal status prior to being taken captive by French traffickers. As he explained, the man who claimed ownership over his mother in Bahía freed her before he was born, making him free as well.[97] For the Afro-descended fisherman who had spent the previous decade and a half in captivity and slavery, his testimony was about more than the geopolitical concerns of Spanish officials. It was about his future.

Law and legal recognition, Costa soon learned, proved to be two different things. Written in the margins of Costa's testimony was a brief note to the Council of the Indies about the "Black that passed over to this island escaped from Tortuga." The marginal note repeated a select part of Costa's testimony, that he "had been taken captive more than thirteen years ago by the French enemies" and that the French treated him like a slave. Armed with that evidence, the Audiencia of Santo Domingo sold Costa into slavery at public auction, pocketing the money for the royal treasury. They also ordered that Andrés and Marcos be returned to Campeche on the first ship sailing from Santo Domingo for Veracruz. Andrés and Marcos were protected from sale into slavery in Hispaniola by various laws barring Indigenous slavery in the Spanish Caribbean, while Costa found himself enslaved despite his claims of being free.[98] As Costa was trafficked thousands of miles away from anyone who could corroborate his claims, his case underscores the racialized vulnerability experienced by captives of African descent in the seventeenth century, even in moments when they liberated themselves from captivity. His status as "a Black" refracted the violence of his forced removal from his home community and ended in his enslavement in Santo Domingo. This becomes even more apparent when Costa's experiences are compared to those of European prisoners of war, such as Raimundo Burgos, who received transportation back to Europe following their testimonies. Centering Costa's fate at the hands of the Audiencia of Santo Domingo underscores the stakes involved in captive testimonies for people of African descent. Attending to this fact is important for the next chapter, which examines Spanish responses to captive testimonies about the raiding and captive-taking of Spain's European rivals.

Spanish officials learned a great deal from self-liberated captives over the first half of the seventeenth century. Extensive networks of raiding and captive-taking had developed throughout the Caribbean by the 1640s. From Cuba to Campeche, traffickers engaged in raids and profited off of the sale of captives in nascent colonies during a moment of Atlantic-wide warfare and crisis. For the nascent colony of Tortuga, trafficking networks brought access to captives and outlets for the dyewood, tobacco, hides, and sugar that the colonists forced captives to produce. The colonists who established themselves on Tortuga did so because traffickers had developed anchorages in the region in the late sixteenth and early seventeenth centuries, and they benefited from the continued arrival of traffickers even after official colonization under the auspices of the Providence Island Company. Colonies in the western Caribbean exacerbated raiding and captive-taking throughout the region, and it was a situation that Spain responded to with force. As the next chapter will show, the regional trade in captive people incentivized cycles of increasingly more violent European warfare in the greater Caribbean. For some captives of African and Indigenous descent, the chaos of warfare at mid-century created opportunities, while for those who formed Maroon communities, cycles of European warfare ended their bids for autonomy in places like Tortuga and Providence Island.

CHAPTER 4

_____

"As He Himself Confessed"

Contested Spaces and Serial Displacement

In 1635, Francisco Biafra gave testimony to Spanish officials in Portobelo about his captivity on, and subsequent escape from, Providencia. His eyewitness testimony proved critically important for his interrogators by providing strategic details about the island's fortifications, population, and number of ships anchored in the harbor. Several months later, Spanish officials launched the first of three separate invasions of Providencia and neighboring San Andrés.[1] To that end, Biafra's testimony was not unique. Between 1629 and 1653, Spain authorized seven different invasions of St. Christopher, St. Martin, Tortuga, and, again, Providencia, each planned with the aid of testimonies from other self-liberated captives like Biafra. While it was perhaps with some satisfaction that Biafra provided strategic information for a Spanish assault on his former captors, it was undoubtedly with a sense of hope that he gave, unasked, the names of six men: Martin Balanta, Andrés Golofo, Francisco Angola, Juan Angola, Baltasar Folupo, and Juan Arará. Those six men remained captives on the island after they were unable to rendezvous at the beach, as planned, on the night that Biafra and the others escaped.[2] In Portobelo, Biafra used his testimony to bring their status as captives to the attention of the Spanish officials who planned an invasion of Providencia. Although Biafra anticipated the Spanish liberating his stranded companions from captivity, the fate of the six men in the wake of the three separate Spanish assaults on Providencia and San Andrés over the next six years is hard to trace in the archival record.

Perhaps the Spanish force that invaded Providencia in 1640 took Biafra's six companions and distributed them among the soldiers tasked with manning the newly built Spanish presidio on the island. If that had been the case, they might have known a woman named Catalina Angola who lived in the

home of the presidio's captain, Salvador de la Peña. Like Biafra and his companions, Catalina had been taken captive by northern European traffickers
and sold into slavery among the English on Providencia. How many years
she labored for English puritans on the island before the Spanish invasion
is unclear, but she witnessed at least some of the violence and turmoil that
accompanied the various Spanish attempts to dislodge the English colony.
By 1646, Catalina had given birth to three children, two daughters and a son
named after his father. After years of dislocation and uncertainty, the intimate
ties that Catalina forged with Peña led to her and her children being granted
their freedom.[3] Creating a home on a strategically important but undersup-
plied Spanish presidio, however, provided little security from the waves of
captive-taking and violence ebbing and flowing in the wider Caribbean. In
1666, at least one of Catalina's children—the son named Salvador—had been
taken captive by English traffickers and sold into slavery in Jamaica. Captivity and serial dislocation, in this case, were intergenerational. When Salvador
eventually escaped from Jamaica, he did so in the company of six others who
also had been taken captive from Providencia, although none of them bore
the names of Biafra's six companions.

While the outcome of Biafra's testimony for his six companions might
not have been what he wanted, his description of the island proved useful for
Spanish officials in Portobelo. Over the decades leading up to mid-century,
testimonies of self-liberated captives like Biafra facilitated numerous Spanish
assaults on English, French, and Dutch settlements in the greater Caribbean.
Scholars tend to analyze the series of Spanish responses to foreign colonial
interlopers as limited or singular, studying each invasion within the context
of the history of a single island, for example. The rapid succession of Spanish
invasions across the Caribbean between 1629 and 1653, however, were not
singular occurrences. Seen together, those invasions reveal a concerted Spanish reaction to the increased raiding and captive-taking that accompanied
the establishment of English, French, and Dutch colonies in the Caribbean
beginning in the mid-1620s. Put simply, maritime predation incited Spanish retaliation against specific spaces in the greater Caribbean. Raiding and
captive-taking by northern European traffickers in the greater Caribbean, in
other words, sparked violent reactions by Spanish Caribbean officials who
acted on the strategic information provided by self-liberated captives.

Analyzing the numerous Spanish invasions between 1629 and 1653 in
a single frame shows what this inter-imperial competition meant for captive people, particularly those captives of African and Indigenous descent.[4]

Centering captives in the history of the multiple Spanish invasions of rival colonies, however, does more than just underscore the human consequences of the decades of Caribbean violence leading up to mid-century. Rather, captives like Biafra and his six companions were cause and consequence of moments of inter-imperial violence and contestation in two ways. First, captive testimonies impelled the Spanish to invade specific colonies, and their testimonies provided critical intelligence for those invasions. Second, in several instances, Spanish imperial planners then used the sale of Afro-descended captives seized during invasions to recoup the expenses of those very same invasions. The testimonies of captives like Biafra, in other words, force a shift in historical perspective that accounts for both the experiences of individuals caught in the middle of rival claims to Caribbean spaces and their influence on those wider events.

Scholars tend to situate the various Spanish invasions of rival colonies between 1629 and 1653 within a wider set of questions about colonialism and European imperial competition.[5] A focus on imperial competition, however, has resulted in a focus on imperial outcomes—territorial gains or losses, wider Atlantic warfare, or the consolidation of state power over colonial expansion—often at the expense of discussing how individuals encountered and influenced the turmoil of these decades. Accounting for the role of captives, in particular, also contributes to a growing literature that has expanded how historians understand the profitability of the slave trade more broadly. Recent scholarship shows that the profits earned through the sale of enslaved people via the transatlantic slave trade were not the only means through which individuals made the slave trade profitable, with economic activities like the resale of captives through the intra-Caribbean slave trade or using the commercial networks of the transatlantic slave trade to conduct other business, such as smuggling or specimen collecting, all contributing to the wealth earned through the slave trade.[6] The sale of African and Indigenous captives seized during the invasions of rival colonies adds further nuance to the extensive ways in which the trade in human captives produced wealth in the Atlantic world. The experiences of people like Francisco Biafra or Catalina Angola, in other words, reveal how raiding and captive-taking were not ancillary to imperial competition over Caribbean spaces in this moment but were central to it.

Captives of African and Indigenous descent responded to their captivity in myriad ways in the decades leading up to mid-century. Some, like Biafra, used the aqueous environment of the Caribbean to escape to Spanish territory, where they provided vital information for military interventions against their former captors. Others liberated themselves from slavery but remained on the islands where they had been trafficked, forming Maroon communities in remote locations. A small number of men taken captive from Spanish territory even joined their English, French, or Dutch captors as sailors aboard ships armed for raiding.[7] Gender and age mediated the options available to captives. Young men, for example, predominated among those who escaped by sea, and they were alone in their ability to join the maritime crews of their captors. For women, children, and the elderly who wished to escape their enslavement, Maroon communities offered one option.[8]

Despite the myriad responses to captivity by people of African and Indigenous descent, their experiences during moments of inter-imperial warfare were profoundly shaped by the implications of the wider commodification of racialized labor in the Atlantic world. Decades of regional instability and violence meant that islands like Tortuga and Providencia switched hands multiple times. African and Indigenous captives caught in the middle of these European contests over territory were often commodified anew during moments of violence, either carried away by their captors in advance of Spanish attacks, only to be trafficked into slavery elsewhere, or seized and sold as "slaves of the king" by incoming Spanish officials and soldiers. And, because these islands suffered repeated invasions over several decades, the serial dislocations associated with inter-imperial competition crossed generations. Only by analyzing the disruptive violence of the years between 1629 and 1653 as a whole and by accounting for the experiences of captives in those contested spaces does the wider, intergenerational story emerge.

Invading St. Christopher, 1629

The testimonies of former captives who escaped to Spanish settlements in the greater Caribbean provided Spanish officials with a disturbing portrait of the activities of their European competitors in the region. Officials gained insight into the place of specific island colonies in networks of raiding and trafficking that transected the Caribbean by the early seventeenth century. Spain's Council of War also learned about the state of defenses on those island colonies. The experiences of a French sailor named Thomas Cordero exemplify how trafficking networks exposed colonists on St. Christopher and Nevis to not only opportunity in terms of trade but also peril in the form of a well-timed Spanish assault on the island in 1629. A native of Le Havre, Cordero had worked from a young age as a sailor in regional trade between France and Spain. By twenty-two he was sailing on the ship of a French wine merchant heading back to Le Havre when the crew of another French vessel attacked and boarded them. According to Cordero, "because they carried no weapons," he and his companions on the wine merchant's ship did nothing to defend themselves and their attackers easily overcame them. Together, the pair of ships crossed the Atlantic and stopped first at the Kalinago islands of St. Lucia and Martinique, where the French crew traded with the Kalinago, before continuing on to St. Christopher to sell the stolen ship along with the cargo of wine. They also sold the captive crew members as servants on the island. Cordero found himself forcibly employed in hunting turtles and seals for the provisioning trade to St. Martin by a French boat owner on St. Christopher.[9] He might have remained in that employment indefinitely if not for the arrival of a Portuguese pilot named Manuel Franco Camarino.

Camarino's ordeal began when he signed on to pilot a slaving vessel from Angola to New Spain. Shortly after the crew departed Havana, where they delivered the remaining enslaved Central Africans, the vessel encountered rough seas near Santo Domingo. Although just over 750 nautical miles separate the two port cities of the Greater Antilles, the slaving vessel was blown so far off course that it went down near Anguilla in the eastern Caribbean. Of the original crew, eighteen survived the shipwreck and were rescued by a French ship captain, who deposited them into the hands of authorities on St. Christopher and, ultimately, the island's prison. During his time in prison, Camarino made the acquaintance of an unnamed Portuguese-speaking woman of African descent who earned additional income by cooking meals for the prisoners of the jail.[10] According to his later testimony, it was through his friendship with her that Camarino gained important information about the French and English settlements on the island. It was also likely through her that Camarino made plans with Cordero and two other French servants to escape the island. After seven months imprisoned on St. Christopher, Cordero and his companions broke Camarino out of prison, and the group escaped to neighboring Puerto Rico in a stolen fishing boat.[11] Once in Spanish territory, Camarino and Cordero gave extensive testimonies to Spanish officials about what they had experienced and seen on St. Christopher, including details about the island's fortifications and population. That intelligence would prove fatal for French and English colonists on the neighboring island.

The presence of both Cordero and Camarino on St. Christopher in the late 1620s underscores the danger posed to English and French colonists on the island by serving as a welcoming port for traffickers. This was especially true considering the close proximity of Spanish Puerto Rico. The French ship captain who seized Cordero and the vessel he worked on clearly knew that he would find a market at St. Christopher for the pilfered wine and a place to dispose of Cordero and his companions. Northern European traffickers continued to use St. Christopher as an anchorage over the first half of the seventeenth century and frequently sold captives seized during maritime raiding at the island, including captives of European descent.[12] The decision to keep Camarino and the other shipwreck survivors imprisoned on St. Christopher was undoubtedly with an eye toward using him in a prisoner exchange that would open the possibility of further smuggling with nearby Spanish ports.[13]

The time Camarino, Cordero, and others like them spent on St. Christopher, however, meant that they gained a strategic understanding of the state of the island—one that they willingly shared with officials in Puerto Rico when they escaped. Camarino, for example, testified to the growing commercial importance of St. Christopher, describing a constant traffic of ships of one, two, and three hundred tons over the course of his seven-month imprisonment.[14] Camarino also described the fortifications and defenses, going so far as to warn Spanish officials that many of the men capable of bearing arms on St. Christopher had military experience. Most, according to Camarino, were veterans of the early stages of the Thirty Years' War.[15] Cordero confirmed much of what Camarino said but added a more detailed perspective of the island's social dynamics and fortifications. According to Cordero, shortly before he and his companions escaped to Puerto Rico, the English and French had come to blows "over the command and lordship of the island and many English had died."[16] These testimonies revealed the centrality of St. Christopher to regional trade networks but also underscored the instability caused by discord between the English and French residents on the island. St. Christopher was, in other words, a dangerous neighbor but also one weakened at that moment by internal fighting over territorial boundaries.

The strategic information provided by captives who had escaped from St. Christopher turned into action when an armada of thirty-five Spanish warships approached Nevis in September 1629. Over the previous spring and early summer, Spain's Council of War consulted the testimonies of Camarino, Cordero, and others in order to draft the orders that the admiral of the armada, Fadrique de Toledo, opened while crossing the Atlantic.[17] Tasked with delivering supplies to Cartagena de Indias and destroying any Dutch fleets they encountered, Fadrique was also ordered to dislodge foreign settlements in the Lesser Antilles. He approached Nevis first. Less densely populated and possessed of weaker fortifications, Fadrique understood it to be an easier target than neighboring St. Christopher. Perhaps more important, after the English settlers on Nevis capitulated to the Spanish fleet after a day and a half of battle, Fadrique interrogated the island's defenders and select crew members from the ten merchant vessels anchored in the harbor at the time of the attack.

These prisoners described the locations and relative strength of St. Christopher's three main fortifications, adding to and updating the details already acquired by Spain's Council of War. After ordering the destruction of the fort, houses, and tobacco fields on Nevis, Fadrique set sail for St. Christopher. The fleet likely anchored near Charles Fort, and within seventeen days of bombarding the island, the English and French forces on St. Christopher also capitulated.[18] The Spanish attack dispersed the island's French and English population, leaving only around four hundred people who "fled to the mountains," many of whom returned to rebuild their homes and replant their fields once the smoke cleared and Fadrique's sails disappeared over the horizon.[19] Other colonists, however, fled to St. Martin or Tortuga.[20] Less clear is what happened to the enslaved African and Indigenous populations on St. Christopher and Nevis in the wake of the attack. Some undoubtedly fled into the mountains while others were likely seized by Fadrique's forces.[21] The enslaved women and men from St. Christopher who were forced to accompany English and French refugees to Tortuga, however, would soon experience a new round of violence and dislocation in the western Caribbean.

Tortuga and Serial Dislocation, ca. 1634–1635

Imperial competition, especially in hotly contested spaces in the western Caribbean, profoundly shaped the experiences of captives of African descent.[22] The multiple Spanish invasions of Tortuga and Providencia in the decades leading up to mid-century provide a context for thinking through the implications of raiding, trafficking, and European warfare on the lives of African and Indigenous captives on those islands. For the people of African and Indigenous descent on Tortuga, unrest and warfare in the 1630s brought opportunity and peril. Much like St. Christopher, Tortuga had served as an anchorage for traffickers in the half century before the island was claimed by the Providence Island Company, and the colony continued to welcome traffickers of all nations even after the arrival of Governor Anthony Hilton and the English and French refugees from Nevis and St. Christopher. Many of those traffickers raided Iberian shipping, especially ships out of Cartagena, along with coastal communities, in order to seize African and Afro-descended captives whom they trafficked into slavery on Tortuga. The activities of those traffickers incited a violent Spanish assault in 1635, in which nearly two hundred Europeans were killed and between forty and fifty people of African descent were taken captive by Spanish forces and sold into slavery in Santo Domingo.[23] Slavery in Santo Domingo was just one among several different trajectories for Africans and their descendants caught in the middle of European territorial contestation in the 1630s, while Indigenous captives, especially Maya from the Yucatán, were returned to the region of their captivity. For some, the 1635 assault on Tortuga was neither the first nor the last time their social worlds were upended by inter-imperial violence over the first half of the seventeenth century.

The majority of the enslaved population on Tortuga on the eve of the 1635 Spanish invasion arrived as captives taken in raids on Iberian shipping. The informal nature of captive-taking and trafficking to Tortuga, coupled with the subsequent Spanish invasions, prohibits quantifying the sale of captives into slavery in the decades before mid-century. Some figures provided by Dutch observer Johannes de Laet can, at least, convey the scale of maritime predation against Iberian shipping in the years leading up to the Spanish invasion of Tortuga. According to De Laet, between 1623 and 1636, ship captains operating with commissions from the Dutch West India Company alone had seized 3,256 captive Africans from 547 Iberian ships. Some of the traffickers commissioned by the Dutch company used Tortuga as a Caribbean port, where they sold the Africans seized in maritime raids, referred to as "prizes," for around 250 Dutch florins per person.[24]

Spanish Caribbean reports confirmed the brisk trade conducted out of Tortuga in tobacco, foodstuffs, and dyewood with passing vessels that, as officials in Santo Domingo complained, frequently raided Spanish "frigates and boats ... in order to rob them."[25] Nor was the Dutch company alone in issuing commissions against Iberian shipping. According to estimates from historians Linda M. Heywood and John K. Thornton, between 1631 and 1639, no fewer than sixteen Portuguese transatlantic slave ships were seized by ship captains operating under the auspices of the Providence Island

Company. The year that Anthony Hilton arrived as governor of Tortuga, in other words, the same company that had invested in his colony was also supporting maritime raids against Iberian shipping that ended in the captivity of more than three thousand African women, men, and children.[26] Archival records prohibit knowing precisely how many captives ended up in Tortuga on the eve of the 1635 Spanish invasion, but the records that do survive point to the proliferation of captive-taking by traffickers in the greater Caribbean and the likelihood that Tortuga served as a welcome and important market for that trade.

Raiding by traffickers in the waters between Cartagena and Portobelo during the 1620s and 1630s provides a glimpse into the intra-Caribbean slave trade as both nonlinear and intensely violent. It is worth pausing to consider why so much maritime predation occurred between these two ports and to reflect on the consequences for Africans caught in the middle of those maritime raids. After 1595, Spain granted monopoly contracts, called *asientos de negros*, to Portuguese merchants who contracted ships to conduct the transatlantic portion of the slave trade to Spanish America.[27] Despite allowing the Portuguese a monopoly on the transatlantic trade, Spain prohibited foreign merchants from conducting the slave trade into interior regions like Peru. Rather, transatlantic slave ships could only legally sail to specific ports like Cartagena and Veracruz. For African captives who disembarked transatlantic slave ships in Cartagena, after surviving the many brutalities of the Middle Passage, this meant that the so-called Middle Passage marked only one in a long series of voyages into slavery in the Americas.[28]

West or West Central African captives who disembarked at Cartagena often faced lengthy journeys over sea and land to Peru—journeys always threatened by maritime raids. Once disembarked in Cartagena, African captives destined for Peru would spend a period of time, from several days to weeks, in either overcrowded sheds or makeshift hospitals called *casas del cabildo*. Slave traders purchased many newly arrived African captives in Cartagena in order to resell them in the Peruvian city of Lima, where Spanish residents paid two to three times more for enslaved Africans than buyers in Cartagena.[29] Captive Africans destined for Lima traveled by sea from Cartagena to Portobelo, a journey that took nine to ten days. That journey left the smaller merchant vessels carrying African captives vulnerable to maritime raids.[30] Reports from Lima confirmed that traffickers seized "boats transporting Blacks arriving [there] from Cartagena" throughout the 1620s and 1630s.[31] For captive West and West Central Africans, those maritime raids marked one moment of violent captivity in a long, complicated trajectory from ports in Upper Guinea or Angola to enslavement in various destinations in the Americas.[32]

For those African captives seized in the maritime passage between Cartagena and Portobelo and trafficked into slavery in Tortuga, the 1635 Spanish invasion of that island marked another moment of serial dislocation that defined slavery in contested spaces. For both newly arrived African captives and those Africans and their descendants who joined English and French refugees from Nevis and St. Christopher, the invasion of Tortuga mirrored other moments of dislocation, although the violence of the Spanish assault in 1635 was more extreme. As with St. Christopher, Spanish officials planned the assault on Tortuga with information gathered from the testimonies and reports of individuals who escaped the island.

In the case of Tortuga, the account of an Irish servant who defected to Hispaniola from Tortuga proved especially useful. Referred to as Juan Morfa Geraldino y Burco in Spanish documents, the former servant described the lack of military discipline on Tortuga and volunteered his services as a guide for an invasion. In December 1634, Spanish officials in Santo Domingo drew up plans for Morfa to guide the admiral of the galleys, Ruy Fernández de Fuenmayor, along with 250 soldiers against Tortuga.[33] The resulting invasion the next year proved far more violent than Fadrique's assault on St. Christopher and Nevis. Over the course of five days, Spanish forces killed, according to one report, 190 people and took thirty more as prisoners of war.[34] The violence of this moment cut both ways. According to Dutch navigator and chronicler David Pieterszoon de Vries, a Dutch shipmaster named Pieter Jansz Maertman was careening at Tortuga when the Spanish invasion started. In the course of the fighting, Maertman took several Spanish soldiers as prisoners before fleeing to western Hispaniola. As Maertman told de Vries, he presented the Spanish prisoners to Tortuga's ousted English governor, Christopher Wormeley, "in order that some of them might be ransomed" for a profit.[35] Wormeley refused to offer the soldiers quarter and instead ordered their execution.

For captives of African descent, uncertainty compounded the extreme violence of this moment of inter-imperial warfare. Some, however, turned the disorder caused by the Spanish invasion to their advantage by escaping their enslavement and either rowing to Hispaniola or gathering in remote areas of Tortuga. Hispaniola, however, offered a precarious existence for the people of African descent who fled there after the invasion. Spanish officials had received reports about a number of Tortuga's inhabitants who had made their way to the larger island before the invasion of Tortuga, and they scoured the landscape for European prisoners and African captives. According to some reports, nearly seventy Africans from Tortuga had fortified themselves in western Hispaniola, and when Spanish forces attacked, they took fifty-nine people as captives. Over the next several months, Spanish residents in Santiago armed themselves and raided the northwestern coast, seizing an additional fourteen people of African descent who had fled Tortuga for Hispaniola.[36]

In the short term, remaining on Tortuga offered a better chance at evading capture by Spanish forces than Hispaniola. Remote areas of Tortuga had long provided people of African and Indigenous descent with geographic isolation from the Spanish and, later, the English, Dutch, and French. As Spanish forces burned the houses and fields of Tortuga's residents, many among the island's enslaved population formed Maroon communities in the north. Those Maroon communities were large enough that, only three years after the Spanish invasion, reports circulated among investors in the Providence Island Company in London that the English planters who had returned to resettle the island had abandoned it again due to threats from the island's Maroon communities.[37] By 1638, in other words, the Maroons of Tortuga prevented some of their former enslavers from reestablishing plantations that had been destroyed during the Spanish invasion three years earlier. Maintaining their autonomy in an inaccessible geographic space, the Maroon communities formed in this moment of territorial contestation continued long-standing practices of resistance to slavery in Tortuga and Hispaniola. Within two decades of the 1635 Spanish invasion, as will be seen, those who claimed their autonomy by establishing communities in northern Tortuga would once again see the island invaded and their autonomy threatened.

Not all enslaved people on Tortuga escaped their enslavement during the confusion that accompanied five days of fighting on the island. Tortuga residents had some advance warning of Ruy Fernández's approach, and the majority of colonists escaped in canoes to western Hispaniola under the cover of darkness. Those colonists undoubtedly forced as many enslaved people as they safely could on board the canoes—as moveable property in the eyes of English and French colonists, enslaved people would have provided some compensation for the value of what colonists had just lost on Tortuga. For people of African descent taken captive by the Spanish on Tortuga, the commodification of racialized labor in the greater Caribbean meant that the invading Spanish forces also viewed them as a potential source of profit. Early reports from the Spanish invaders placed the number of enslaved Africans taken prisoner on Tortuga at somewhere between thirty and forty. Spanish forces searched the island for any additional enslaved Africans who had fled the violence, and by 1636, the governor of Santo Domingo claimed that a total of forty-nine people of African descent had been seized during the invasion and subsequent search of the island's interior.[38] Officials in Santo Domingo viewed the African captives through the lens of racialized commodification in which their sale, along with the seventy-three people of African descent seized by patrols in western Hispaniola, would cover the "very considerable" costs associated with the invasion.[39] Half of the proceeds from the sale of the African women, men, and children taken captive went to covering the costs of the soldiers' salaries, one quarter to the officers, and the final quarter to replenish the royal treasury of Hispaniola.[40] If the value of enslaved Africans in Santo Domingo correlated at all to what their value would have been in Cartagena in the 1620s or 1630s, the proceeds would have been well over 35,000 pesos.[41] It was a considerable sum of money for a treasury described as "wanting" after the invasion.[42] The human toll in terms of severed ties of family and friendship, on the other hand, is immeasurable.

Whether the African captives remained enslaved in Santo Domingo or experienced transshipment to another, potentially more lucrative Spanish American port is unclear from surviving archival sources. As will be seen, it is likely that at least some of the African captives who were sold into slavery in Santo Domingo had been legally free before traffickers took them captive and sold them in Tortuga. Most had undoubtedly experienced several forms of violent dislocation, some with their initial captivity in West or West Central Africa and others during the maritime raid that resulted in their captivity and sale in Tortuga. The people of African descent seized during the invasion of Tortuga, in other words, experienced European territorial contestation in the greater Caribbean as one among many moments of dislocation and commodification.

Despite the wealth generated by the sale of the African captives, officials in Santo Domingo had expected to encounter a larger enslaved population on Tortuga. As it turned out, many of the people of African descent whom Spanish officials had anticipated seizing in Tortuga had already been sold and transshipped off the island on the eve of the 1635 invasion. Although the enslaved Africans trafficked off of Tortuga before 1635 avoided the violence of the Spanish assault, their sale into slavery in Providencia placed them squarely in the center of a series of Spanish assaults during the 1630s and 1640s.

Marronage and Violence on Providencia

African captives trafficked from Tortuga to Providencia during the early 1630s arrived on an island not dissimilar from the one that they had left. On Providencia, they encountered, for example, an enslaved majority composed of people of African and Indigenous descent seized during maritime raids against Iberian shipping and from Spanish coastal communities. Individuals like Francisco Biafra and his companions, whose escape from Providencia opened this chapter, labored building fortifications and in the fields of the island's settlers. Biafra and many like him arrived in Providencia through networks of raiding and human trafficking that bound Providencia and Tortuga under the auspices of the Providence Island Company. Company investors, of course, had imagined a very different kind of colony. They planned and invested in a puritan settlement of English families engaged in planting, trade, and proselytizing among the Indigenous Miskito populations of the coastal regions of modern-day Nicaragua. The colony that eventually developed on Providencia would look nothing like what investors had imagined.

In part, the failure of the company's puritan experiment was tied to the role Providencia played in networks of raiding prior to English colonization. Traffickers had used Providencia and San Andrés in the decades before the Providence Island Company sent English puritan families to colonize them. The company learned of the geographic location of the island, after all, from Daniel Elfrith—a ship captain with a long career of raiding and trafficking. Elfrith claimed that he "discovered" Providencia, which echoes similar claims made about St. Christopher by d'Esnambuc and du Roissy.[43] In both cases, the islands were long known to traffickers and continued to serve as nodes in networks of raiding even after colonization. And much like St. Christopher, reliance on traffickers imperiled the colonists on Providencia. Historians have analyzed how religious and political tensions, Spanish reprisals, and the island's enslaved majority led to Providencia's failure as a puritan colonial experiment by 1641.[44] Spanish archival and secondary sources add depth to this analysis by revealing what the instability on Providencia and the eventual collapse of the colony meant for captives of African descent within the wider regional context of raiding, human trafficking, and territorial contestation.

The experiences of captivity and human trafficking that resulted in Francisco Biafra's sale into slavery in Providencia were far from unique. Rather, the dramatic episode involving traffickers seizing the boat that Biafra labored on along with the rest of the crew off the coast of Cartagena occurred with alarming regularity throughout the 1630s. The Spanish forces who invaded Providencia in 1641, for example, encountered no fewer than 150 enslaved Africans who had been "taken from residents of Cartagena" among the nearly four hundred people of African descent on the island at the time.[45] English, Dutch, and French traffickers sailing with commissions from the Dutch West India Company or the Providence Island Company haunted the sea lanes around Cartagena in order to intercept ships involved in the intra-Caribbean and transatlantic slave trades.[46] As Biafra's experience illustrates, many of those same traffickers had no compunction against seizing anyone of African descent whom they came across in or near those coastal waters.

By the mid-1630s, maritime predation and trade to Providencia resulted in an enslaved majority and the attention of Spanish officials in the Caribbean and Spain. Between 1635 and 1641, social turmoil and three separate Spanish attacks rocked the population of Providencia. Enslaved and indentured people responded, much as they had on Tortuga, in myriad ways to those chaotic six years. Both enslaved and indentured people, as well as disaffected sailors, used the maritime traffic of the island to escape to Spanish territory. Biafra's testimony following his escape from Providencia, for example, found its way to the governor of Cartagena, Francisco de Murga y Ortiz de Orué, in the spring or early summer of 1635.

Well aware of the extensive raiding conducted by English, Dutch, and French vessels on Cartagena's maritime trade, Murga assembled the first of three attempts to eliminate the English colony. The arrival of that force of three ships and 250 infantrymen in late July mobilized the population of Providencia. Heavy cannon fire from the island's fortifications forced the Spanish to withdraw, but not before the Spanish commander and military engineer gathered valuable information about the island along with thirteen prisoners from neighboring San Andrés, twelve Englishmen and an Englishwoman.[47] Among the defenders of Providencia were enslaved men of African descent who had been promised their freedom by anxious English settlers in exchange for their military service. The fact that freedom was not, in fact, forthcoming for the African men who took up arms for the English against the Spanish in 1635 doubtless contributed to the growth of Maroon communities on the island in the following years.[48]

Providencia continued to serve as a market and base for maritime predation against Iberian shipping and Spanish coastal communities in the years after the failed 1635 attack. One metric of the island's continued ties with traffickers was the rapid growth of the enslaved population, with consequences for Providencia's social stability. According to an English mariner, by July 1637 "every one of the soldiers [on Providencia] who has anything has in his service three or four Blacks."[49] Although likely hyperbolic, the English mariner's assertion that even English soldiers claimed ownership over multiple African captives nevertheless highlights the obvious demographic majority of Africans and their descendants. The day-to-day lived experience of slavery for the island's majority population, however, is difficult to flesh out with available archival documents. That said, Africans and their descendants engaged in widespread resistance to their enslavement in the years after the 1635 Spanish attack.

One observation about that resistance comes from the testimony of an English sailor named Joan Fierrio Lopez in the early summer of 1640. Lopez claimed that he had fled Providencia after the ship captain he signed on with in London declared his intention of turning to raiding after the delivery of supplies and colonists to the island. Before his escape, Lopez heard from residents that there were nearly five hundred enslaved Africans on the island and that "they had rose in rebellion multiple times and that now some had run away."[50] Scholars have argued that African resistance in the form of marronage and rebellion stemmed, in part, from the antislavery rhetoric of one of the island's ministers, a man named Samuel Rishworth, and in part from the social turmoil caused by religious and political tensions among the English colonists on the island.[51] No doubt these were powerful factors influencing the actions of some of the people of African descent who were held captive on Providencia. The sense of betrayal experienced by the men of African descent who had taken up arms for the English against the Spanish in 1635, and were not subsequently freed, likely also contributed to the multiple enslaved rebellions that erupted on Providencia over the years between 1635 and 1640. If their English captors refused to honor the promises of freedom, in other words, African captives on Providencia would take it by force.

Reports of a large, restive population of African descent on Providencia alongside continued maritime predations by ships that called at that island encouraged two more Spanish attacks, one attempt in 1640 and a second, successful invasion in 1641. During the summer of 1640, Spain's Council of War ordered several galleons of the flota under the command of Francisco Díaz Pimienta to break off from the main fleet and remove the English colony on Providencia. That same summer, however, Cartagena's governor, Melchior de Aguilera, launched his own invasion of Providencia with several of the vessels from the fleet that had been dispatched to recapture Brazil from the Dutch. Melchior's fleet from Cartagena arrived at Providencia first, but the attempted invasion proved disastrous for the Spanish forces, as contrary winds and an ill-informed attempt to approach the island's fortified central coast led to the deaths of many of the Spanish invaders.[52]

The second invasion the following spring had more luck. In part, the success of the second invasion stemmed from the far better intelligence about the English-held island—information that Spanish officials had received from a French sailor who had been caught smuggling in Jamaica after spending some time on Providencia. The Frenchman reported on the strength of English defenses and suggested that the fleet under Díaz approach the southeastern section of the island where there were fewer fortifications. Crucially, the Frenchman also urged Díaz to launch his attack in the spring months, since "the pirates will have left [in search of prizes] and there would be fewer people" defending the island.[53] As a result, Díaz led eleven ships out of the bay of Cartagena on May 6 with two thousand soldiers and sailors under his command.[54] The attack came on the morning of May 24, and by the end of that month the English capitulated to the larger Spanish force. Díaz offered quarter to the English colonists and ordered them transported to Spain as prisoners of war.[55] For the population of African descent, the violence and disruption of the two successive invasions continued into the days and months after the Spanish occupation of Providencia. The decision to place a presidio on Providencia in order to prevent the island from being reoccupied by Spain's European competitors would have dramatic consequences for Providencia's population of African descent, especially for the women on the island, whose domestic and reproductive labor served to transform a rugged garrison into a settlement composed of households.[56]

Demography and Trafficking on Providencia

When Francisco Díaz Pimienta surveyed the ruins of the English colony on Providencia in 1641, he asserted that a Spanish presidio on the island would flourish. Perhaps more importantly, with the examples of St. Christopher and Tortuga in mind, Díaz also argued to his superiors that Spain's northern European enemies would simply return and reoccupy the island if Spain failed to place a presidio there.[57] As he wrote to the Council of War, Providencia was "such a fertile island that with twenty-five Blacks and an overseer to cultivate the land and raise cattle, they could provide rations" for the

Iberian troops stationed there "throughout the year."[58] Díaz's advice to send twenty-five enslaved Africans to the newly established presidio on Providencia, however, seems odd in light of reports about the number of African captives on the island when the Spanish seized it from the English. Why would the presidio's new commander, Captain Gerónimo de Ojeda, and the 150 soldiers serving under him need twenty-five enslaved people from Cartagena to cultivate foodstuffs and tend livestock when Díaz reported that Spanish forces had taken 381 Africans and their descendants captive during the invasion? Put more simply, what happened to the majority enslaved population on Providencia in the wake of the Spanish invasion in 1641?

For Africans and their descendants on Providencia, the decade leading up to 1641 had been marked by violence, instability, and dislocation. Rather than allow African diasporic communities to remain together on the island, the militarized rationale of keeping Providencia under Spanish control required reshaping the island's laboring population. One form of that reshaping involved the sale of some of the women and children of African descent—whom Spanish officials viewed as less useful for working on fortifications and building roads—off of the island. Crucially, however, Spanish officials sold many other people of African descent off of the island as well because they had been Maroons prior to the 1641 invasion. Their intimate knowledge of Providencia and their success in evading their English captors made them dangerous captives for the small Iberian force that retained the island outpost. Other women of African descent labored in the households of the soldiers posted on the island—domestic and reproductive labor that proved essential in the process of converting the garrison outpost into a colonial settlement.

The demographic profile of Providencia that emerged from the testimonies of captives and disaffected sailors made Spanish officials expect that the invasion of Providencia would pay for itself in the form of enslaved African captives. Officials in Santo Domingo, after all, had profited from the sale of captives of African descent taken during the 1635 invasion of Tortuga, and Spanish officials had every reason to assume that the same would hold true for the 1641 invasion of Providencia. Spanish forces did encounter a significant number of people of African descent on the island in 1641. According to Díaz's report, the English had "381 Blacks of both sexes including children and boys" on the island.[59] That number far exceeded the African captives seized by Spanish forces on Tortuga. At the same time, English prisoners confessed to the Spanish that, in the years leading up to the 1641 invasion, many African captives on the island had been trafficked off the island. Beginning in 1637, the Providence Island Company responded to reports about the restive African majority on Providencia by ordering ship captains to traffic Africans and their descendants to St. Christopher, Bermuda, and Virginia.[60] The policy continued through the final years of the 1630s, with reports of African captives from Providencia being sold as far away as New England in 1638 and 1639.[61]

Among the people of African descent trafficked off of Providencia between 1635 and the Spanish invasion in 1641 would have been individuals taken captive by traffickers throughout the Caribbean, including Cartagena and its hinterlands. The nonlinear, intercolonial nature of the Anglo-Atlantic slave trade in the first half of the seventeenth century meant that some of Francisco Biafra's companions might have ended up enslaved in English North America. The paucity of archival evidence from Virginia or New England during this period, however, means that we know little about the enslaved Africans in North America who bore Hispanic names and surnames.[62] Reports indicate that over the 1630s European traffickers seized nearly 1,600 African captives and sold them into slavery to English colonists in Providencia, yet by 1641 there were only 381 enslaved Africans on the island. The disparity between those numbers indicates that many among the charter generations of slavery in North America were transshipped through Providencia. Perhaps some of those enslaved Africans met Francisco Biafra or some of his companions, shared in their experience of being taken captive, and had developed communal ties on Providencia before being trafficked off of the island.[63]

The intercolonial slave trade between Providencia and surrounding English colonies severed the communal ties forged by people of African descent on the island over the course of the 1630s, often not for the first or last time. European territorial contestation in the form of the 1641 Spanish invasion continued that process of dislocation for many of the island's inhabitants. For some, however, the invasion might have meant returning to networks of kinship from which they had been removed by northern European traffickers. Of the African population on Providencia, for example, there were 150 people who had been taken captive by traffickers from Cartagena and its environs and sold into slavery on Providencia. The Spanish invasion meant a return to Cartagena for those 150 African captives. According to Díaz, those individuals "were restituted to their owners in Cartagena" along with over two hundred head of cattle, also taken from Cartagena by northern European traffickers.[64] Some of the African captives likely testified to their status before captivity, perhaps with a desire to return to loved ones, community, or a particular labor situation in Cartagena. The maritime labor that Biafra and his companions performed for the woman who claimed ownership over them, for example, might have been preferable to the kinds of hard labor expected of them by the English on Providencia. As historian David Wheat has argued, a desire to return to a life of relative autonomy in the waters near Cartagena likely motivated Biafra to testify before Spanish officials in a way that guaranteed his return to that former life.[65]

The Spanish forces that invaded Providencia did not always need the testimonies of African captives to determine their fate. Perhaps some among the African captives from Cartagena preferred not to return to slavery or to a specific person who claimed ownership over them in the port city. In those cases, however, some captives had to contend with bodily markings that would have betrayed their claims to a specific status. Díaz, in other words, could have read the brands applied to enslaved people by Cartagena residents to know an individual's history of enslavement.[66] Burned flesh marked ownership, and for the people of African descent taken captive and sold into Providencia, those bodily mutilations either belied or reinforced their own articulations about their status and personal history.

Among the people of African descent on Providencia who resisted Spanish attempts to re-enslave them were the island's Maroons. In the years leading up to the Spanish invasion, Africans and their descendants used the social and religious discord on Providencia to escape their English captors and form Maroon communities on the island. Self-liberated Africans built cabins and cultivated food in the hilly interior of the island. In a survival strategy adopted by numerous Maroon societies in the Americas, they also occasionally raided the dwellings of their former enslavers.[67] In the case of Providencia, Maroons used Sundays, when English colonists were attending church services, to both take food and supplies and encourage others to escape.[68] By the time Spanish forces arrived in 1641, in other words, the Maroon communities of Providencia had accumulated strategies of community-building that facilitated their continued autonomy on the island.

As Díaz and the Iberian forces surveyed the island, they also launched raids against the Maroons who had escaped from and evaded the English. Spanish officials clearly understood the danger posed by the people whom they "captured in the mountains" during those raids.[69] In a moment when Díaz requested that the governor of Cartagena send enslaved Africans to Providencia to cultivate foodstuffs and work on the fortifications, he also announced his intention of selling the Maroons off of the island. Díaz, in other words, sought to exchange a population of Maroons who had used their knowledge of Providencia's topography and ecology to maintain their autonomy for enslaved Africans who were unfamiliar with the island. In a revealing twist, the Maroons taken captive during Spanish raids in the interior of Providencia remained on the island for longer than Díaz intended. As he wrote to Spain's Council of War in December 1643, he had not sent many of the Maroons to Cartagena yet because the ships that had arrived to carry them off did not have sufficient armaments. Whether Díaz chose "not to risk" sending the Maroons because he feared that they would be seized by traffickers in the open waters between Providencia and Cartagena, or because he feared for the safety of under-armed sailors tasked with transporting the Maroons, is not clear from his letters.[70] Either way, Díaz understood quite clearly the impossibility of forcing the Africans and their descendants who had gained and maintained their autonomy on Providencia back into slavery on that same island.

For the remainder of the 381 African women, men, and children formerly enslaved by the English, Spanish plans to commodify racially stigmatized captives to fund the invasion would threaten the ties of kinship and community that they had built over the previous decade. Mirroring the actions of officials in Santo Domingo following the 1635 invasion of Tortuga, Díaz divided the people of African descent who had been taken captive during the invasion of Providencia into groups: a portion served as recompense for the soldiers and officers, while another portion were declared "slaves of the king."[71] The latter group fell under the supervision of Captain Gerónimo de Ojeda, who put many of them to work rebuilding the island's fortifications and roads. That labor was gendered. Many of the women who had been declared "slaves of the king" were deemed "of little service" for the physically demanding tasks involved in building fortifications and clearing roads. They were either sold or granted to soldiers in order to create households. In 1648, for example, Ojeda authorized the sale of ten women "slaves of the king," pocketing the proceeds for the royal treasury. That sale, according to Ojeda, left twenty-three men, four women, and six children as "slaves of the king" on Providencia.[72] Ojeda does not explain why those four women were not sold off the island, nor the ties of family that account for the presence of six enslaved children among those claimed in the name of the king. Considering reports on the paucity of women on Providencia, the sale of ten women from among the enslaved community would have been a dramatic loss that added to the burden of childcare and domestic labor for the enslaved women who remained on the island.

The people of African descent parceled out to soldiers and officers as recompense for their service confronted the constant threat of sale alongside the declining material conditions of the Spanish presidio over the course of the 1640s and 1650s. As Ojeda had done with the women "slaves of the king," some Spanish officers and soldiers viewed the enslaved women and children granted to them as pay as a burden in the rugged life of the presidio and chose to sell them off of the island within the first couple of years of the Spanish conquest. In July 1646, for example, Ojeda explained that he "risked [sending off the island] twelve *piezas*, seven boys and five women" whom he expected to sell for "the price that they usually sell for in the city of Cartagena." Nor was Ojeda alone. That same year the island's official accountant, Juan de Araña, also sold a boy and another woman.[73]

Not all captive women of African descent were sold off of the island because of their gender, especially those who had been assigned to Spanish and Portuguese soldiers on the island. Their gender did, however, shape their lived experience on Providencia under Spanish authority. Despite the initial enthusiasm for a presidio on the island, Ojeda complained repeatedly during the 1640s about how neither Cartagena nor Portobelo sent sufficient supplies, settlers, and laborers to maintain the island's defenses or establish a civilian population. The lack of foodstuffs, for example, meant that cultivating crops fell to the soldiers, who established ranches "where they plant everything necessary for their sustenance" at a distance of a league or more from the fortifications.[74] Scattered across the windward coast of Providencia, soldiers relied on the labor of African captives, especially women seized during the invasion, for domestic and agricultural labor.

Roots in the Island

Life on Providencia following the Spanish invasion was hard. The survival of the presidio at Providencia depended on the population of African descent, who supported the military presence through cultivating foodstuffs, building fortifications and roads, and, in the case of women of African descent like Catalina Angola, maintaining the households of the soldiers. How those women felt about their enslavement to single, male soldiers in a rugged, frontier environment remains unknowable within the archival traces that remain of their lives.[75] Racialized and gendered vulnerability shaped their experiences but so, too, did opportunities to establish ties of intimacy and obligation. For Catalina, for example, enslavement in the home of a Spanish soldier resulted in her freedom. Nor was Catalina's experience unique in terms of the wider gendered experience of slavery for African women and their descendants in the Spanish Caribbean.[76] Declining material conditions on Providencia made the domestic and reproductive labor of women like Catalina critical to the Spanish imperial project of maintaining the presidio. Crucially, Spanish dependence on women of African descent to create stable households gave Catalina and other women opportunities to secure their freedom and that of their children.

Households promised to root Spanish and Portuguese soldiers to the island and convert the garrison into a stable colony.[77] By 1646, the material conditions for everyone on the island were so poor that many of the soldiers tasked with maintaining the island fled instead. According to the father of Catalina's children, Captain Salvador de la Peña, "many soldiers have escaped the island because they are poorly contented with what little salary they receive," and that "in order to have anything to eat, it [was] necessary for the soldiers to plant it or for those same soldiers to go to the sea to fish."[78] Peña viewed mixed-race households as essential to solving the problem of desertion. His report was clearly influenced by his own household. Peña had fathered three children with Catalina—five-year-old María, three-year-old Juana, and a one-year-old son named Salvador Francisco. Peña's actions within five years of the Spanish invasion of Providencia reflected an emotional connection with the mother of his children that went beyond his dependence on her domestic labor. In 1646, Peña petitioned the Crown for two things: a boat to chase down soldiers who deserted the island in canoes and permission for soldiers like himself to purchase their families out of slavery.

The two requests reflected both the material conditions of the Spanish presidio and the importance of women of African descent to its survival. As Peña explained, "some soldiers have five or six mulatto children with Black women." Those women who had been seized from the English following the Spanish invasion of Providencia had been assigned to maintain the households of individual soldiers. In his petition, Peña requested that the Crown lower the cost of purchasing enslaved women and their children so that soldiers could afford to free their families. Even as a captain in the presidio, Peña lamented his inability to afford the purchase of his three children and their mother. Peña argued that permitting soldiers like himself to free their families would end the waves of desertion plaguing the presidio because soldiers "would have roots in the island."[79] Stable households would convert the struggling presidio into a settlement and, crucially, create a population committed to its own defense. At the center of this logic were women like Catalina. At least twice in her life, Catalina had been seized and treated as a spoil of war. Despite her liminal status and vulnerability, Catalina and others like her maneuvered within this world shaped by captivity and violence in order to secure family and community.

By the fall of 1646, the Crown granted Peña's petition. The father of Catalina's children purchased her and their three children, María, Juana, and Salvador Francisco. As predicted, garrison conditions stabilized over the next twenty years as the mixed-race children of frontier households grew into adulthood. This relative peace was short-lived. By 1666, mixed-race families on Providencia would face violent dislocation in the form of a Jamaican-sponsored raid in which northern European sailors treated the Afro-descended residents of the island, like Catalina and her children, as racialized captives. After the 1666 raid, for example, Catalina's youngest child, Salvador Francisco, was sold into slavery in English Jamaica. As Chapter 6 traces, the efforts of Catalina to secure the free status of her children proved illusory within a wider Caribbean world defined by captive-taking and racialized vulnerability.

The Invasion of Tortuga, ca. 1653

The nearly twenty-five years of Spanish retaliations against specific island colonies in the Caribbean culminated with a second invasion of Tortuga in 1653. Like the invasions that preceded it, Spanish officials in Santo Domingo planned this second invasion of Tortuga with information provided by captives who had escaped the island. Central to that planning in the summer and early fall of 1653 were claims about the utility of the large population of African and Indigenous people held captive on the island. Rather than a potential source of profit to fund the invasion, as had been the case in Tortuga in 1635 and Providencia in 1641, Spanish officials in Santo Domingo instead argued that the African and Indigenous populations on Tortuga would ally themselves with the Spanish against their French and English captors. According to Spanish officials, African and Indigenous captives held on Tortuga had been "robbed" from Spanish territories and, they assumed, would still retain a sense of fidelity to Spain.

Populations of African and Indigenous descent, however, did not respond to the second invasion of Tortuga in 1653 in the ways anticipated by officials in Santo Domingo. This was especially true for the members of Maroon communities, many of whom undoubtedly kept alive memories of the 1635 invasion in which Spanish soldiers rounded up people of African descent and sold them off the island. Nor were individuals who had been "robbed" from Iberian domains and trafficked into slavery in Tortuga exempt from forms of racialized commodification when they escaped to Spanish territory. Alliance, in other words, did not mean freedom for the people of African and Indigenous descent who did help the Spanish. The 1653 Spanish invasion of Tortuga exposes the intersection of race, slavery, and subjecthood at this moment from the perspective of African and Indigenous captives who escaped the island as well as those seized by Spanish forces during the invasion.

Political and social instability defined the eighteen years following the Spanish invasion of Tortuga in 1635. That instability proved detrimental to the foundation of a European colony, even as it provided space for the African Maroon communities to retain their autonomy on the island. Since Spain failed to plant a presidio on Tortuga after 1635, English and French colonists returned in the wake of the invasion, much as colonists had done in the aftermath of the 1629 invasion of St. Christopher. The process of recolonizing the island, however, confronted the opposition of the island's Maroon communities who had prevented English colonists from reclaiming their homes and plantations immediately following the Spanish invasion. That success was temporary. By 1640 a French Huguenot named François le Vasseur governed an island society composed of predominately French and English colonists who had established themselves on Tortuga. His tenure proved despotic and short, ending in his murder at the hands of two associates on the island.[80]

Eager to keep Tortuga within France's Caribbean possessions and to expand the authority of the Knights Hospitaller of Malta, the new governor-general of the French West Indies, Philippe de Longvilliers de Poincy, sent a French ship captain named Timoléon Hotman, the Chevalier de Fontenay, to replace the murdered le Vasseur in 1652. The new French governor proclaimed his authority over a multinational and multiethnic population, including English colonists who had returned to the homes and plantations they lost during the 1635 invasion. Fontenay and the French colonists on Tortuga remained wary of the English colonists on Tortuga, who they rightly assumed wanted the island placed back under English leadership. The mutual suspicions between the island's European population put it on weak defensive footing as the maritime and territorial raids of traffickers drew the attention of neighboring Spanish officials in Santo Domingo.

As the French struggled to maintain political control over Tortuga, European traffickers continued to raid surrounding Spanish shipping and sell their pilfered goods at the island. According to the account of one Spanish lawyer, Pedro Luis de Salazar, during a voyage from Cuba to Santo Domingo, "he was robbed . . . by these corsairs [from Tortuga] twice in one day, and the first corsair having taken everything he had, the second took the very clothes off of his body."[81] With access to colonial markets in French, Dutch, and English colonies, traffickers also raided towns and haciendas in regions where, decades earlier, they had traded with local allies. According to the inhabitants of Baracoa, located on the northeastern tip of Cuba, northern Europeans had raided their town no fewer than four times between 1638 and 1653.[82] During those raids, traffickers sacked homes and haciendas, and "profaned" a church by stealing the "sacred vessels and other ornaments of divine worship."[83] Santo Domingo witnessed a rise in raiding as well. In 1644, three ships of traffickers raided the town of Azua, located west of Santo Domingo along the southern coast. Guiding the assault was a man of African descent who had formerly lived in Azua—likely as a slave—before joining the raiders of his own accord. Ten women of European and African descent were seized during the raid and carried away by traffickers.[84] What became of those women is unclear from surviving archival documents, but reports of the brazen assault joined a chorus of complaints throughout the region in the 1630s and 1640s about raiding and captive-taking by northern European traffickers. At the center of those complaints was Tortuga, where many of those traffickers conducted business.

As with earlier Spanish attempts to dislodge foreign settlements from the greater Caribbean, the testimonies of individuals who escaped Tortuga provided essential information to the Spanish officials charged with planning invasions. Among the people taken captive and trafficked into slavery on Tortuga during the tumultuous decades leading up to mid-century was Francisco da Costa, the Afro-Brazilian who had been taken captive off the coast of Bahía in Brazil and sold as a slave to Fontenay. Standing before officials in Santo Domingo after his escape, Costa testified to his experiences on Tortuga and the state of the island's population, commerce, and defenses. His observations were encouraging for Spanish officials. According to Costa, the French and English population of Tortuga was composed of two different settlements, the majority "English and French boys without beards" who survived by selling cassava, potatoes, and tobacco to passing ships.[85] From his experience in the rugged interior of Tortuga after he fled enslavement in Fontenay's home, Costa also highlighted for Spanish officials the possibility of an alliance with the island's Maroons and captive population.

Nor did Spanish officials in Santo Domingo have to take Costa's word for it. Other captives who had escaped labor coercion on Tortuga testified that the multinational and multiethnic population of the island would not present a unified defense. Some captives declared that one-third of the island's population was of African and Indigenous descent and that they would welcome Spanish forces. Others testified to discord among the English, French, and Dutch residents of the island.[86] One report highlighted the military advantage for the Spanish as a result of the political discord on Tortuga, explaining that "the French [were allowed to] have firearms in their houses while the English [did] not have any weapons in their houses."[87] For Spanish officials in Santo Domingo, reports like these pointed to the possibility that not all of the island's European colonists would take up arms against the Spanish—in the case of the English because they might have lacked arms altogether. As it turned out, at least fifty English colonists refused to defend French rule over Tortuga, declaring instead their loyalty to the king of Spain in order to remain on the island after Spanish forces from Santo Domingo invaded in 1653.[88]

If the testimonies of former captives predicted that not all European colonists on Tortuga would resist the Spanish, their assumptions that the island's African and Indigenous population would join the Spanish proved more ambiguous. In late November and early December, Spanish commander Gabriel Roxas Vallé y Figueroa and three hundred soldiers from Santo Domingo began a ten-day siege of Tortuga that ended with Fontenay capitulating.[89] Rather than receiving the overwhelming support of the island's population of African and Indigenous descent, reports following the French capitulation mirrored earlier Spanish invasions of St. Christopher, Providencia, and the 1635 invasion of Tortuga. The presumed aid of the African and Indigenous people of Tortuga, in other words, did not materialize; instead, racialized captives experienced commodification. According to reports of the invasion, the Spanish forces seized "only seventy Black slaves," although they learned from prisoners that "there was a much greater number in the mountains."[90] In the months following the invasion, Spanish officials in Santo Domingo pledged to "use all diligence" to hunt down the remaining Maroons on the island.

For Africans and their descendants, the violence of the Spanish invasion and subsequent efforts against Maroon communities paralleled Spanish actions in the aftermath of the 1635 invasion. Maintaining their autonomy, in other words, would require renewed efforts to defend themselves and their loved ones from captivity and commodification. Events in Europe meant that the Maroons of Tortuga would gain a small reprieve. In 1655 a massive English fleet arrived off the coast of Santo Domingo. Oliver Cromwell's Western Design force arrived with the intention of a full-scale invasion of the Spanish Caribbean, and the Iberian soldiers stationed at Tortuga abandoned the smaller island in order to defend Hispaniola. For the Maroon communities, this moment of inter-imperial competition provided a small reprieve as Spanish forces became occupied with defending first Hispaniola and then Jamaica from the English. The reprieve was brief. Events both near and far from Tortuga would bring the island to the attention of northern European traffickers and European imperial planners in the coming decades.

In a memorable phrase, historian Eric Williams long ago described the greater Caribbean as "the cockpit of Europe, the arena of Europe's wars."[91] It was a region, in other words, where European powers came to almost continual blows over territory and trade. The repeated Spanish invasions of rival European colonies discussed in this chapter fit within this general view of the Caribbean as both violent and contested. Spanish responses to foreign settlements in the Caribbean started with the 1629 invasion of Nevis and St. Christopher. While many of the English and French colonists returned to rebuild their homes in the aftermath of that 1629 assault, others planted elsewhere, including the island of Tortuga. Within five years of their arrival on Tortuga, however, refugees from the Lesser Antilles again faced Spanish forces. The 1635 Spanish assault on Tortuga provides a window onto the racialized vulnerability of people of African descent during moments of inter-imperial violence. As Spanish soldiers from Santo Domingo destroyed homes and fields on Tortuga in early 1635, they also seized people of African descent in order to finance the invasion, subjecting those captives to another moment of commodification and dislocation. Spanish officials expected the number of enslaved people on Tortuga to be higher, but many had already been trafficked off the island. Those Africans and their descendants who were trafficked from Tortuga to Providencia, however, experienced a series of Spanish attacks on that island between 1635 and 1641. For those captives who fled during the violence on Tortuga, their autonomy was short-lived. In 1653, the Spanish invaded Tortuga again. Spanish imperial planners for this second invasion had anticipated the island's African and Indigenous population coming to the aid of Iberian forces. Maroons on Tortuga, however, held the memory of how Spanish soldiers commodified the island's Afro-descended population after the 1635 Spanish raid, and they chose not to fight for the Iberian soldiers who posed a potential threat to their autonomy.

Isolating the series of Spanish invasions of rival colonial settlements between 1629 and 1653 places the causes and consequences of those Spanish invasions within specific practices of raiding, captive-taking, and human trafficking. Spanish officials in Spain and the Caribbean responded to the actions of traffickers by organizing invasions of specific islands, often with strategic information that they received from the testimonies of individuals who had escaped captivity on those islands. Read carefully, those testimonies can offer a glimpse into the lived realities of slavery in contested spaces for the people of African and Indigenous descent taken captive and trafficked into places like St. Christopher, Tortuga, and Providencia. Crucially, viewing the Spanish invasions in a single frame allows us to see how some racially stigmatized captives experienced serial dislocation as a result of European territorial contestation. From their perspective, a Spanish assault on an island colony like Tortuga or Providencia was not a singular event but part of a longer trajectory in which warfare and racialized slavery severed communities and dispersed captives throughout the Atlantic.

CHAPTER 5

"A Trail Would Be Blazed"

Reform, Commercial Competition, and War

The decades around mid-century saw different European metropolitan efforts to monopolize and regulate the intra-Caribbean and transatlantic slave trades—efforts that refracted in a Caribbean world accustomed to raiding and human trafficking. Gaspar de Espinosa was all too familiar with the violent, informal nature of the trade in human captives transecting the waters of the eastern Caribbean at mid-century. During the late 1650s, Espinosa worked as an unofficial translator for the governor of Puerto Rico, José Novoa y Moscoso Pérez y Buitron, who called upon him when English and Dutch ships arrived to trade. The work was steady, providing Espinosa with a livelihood sufficient, for example, to purchase an enslaved African woman for 100 pesos from a Dutch trafficker sometime in 1657. Espinosa's unflinching entrance into the economy of human trafficking seemed incongruent with his own past—he had gained the linguistic skills that afforded his survival in Puerto Rico from his own experiences as a captive trafficked into slavery.

Described as a "free mulatto of the Portuguese nation," Espinosa entered the Caribbean after having been taken captive by Dutch traffickers off the coast of Brazil in the early 1650s. He worked on that Dutch ship for two years before the captain sold him into slavery in English Barbados, where he labored for two more years before escaping to Puerto Rico. In Puerto Rico, Espinosa carved out a position for himself within the island's informal economy, using the English and Dutch that he had learned as a captive in order to facilitate trade with traffickers from throughout the Lesser Antilles.[1] His good fortune would not last long. Within several years, Espinosa was taken captive for a second time and sold into slavery among the French on neighboring St. Croix. By 1664, Espinosa escaped enslavement again and made his way back to Puerto Rico.[2] The circumstances that Espinosa had exploited in the late 1650s had changed significantly over the years that he was enslaved in St. Croix. Espinosa's former employer, for example, had been removed from his post as governor, and royal officials brought charges against the ex-governor and members of his commercial network on the island.[3] The removal of Novoa from Puerto Rico, however, did little to dissuade the island's English, French, and Dutch neighbors during the early 1660s, especially as certain islands in the Lesser Antilles emerged as entrepôts in the transatlantic and intra-Caribbean slave trades by mid-century.

By 1662, the profitability of the intra-Caribbean slave trade conducted by traffickers became the model for a new monopoly slave-trading contract, called the *asiento de negros*, which Spain issued to a pair of Genoese merchants named Domingo Grillo and Ambrosio Lomelín.[4] Rather than conduct the transatlantic slave trade themselves, Grillo and Lomelín negotiated for permission to purchase enslaved Africans in the Caribbean from any nation at peace with Spain and to fulfill their contract by transshipping those captives to specific Spanish American ports. This asiento created commercial competition between the new English and Dutch monopoly slave-trading companies that supplied the asiento holders, but it also created conflict between those companies and the traffickers, merchants, and governors who had long engaged in regional, informal networks of human trafficking.[5] As a skilled translator in Puerto Rico in 1664, it is easy to imagine that Espinosa found opportunities for himself at the center of this competitive, multinational trade in human captives. As a man of African descent, however, it is also easy to imagine Espinosa's continued vulnerability at the center of this violent commercial world.

Gaspar de Espinosa's involvement in regional networks of informal trade, as translator and captive, spanned two formative, complicated decades in the development of the transatlantic and intra-Caribbean slave trades. His initial captivity in Brazil in the early 1650s occurred during a decentralized and largely self-organized period in the transatlantic slave trade, while his return to Puerto Rico in 1664 coincided with the development of an increasingly more systematic intra-Caribbean and transatlantic slave trade through the Grillo and Lomelín asiento and the actions of English and Dutch monopoly slave-trading companies. Within a year of his return to Puerto Rico, global commercial and political competition escalated into open warfare between England and the Netherlands.[6] The Second Anglo-Dutch War (1665–67) had appalling consequences for enslaved and free people of African descent in the Caribbean, as invading forces used the war to legitimize raids against specific islands for the purpose of seizing racially stigmatized captives. Officials, merchants, and monarchs in Europe attempted to formalize—and increase the profitability of—the transatlantic and intra-Caribbean slave trades during and after the outbreak of war in 1665. Those efforts overlapped with the efforts of white elites on islands like Barbados to expand sugar production through the exploitation of enslaved labor.[7] For Espinosa, few parts of the world that he knew in the 1650s would have been recognizable a decade later. The networks of informal trade driven by the trafficking of human captives still crisscrossed the eastern Caribbean, but by the mid-1660s, the interests of competing European monopoly companies and widespread imperial competition had increased the scale and intensity of captive-taking alongside the growth of the intra-Caribbean and transatlantic slave trades.

This chapter situates the multiple captivities of Gaspar de Espinosa in the wider Caribbean and Atlantic worlds. As Espinosa's brief career as a translator makes clear, informal trade with northern European traffickers was well established in Puerto Rico by the 1650s. The brazenness of Novoa's involvement in regional informal trade—which included sending an ill-fated ship on a smuggling run to English St. Christopher during a period of war between England and Spain—led to his removal from office and the growing realization among members of Spain's Council of the Indies that the intra-Caribbean and transatlantic slave trades needed reform. At the same time, merchants involved in the English and Dutch monopoly slave-trading companies began transporting increasing numbers of enslaved people from West Africa, many of whom ended up disembarked at specific islands in the Caribbean before being re-embarked for Spanish Caribbean markets through networks of informal trade. The increase in transatlantic shipping to islands like Curaçao drew traffickers to the southern Caribbean, creating moments of extreme maritime violence for the women, men, and children who survived the Middle Passage. Despite the risks of maritime predation, networks of informal trade out of Dutch and English Caribbean entrepôts became the model for the Grillo and Lomelín asiento that was intended to reform the decentralized nature of the intra-Caribbean slave trade. Rather than reform, the new asiento sparked regional and Atlantic-wide competition over human trafficking to Spanish Caribbean markets. At the same time, changes to the administration of the Anglo-Caribbean after the restoration of the Stuart monarchy, especially the creation of admiralty courts based in the Caribbean, incentivized increased captive-taking by traffickers who sought to make a voyage.

The story of Espinosa's multiple captivities and his work as a translator in a regional network of informal trade seems quite small when cast alongside the sweeping changes taking place in the Caribbean and wider Atlantic world during the 1650s and 1660s. But small stories often provide important insights into larger historical narratives.[8] In this case, Espinosa's experiences in the eastern Caribbean reveal the surprising continuity of practices of captive-taking and human trafficking through the 1650s and 1660s. Traffickers continued to raid and traffic captives into slavery through the 1660s, often with the tacit support of regional governors. For example, St. Christopher remained an important node for informal trade that supplied islands like Puerto Rico with enslaved captives, foodstuffs, and manufactured goods. Significantly, informal trade continued despite efforts by agents of the Grillo and Lomelín asiento and the newly created English monopoly slave-trading company, the Royal Company of Adventurers Trading to Africa, to end it. In short, as Espinosa's experiences illuminate, metropolitan efforts to rationalize the intra-Caribbean slave trade did not make the Caribbean any less predatory during the 1660s. In fact, forces of regional and global economic competition, especially between the English and the Dutch, would make the Caribbean a more volatile place, especially for people of African and Indigenous descent, like Gaspar de Espinosa. European commercial competition, in other words, coincided with the continuation of older practices of northern European traffickers who sought to make a voyage in the Caribbean, intensifying maritime predation and violence against populations of African descent in the region.

Puerto Rico and the Eastern Caribbean, ca. 1620–1650

The world that Gaspar de Espinosa entered when he and his companions escaped from Barbados to Puerto Rico in 1657 was shaped by informal trade in the eastern Caribbean. Traffickers had called on the island of Puerto Rico since the late sixteenth century, and over the first half of the seventeenth century, commercial ties between Puerto Rico and neighboring northern European settlements in the Lesser Antilles intensified.[9] Between the 1590s and 1620s, the Puerto Rican economy expanded through the production of tobacco, cattle hides, and ginger. Ginger, in particular, tied Puerto Rican residents to foreign commercial partners as early as the 1590s. Cultivated between January and May, ginger needed to be dried before it could be shipped, which meant that ginger sent with the March fleet would rot before it arrived in

Europe.[10] Alongside the fact that demand for ginger was highest in northern Europe, the production of the crop drew Puerto Rico further into the commercial orbit of northern European merchants and ship captains by the 1590s.[11]

The increase in ginger production also increased the demand for enslaved Africans to cultivate the crop, intertwining the trade in ginger with the trade in human captives. The turn to the exploitation of enslaved Africans for the production of a cash crop in the Caribbean, in other words, did not begin with sugar but had antecedents in this vibrant, informal economy based around products such as hides, foodstuffs, and, especially, ginger.[12] The nature of Puerto Rico's economy by the first half of the seventeenth century also shifted local attitudes about trading with foreigners. While traffickers in the late sixteenth century periodically resorted to violence in order to force trade, conditions had changed significantly by the mid-seventeenth century. In 1579, for example, the French trafficker Jean Hacquet resorted to kidnapping the governor of Puerto Rico in order to coerce island residents into purchasing the African captives chained in the hold of his ship. By the time Gaspar de Espinosa arrived in Puerto Rico in the 1650s, however, island residents were habituated to an informal trade in which local officials participated. As a go-between for English and Dutch traffickers, Espinosa understood better than most the importance of informal trade to Puerto Rico's economy. As a translator working for the island's governor, he was also familiar with the degree to which local officials participated in regional, informal trade networks.

Local participation in informal trade in Puerto Rico led to the creation of various strategies for defending or concealing a trade that was considered illegal by Spain. The importance of informal trade for Puerto Rico in the first half of the seventeenth century, in other words, did not make it any less clandestine. Any trade between non-licensed foreign merchants and Spanish subjects in the Americas was considered illegal. This was true even if trade with non-licensed foreign vessels was often the only way for Puerto Rican residents to sell island produce or purchase necessities. Over the course of the seventeenth century, traffickers and their Puerto Rican trade partners developed various methods for covering or justifying their commerce. Sometimes those justifications had merit. For example, Puerto Rican officials explained the presence of foreign vessels by citing the extreme want or deprivation of island residents. This proved especially common after one of the eastern Caribbean's frequent and devastating hurricanes.

In August 1657 a powerful hurricane struck Puerto Rico, destroying crops and resulting in, according to island residents, "much hunger" and a "great lack of supplies." Espinosa and his companions arrived in Puerto Rico around the same time as this hurricane, which meant that Espinosa's skills as a translator were put to immediate use. According to island residents, numerous small vessels transporting "cassava, fish, and turtle" sailed to Puerto Rico from neighboring English, French, and Dutch islands in the aftermath of the hurricane.[13] As Governor Novoa explained, Puerto Rico "had no commerce nor licensed ship in the eight years" prior, and "due to the storm" he allegedly had no choice but to allow commerce with foreign merchants.[14] The foodstuffs that those ships transported to Puerto Rico no doubt helped island residents survive a season of failed crops following the 1657 hurricane.

The provisioning trade served as a useful cover for informal trade because of the frequent need for foodstuffs in Puerto Rico and the fact that the richest fisheries in the eastern Caribbean were also near islands occupied by traffickers. Traffickers had long used small islands near the fisheries and turtling grounds of the eastern Caribbean as maritime bases from which they launched raiding and trafficking voyages, as Espinosa knew too well from his experience as a captive in the Virgin Islands. In the decades leading up to mid-century, traffickers used the islands of St. Croix and Tortola for careening, refreshing their supplies, fishing, and turtling. Traffickers operating out of those islands also regularly seized fishermen and sailors in order to exploit their maritime labor and, when those captives were of African or Indigenous descent, to traffic them into slavery.[15] A French sailor named Michel Duyori described being taken captive by traffickers in 1662 and forced to labor for his captors in the fisheries of St. Croix, catching and processing the maritime protein that might have been used to provision neighboring Puerto Rico.[16]

If so, Duyori's captors had more than fish to traffic at Puerto Rico. Gaspar de Espinosa, too, had experienced captivity and slavery on St. Croix. Two years after Duyori's escape, Espinosa joined a fisherman named Domingo Hernández and escaped to Puerto Rico in a small boat with three women of African descent. Hernández had been taken captive at sea by traffickers off the coast of New Granada and, despite being born free, was sold into slavery in St. Croix. The circumstances surrounding Espinosa's second captivity are unclear, but he too had been sold into slavery. The three women who joined them in their escape had each been taken captive in raids along the Spanish Main and then sold in the Virgin Islands.[17] The same islands that brought provisions to Puerto Rico at mid-century, in other words, were deeply embedded in practices of captivity and trafficking.

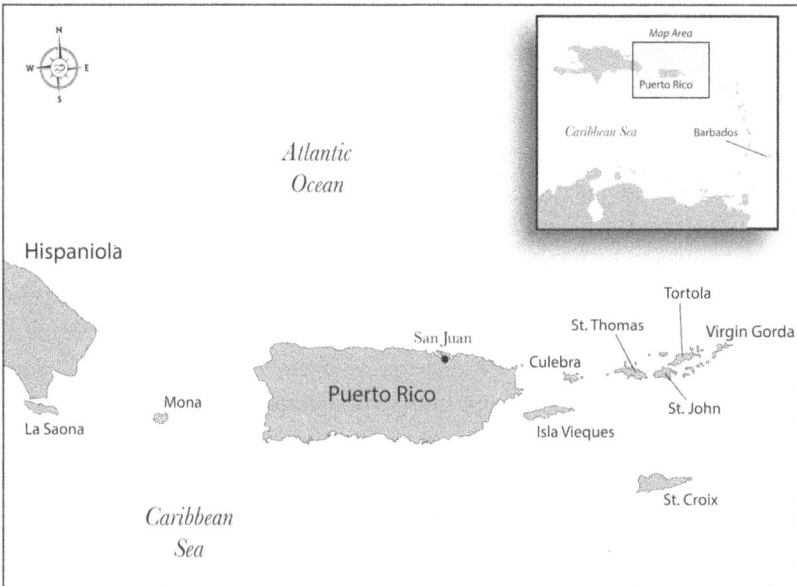

Map 7. Puerto Rico and the Virgin Islands

By the 1650s, maritime escapes like that of Hernández and his companions could, paradoxically, also facilitate the trafficking of other captives of African descent into slavery. The context surrounding this was the signing of the Peace of Münster (1648) between the Dutch Republic and Spain, which ended eighty years of nearly continuous war between the two powers and led to the recognition of an independent Dutch Republic.[18] Crucially, the peace also meant that Spain afforded the Dutch diplomatic recognition in the Caribbean, which included, among other things, allowing Dutch ships in distress to enter Spanish ports and maintaining diplomatic correspondence with regional governors. The articles of peace explicitly forbade direct commerce between Spanish American subjects and unlicensed Dutch merchants, but the thawing of hostilities in the Caribbean nonetheless opened multiple avenues for informal trade.

One of those avenues involved Dutch slaveholders who sought the restitution of self-liberated captives who made their way to Puerto Rico. The Peace of Münster did not grant the Dutch permission to demand the restitution of self-liberated enslaved people, and, as the next chapter will show, Spanish Caribbean governors would refuse to participate in regional treaties of rendition in the 1660s and 1670s. In this inchoate moment, however, Dutch traffickers relied on a regional, vernacular understanding of the rights of so-called property owners to approach Spanish Caribbean officials to seek the return of individuals who escaped to neighboring Puerto Rico. In 1658, for example, a Dutch captain sailed into San Juan to demand the restitution of "some Blacks who had escaped from him." He was unsuccessful in redeeming the self-liberated captives, but he did succeed in selling four African captives into slavery in Puerto Rico during the course of his negotiations with Novoa.[19] Who those African captives were or where they came from prior to their captivity is obscure, but their experiences underscore how the maritime proximity of islands in the eastern Caribbean enabled both avenues for escape for some and methods for human trafficking for others.

If hurricanes and European peace treaties helped facilitate informal trade in the eastern Caribbean, so too did war in the form of prisoner of war exchanges following England's invasion of Jamaica in 1655. Traffickers had long used the transportation of prisoners of war as a pretext for entering Spanish Caribbean ports and engaging in trade. Often those prisoners were actually sailors or passengers from ships seized at sea by the same traffickers, who then used those captives to gain entry to Spanish American ports where they often also engaged in informal trade. The English invasions of Hispaniola in 1654 and Jamaica in 1655, produced a flood of Spanish prisoners whose captivity facilitated informal trade. Residents of Puerto Rico, for example, described a constant traffic of small ships beginning in 1655 "that brought crabs and turtles" as well as "a quantity of Spanish Christians and among them some priests whom the English had taken captive."[20] For his part, Novoa defended his decision to allow these ships anchorage in San Juan. As he explained, the ships that brought Spanish captives to Puerto Rico sailed under Dutch flags and carried Spanish prisoners of war from English islands like St. Christopher "at great risk to themselves" and without carrying any merchandise beyond "some fish caught on the way here." More importantly, Novoa argued that the Dutch saved Spanish and Irish Catholics from terrible fates in Jamaica or St. Christopher where, he wrote, "the English trade in them like slaves."[21]

Regardless of how English residents of St. Christopher or Jamaica used Spanish prisoners of war, other evidence contradicts Novoa's claims that only the Dutch engaged in the transport of prisoners of war or that such exchanges were not accompanied by further informal trade and human trafficking. English and French traffickers also entered San Juan on the pretext of transporting prisoners of war, but they did so by flying Dutch flags. Among the prisoners of war that Dutch, English, and French traffickers transported to Puerto Rico, moreover, were captives of African and Indigenous descent who were sold into slavery, often at the hands of Novoa's financial agents.[22] Like Espinosa, some of those captives had been free before traffickers took them captive "off the coasts of Brazil and other parts" and sold them into slavery in Puerto Rico and throughout the Lesser Antilles.[23] As in earlier decades, the transportation of Spanish prisoners of war seized during the fighting in Jamaica served as cover for the trafficking of captives of African and Indigenous descent into slavery.

Puerto Rican residents, including Gaspar de Espinosa, participated in robust informal trade with neighboring islands that centered around captive slavery. Espinosa's work translating for negotiations between Puerto Rican elites and the English and Dutch traffickers who arrived to trade during the late 1650s underscores these commercial ties. For his part, the role afforded Espinosa access to informal trade that, as his purchase of an enslaved African woman makes clear, he invested in shortly after his arrival on the island. Facilitating commercial transactions with Dutch and English traffickers for Puerto Rico's governor and his closest associates also gave Espinosa the patronage of the most powerful men on the island.[24] In the violent, unstable world of the mid-century Caribbean, that patronage might have offered Espinosa a modicum of security, even if he achieved it by translating for the same kinds of multinational traffickers who had taken him captive in Brazil four years earlier. Neither his lived experience nor his racial background kept him from adapting to the circumstances in which he found himself in Puerto Rico.

Nor should that be surprising. Espinosa took advantage of opportunities where he could in a wider Caribbean world shaped by informal trade and human trafficking. But, however much Espinosa had carved out a life for himself, he arrived at Puerto Rico at an inauspicious time. Within several years of his arrival, practices of human trafficking in the greater Caribbean would inspire European monarchs and merchants to enact profound changes to the intra-Caribbean and transatlantic slave trades. Those changes would have dramatic consequences for individuals like Espinosa. A granular focus on a 1657–58 trafficking venture to Puerto Rico reveals this Caribbean world on the verge of transitioning from a decentered, violent trade in human captives to a supposedly more rational, organized asiento trade. As Espinosa would discover, however, a more rational, organized trade did not make the Caribbean any less violent or precarious.

Henrique Fon, Curaçao, and the Intra-Caribbean Slave Trade

Shortly after his escape to Puerto Rico in 1657, Espinosa received a summons from one of the governor's closest confidants, Francisco de Olivares, who asked for his assistance translating for a recently arrived Dutch ship. The Dutch captain, named Henrique Fon, claimed that the water casks on his ship had run dangerously low while enroute to New Netherland from the island of Curaçao. Taking advantage of the peace between Spain and the Dutch Republic, he explained that he sailed to Puerto Rico seeking water and other supplies to continue his voyage. Rather than purchase his supplies and ready his ship to leave, however, Fon accepted an invitation from Olivares to come ashore. Over several weeks in San Juan, Fon met and "developed friendships" with many island residents but "particularly [with] the royal officials," such as Governor Novoa.[25] Fon had arrived at an opportune moment. In the wake of the recent hurricane, Puerto Rican residents needed European manufactured goods, especially construction materials like wooden shingles.[26]

After several weeks on the island, Fon sailed to Europe with a lengthy shopping list compiled by Novoa, Olivares, and other Puerto Rican elites.[27] Understanding the value of his nascent friendships in Puerto Rico, Fon returned promptly with the goods that "were requested by the people with whom he had developed friendships."[28] The Dutch captain clearly knew what he was doing when he cultivated relationships of trust and commerce with Puerto Rico's elites. Shortly after unloading the European merchandise, Fon negotiated a contract with Novoa and his commercial circle to purchase enslaved Africans and transport them to Puerto Rico. Rather than a transatlantic venture to Atlantic Africa, Fon took his contract and sailed south to the Dutch island of Curaçao to purchase enslaved Africans for his Puerto Rican associates.

Curaçao was an island in transition at mid-century, shifting from a waystation where traffickers sold captive people in exchange for dyewood to an entrepôt in a more formalized intra-Caribbean slave trade. The Dutch island would emerge as a major hub in the intra-Caribbean and transatlantic slave trades by the 1660s, but that future was still aspirational when Fon signed a contract with Novoa and his associates. The Dutch had laid claim to the arid islands of Curaçao, Aruba, and Bonaire in 1634 and experimented over the next decade with ways of making them profitable.[29] Bonaire contained promising salt pans while residents on Aruba raised horses for a burgeoning intra-Caribbean trade, especially to Barbados. All three islands boasted stands of dyewoods that, especially on Curaçao, promised a profitable commerce for ships returning to Europe.[30]

As Governor Matthias Beck of Curaçao explained to the directors of the Dutch West India Company (WIC), "most profitable . . . on all three islands" was dyewood that could be "cut and made accessible so that the ships can fetch it whenever possible."[31] Dyewood cutting had long served as a method for traffickers to make their voyages, and the rise of dyewood cutting in Curaçao also tied the island to networks of captive-taking and human trafficking. After all, many of those ships also carried captives who had been seized during raids on Iberian transatlantic shipping and Spanish American coastal communities. As in other parts of the Caribbean, exchanging captives for a hold full of dyewood allowed traffickers to make their voyages while it also led to a growing population of captives on Curaçao. For residents of the Dutch island, the presence of captives seized during raids connected them with intra-Caribbean trade. As early as 1639, a Dutch captain contracted to transport twenty-five captives of African descent to English St. Christopher.[32] By 1641, in fact, the directors of the WIC ordered traffickers sailing under Dutch commissions to transport all of the captives of African descent seized in regional raiding to Curaçao.[33] Fon had good reason to believe that he could fulfill his end of the slave-trading contract at Curaçao—the informal trade in captives out of Curaçao was, after all, well established by the time he sailed south from Puerto Rico in 1658.

The notoriety of the trade out of Curaçao, in fact, drew the attention of Spanish merchants and ship captains in the region. A year before Fon arrived in Curaçao with money and goods invested by Puerto Rican elites for the purchase of enslaved Africans, a Basque ship captain named Juan de Aguira became involved in trafficking captives from Curaçao for Spanish Caribbean ports. An analysis of Aguira's experiences illuminate the nature of the captive trade out of Curaçao as well as the promise of that trade for making the Dutch islands profitable to the WIC. As Governor Beck explained to the WIC directors, Aguira's commercial connections with Curaçao represented a future wherein "a trail would . . . be blazed" in the intra-Caribbean slave trade.[34] That so-called trail would involve a direct trade in enslaved people of African descent from Curaçao to Spanish ports throughout the Caribbean. Although initially many of the people caught up in this trade had been taken captive within the Caribbean itself—either off of Iberian transatlantic ships or from coastal communities—by the late 1650s, the prospects of the intra-Caribbean slave trade coincided with increased Dutch slave-trading activity in Atlantic

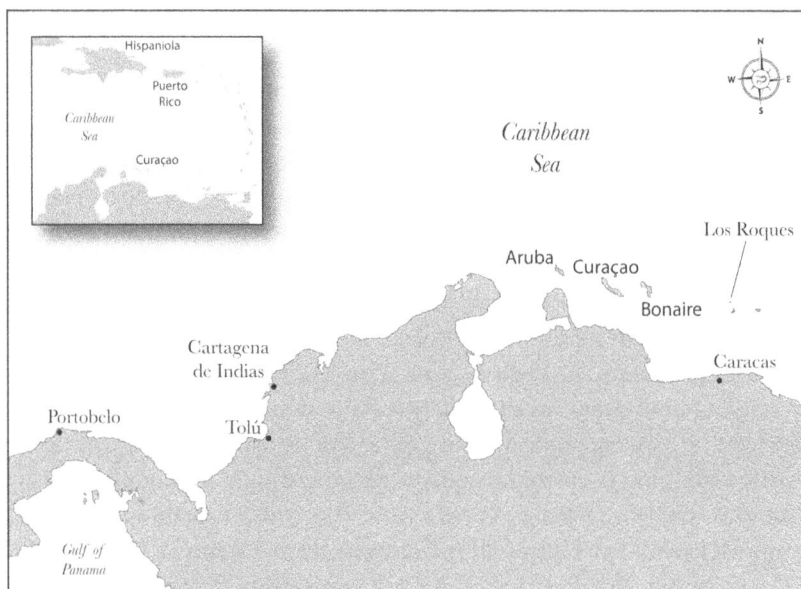

Map 8. Curaçao, Aruba, and Bonaire

Africa.[35] Aguira and Beck's commercial arrangements, in many ways, fore-shadowed the structure of the subsequent Genoese asiento contract, in which Curaçao emerged as an entrepôt in the formalized, intra-Caribbean trade. The experiences of captive people trafficked to and from Curaçao in the late 1650s, moreover, reveal how ongoing raiding and predation continued alongside the beginnings of a supposedly more systematic slave trade.

The increase in the Dutch transatlantic slave trade to Curaçao in the late 1650s led Governor Beck to attempt to establish a direct trade with neighboring Caracas, and although his offers would be rejected, his efforts drew the attention of regional traffickers like Aguira. In the summer of 1657, Beck sent two commissioners, Balthasar van Essen and Johan Rombouts, south to Caracas in order to present his Spanish counterpart with an offer for establishing trade between the two ports. The *Bontekoe* had recently arrived in Curaçao with 281 African captives on board, the survivors of a Middle Passage that claimed the lives of sixty-six of their shipmates.[36] Unconcerned with the human toll of the voyage, Beck saw an opportunity in the *Bontekoe*'s arrival to engage his Spanish neighbors in an informal trade. Although Caracas governor Andrés de Vera y Moscoso refused open trade, citing Article VI of the Peace of Münster, which expressly forbade direct trade between Spanish subjects and the Dutch in the Americas, the commissioners' trip was not in vain.[37] While they were in Caracas, a local ship captain approached the Dutch intermediaries with a plan for working around the trade restrictions. According to the commissioners' report, Juan de Aguira suggested that the Dutch trade with him out of view of Spanish port officials in Caracas. Aguira informed the commissioners that he had a ship that he planned to take to Los Roques, a series of sandy islets off the coast of Venezuela, in order to catch turtles. He planned to be in the vicinity of Los Roques for at least three weeks and suggested that if "they be pleased to meet him there for trading," he would bring "tobacco, hides, and other prepared goods" to exchange for enslaved Africans.[38]

Fishing and turtling had long served as cover for informal trade by allowing ships to rendezvous and conduct business in isolated or peripheral spaces. Los Roques had served as an anchorage for traffickers in the decades leading up to the 1650s, something Aguira likely knew from experience. The Basque ship captain viewed the meeting at Los Roques as a chance not just to engage in a single act of informal trade but also for establishing long-term connections with Dutch Curaçao. As he explained to the Dutch commissioners, Los Roques would allow them to "have a better opportunity there to discuss other business."[39] Despite careful planning, Aguira's plans were thwarted when Governor Moscoso asked him to transport several Spanish officials to Portobelo on his way to turtling in Los Roques. Aguira realized that carrying merchandise would arouse the officials' suspicion and cancelled his plans.

Rather than allow his lack of merchandise to foreclose the possibility of trade with the Dutch, Aguira decided to sail to Curaçao himself to explain his situation directly to Governor Beck. If the Basque ship captain assumed that his knowledge of Spanish Caribbean trade would compensate for his failure to bring trade goods to Los Roques, he was right. In the case of Aguira's first trip to Curaçao, information proved more valuable than the tobacco, hides, or money that he had promised Beck's commissioners. Once in Willemstad, Aguira explained that the most important Spanish Caribbean port for the transatlantic slave trade was Portobelo but that Spain limited the trade there and elsewhere to licensed Spanish merchants who paid a royal tax of 113 pieces of eight for each enslaved person disembarked at that port. The workaround for those restrictions, according to Aguira, was for him to sail on a WIC ship along with five or six Spanish sailors. Once they arrived in Portobelo, Aguira assured Beck that he could gain entrance to Portobelo and secure the sale of enslaved Africans "under the pretext of having hired a Dutch ship and crew" to transport supposedly Spanish-owned merchandise and enslaved Africans.[40] At Portobelo, Aguira argued that any enslaved Africans would sell at "a price high enough that it [would] sufficiently cover the expense" and earn for the company "two hundred reals or pieces of eight" per enslaved African between the ages of eighteen and thirty years of age.[41]

For Beck, who confronted the diminishing quality and quantity of dyewood on Curaçao, Aguira's offer opened new opportunities for the arid Dutch island. As a token of his goodwill, Beck sold three children of African descent, two small girls and a boy, to Aguira for what he described as "a civil and reasonable price" that he hoped would "encourage and induce" the Basque captain to return for future trade.[42] Whether Aguira trafficked those three children into slavery in Portobelo or elsewhere is unclear from the surviving archival record. Four years later, however, a companion of Henrique Fon's named Jacobo Mandix attempted precisely the kind of trafficking that Aguira suggested at Portobelo. Unfortunately for the Dutch ship captain, port officials in Portobelo in 1661 confiscated his ship and the enslaved Africans on board rather than allowing Mandix to engage in trade.[43] Regardless, beginning with Beck's sale of three African children to Aguira, Dutch commercial connections in the Caribbean would result in far more people of African and Indigenous descent being trafficked to and from Curaçao.

Negotiations like those conducted between Beck and Aguira led to the increase of Dutch transatlantic slaving vessels calling at Curaçao and the creation of regional networks of informal trade in captive people that would become the basis for the Grillo asiento in the next decade. The Basque ship captain was not the only intermediary willing to facilitate the intra-Caribbean slave trade out of Dutch Curaçao, as the examples of Fon and Mandix make clear. The growing interest in establishing an informal, intra-Caribbean slave trade to Spanish American ports led the Dutch WIC to invest in even more transatlantic slave-trading voyages to Curaçao. This transformed Curaçao from a self-organized waystation for people taken captive during raids against Iberian shipping and coastal communities to an official entrepôt for the transatlantic slave trade. Between 1657 and 1659, in fact, six transatlantic slave ships of Dutch ownership arrived at Curaçao where they disembarked 1,747 African women, men, and children.[44] Between 1660 and 1670, that number would increase nearly tenfold, with a total of 16,617 African women, men, and children transported to Curaçao in a total of sixty-one voyages. Crucially, in earlier decades between 1634 and 1650, not a single transatlantic slave ship sailed from Atlantic Africa with Curaçao as their final destination. The commercial negotiations between Beck and Aguira, in other words, fore-shadowed a dramatic transformation in the intra-Caribbean slave trade that would be institutionalized five years later with the creation of the Genoese asiento. Even before Spain granted an official asiento that created a formal intra-Caribbean slave trade, Curaçao was in the process of transitioning into a slave-trading entrepôt.

The context around the role of Curaçao in the transatlantic and intra-Caribbean slave trades explains the decision of Henrique Fon to sail to Curaçao to purchase enslaved Africans for his Puerto Rican associates. It was good timing—his arrival coincided with that of a slave ship named the *Den Coninck Salomon*, which arrived in Curaçao with 241 enslaved women, men, and children shackled belowdecks. The merchant responsible for the voyage of the *Den Coninck Salomon*, Henrico Mathias, maintained close commer-cial connections with a Sevillian merchant named Jacinto Vasques, repre-sentatives of the WIC, and Governor Beck in Curaçao.[45] These ties were not unusual—multinational trade and trans-confessional interactions defined the burgeoning slave trade in this period, as much in the Caribbean as in Atlantic Africa.[46] For the enslaved Africans trafficked on the *Den Coninck Salomon*, 241 people survived a Middle Passage in which they bore witness to the death of one of their shipmates 121 times.[47] Their respite from West African warfare and the horrors of the Middle Passage would be brief and punctuated by the separation of individuals who might have formed kinship ties with their ship-mates. Shortly after their arrival, 160 of the 241 Africans from the Gold Coast transported on the *Den Coninck Salomon* were forced onto Fon's smaller ship for the month-long voyage north and into slavery in Puerto Rico.[48]

Curaçao's burgeoning role as an entrepôt in the transatlantic and intra-Caribbean slave trades meant that the Caribbean waters around the Dutch island became more violent and unpredictable as traffickers cruised the southern Caribbean in the hope of intercepting a vessel and seizing the cap-tives on board. This made the voyages of Africans transported from Atlantic Africa to Curaçao especially dangerous. Traffickers, as they had done with the intra-Caribbean slave trade between Cartagena and Peru in earlier decades, congregated in the waterways connecting Curaçao with transatlantic trade. The experiences of the 219 women, men, and children aboard the Dutch slave ship the *St. Jan* underscore the human consequences of this moment when the renewal of the Dutch transatlantic slave trade confronted a Caribbean world accustomed to raiding and captive-taking.

The voyage of the *St. Jan* embodied the banal horrors that accompanied the transatlantic slave trade from the beginning. The ship arrived along the Slave Coast in mid-March 1659, sailing between the trading fort of El Mina in modern-day Ghana and the Niger River in order to purchase enslaved Africans. By the end of May, 219 women, men, and children had been loaded aboard the *St. Jan*, but the Dutch captain, Adriaen Blaes van der Veer, struggled to find food supplies for the voyage.[49] The combination proved deadly for the enslaved Africans belowdecks. By the time the *St. Jan* arrived in Tobago in the eastern Caribbean nearly four months later, the Dutch crew had gone three weeks without rations, while the enslaved Africans suffered far worse. Of the 219 people who left Atlantic Africa in May 1659, only ninety reached the Caribbean alive.[50]

Nor were the sufferings of the survivors over once their floating prison entered Caribbean waters. On the way to Curaçao, the *St. Jan* wrecked on the reefs surrounding Los Roques, killing four African captives. According to the testimony of the ship's captain, "after perceiving our danger, I saved myself in the boat, together with all of the crew," and sailed for Curaçao, leaving the eighty-six African survivors of the *St. Jan* with the ship's wreckage on Los Roques. The "danger" that the Dutch captain and crew escaped was not drowning but, rather, the retaliation of the eighty-six African survivors suddenly liberated from their maritime confines. The African survivors of the *St. Jan*, in other words, used the ship's destruction to claim their freedom from slavery. Shortly after the Dutch crew from the *St. Jan* arrived in Curaçao, Beck dispatched another WIC vessel to "rescue" the eighty-six survivors. When the captain of that vessel, the *Jonge Bontecoe*, arrived at Los Roques, however, he claimed that his small crew "stood in fear" of the eighty-six Africans on Los Roques and chose to wait for the arrival of reinforcements.[51] Those reinforcements did not arrive in time. Cruising near Los Roques was a Danish trafficker named Jan Pietersen with a multinational crew of English, French, and Dutch sailors. Pietersen and his crew attacked the *Jonge Bontecoe*, raided the ship, and violently subdued the eighty-six African survivors of the *St. Jan*. According to Dutch reports, Pietersen and his crew seized "84 slaves and 2 nursing children"—infants born during the *St. Jan*'s brutal transatlantic voyage. After surviving enslavement in Atlantic Africa, four harrowing months in the Middle Passage, a shipwreck, and seizure at the hands of multination traffickers, the eighty-six survivors of the *St. Jan* found themselves captives on a new ship that trafficked them into slavery in English Jamaica.[52]

The experiences of the survivors of the *St. Jan* resulted in part from the continuation of older practices of raiding, captive-taking, and human trafficking in the Caribbean in the 1650s. As Governor Beck lamented, the English and others had an "envy for these places and the incipient trade," which made the waterways surrounding Curaçao increasingly dangerous in the years leading up to the 1660s.[53] Traffickers like Pietersen and his crew predated in the waters around Curaçao and found markets throughout the Caribbean for the human captives whom they seized. This was especially true, as will be seen, in English Jamaica, where Beck tried and failed to negotiate for the restitution of the eighty-six survivors of the *St. Jan* in 1660.[54] As ship captains like Aguira and Henrique Fon sailed to Curaçao with increasing frequency, maritime predators too stalked the waters around the Dutch island.

Nor was Curaçao the only island emerging as an entrepôt in the intra-Caribbean and transatlantic slave trades in the late 1650s. English, Dutch, and French settlements in the northern Lesser Antilles also engaged, to varying degrees, in a regional trade in human captives. During the decade leading up to 1660, European merchants and metropolitan officials attempted to formalize the intra-Caribbean slave trade. Those efforts coincided with ongoing maritime predation in ways that reflected older practices of captive-taking and human trafficking. The decentralized nature of the trade would lead to changes in the Spanish asiento system by the 1660s, but only after evidence of widespread informal trade and inefficiencies in the transatlantic slave trade were brought to the attention of imperial officials. For Gaspar de Espinosa, that imperial attention would have dramatic repercussions for the life he had built for himself in Puerto Rico. The events leading up to his second captivity revolve around the sinking of a Spanish ship called the *Carlos Quinto* and the imprisonment of his patron, the governor of Puerto Rico.

The *Carlos Quinto* and the Fall of Novoa

The ill-fated voyage of the *Carlos Quinto* encapsulates the entangled nature of informal trade and maritime violence that would draw the attention of imperial officials intent on reforming trade in the Caribbean. The voyage of the 250-ton *Carlos Quinto* ended tragically when it sank during a storm, killing all but one of the ship's 115 soldiers and sailors. The disastrous loss of life left numerous widows across the island.[55] The maritime calamity would also end the political career of Puerto Rico's governor. The fall of Novoa severed Gaspar de Espinosa's access to political patronage on the island, and shortly after the *Carlos Quinto* disappeared beneath Caribbean waters, Espinosa would be taken captive for a second time. Beyond the tragic end to the voyage, an examination of the *Carlos Quinto* casts light on the changing nature of trafficking and informal trade in the years leading up to the 1660s. The eighteen-gun ship went down during a voyage that blended privateering against the traffickers who had raided Puerto Rican residents with direct, informal trade to purchase enslaved Africans and clothing from the English in the Lesser Antilles. The *Carlos Quinto*, in other words, was both privateer and merchant vessel on its last run. Residents of Puerto Rico had invested heavily in the voyage, despite the danger involved in sending off the island's largest ship in the midst of open war between England and Spain. England had invaded Spanish Jamaica three years before, and the resulting conflict over control of Jamaica was ongoing when the *Carlos Quinto* sailed away from San Juan in 1657. Crucially, the *Carlos Quinto* hunted so-called pirates, specifically in the Virgin Islands, while it was directed to trade with the English at St. Christopher. Untangling the planning and execution of the *Carlos Quinto*'s last voyage reveals the elaboration of networks of informal trade between the governors of Puerto Rico and St. Christopher.

Novoa and his associates made the arrangements for the *Carlos Quinto*'s 1658 voyage from what they had learned of opportunities to purchase enslaved Africans at St. Christopher. The plans for the *Carlos Quinto*'s voyage might have begun two years earlier at an obscure port several leagues west of San Juan. In 1656, a ship flying Dutch colors approached San Juan, but before entering the harbor, a pilot rowed out to meet it and guided the ship to a place called Puerto de Toa. Located at the base of the small peninsula that shielded the port from view of San Juan, Novoa and his associates frequently used Puerto de Toa to engage in informal trade with northern European vessels.[56] The ship that arrived in 1656, however, carried very little merchandise. Rather, the captain, an Englishman named John Easton, brought letters instead. Perhaps Captain Easton delivered communiqués from St. Christopher that inspired Novoa to purchase the *Carlos Quinto* using funds from the royal treasury two years later. The continual arrival of smaller vessels to Puerto Rico from the neighboring Lesser Antilles, as seen above, might also have provided Novoa with diplomatic and commercial connections with neighboring St. Christopher.[57] Either way, Novoa and the residents of Puerto Rico who invested in the venture of the *Carlos Quinto* in 1658 had good reason to believe that the ship's crew would be able to purchase enslaved Africans and

European manufactured goods in St. Christopher. The voyage of the *Carlos Quinto*, however, was not just commercial. Novoa also ordered the captain and crew to cruise against so-called pirates, an essential part of the plan.

Shortly after setting out from San Juan, the *Carlos Quinto* took two maritime prizes. The first, a small English ship, surrendered near the island of Virgin Gorda, the third-largest of the Virgin Islands archipelago. The second prize, a French boat engaged in turtling, was seized near Isla Vieques off of Puerto Rico's eastern seaboard. The captain and crew of the *Carlos Quinto* undoubtedly knew they would find foreign vessels in the waters around Vieques and the Virgin Islands since the scattering of small islands in the northeastern Caribbean had long served as maritime bases for multinational traffickers.

The island of St. Croix, for example, had a history similar to that of St. Christopher—by the late 1620s the island was inhabited by Dutch, English, and French mariners and settlers who used its location and maritime resources to engage in raiding and trafficking.[58] Isla Vieques, similarly, had hosted multinational mariners over the course of the late sixteenth and early seventeenth centuries. For the *Carlos Quinto*, in other words, both Vieques and the Virgin Islands offered opportunities to seize prizes. Neither prize, however, justified the expense of purchasing, manning, and outfitting the *Carlos Quinto*, but privateering was never intended to earn Puerto Rico's residents a return on their investments. The small prizes did, however, provide cover for the use of a ship, supplies, and soldiers in an intra-Caribbean slave-trading venture. Crucially, the presence of traffickers between Puerto Rico and St. Christopher might have necessitated the use of an eighteen-gun ship in order to conduct informal trade. As the example of the *St. Jan* underscores, traffickers continued to predate along maritime routes of trade throughout the Caribbean in the late 1650s.

Disaster struck the *Carlos Quinto* between the Virgin Islands and St. Christopher when the ship encountered a violent tropical storm. The loss of life was near total, with only a single crew member returning to Puerto Rico. The sinking of the *Carlos Quinto* also ruined the financial prospects of many Puerto Rican residents, especially the newly widowed women and orphaned children awaiting the return of their loved ones. The financial investment in the informal intra-Caribbean slave trade represented by the *Carlos Quinto*'s voyage must have been considerable, if anecdotal evidence collected during the official Spanish investigation of Novoa's conduct is to be believed. Numerous members of the *Carlos Quinto*'s crew had carried significant personal financial resources in order to purchase enslaved Africans at St. Christopher.[59] The ship's surgeon, Nicolas de Arisenendi, explained to a friend before embarking that he had "brought all the money that he had to purchase slaves."[60] Those who remained on shore also entrusted their money with sailors and soldiers whom they expected to trade on their behalf. Gaspar de Espinosa, for example, invested his own earnings in the voyage. When an artilleryman named Pedro de Berueta approached Espinosa for a small cash loan, the translator allegedly responded that "he did not have any [money] because he sent it all on the *Carlos Quinto* so that it would bring him some slaves."[61] Records of just how much money and island produce the *Carlos Quinto* carried do not survive. References to individuals investing all the money that they possessed, however, point to Puerto Rican expectations that they would be able to purchase a significant number of enslaved African women, men, and children at St. Christopher. As will be seen, the jointly held English and French island would emerge as an entrepôt in the intra-Caribbean slave trade organized under the Grillo asiento in the next decade. Yet, as the voyage of the *Carlos Quinto* reveals, St. Christopher occupied the role of entrepôt well before England became involved in the licensed intra-Caribbean slave trade.

The sinking of the *Carlos Quinto* unraveled the political career of Governor Novoa in Puerto Rico and raised the stakes among Spanish imperial planners for reforming trade in the Caribbean. In the context of the 1655 English invasion and occupation of Jamaica, defense of Spanish territories in the greater Caribbean preoccupied Spanish officials on both sides of the Atlantic. Rumors that the *Carlos Quinto* sank while on a venture involving informal trade with the English enemy rather than in the defense of Puerto Rico drew official scrutiny of Novoa and his commercial circle. The subsequent investigation revealed the degree to which Novoa and his associates condoned and participated in regional, informal trade. Worse for the governor, however, were multiple testimonies from island residents about English merchants and mariners who passed freely around Puerto Rico. The loss of the *Carlos Quinto* along with 115 soldiers and sailors during a moment of inter-imperial warfare was bad—especially when Novoa had received repeated orders from Spain to send all available men and supplies to help with the Spanish defense against the English invasion of Jamaica.[62] But, in the context of that English invasion, maintaining close commercial ties with the enemy and allowing them access to Puerto Rican ports proved beyond the pale. The investigation into Novoa's tenure as governor ended with a sentence to pay 340,000 pesos and to serve at his own cost for three years at the pre-sidio of Oran in modern-day Algeria. Unable to pay such a high fine, Novoa was arrested along with other Puerto Rican officials, including Olivares, and imprisoned in Madrid.[63] While Novoa's career ended ignobly as a result of the networks of informal trade that transected the eastern Caribbean, the nascent intra-Caribbean slave trade that he facilitated drew a different kind of attention from merchants and imperial planners in Europe.

Within two years of Novoa's removal from office, Spain formalized the networks of informal trade by issuing a new asiento contract to Grillo and Lomelín. The terms of that asiento echoed the way in which the intra-Caribbean slave trade had developed over the final years of the 1650s, with the new asiento factors responsible for the purchase and transportation of enslaved Africans from regional Caribbean entrepôts to select Spanish American ports. Imperial planners and merchants, in other words, sought to co-opt the decentralized trade that traffickers had created over the previous half century. Monopoly companies, unsurprisingly, confronted colonial pop-ulations throughout the Caribbean that were habituated to informal trade and human trafficking. To succeed, the English and Dutch monopoly slave-trading companies would need to change ingrained patterns of trade and behavior. That they failed to do so should hardly be surprising, but what this moment of transition meant for traffickers, captives, and regional networks of trade can only be understood by analyzing what the new asiento holders and their Anglo-Dutch trade partners attempted to create in the early 1660s. For Espinosa and others like him, the new asiento created a more precarious and violent Caribbean.

The Asiento, Monopoly Companies, and Jamaica

The trade networks exposed by the official investigation into Novoa's tenure as governor of Puerto Rico contributed to the growing realization in Spain that the transatlantic slave trade to Spanish America needed reform. This was especially true after the end of the Iberian Union, when Portugal split from the Hapsburg monarchy and lost their monopoly over the transatlan-tic slave trade to Spanish America. The two decades between 1640 and 1662 represented an era of "close to *de facto* free trade" throughout the greater Caribbean, especially in enslaved African and Indigenous captives.[64] The end of the Iberian Union meant that, between 1640 and 1651, for example, not a single license for the transatlantic slave trade was issued by the Council of the Indies, creating what historian Marisa Vega Franco calls a "period defined by clandestine trade" in enslaved people.[65] During these years after the dissolution of the Portuguese trade, northern Europeans carried on an increasingly vigorous trade to Spanish America, often trafficking people taken captive in one part of Spain's American territories into slavery in peripheral Caribbean markets. As the example of Aguira's plans to traffic enslaved Africans from Curaçao to Portobelo makes clear, even vital ports like Portobelo were potentially receptive to informal trade by the 1650s. Crucial too was the flourishing informal trade with northern Europeans, which posed serious economic and security concerns in the eyes of Spanish officials following the recent English invasion of Spanish Jamaica.

The decision to create a new asiento contract represented the formalization of the kinds of self-organized, intra-Caribbean trade in human captives that had previously been considered illicit by Spain. The changing nature of the transatlantic slave trade to Spanish America after mid-century presented an opportunity for a pair of Genoese merchants with ties to the Hapsburg court. Domingo Grillo and Ambrosio Lomelín saw a chance to create a new, and highly profitable, role for themselves out of the informal, intra-Caribbean slave trade of the 1650s. In 1662, after several years of difficult negotiations with Spanish officials, Grillo and Lomelín received an exclusive charter for the slave trade to Spanish America. The new asiento represented something radically different from earlier charters, the terms of which would be replicated in future English, French, and Dutch asientos. Rather than engage directly in the purchase of African captives at trading forts in West and West Central Africa, Grillo and Lomelín received permission to buy enslaved Africans in the Americas from any nation at peace with Spain.[66] The two merchants planned to purchase enslaved Africans from regional entrepôts like Curaçao, Barbados, or Jamaica, and to transship those enslaved women, men, and children to select ports in Spanish America, formalizing what traffickers had been doing over the previous decades. As historian Alejandro García-Montón argues, the new asiento created a "new international commercial sphere" in which Grillo and Lomelín acted as "gatekeepers."[67] This was a dramatic change to the official slave trade to Spanish America, even if it echoed established patterns of informal trade in the Caribbean. The new asiento, in other words, formalized the networks of informal trade that had developed over the decades leading up to the 1660s and placed Grillo and Lomelín as intermediaries in the burgeoning inter-imperial, intra-Caribbean slave trade.

For merchants in the English and Dutch monopoly slave trading companies, the Genoese asiento promised access to legal trade with Spanish America and an increase in the profitability of the transatlantic slave trade, but English efforts to negotiate a contract with the Genoese were initially stymied by Caribbean violence. Soon after finalizing their contract in 1662, agents for the Grillo and Lomelín asiento brokered a subcontract with the Dutch West India Company for the purchase of enslaved Africans from Curaçao. Agents for the asiento holders also approached the WIC's English counterpart, the Royal Company of Adventurers Trading to Africa, to negotiate a subcontract for the purchase of five thousand enslaved Africans annually. The English Royal Adventurers, however, faced opposition in their efforts to secure a role in the new asiento trade. In the midst of negotiations with Grillo and Lomelín's agents, the Spanish king ordered the Genoese merchants to cease all commercial dealings with the English company.[68]

The order came after an ill-timed English Jamaican raid on neighboring Santiago de Cuba sanctioned by Jamaica's royal governor. As Philip IV argued, the terms of the asiento stipulated that Grillo and Lomelín could only subcontract the transatlantic transportation of enslaved Africans from nations at peace with Spain.[69] A state-sponsored attack on Santiago de Cuba strained any argument that peace existed between English and Spanish subjects in the Caribbean. The attack on Santiago de Cuba, as will be seen, underscored the challenges that the Royal Adventurers would face in disciplining English subjects in the Caribbean to the control of a monopoly company over the next decade. Efforts to formalize the intra-Caribbean slave trade, in other words, confronted preexisting practices of maritime raiding that persisted in the face of official attempts to appropriate the region's economy in human trafficking. In the case of the English, conflicting imperial policies in the metropole prolonged the tacit support of maritime predators in the greater Caribbean.

The attack on Santiago de Cuba that disrupted the Royal Adventurers' plans reveals the continuation of older practices of raiding and captive-taking in the Caribbean even during a moment of widespread reform. Although commanded by a vice admiral of the Royal Navy, the force that raided Santiago de Cuba was composed of traffickers recruited from throughout the Caribbean. In the early fall of 1662, Robert Gordon sailed to the Virgin Islands in search of crew members for his ship. As the islands were a popular rendezvous for traffickers, Gordon had good reason to believe that he would find sailors willing to join a venture against Spanish territories among the small islands to the northeast of Puerto Rico. At each anchorage, Gordon announced to the sailors and others that the English governor of Jamaica was preparing an invasion of Santiago de Cuba, and he offered anyone willing a spot on his vessel. Shortly after, Gordon returned to Jamaica to join the invasion force with a full complement of multinational sailors recruited from the Virgin Islands.[70] The invasion force that Gordon and his recruits joined was large, especially during a time of relatively rare peace in the Caribbean— eleven ships with over a thousand men, many of whom were ship captains like Gordon, who sailed with composite crews who signed on with the hope of gaining plunder. Under the command of the vice admiral of the Royal Navy, Christopher Myngs, the fleet sailed from Jamaica for neighboring Cuba on October 1, 1662. Six days later, Myngs's forces overwhelmed the defenses of Santiago de Cuba. On shore, Myngs and his force of a thousand sailors and soldiers of fortune dismantled the Cuban port city's fortifications, ransacked homes, and set fire to the main cathedral.[71]

The raid was financially successful for the sailors and soldiers who signed on to attack Santiago de Cuba, and, perhaps surprisingly, they received a warm welcome when they returned to Jamaica. Crucially, despite ruining the efforts of the Royal Adventurers, the raid occurred during a moment of political uncertainty before Spain and England had negotiated a peace treaty. After more than a week of violence, Myngs and his forces sailed back to Jamaica with nearly £200,000 in the form of captives of African descent, pillaged goods, and six small merchant vessels seized from the harbor.[72] According to Myngs, his forces succeeded in "blowing up the main castle" in Santiago de Cuba. At the same time, the English vice admiral lamented the fact that although his forces spent five days "pursuing the enemy," their efforts "proved not very advantageous [since] their riches [had been] drawn off."[73] Nothing would have been surprising about Myngs's invasion of Santiago de Cuba or his description of plundering the Cuban port city's inhabitants in the context of the Anglo-Spanish warfare that had been sparked by England's invasion of Jamaica in 1655.

Myngs's raid, however, took place after outright hostilities between England and Spain ended in 1660 but before Spain and England finalized the terms of a peace—a situation that the governor of Jamaica, Thomas Windsor, took advantage of in the fall of 1662.[74] At the same time, Windsor's actions directly contradicted the goals of the Royal Adventurers and cost the company a chance at an early subcontract with the new asiento holders. That he acted within the bounds of his royal commission reflected larger unresolved tensions within the inner circle of the restored Stuart monarchy. Those unresolved tensions contributed to chaotic, uneven policies in the Caribbean, with dramatic repercussions for communities of African descent, including the unspecified number of individuals seized during Myngs's raid. As the next chapter will show, some of those individuals had been free before being taken captive and trafficked into slavery in English Jamaica.

The flexibility written into Windsor's commission as governor of Jamaica reflected the strategy of imperial planners in England to use maritime violence in the Caribbean to force Spain to concede more at the negotiating tables. England and Spain had been at war since Oliver Cromwell launched the Western Design in a quixotic bid to unseat the Spanish monarchy in the Americas in 1655. The restoration of the Stuart monarchy to the English throne in 1660, following Cromwell's protectorate, brought a temporary reprieve from open warfare and, for English planners, a chance to negotiate for peace and open trade with Spain and Spanish America. The return of Charles II to the English throne ended outright hostilities between England and Spain, but neither side agreed on the conditions of the subsequent peace. For their part, negotiators for Spain wanted the peace treaty to revert to the terms of the 1630 Treaty of Madrid, which, among other things, reestablished Anglo-Spanish trade in Europe and released prisoners of war. Crucially for the negotiations, the 1630 Treaty of Madrid did not explicitly recognize English territorial sovereignty over the lands that England claimed and colonized in North America.[75] English negotiators refused to revert to the old treaty's terms and continued pushing for Spanish diplomatic recognition of England's colonies in the Americas. Some among Charles II's advisors encouraged the continuation of belligerence in the Caribbean, arguing that ongoing maritime predations could force Spain to agree to their terms and, possibly, concede on even more, such as granting the English access to trade in Spanish America. Other royal advisors disagreed, citing the economic damage suffered by English merchants who had been prohibited from trading with peninsular Spain during the war.[76]

Disagreement in the Stuart court over peace with Spain manifested itself in Windsor's decision to use violence against Jamaica's Spanish neighbor for refusing to allow open trade between the two islands. The instructions that Windsor received at the start of his term as governor encouraged him to establish peaceful trade with neighboring Spanish territories, but they also granted him the authority to use force if his overtures were rejected.[77] When neighboring Spanish governors rejected Windsor's proposals for an open trade considered illegal in Spain, Windsor used force. As Windsor wrote in his orders to Myngs, he had sent messages to his Spanish Caribbean counterparts when he arrived in Jamaica but they held to "their former practice of denying us traffique, thereby ingrossing to themselves the riches of the Indies, contrary to the use and custom of all governments and the lawes of nations."[78] It was a feeble justification. England, of course, maintained the right to "ingross" the profits produced by their colonies by denying Dutch merchants "traffique" in the form of the Navigation Acts.[79] Windsor also understood that trade restrictions did not violate any nascent ideas about the law of nations. Rather, Windsor sponsored Myngs's assault on Santiago de Cuba as a continuation of the kinds of maritime belligerence that some in England believed would force Spain to agree to additional concessions at the negotiating tables in Europe.

Myngs's raid would have consequences around the Atlantic world, although perhaps not in the way some English royal advisors intended. The raid prevented the Royal Adventurers from signing a subcontract with the new asiento holders in 1662, cutting the English company out of the trade temporarily and making the WIC the primary supplier of enslaved Africans for the trade to Spanish America. The raid also drew increasing numbers of men like Robert Gordon and his multinational crew from the Virgin Islands to Jamaica, where they hoped to receive royal commissions to raid Spanish American shipping and territories. The combination of increased maritime predation alongside a growing demand for enslaved Africans among European colonists in the early 1660s created an increasingly unstable world for people of African and Indigenous descent in the greater Caribbean. The captives seized in Myngs's raid on Santiago de Cuba would be enslaved next to individuals in English Jamaica who had similarly experienced violent captivity and trafficking, such as the captive women, men, and children seized from the wreckage of the *St. Jan* in 1659.

Traffickers and Raiding in the Early 1660s

Myngs's raid and wider administrative changes in the Anglo-Atlantic incentivized an increase in raiding and captive-taking by traffickers who sought to make a voyage in the early 1660s. Unlike Myngs's larger raid, the majority of maritime predation in the early 1660s involved frequent small-scale raids that yielded fewer captives but proved a constant source of violence and instability in the Caribbean. The end of hostilities, in fact, meant that traffickers preferred taking people of African descent as captives rather than seizing ships or goods from Spanish Caribbean settlements. This was especially true after the establishment of admiralty court jurisdiction in the Caribbean after 1662. Admiralty courts had long adjudicated prizes in Europe, deciding whether the seizing of a specific ship violated international law. Seizing a neutral vessel in a time of war, for example, constituted a violation of international maritime law and resulted in the seized vessel and goods being returned to their previous owners. Prior to the English Restoration, however, English subjects in the Americas had to send prizes across the Atlantic to be adjudicated in England. This changed in 1661 when English royal governors received the authority to create prize courts to adjudicate prize cases in the Caribbean itself, thereby speeding up the process of dividing spoils among crew members.[80] As some mariners would discover, however, the admiralty courts in Jamaica also provided Spanish shipowners with legal recourse to challenge the seizure of their vessels.

In the summer of 1664, for example, the admiralty court in Jamaica adjudicated a case involving an English captain who had captured a Spanish ship and brought it into Port Royal as a prize. In the end, the Spanish shipowner received compensation for his vessel, which was seized during an official peace and therefore was not a legal prize, with grim consequences for the English captain. As Governor Thomas Modyford explained, after the decision was rendered "the Creditors of the Man of War [who] hoped to be paid out of this prize, pressed [the captain] so hard ... he fled [Jamaica] in the night."[81] Put simply, English admiralty courts in the Caribbean presented traffickers with a layer of oversight in which their prizes could be and occasionally were deemed illegitimate. For ship captains who received merchant financing for their voyages, the loss of a prize was financially ruinous. In this environment, however, human trafficking continued to be a profitable way for ship captains and mariners to covertly make a voyage in the early 1660s.

Reports from Spanish Caribbean sources reveal how captive-taking and human trafficking served as an alternative to taking ships for traffickers who sought to avoid financial ruin. In the summer of 1664, officials in Santo Domingo received reports about two Jamaican vessels crewed by an assortment of "English, Dutch, and Pechilinga [Fleshing]" sailors that captured and robbed fishing boats sent out to provision Hispaniola's principal port city. The testimony of a Spanish fisherman taken captive and released by the traffickers offers a window into how admiralty changes in the Anglo-Caribbean incentivized captive-taking and human trafficking in the early 1660s. Diego Sanchez worked as a fisherman on a boat owned by a resident of Santo Domingo when it was seized by one of the two vessels off the coast of La Saona in early July 1664. Located midway between Hispaniola and Puerto Rico, La Saona had long served as an anchorage for traffickers. In this case, the traffickers at La Saona were less interested in seizing the ship Sanchez worked on than in using him to obtain very specific information. Sanchez described how his captors demanded to know the locations of Spanish haciendas along the coast of Hispaniola, torturing him and the other Spanish fishermen over the course of several days. Under coercion, Sanchez and his companions guided their assailants to two haciendas, the first belonging to a widow named Doña Violante Ponçe and the second owned by Lope de Morla. Between the two estates, Sanchez's captors seized nine people of African descent, including an elderly man and a mother with her two children.[82] The nine victims of this violent raid found themselves transported back to Jamaica and trafficked into slavery on the English island.

The traffickers who took those nine people of African descent captive in Hispaniola made a calculated choice that reflected changing administrative and commercial conditions in Jamaica. A statement made by one of the traffickers highlights the economic incentives that drove small-scale captive-taking and human trafficking in this moment. According to Sanchez, one of the traffickers admitted that he and his companions had "nowhere to go unless they took a good prize."[83] It is worth speculating about what he meant and how financial pressures from merchant financiers shaped the choices that those traffickers made in the summer of 1664. Investors expected a quick profit from raids in return for the funds, usually between £100 or £200 per vessel, that they invested in outfitting ships. The two ships sailed by Sanchez's captors, at a hundred and seventy tons, respectively, were larger than most Jamaican-built vessels, which indicates that these ships were themselves former prizes. As historian Nuala Zahedieh shows, prizes of this sort were sold "at knock-down prices" in Jamaica because the admiralty courts there tended to sell ships deemed legal prizes well below market value.[84] For traffickers who needed to make their voyage by returning with a profit for investors, however, the chance of a prize being deemed illegitimate or being sold at a low price incentivized seeking other sources of profit, namely, people who could be trafficked into the voracious slave markets of early English Jamaica. The nine individuals seized by Sanchez's captors, for example, would have sold for around £19 for each adult and slightly less for the elderly man and the two children.[85] Crucially, trafficking captives into slavery could also be done more covertly than attempting to sell a prize ship in Port Royal's harbor, thereby evading the jurisdiction of the admiralty court altogether. For enslaved and free people of African descent, these mundane economic calculations on the part of traffickers resulted in violent raids and forced dislocation from family and communities of belonging throughout the Caribbean.

The administrative changes that incentivized captive-taking—the creation of admiralty courts and the presence of representatives of the Royal Adventurers in Jamaican markets—meant that traffickers developed covert methods of trafficking human captives into slavery after 1660. The traffickers who seized the nine captives from Hispaniola likely trafficked those women, men, and children into slavery in Jamaica through one of various guises. Between the admiralty courts and the monopoly over the slave trade to Jamaica claimed by the Royal Adventurers, the risk that the captives might be deemed illegitimate "prizes" was high. One method used for trafficking captives beyond the purview of English officials in Port Royal involved using the maritime geography surrounding Jamaica to conduct trade. Many traffickers, for example, used the Cayman Islands as an isolated anchorage to conduct technically illicit trade. As early as the 1640s, multinational mariners had used the Cayman Islands for careening, exchanging information, and forming partnerships. By the 1660s, the islands hosted permanent settlements removed from imperial oversight.

A French sailor named Jean Pixon, for example, claimed that he lived among French sailors in the Caymans in the early 1660s before sailing for Tortuga.[86] At the same time, an English captain named Samuel Hutchinson claimed that an Englishman named "Captain Ary" served as the leader of the sailors and others who congregated at the Caymans.[87] Officials in Jamaica, however, viewed the populations in the Caymans as "diverse Soldiers, Planters, [and] Privateers" who had fled Jamaica and used shelters in the Cayman Islands to hide from "his Majesty's displeasure, or punishment for their past irregular actions, or [prosecution] by their Creditors."[88] Undoubtedly some of the individuals living in rudimentary shelters on the Caymans did so because acts of maritime violence or outstanding debts made a return to English society in Jamaica potentially hazardous. Others, like Jean Pixon, had no previous ties to Jamaica at all.

For traffickers, like those who had taken the nine captives in Hispaniola in the summer of 1664, the Cayman Islands provided cover for trafficking those captives into slavery. Not only were the islands removed from imperial oversight, but they had long-established trade ties with Jamaica that served as a cover for other kinds of trade, including human trafficking. English mariners from Jamaica, after all, fished and hunted turtle in the waters around the Caymans, selling fresh and salted maritime protein to the burgeoning population of Port Royal.[89] Provisioning, in other words, served as the perfect cover for human trafficking. The example of one Jamaican trafficker named Thomas Stedman offers a glimpse into the practice of trafficking captives through the Caymans.

Stedman frequently conducted business at those small islands, such as when he sold a boy of African descent to a Bermudian merchant and shipbuilder named Anthony Peniston. In 1664, Peniston sent his ship, the *Blessing*, to the Caymans where the ship's captain, John Bristow, purchased the boy, likely taken captive during a raid in neighboring Cuba.[90] That same year, Peniston arranged for the purchase of two Indigenous captives from Stedman at the Caymans.[91] For Stedman and Peniston, the Cayman Islands provided a maritime rendezvous removed from the oversight of imperial officials where they could engage in the trafficking of captives seized during small-scale raids against Spanish Caribbean shipping and settlements. For the Afro-Cuban boy or the two Indigenous captives trafficked through the Caymans, imperial oversight in neighboring Jamaica added additional time to their maritime journeys before being trafficked into slavery elsewhere. Their experiences proved far from uncommon in the early 1660s.

English colonists in places like Jamaica proved ready customers for traffickers who brought captives to sell because of a growing resentment toward the monopoly of the Royal Adventurers. Traffickers and colonists, in other words, had mutually reinforcing reasons to subvert the monopoly of the company. For their part, English colonists proved willing accomplices with traffickers because many believed that the Royal Adventurers' monopoly on the slave trade unfairly drove up the cost of purchasing enslaved Africans. English colonists throughout the Caribbean also resented the Royal Adventurers because of the Grillo and Lomelín asiento. By 1664, the Royal Adventurers had finalized a subcontract with the new asiento holders that allowed them to use islands like Jamaica and Barbados as entrepôts in the intra-Caribbean slave trade to Spanish America. In response, English colonists complained that the Royal Adventurers favored Spanish American markets, leaving Anglo-Caribbean colonies without as many enslaved African women, men, and children as Anglo-Jamaicans wanted to purchase.[92] Disgruntled colonists throughout the English Caribbean became ready buyers of captive people from traffickers through various means, including those used by Stedman at the Caymans. Traffickers, too, found captive-taking provided greater returns than seizing Spanish ships as prizes, creating a violent and precarious environment for vulnerable populations throughout the Spanish Caribbean. Escalating tensions and commercial competition between the English and Dutch, meanwhile, would soon erupt into a destructive war with devastating consequences for populations of African descent in the Caribbean.

Anglo-Dutch Competition and the
Intra-Caribbean Slave Trade

By the summer of 1664, Gaspar de Espinosa had experienced being taken captive and trafficked into slavery for a second time. Details of his second captivity are sparse, although he was clearly enslaved in St. Croix before he escaped to Puerto Rico with four other people of African descent.[93] As a translator of African descent who frequently served as an intermediary for traffickers, it is easy to imagine Espinosa being taken captive during a negotiation gone wrong. The years following the sinking of the *Carlos Quinto* provided multiple opportunities for just that sort of perilous interaction. Despite the removal of Novoa and creation of the Grillo and Lomelín asiento, Puerto Rico's English and Dutch neighbors persisted in their attempts to secure an informal trade with the Spanish island. Perhaps, too, traffickers simply seized Espinosa during one of their raids on Puerto Rico. The Virgin Islands and Vieques, after all, provided secure anchorages in close proximity to Puerto Rico for just those kinds of multinational maritime predators. Whatever the conditions of his second captivity, Atlantic-wide efforts to formalize the intra-Caribbean slave trade under the auspices of the new asiento and English and Dutch monopoly slave-trading companies did not make the Caribbean any less predatory for individuals like Espinosa. Recentering Puerto Rico in the wider history of changes to the intra-Caribbean and transatlantic slave trades in the 1660s reveals the continuation of practices of raiding and informal trade in the region.

As the Royal Adventurers and the WIC competed for subcontracts from the new asiento holders, regional rivalries also played out in the Caribbean. In the eastern Caribbean, for example, the governor of St. Christopher vied with neighboring Tortola over the informal trade in captive Africans to Puerto Rico. In May 1663, Lieutenant-Governor William Watts of St. Christopher sent an intermediary to Puerto Rico with an offer. Watts had a long career as a merchant sea captain, giving him an intimate knowledge of the

wider networks of informal trade in the Lesser Antilles and greater Caribbean, including the long-standing commercial ties between Puerto Rico and
St. Christopher.[94] With that in mind, Watts dispatched an intermediary, a
man who claimed to be a Dominican priest named Padre Martin, to discuss
the possibility of trade with Puerto Rico's new governor, Juan Pérez de Guzmán y Chagoyen. Padre Martin explained to Pérez de Guzmán that Watts
sent him to establish an annual trade with Puerto Rico for five hundred to a
thousand enslaved Africans in exchange for "gold, silver or fruits of the country."[95] The English governor's offer pre-dated the Royal Adventurers securing
a subcontract with the Genoese and likely pointed to Watts's efforts to secure
St. Christopher as a regional entrepôt in anticipation of successful negotiations between the English company and the new asiento holders.

It turned out that Watts had local competition in his efforts to establish
an informal trade with neighboring Puerto Rico. The next year, in July 1664,
Pérez de Guzmán received a similar offer in the form of a letter from the
merchant proprietor of neighboring Tortola. Addressed to Pérez de Guzmán,
Willem Hunthum offered a direct trade in enslaved Africans to Puerto Rico
as well. As he explained in the letter, "every year slaves from two or three
ships" were sold in Tortola, and a commerce between the two islands was
something that Hunthum concluded "might serve you."[96] For his part, Puerto
Rico's new governor rejected both offers to establish an informal trade with
his English and Dutch counterparts.

Despite ending in failure, the offers presented by both Watts and Hunthum
point to a significant blurring between licensed, intra-Caribbean trade and
networks of informal trade in human captives. Both offers, for example,
exceeded the parameters of the Grillo and Lomelín asiento, which only allowed
asiento factors to transport enslaved Africans to the ports of Cartagena, Veracruz, and Portobelo in the early 1660s. Puerto Rico would not receive permission to admit asiento ships until 1667.[97] In the case of Hunthum's offer, the
merchant proprietor of Tortola also attempted to reinstate older practices of
human trafficking in Puerto Rico. In his letter, Hunthum requested that "if it
happens that some slaves escape from this Island that you secure them and
give me notice."[98]

Rendition of self-liberated captives had served as a cover for informal
trade during the tenure of Pérez de Guzmán's predecessor, Novoa, and
Hunthum likely understood this request as a way to continue that practice
while creating a more secure slave society on maritime Tortola. As Espinosa
would discover when he escaped from the island of St. Croix during the

summer of 1664, the maritime mobility of people of African descent would make Pérez de Guzmán respond, just not in the way his Dutch counterpart expected. And, as Espinosa's experience as a captive trafficked into slavery in the Virgin Islands makes clear, the enslaved Africans offered by both Watts and Hunthum undoubtedly also included individuals taken captive in different parts of the greater Caribbean and trafficked into slavery. Despite efforts to formalize the intra-Caribbean and transatlantic slave trades in the 1660s, regional networks of informal trade shaped by raiding and captive-taking continued to influence the experiences of individuals in the greater Caribbean to a profound degree.

Within a year of Espinosa's escape from St. Croix, warfare engulfed the Caribbean. The causes of the Second Anglo-Dutch War (1665–67) were global in scope as the two Protestant rivals competed over trade in Asia, Africa, and the Americas during the 1650s and 1660s.[99] In the Caribbean, the same practices of raiding and captive-taking that had stymied the efforts of European officials to formalize the intra-Caribbean and transatlantic slave trade also refracted the violence of inter-imperial warfare. Caribbean governors used raiding and captive-taking as a method for waging war, mobilizing traffickers and soldiers of fortune to target specific islands that served as regional entrepôts as well as the plantations settlements of their rivals. The resulting violence institutionalized captive-taking as a method of waging war in the Caribbean, with dramatic and devastating consequences for populations of Africans descent. At the declaration of war, for example, Governor Thomas Modyford of Jamaica launched an attack on Dutch islands in the eastern Caribbean that had attained a level of regional notoriety in the intra-Caribbean slave trade. As had been the case when ship captains like Robert Gordon signed onto the invasion of Santiago de Cuba in 1662, the ship captains, soldiers, and sailors who joined the English invasion of the Dutch islands of St. Eustatius and Saba in 1665 did so on the promise of reaping substantial financial rewards in the form of captive people of African descent.[100]

The English assault on St. Eustatius and Saba would have profound consequences for the 942 people of African descent taken captive off of those islands. The soldiers of fortune who took those people captive divided them based on their perceived value, claiming as their pay those young, healthy, and experienced captives who they assumed would fetch high prices in Jamaica. The soldiers selected nearly five hundred individuals who would endure the maritime passage back to Jamaica in vessels equipped for warfare and not the transportation of captives. The remainder of the women, men, and children seized off of the Dutch islands found themselves sold into slavery in St. Christopher and Nevis, separated permanently from the individuals trafficked back to Jamaica.[101] For the captives, the sorting process by the English paralleled other moments during slavery when their bodies were physically handled and appraised, with prices based off of their anticipated productive capacity. Nor would it be the final time that the individuals sold in St. Christopher and Nevis would experience violent dislocation.

By 1666, France joined the war with their Dutch allies and French forces invaded the English settlements of the jointly held island of St. Christopher.[102] Enslaved people of African descent, including the captives recently trafficked from St. Eustatius and Saba, experienced the brunt of this violence as French soldiers targeted English plantations on the island. The French committed "many wastes, damages, and devastations," according to English residents of St. Christopher who complained that they "accommodated themselves . . . as victorious soldiers do."[103] Over the remaining year of the war, French forces allegedly took nearly 1,700 people of African descent captive from the English islands of St. Christopher, Nevis, Antigua, and Montserrat.[104] For the women, men, and children seized off of St. Eustatius and Saba, the Second Anglo-Dutch War meant repeated encounters with rapacious European soldiers, forced separations from family, and the uncertainty of being trafficked into slavery on distant, foreign islands. The institutionalization of captive-taking as a method for waging inter-imperial war in the 1660s resulted in the widespread suffering of the people who were viewed as so-called "prizes" by invading armies.[105] It was a practice, moreover, that outlived the monopoly slave-trading companies whose economic competition in the greater Caribbean contributed to the outbreak of war in the first place.

For the English Royal Adventurers, the prospects of engaging in the intra-Caribbean slave trade via the new asiento crumbled against the realities of commercial competition with the Dutch and widespread Caribbean raiding. English crews did not confine their raids to Dutch targets when war broke out. Older habits of attacking and raiding Spanish islands persisted perhaps most dramatically with the voyage of Edward Mansvelt and Henry Morgan from Jamaica in 1666. Rather than use their forces against a Dutch foe, Mansvelt and Morgan launched an assault on the Spanish presidio at Providencia, where they seized captives of African descent and trafficked them into slavery in Jamaica. Among those captives was Catalina Angola's son, Salvador Francisco de la Peña. For everything that happened over the course of the 1660s, in other words, practices of raiding and captive taking persisted. For people taken captive in this violent world, however, the 1660s and 1670s witnessed broad changes that would alter their prospects in slavery and freedom. While the creation of the Grillo and Lomelín asiento led to commercial competition and increasing violence, it also created new forms of oversight in Spanish Caribbean cities and ports. For captives who escaped captivity in neighboring English, French, or Dutch settlements, such as Salvador Francisco, the results of this new system of oversight would prove highly ambiguous.

CHAPTER 6

"Free as Any Children of Adam"

Warfare, Racialized Vulnerability, and the English Invasion of Jamaica

Standing before Spanish officials in Havana in 1668, a woman of African descent from Brazil named Madalena explained how she and her daughter arrived on the island of Cuba in a stolen fishing vessel along with eleven other people. As she explained, the group had escaped captivity in Port Royal, Jamaica, with the aid of a Cuban fisherman whom they had liberated from the island's prison. Among the captives, Madalena had spent the most time in unfreedom. In 1658, she had been taken captive off of a boat in the Bay of All Saints in Brazil by French traffickers who transported her to the island of Tortuga where they sold her into slavery. She spent two years enslaved on Tortuga, during which time she gave birth to her daughter, before she was sold again to a French merchant residing in Port Royal. Madalena lived and labored in the bustling English port city for the next seven years before her escape. Now, a decade later, Madalena defended her free status before Spanish officials, declaring that she "was born free and, as such, still is." Crucially, this meant that her daughter inherited her mother's free status, regardless of the circumstances surrounding her birth.[1] Captivity by French traffickers and the experience of being commodified twice in less than ten years, as she argued, had not made slaves of Madalena or her daughter.[2]

At least one man in the room had reason to disagree with Madalena's articulation of her status. Listening to her testimony was Nicolás Castellón y Sánchez Pereira, the resident judge who represented Grillo and Lomelín in issues surrounding the newly created monopoly on the slave trade to Spanish America. Castellón claimed legal ownership over the Afro-descended captives who arrived from neighboring Jamaica on behalf of the new asiento holders. To Castellón, the Cuban fisherman who piloted the stolen boat was undoubtedly attempting to smuggle the Afro-descended passengers into slavery rather than free them from captivity. And, he argued, by virtue of the asiento contract, Grillo and Lomelín had the right to "all of the Blacks that are introduced [in Cuba] and the value of them," including captives trafficked by smugglers.[3]

Madalena's claims to freedom also fell on deaf ears among the other men in the room, some of whom argued that she, her daughter, and her ten companions should be granted their freedom—an argument that assumed they had become slaves in the course of being taken captive in the Americas and trafficked by northern Europeans. Rather than acknowledge her free status prior to captivity, Governor Francisco Oregón y Gascón argued that Madalena should be granted her freedom because she escaped from enemy heretics and sought to live among Catholics in Spanish territory. In making this argument, Oregón articulated a new Spanish Caribbean policy intended to weaken northern European colonies in the region by encouraging individuals enslaved by Protestants to escape. In the face of those officials, Madalena continued to articulate her free status, rejecting outright the logic that captivity and trafficking had ever made her a slave.

Madalena's testimony in 1668, and the competing interpretations of her status, lay bare the racialized vulnerability experienced by captives of African descent who were trafficked across imperial jurisdictions. Madalena's removal from the community of her birth—where family, neighbors, and community members would have attested to her free status—led officials in Havana to treat her like a slave. Nor was Madalena's case unique. Focusing on the years surrounding the English invasion of Jamaica in 1655 and Madalena's testimony in 1668, this chapter explores the intersection of mobility, racialized vulnerability, and status for captives of African descent trafficked to and from the island of Jamaica. Focusing on the experiences of people taken captive and trafficked during this period reveals how territorial contestation in the form of the 1655 English invasion of Jamaica exposed different notions of race and status between the Spanish and English, while changes to the nature of the transatlantic slave trade to Spanish America meant that people who escaped captivity, like Madalena, became vulnerable to racialized interpretations of their legal status. The confluence of warfare and new slave-trading methods, in other words, had important consequences for free people of African descent trafficked away from the communities where their free status was recognized.

An analysis of the experiences of people taken captive and trafficked away from communities of belonging intersects with a growing body of scholarship on the movement of people of African descent across imperial borders in the seventeenth and eighteenth centuries. Historians have shown, for example, that self-liberated Africans and their descendants drove the creation of a sanctuary policy in Spanish America in which enslaved people who escaped from English, French, and Dutch colonies and sought baptism in the Catholic church were granted their freedom. By the late seventeenth century, the Spanish sanctuary policy provided important avenues for freedom for enslaved people who could escape and travel to Spanish territory.[4] Some scholars have interpreted the experience of Madalena and her companions through the lens of this sanctuary policy, arguing that everyone in the group save one received their freedom.[5] The experiences of the escapees from Jamaica, however, were more complicated and their eventual fate more ambiguous because of the profound changes enacted to the intra-Caribbean and transatlantic slave trades during the 1660s. Religion and vassalage, in other words, were not the only factors that influenced what happened to individuals of African descent who sought sanctuary in the second half of the seventeenth century. Rather, people of African descent encountered a Spanish Atlantic profoundly shaped by the unprecedented authority that the Spanish Crown granted to representative factors of the Grillo and Lomellín asiento. The formalization of the slave trade under the new asiento, as scholars Tatiana Seijas and Alejandro García-Montón have argued, "Africanized" slavery in Spanish America as other forms of licensed trade in bound labor were subsumed by the Grillo and Lomelín monopoly.[6] These wider changes meant that the statuses of Madalena and her companions were contested by representatives of the asiento in Cuba who viewed the group not as potential converts or vassals but as Blacks and slaves.

Territorial contestation between the English and the Spanish and subsequent changes to the intra-Caribbean slave trade unsettled many of the recognized social and corporate statuses that undergirded the position of Africans and their descendants in Spanish Caribbean society. This was particularly true for individuals who moved between Spanish and English spheres by coercion or by choice. A granular examination of the experiences of two groups of captives reveals the differences between Spanish and English practices surrounding race, martial service, and subjecthood at mid-century. Crucially, however, a close focus on a relatively small number of people also shows the vulnerability experienced by people of African descent who were removed from the local Spanish American circumstances that anchored their corporate, social, and economic identities. As these cases show, captivity and trafficking meant that the statuses that captives held collapsed from relatively fluid interpretations based on a number of factors to the singular category of Blackness and slavery. This chapter explores the limits of racial fluidity for two groups of people of African descent in the context of mid-century warfare and dislocation. Crucially, as Madalena and her companions experienced, territorial contestation and changes to the intra-Caribbean slave trade would have profound consequences for people trafficked across imperial borders.

Race and Status in the Mid-Century Spanish Caribbean

The English invasion of Spanish Jamaica and the subsequent development of the island colony were deeply entangled with practices of captivity and human trafficking. By the time Madalena and her companions fled to Cuba, northern European traffickers had been selling captives into slavery among the English in Jamaica for over a decade. During the five-year struggle between English and Spanish forces over Jamaica that began with the English invasion in 1655, English soldiers also seized captives from among the racially diverse populations of Maroons and soldiers defending the island. Those captives found themselves trafficked off of the island and into slavery elsewhere. The experiences of one group of people taken captive during English efforts to seize Jamaica who were from a region near the Porus Mountains and trafficked off of the island show how captivity and human trafficking shaped not just the English invasion but the experiences of people of African descent during this moment of territorial contestation. Understanding the treatment that Madalena and her companions experienced in English Jamaica, as well as their continued racialized vulnerability in Cuba, requires tracing how captivity and race shaped the English invasion of Jamaica and the subsequent development of the island colony.

The English invasion of Jamaica began with much bigger ambitions than simply seizing a single Spanish island in the Greater Antilles. Oliver Cromwell, Lord Protector of England during the interregnum, had dispatched a fleet in 1654 with dreams of dislodging the Spanish entirely from the Americas. Under the command of Admiral William Penn and General Robert Venables, the English force attacked Hispaniola first, assuming that an easy victory there would allow them to seize surrounding Spanish Antillean spaces and,

eventually, the mainland territories of Mexico and Peru. The invasion of Hispaniola proved disastrous, as poor planning, the virulent Caribbean disease
environment, and the effectiveness of the Spanish defense killed thousands
of English soldiers.[7] With the surviving men, many of whom were sick and
dispirited, Venables and Penn set their sights on Jamaica, where they anticipated an easy victory that would save them from returning to England empty-
handed. The inhabitants of Jamaica's capital city, Santiago de la Vega, fled to
the mountains when the English landed while the governor, Juan Ramírez de
Arellano, entered into negotiations. When the intent of the English to occupy
Jamaica permanently became clear, a contingent of Spanish residents refused
to abandon Jamaica and launched the beginning of a five-year struggle to
hold the island.[8]

Under the command of Cristóbal Arnaldo de Ysassi, the Spanish resistance in Jamaica relied on alliances with autonomous communities of African
descent in the interior of the island, some of which were composed of individuals who had used the English invasion to escape slavery. Soldiers of African and Indigenous descent dispatched from other parts of Spain's American
territories also undergirded the Spanish military efforts. Guerrilla warfare in
Jamaica turned in the favor of the English in 1659 when English troops located
one of the island's three autonomous Black communities, led by a man named
Juan Lubolo. To prevent English raids on their community, Lubolo and his
followers allied with the English and assisted in the successful raid of a neighboring community near a region between the Mocho Mountains and Porus.
An analysis of the context surrounding the Porus captives, from their role
in Spanish Jamaican society before the invasion through their experiences
as captives trafficked off of the island in 1660, reveals the centrality of race,
captive-taking, and trafficking in the wider history of the English invasion of
Jamaica.[9]

Recent scholarship on sixteenth- and seventeenth-century Spanish America has shown race to be relatively fluid in colonial contexts where other cat-
egories of social organization, such as economic status, familial and political
connections, or religious affiliation, often proved more important. This was
especially true in the greater Caribbean, where Africans and their descendants
formed demographic majorities in many regions. As the foundation of colonial society, racial status tended not to curtail the social and economic status
of people of African descent within their communities of belonging in the
sixteenth and seventeenth centuries in the same way that it would by the eighteenth century.[10] Corporate identities, in other words, often mattered more

in social, legal, and economic interactions than race alone. For individuals of African descent in Spanish America who belonged to larger organizations that provided them with recognized social status or legal privileges, such as military service, corporate identities allowed them to access the rights and privileges associated with vassalage to the Spanish monarchy.[11] This stood in contrast to English ideas about race and status in this period.[12] Those views had been shaped by decades of raiding and captive-taking by English ship captains and crews who viewed people of African descent as so-called prizes who could be seized and sold into slavery—often regardless of their status before being taken captive.

As with other parts of the Spanish Caribbean, race was a relatively fluid category in the social landscape of Spanish Jamaica on the eve of the English invasion. Throughout the first half of the seventeenth century, Africans and their descendants performed the free and enslaved labor essential for ranching and agricultural production in Jamaica's rural hinterlands. Disruptions to the transatlantic slave trade in the 1640s and 1650s meant that the majority of the enslaved population in Jamaica had resided among Iberians long enough to be considered *ladinos*, or Africans acculturated to Spanish language, religion, and custom.[13] People of African descent formed the demographic majority in Jamaica by the first half of the seventeenth century, and, as with other parts of the Spanish Caribbean, it was often their economic, social, or corporate position rather than their race that defined their status. Some long-standing elite creole families in Spanish Jamaica were of African descent, including the Ysassis, a family that played an important role in Spanish efforts to retain the island following the English invasion. Their social prominence and economic standing allowed male members of the family to attain prestigious positions in Jamaica and Cuba. In fact, the racial background of a scion of the family, Cristóbal Arnaldo de Ysassi, was noted only when opponents of his military leadership used it to insult him late in the war against the English.[14]

Prior to the English invasion, the Spanish Jamaican captives from Porus lived and labored on strategically important *hatos*, or open-range cattle and sheep ranches, of Guatibacoa, in central Jamaica.[15] Their roles as agricultural producers were central to the Spanish Jamaican economy and the resilience of the Spanish defense against the English invasion. The Porus region, just west of the island's largest town of Santiago de la Vega, provided urban residents and passing ships with meat, agricultural products, and cattle hides. Spanish Jamaican society was overwhelmingly rural in the early seventeenth century, with populations in the countryside surpassing the urban center of

Santiago de la Vega.[16] Food production in Spanish Jamaica's many rural *hatos* proved invaluable during the five years of guerrilla warfare following the English invasion in 1655, when the Spanish resistance withdrew to Jamaica's mountainous interior and pursued a campaign of hit-and-run tactics against the English. That strategy depended, in part, on the ability of the Spanish resistance to move unhindered through the island's interior and their access to foodstuffs from the local *hatos*.[17] Guatibacoa, for example, situated at the southern end of an agricultural corridor in the center of the island, created space for the movement of Ysassi's troops between the northern and southern coasts, while the predominantly Afro-descended communities at Guatibacoa and elsewhere provided the Spanish resistance with meat and other foodstuffs.[18] In terms of the Africans and their descendants who lived in the Porus region, their communities occupied a central role in Spanish Jamaican society in the decades leading up to the invasion, and their role in supplying Ysassi and his forces allowed the Spanish to maintain a toehold on the island over five years of guerrilla warfare.

Race and Status During the English Western Design, ca. 1655

The English invasion of Hispaniola and Jamaica brought different views of race, subjecthood, and status into conflict. English assumptions about the status of Blacks in the Spanish Caribbean had dire consequences for the soldiers and sailors involved in the Western Design. Free people of African descent in the Spanish Caribbean, as seen above, were considered vassals of the Spanish Crown, and some attained positions of prominence. As Cromwell and his advisors planned the Western Design, however, they imagined that Africans and their descendants were uniformly enslaved and would welcome the arrival of English forces in order to overthrow the Spanish.[19] When English soldiers attempted to seize Santo Domingo in 1654, however, men of African descent defended their homes and communities from the English invaders. The flattening of all Afro-descended people on Hispaniola to the condition of slavery on the part of English planners backfired in a region where the interests of free Blacks could and did align with the maintenance of Spanish sovereignty over the island. The narrowing of all martial options to resistance to slavery on the part of English planners ignored the more complicated racial dynamics in the Spanish Caribbean and, among other factors, resulted in the defeat of the Western Design forces at Hispaniola. Nor were free people of

African descent alone in taking up arms against the English—enslaved African men also chose to defend their families and communities from English forces. Clearly, the assumptions that English planners took into the Western Design had less salience for some people of African descent with communal, familial, and religious ties in the Spanish Caribbean.

In other cases, international war in the Caribbean provided avenues for securing the subject position of men of African descent and their dependents in Jamaica and beyond. For enslaved men of African descent in Jamaica, the English invasion offered them the opportunity to secure their freedom in exchange for military service among Ysassi's Spanish resistance.[20] Over the course of the conflict, moreover, New Spain sent over a thousand soldiers, many of whom were of African and Indigenous descent, to Jamaica in three separate voyages between 1656 and 1659.[21] One such soldier, a man from New Spain named Domingo Rolón, was sent with his mixed-race regiment, called the *tercio mexicano*, to Jamaica. Once there, Rolón attained the rank of captain and fought at the Battle of Río Nuevo in June 1658. Rolón had "done much damage to the Enemies" in that battle before he was killed in action. In recognition of his service, the Spanish Crown ordered that Rolón's widow, an enslaved woman of African descent named Gracia de Fuentes, be given her freedom and "two Reales a day in order to sustain herself."[22] Rolón's service followed a well-worn path to freedom and economic advancement deployed by men of African descent throughout Spain's American territories.[23] Gracia de Fuentes found her freedom and economic survival tied to her husband's role, and ultimately his death, serving the Spanish Crown. International warfare in Jamaica, then, provided men of African descent and their dependents with a means to "claim the honor and reputation of loyal vassals," along with the corporate status and protection that that subject position implied.[24] As will be seen, however, that corporate status often relied on the ability of Africans and their descendants to remain rooted in local contexts where that status was recognized.

The English participants in the Western Design brought their own nascent ideas about racial hierarchies and the military service of people of African descent to the five-year engagement in Jamaica. Crucially, English mariners and ship captains had raided Spanish Caribbean towns and shipping for the previous half century, taking Africans and their descendants as captives and trafficking them into slavery. Embedded in the interactions between English soldiers and Spanish Jamaica's racially stigmatized defenders, in other words, was the notion of the commodifiability of captives of African descent. For

their part, many of the English soldiers also insisted on strict racial hierarchies to protest being forced to perform what they saw as degrading manual
labor during the English invasion and occupation of Spanish Jamaica. As
Kristen Block argues, the effective resistance of predominantly soldiers of
African descent on Hispaniola reshaped English expectations from assuming
that they could rely on racialized others as allies to "insisting on their subju-
gation, casting them as rebellious slaves," regardless of their prior legal status
within the Spanish Caribbean.[25]

Racialized slavery in the English Caribbean and widespread practices of
captive-taking shaped English views of race and status during the invasion
of Jamaica. Over the course of the English invasion and subsequent warfare
over the island, for example, English soldiers and mariners seized captives of
African descent at sea and on the island. As the governor-general of Jamaica,
Edward D'Oyley, explained, enslaved captives were seen as "the prize of soldiers, who receive[d] no pay" otherwise.[26] The English soldiers dispatched as
part of the Western Design, in other words, immediately embraced the commodification of racially stigmatized Spanish Caribbean war captives. From
viewing Africans and their descendants in the Spanish Caribbean as possible
allies to "rebellious slaves" and "prizes," nascent English expectations and
racial ideologies differed sharply from prevailing Spanish Caribbean practices
and would have dire consequences for the Porus captives.

The conflict over control of Jamaica turned in 1659 when English troops
located the community of Juan Lubolo. Well defended with ample gardens
and fields in the Lluidas Vale, Lubolo's community had provisioned and
offered other forms of aid to Ysassi's forces. The discovery of their town by
the English threatened Lubolo's community with continual harassment by
the English. As a result, Lubolo and his community negotiated an alliance
with the English in which they would remain free and in possession of their
territory in exchange for assisting the English in rooting out the remaining
Spanish resistance.[27] In early 1660, Lubolo's forces and the English launched
joint assaults against two neighboring villages. The raid against the community near Porus resulted in the seizure of between fifty and sixty captives,
who were subsequently sold to English merchants in Port Royal. These captives constituted 17 to 27 percent of the population of African descent on
the island, and 41 to 60 percent of those remaining loyal to the Spanish after
Lubolo's defection.[28] Their capture turned the tide in favor of the English
war effort and significantly altered Jamaica's social landscape.[29] According
to Mavis C. Campbell, Afro-Jamaicans from Lubolo's community moved

into the recently depopulated region and west toward Clarendon shortly after they raided the territory.[30] International warfare created conditions for Lubolo and his community to achieve a corporate status under the English. The recognition of the autonomy of Lubolo's community came at the expense of the Porus captives' freedom and with the caveat that Lubolo's community would police the boundaries of English Jamaica's nascent plantation system by capturing and returning any self-liberated slaves to the English.

Prisoners of War, Captives, and Trafficking

For the fifty women, men, and children seized from Porus in the summer of 1660, their captivity severed their ties to Jamaica and subjected them to being trafficked into slavery. After their sale in Port Royal, the Porus captives were forced aboard the larger of two English ships sailing to Portobelo. During the five years of guerrilla warfare in Jamaica that followed the invasion, they had joined the Spanish resistance, defended their communities and livelihoods against English forces, and sought to secure their positions as vassals of the Spanish Crown through their martial service.[31] But as captives, the Spanish Jamaicans were forced below the decks of a four-hundred-ton merchant vessel perversely called the *Blessing*, where they found room wherever they could between the bales of imported silks and other commodities. They likely had no sense of the *Blessing*'s destination, but, as people of African descent forced into the hold of an English ship, they undoubtedly understood the precarity of their situation. As captives with an intimate knowledge of Jamaican geography and martial experience against the English, the Porus captives were trafficked off of the island rather than sold locally.

The captives spent a month at sea before the English captain, a man named Robert Breton, attempted to sell them into slavery in Portobelo.[32] Breton was a notorious trafficker with a long history of engaging in a variety of legal and illegal trade throughout the Iberian Atlantic. A Sevillian pilot who accompanied Breton to Portobelo recalled having "spoken with [Breton] in Spain, in Madrid, Sevilla, and Cadiz" in the years before their voyage together.[33] Officials in Panama likewise declared that Breton was "a person well known" on that coast for engaging in informal trade.[34] Breton, in turn, relied on his knowledge of regional markets as well as diverse tactics common among traffickers in his attempt to sell the Porus captives into slavery in another part of Spanish America. Portobelo was an obvious market for Breton to approach first. Northern European merchants had used the Panamanian coastline to conduct illicit trade since the latter half of the sixteenth century, but the decline of the legal slave trade after 1640 led to the rise of Portobelo as a potentially receptive market for English and Dutch slave traders.[35] As Alejandro García-Montón has shown, royal officials in Portobelo often facilitated the illicit slave trade with northern European merchants who "began arriving regularly along Portobelo's coast from late 1657 onward."[36] Although most of the informal slave trade of the 1650s was carried out by Dutch merchants, the fact that Breton was "well known" in Portobelo indicates that the Porus captives likely were not the first people of African descent the English captain trafficked to Panama.

International warfare in Jamaica gave Breton a legal cover for approaching the Panamanian coast. Prisoner of war exchanges had long served as a pretext for engaging in informal trade, and the five-year struggle over possession of Jamaica created numerous prisoners of war. As with other moments in the Caribbean, Breton carried not prisoners of war but individuals who had been taken captive at sea during extensive English raids of Spanish shipping and surrounding port cities over the course of the war. Those repeated, small-scale raids produced a steady flow of captives into English Jamaica, some of whom were trafficked into slavery while others were used in prisoner of war exchanges.[37] The experiences of one of the prisoners on board Breton's ship, an Afro-descended man named Tomás Gutierrez, provides a window into the intersection of raiding and racialized vulnerability for captives of African descent. Alongside Gutierrez were three other prisoners—a priest taken captive off of a merchant vessel carrying cacao from Caracas to New Spain, a man from New Spain named Antonio Vazquez who had been held captive in Jamaica for the previous three years, and an Iberian pilot who claimed to be a captive named Joseph Vargas Machuca but turned out to be a known criminal named Diego Lobatón. Among the four, only Gutierrez experienced the instability of his status as a man of African descent trafficked away from his community of belonging.[38]

For people of African descent, the vulnerability to being sold into slavery heightened the stakes involved in prisoner of war exchanges. According to his testimony, Gutierrez had been born free and worked as a shoemaker in Coro, Venezuela. As he explained to authorities in Portobelo, he and a companion had been gathering plantains along the coast when they were taken captive and "carried to Jamaica on an English frigate" where the

English stole his *carta de libertad*, or freedom letter. As Gutierrez explained, the theft of the documentary evidence of his free status left him exposed to being enslaved in Jamaica or sold elsewhere.[39] Of the four prisoners, Gutierrez emphasized that he volunteered to join Breton's venture to Portobelo. According to his testimony, he "embarked of his own pleasure in the said ship . . . as a result of his desire to return to *su tierra*" or his country.[40] While it is possible that Gutierrez's claims of volition were true, this moment in his testimony likely indicates Gutierrez's recognition of his own vulnerable status in this fraught encounter with Spanish authorities at Portobelo. The interrogation allowed Gutierrez to underscore his status as a free man before his captivity, making him a prisoner of war rather than an enslaved man treated as seized property during warfare. The distinction was essential for Gutierrez to maintain his freedom, but he lacked the *carta de libertad* as evidence of his prior status.

The experiences of Gutierrez and the Porus captives at Portobelo reflect wider patterns of racialization in the Iberian Atlantic as well as their removal from local communities that recognized their status as free. In the case of Gutierrez, Spanish officials debated not whether he was free before his captivity but, rather, the timing of his captivity and the legality of Breton's claims that he was a legitimate "prize" of war. In other words, because the English mariners who seized Gutierrez took him after the end of hostilities in September 1660, Spanish officials at Portobelo argued that he could not legally be considered a prize of war.[41] That legal argument doubtless did little to ease Gutierrez's anxiety. Rather than agreeing with his claim to free status before captivity, authorities in Portobelo debated the timing of the English raid. In other words, Gutierrez's status depended on the nature of his captivity, not his own claims to freedom.

From the surviving archival documentation, Gutierrez's fate is unclear after Breton petitioned for his return according to the laws of war. In a letter sent to the Casa de la Contratación, the governor-general of Panama referenced two Black captives who had been transported by Breton and "would be sold and the proceeds entered into the royal treasury."[42] Whether Gutierrez was one of those two is unclear. Regardless, the legal wrangling over his status reveals the precarity of captives of African descent removed from the local circumstances that undergirded their status as free subjects of the Spanish Crown. Trafficking, in this sense, severed Gutierrez from a social world where his status as a free man would have been common knowledge and set him adrift in a world where his African ancestry made him vulnerable. For an Afro-descended captive like Gutierrez, freedom was a status best guaranteed at the local, rather than the regional, level.

Trafficking the Porus Captives: Mobility and Vulnerability

In the end, Breton had miscalculated in his selection of Portobelo as a receptive port for selling the Porus captives into slavery or smuggling the silks and other goods aboard the *Blessing*. The political environment of Panama had changed by 1661, proving less welcoming to northern European smugglers and slave traders. That year alone, three Dutch slave traders were also prevented from unloading their enslaved captives by the new president of the Audiencia of Panama, Fernando de la Riva Agüero.[43] The Dutch WIC was still a year away from securing a subcontract with Grillo and Lomelín, which made those Dutch slave traders technically smugglers. Frustrated in his attempt to trade in Portobelo, Breton asked Riva Agüero for a supply of beef to continue his voyage, food that might have nourished the Porus captives still chained in the *Blessing*.

Captives trafficked through illicit trade networks, like those from Jamaica on board Breton's ship, often experienced extended periods of time in maritime confinement.[44] For the Porus captives, the detention and interrogation of Breton and the other men aboard the pink added time to the anxious month already spent on board the *Blessing*. If the Porus captives knew that Breton had transported them to Spanish territory, some of the free people of African descent may have hoped that their legal status would ensure their release from captivity. Perhaps others assumed that their service in supporting Ysassi's resistance in Jamaica would have earned them their freedom from slavery and release from English captivity.[45] But the month at sea in the passage between Jamaica and Panama denuded the Porus captives of their previous status. Despite having performed martial service for the Spanish Crown in defending Spanish Jamaica during the invasion, by the time the *Blessing* reached Portobelo the captives from the Porus region of Jamaica had been forcibly removed from the social connections that had previously secured their status. In reports describing the arrival of an English trafficker to Portobelo, the governor-general of Panama characterized the Spanish Jamaican captives from Porus as simply "unos negros . . . que los trae de los Palenques [some Blacks . . . that they brought from the Palenques]."[46]

Breton might have succeeded in smuggling the captives somewhere else along the Panamanian coast, or he might have transported them to English colonists in Virginia.[47] If the Porus captives were sold in Virginia, they might have encountered some of their countrymen from Jamaica. Shortly after Riva Agüero turned Breton away, Cuban patrols seized a small vessel in the waters near the Jardines off of that island's southern coast. On board were nine men of African descent, supporters of Ysassi, who had escaped Jamaica after the Spanish resistance forces abandoned the island. According to one of the men, "all of the Blacks from the Palenques were being seized and sold to those damned English who transported them to Virginia."[48] It is possible that the Porus captives joined those trafficked off of Jamaica and sold in Virginia, but whether anyone in Virginia knew about or commented on who the enslaved captives were or where they had come from is unclear from surviving archival records. Once stripped of their role in the defense of Spanish Jamaica, the Porus settlement captives entered an Atlantic market that commodified their bodies and labor as a people without a past. For the Porus captives, warfare and trafficking laid bare the precarity of racial status and subjecthood in the seventeenth-century Caribbean.

The ambiguity of the status of the Porus captives during the conflict—using martial service to secure vassalage—meant that trafficking reduced their status to that of Maroons or fugitives. That trafficking so dramatically changed the status of the Porus captives underscores the nature of martial service, subjecthood, and legal status as unstable and often dependent on local, rather than imperial, recognition. The experiences of the Porus captives, and that of Tómas Gutierrez, contrast sharply with the martial freedom attained by Juan Lubolo and the members of his community. In exchange for possession of their land and retention of their local leaders, Lubolo and the members of his community agreed to help the English defeat the remaining Spanish resistance.[49] By the terms of that agreement, Lubolo's community attained an autonomous status.

But autonomy was not the same as freedom. Afro-Jamaican men were required to perform martial service for the English in exchange for local autonomy. After Ysassi and the last of the Spanish resistance fled Jamaica, Lubolo and his men were required to help the English fight against the remaining Afro-Jamaican communities and, eventually, to aid in retrieving enslaved Africans who escaped from the growing English plantation economy on the island. In other words, the autonomy of Lubolo's community came at the cost of policing the boundaries of the English colony's growing slave society and was earned through martial service to the English. Freedom papers, in the case of Gutierrez, or having served as loyal vassals, in the case of the Porus captives, ultimately proved less effective than the local, negotiated autonomy attained by Lubolo and his community.

A Christian Algiers and the Intra-Caribbean Slave Trade

The same year that the combined forces of Juan Lubolo and the English took women, men, and children captive from the Porus region in Jamaica, Madalena, whose experiences opened this chapter, found herself sold to a French merchant in Port Royal. English Jamaica had developed a reputation as a "Christian Algiers," due to the parallels between the Caribbean island and Algiers, an infamous North African destination for European captives seized throughout the Mediterranean world by Muslim sailors or so-called Barbary corsairs.[50] Like Algiers for the Mediterranean, Jamaica was in the process of becoming a central node in the trade in captives seized through maritime raids in the Caribbean by the 1660s.[51] During her time on the island, Madalena encountered a flourishing market in captive people who were, according to the English governor, contributing to the "great furtherance" of the colony.[52] English Jamaica deserved its reputation as a Christian Algiers, but unprecedented changes to the intra-Caribbean and transatlantic slave trades in the 1660s would have profound effects on the regional captive economy as well as the experiences of captives like Madalena and her companions. Efforts to formalize the transatlantic and intra-Caribbean slave trades by Spain and England's desire to participate in that trade created conditions in which Madalena and her companions found themselves treated as if they were slaves following their escape from Jamaica to neighboring Cuba.

By mid-century, the creation of a new asiento permitted the purchase of enslaved Africans within the Caribbean from nations at peace with Spain, but it also created ample opportunities for traffickers and others to interlope on the Grillo and Lomelín monopoly on the intra-Caribbean slave trade to Spanish America. In order to regulate the trade in enslaved Africans and to cut down on the informal, extralegal trade that had provisioned much of the Spanish Caribbean previously, the new asiento holders were given permission to position factors throughout Spanish America. These efforts to formalize the intra-Caribbean slave trade had unexpected consequences for captives of African descent like Madalena and her companions. Upon their arrival in Havana, for example, the representative of the asiento claimed ownership over the Afro-descended captives from Jamaica, even though nearly half of them had been free before being taken captive by English traffickers. Nor would their claims to free status prior to captivity be completely respected by Cuba's governor.

A close analysis of the experiences of Madalena and her companions reveals the consequences of the new asiento contract for people of African descent who were taken captive and trafficked across imperial borders. The competing claims of the asiento factor, the governor, and the captives themselves reveal "the combination of disposability and care" that scholar Daniel Nemser calls the "racialized discourse of vulnerability."[53] A focus on their testimonies, however, reveals not just the vulnerability they experienced as the intra-Caribbean and transatlantic slave trades to Spanish America fell under the jurisdiction of the Grillo and Lomelín asiento but also the ways in which the escapees from Jamaica articulated their own understandings of freedom and unfreedom.

Captivity in Port Royal

Just a year after Lubolo and his community finalized their alliance with the English and attacked the Porus community, the woman who opened this chapter arrived in Port Royal, Jamaica. In 1661, the French merchant who held Madalena and her daughter, Dominga, captive in Tortuga sold the mother and daughter to James Martine in Port Royal. Martine's purchase of Madalena and Dominga from another man who claimed ownership over them created a documentary record of their enslavement and covered the illicit provenance of the two captives; should officials in Port Royal ask, Madalena and Dominga were already enslaved when Martine purchased them. It is likely, however, that no one asked about the provenance of the young mother and her child. The English town that Madalena and her daughter resided in for the next seven years was in the process of a rapid transition from a line of warehouses with a poorly built fort to a well-defended and thriving commercial hub. When Madalena arrived in 1661, Port Royal had just under 700 free residents and around 50 enslaved people. A decade later the population had grown to 1,669 people who held 312 individuals as slaves in the town.[54] Small- and large-scale raids throughout the 1660s meant that, much like Tortuga, Madalena and her daughter encountered captives in Port Royal from throughout the Spanish- and Portuguese-speaking world. The social connections Madalena forged in Port Royal with other captives facilitated her eventual escape from captivity among the English.

Over the six years that Madalena spent as an enslaved captive in Jamaica, the English colony had grown considerably. The English built on Spanish foundations. For Afro-descended captives seized from Spanish America and trafficked into places like Santiago de la Vega in Jamaica, certain aspects of the island would have been reminiscent of the towns and countryside from which they had been taken. When the English occupied Santiago de la Vega, they retained the grid design of the streets and the central plazas of the former Spanish Caribbean city. English correspondents initially referred to the town as St. Jago, Anglicizing the original Spanish name, before settling on Spanish Town. The Spanish-era Plaza Mayor remained a focal point of the city's grid design, although the English renamed it the Parade. Flanking the Parade, the houses remained distinctly Spanish in their orientation toward internal courtyards rather than the English style of facing public streets. Captives might have heard Spanish spoken by the Afro-ladinos, such as Major de Campo or Anthony Rodriguez, who had allied themselves with the English during the invasion and were rewarded with plots of land close to the Parade.[55] Some Spanish American captives would have found themselves sold to urban-dwelling English residents, which meant that many of them lived among other free and enslaved people of African descent in housing near the Commons rather than in their enslavers' households.[56] English raiding of Spanish American ships, ports, and towns meant that Spanish American captives in Spanish Town encountered people with whom they shared cultural and linguistic affinities in an urban landscape that was strikingly familiar.

Other Spanish American captives experienced a very different Jamaica from their counterparts in Spanish Town. While many individuals were sold to labor on rural plantations, by the mid-1660s, others like Madalena and her companions joined the growing population of enslaved people in the newly renamed Port Royal.[57] Occupying a spit of land at the entrance to Cagway Harbor, Port Royal quickly emerged as a bustling economic and maritime center for English Jamaica. The brick homes and patios built by Port Royal's mercantile community might have been disorienting for Spanish American captives and the town's streets, which were designed around a triangular shape, beguiling for travelers accustomed to Spanish America's gridded urban centers.[58] Unlike Spanish Caribbean towns, which tended to be built inland to secure against foreigners attacking by sea, Port Royal's orientation was thoroughly maritime. Even fresh water had to be rowed across the harbor from Passage Fort near the Rio Cobre and stored in cisterns in order to maintain the population of Port Royal. Captives in Port Royal labored both for English Jamaica's maritime trades and for English administrators in building fortifications to defend against a feared Spanish or Dutch invasion.

Port Royal's growth during the 1660s relied heavily on the traffickers who brought specie, trade goods, and captives to the town.[59] Scholars have long recognized the importance of maritime raiding for Port Royal's economic development, but the testimonies of Madalena and her companions provide a unique lens onto the experiences of the victims of that raiding economy. Of the eleven people who escaped Port Royal with Madalena and her daughter, five had entered captivity as a result of opportunistic raids starting as early as 1659. The remaining six individuals were seized off of the island of Providencia. Of the four women in the group, only one came from Providencia, underscoring the gendered nature of wartime captivity compared with opportunistic, small-scale raids. Among the men who escaped, only two were seized during a small-scale raid, including Ignacio Hernández and a man named Gregorio Rodriguez. Described as a "mozo," or young man, it is easy to imagine that Ignacio's captors faced little struggle in seizing him. In contrast, the struggle to take Gregorio, an adult man, captive at Rio de la Hacha in 1666 turned violent and resulted in the death of one of Gregorio's companions. Five of the six women who escaped had been seized singly or in groups from as far as Pernambuco and as close as Cuba, their captors undoubtedly viewing women and children as easier targets than adult men.

During her seven years in Port Royal, Madalena would have met some or all of the individuals with whom she would risk her and her daughter's lives in fleeing Jamaica. Passing through the streets of Port Royal while performing errands for Martine, Madalena might have encountered Cathalina and heard about her abduction from Santa Marta. In 1662, Cathalina labored on a rural estate owned by a widow named Graciana de Medina when a group of English traffickers attacked during the night, seizing Cathalina and ten or eleven other people. In relating the story of her captivity to Madalena, Cathalina might have lamented the fact that everyone who had been forcibly transported to Jamaica with her had all been sold to different people. Perhaps this dispersal explains why no one else from the widow Medina's estate escaped alongside Cathalina.

Gregorio Rodriguez experienced a similar kind of abduction as Cathalina when he and two other companions were seized at Rio de la Hacha by an English crew from two large ships that raided the coastline in 1666. Gregorio might have told the two women about his life before captivity, how he sold "cachivaches" or rubbish in the New Granada port town to support his wife. The violence of his captivity, in which one of his companions was killed, might have reminded Cathalina of the nighttime attack that she, too, experienced. Ignacio Hernández undoubtedly related to both of these narratives of captivity, and he might have described his own experience of being taken from a hacienda called the Rincón outside of Cartagena in 1663. He perhaps explained how he and a companion named Juan Patacon were gathering plantains when traffickers seized both boys, selling each to a different buyer in Jamaica. Their shared experiences of captivity, forced transportation, and separation might have helped forge bonds of trust between Madalena and her companions that facilitated the group's escape together.

Among the captives who escaped with Madalena were five men and one woman from the island of Providencia. The struggling Spanish presidio on the former English island was attacked in 1666 by a fleet of privateers under the command of Henry Morgan and Edward Mansvelt under the pretext that the island was still English, even though settlers from the Providence Island Company had been dislodged over twenty years earlier.[60] Among the captives seized by the English force was Salvador Francisco de la Peña, the son of Catalina Angola, the enslaved woman who gained her freedom as a result of Salvador's father's petition to the Spanish Crown in 1646. Salvador Francisco grew up a free man on an island with a large population of mixed-race families alongside his sisters María and Juana. But when the two ship captains attacked Providencia in 1666, at twenty-one years old, Salvador Francisco was taken captive and trafficked into slavery in Jamaica on the pretext of his racial background.[61] Neither his sisters nor his mother joined Salvador Francisco in escaping Jamaica, indicating that the women had avoided being taken captive by Morgan and Mansvelt's forces or that they were sold away from him. For Salvador Francisco and his five companions, the English attack on Providencia destroyed familial and communal ties built up on the island over the previous two decades.

Escape from Port Royal

The labor that Madalena and her companions performed in Port Royal provided them with mobility and social connections that facilitated their escape. For the three adult women who escaped, their enslavement by urban-dwelling merchants gave them ample opportunity to establish friendships with other captives as they performed errands around the city. Many of the male captives labored on Port Royal's fortifications, which positioned them, too, in close proximity with other captives. The likely mastermind behind the escape from Jamaica was Ignacio Hernández. Certainly, Ignacio's mobility and social connections facilitated the communication between captives in Port Royal that was essential for the plan to work.

When a Cuban fisherman named Simon Rodriguez contracted a fever while imprisoned in Port Royal, his English captors called upon Ignacio Hernández to nurse him back to health. The Cuban fisherman had been taken captive when he sailed from Havana in 1666 for a tangle of sandy islands and reefs off of Florida's southern coast. Following the seasonal migrations of sea turtles to the Bahamas, Rodriguez joined a multiethnic assortment of sea workers who hunted the marine creatures to provision regional markets. But in the shallow waters off the coast of Abaco, an English crew took him captive and forced him to labor aboard their vessel, likely in hunting the same turtles Rodriguez sought before being taken captive himself. After a month, Rodriguez's captors left Bahamian waters to sell their catch to the rapidly growing population of Jamaica.

No longer useful, and possibly a source of profit, Rodriguez's captors attempted to sell him in Jamaica "to work for the space of seven years in the countryside."[62] The intervention of Jamaica's governor prevented Rodriguez from being sold as an indentured servant, but he remained a captive in the island's jail, likely so that he could serve in the same kind of prisoner of war exchange that Breton had used to gain entrance to Portobelo. Attending to the Cuban fisherman's bedside, Ignacio recognized the utility of an experienced mariner for escaping the English island. In Rodriguez's testimony about their escape, he referred to the other ten individuals as "companions" of Ignacio's, indicating that it was Ignacio who maintained social ties with the other Spanish American captives and that the idea of escape by sea might have originated with the initial encounter between Simon and Ignacio.

For the Afro-descended captives, deciding to escape Jamaica with Simon Rodriguez meant weighing the risk of being caught alongside their particular vulnerability in a Caribbean context where their racial backgrounds made them a potential source of profit. Could they trust the Cuban fisherman to pilot them to freedom and not to slavery elsewhere? At least one member of the group had reason to fear being betrayed. Six years earlier, in 1662, Juana de Quesada had been in a remarkably similar situation to the one she found herself in while deciding whether or not to trust Simon Rodriguez. That year, while enslaved in Bayamo, Cuba, an enslaved man named Luis convinced Juana to escape with him. The pair fled to the coast where Luis signaled to two ships anchored in the bay and a group of Englishmen rowed to shore. Perhaps to Juana's surprise, Luis and the Englishmen seemed to know one another. But rather than carry the pair to freedom together, Luis betrayed her. He declared that Juana was his slave and arranged her sale to the Englishmen. Over the course of her six-year enslavement in Jamaica, Juana doubtless turned back to that moment in her memory, replaying the hopeful optimism of escaping with Luis and the heartbreaking despair of having been deceived by him.[63] If Juana recounted her experience to her companions, it doubtless underlaid the general anxiety each member of the group felt as they made their plans to escape. Ignacio understood the risks. According to Simon Rodriguez's testimony, Ignacio made the Cuban fisherman promise not to reveal their plans to escape and told him that the rest of his companions were "people in whom he could trust."[64]

The crowded urban character and maritime orientation of Port Royal facilitated the escape of Ignacio and his companions. Scholars have analyzed how common maritime marronage was between the geographically proximate islands of the Lesser Antilles, where the availability of small boats allowed women and men, young and old, a chance to seek freedom at sea.[65] The escape of Ignacio and his companions shows that maritime marronage was not exclusive to the Lesser Antilles and invites a reinterpretation of the meaning of "proximate" in maritime environments. Perhaps the most difficult part of the plan would have been freeing Simon Rodriguez. The Cuban fisherman was likely being held in the "New Prison," a timber structure built on a large lot where Queen Street ran into High Street in the northwestern corner of the Point. The lot belonged to Thomas Lynch and housed prisoners until an official prison was built decades later in 1685.[66] Despite the name, New Prison had a reputation for being quite porous throughout its tenure as a place of confinement, so perhaps Simon Rodriguez was able to slip away easily.[67] To the west of New Prison ran Lime Street and, beyond that, Fishermen's Row, so called because fishermen used the relatively shallow water off the western shore of the Point, called Chocolata Hole, to anchor or moor their smaller vessels. Laboring on Fort Charles, Ignacio and his companions would have seen the shallops, sloops, and rowboats of Port Royal's fishermen lined up along the beach at Chocolata Hole. On the night of their escape, each member of the group made their way to Chocolata Hole where they seized a boat and rowed away from Port Royal under the cover of darkness.

Freedom Claims and Captive Testimonies

True to his word, Simon Rodriguez piloted the stolen boat over four hundred nautical miles between Port Royal, Jamaica, and Puerto de Batabano on the southwestern coast of Cuba. Rather than freedom, the arrival of a Cuban fisherman with eleven people of African descent raised questions, especially from the island's representative of the Grillo and Lomelín asiento, an elite Cuban named Nicolás Castellón y Sánchez Pereira. With a shadow of suspicion over them, Madalena and her companions were marched to Havana where they were confined by Castellón. Their situation was made worse by the fact that their escape to Cuba coincided with a deadly epidemic on that island during which time official business ceased. The disease environment of the port city meant that Ignacio and his companions languished for a year under Castellón's authority before the governor of Cuba, Francisco Oregón y Gascón, received a petition from members of the group and called for their interrogations in October 1668.

The petition, penned in the same notarial hand as the subsequent testimonies and signed by three of the eleven captives, contested the claims of the island's asiento representative. The three signers—Ignacio Hernández, Gregorio Rodriguez, and Leonisio Rodriguez—explained that they had been held captive by the English for many years but, "as loyal vassals" of the Spanish Crown, they "risked their lives to escape tyranny and servitude among English heretics." In contrast to the claims of Castellón, they argued that they were "free as any children of Adam," and that it was simply circumstances that brought them before the governor of Havana to plead for a recognition of their freedom.[68] The petition forcefully rejected the claims of Castellón that the captives were enslaved Africans smuggled into Cuba by Simon Rodriguez. As "free as any children of Adam," the petitioners demanded that the governor of Havana adjudicate their case.

Governor Oregón responded by ordering the captives to explain the situation. The first to testify was the Cuban fisherman, Simon Rodriguez. Still suspected of attempting to smuggle Afro-descended captives into slavery on the island, Simon emphasized the friendship he formed with Ignacio Hernández during his convalescence in Port Royal. Perhaps Simon chose to describe their personal relationship in order to convince Havana authorities that he was not a slave trader. He explained that, in the end, he agreed to transport Ignacio and his companions "to Catholic lands" so that they "could live as Christians."[69] He further emphasized that everyone in the group had risked their lives fleeing English Jamaica, underscoring the sincerity of their desire to reside among Catholics.

Two elements of Simon Rodriguez's declaration—the physical risk of attempting escape and the desire to reside among Catholics—emerged as central in the other captives' testimonies as well. The danger of physical punishment if caught by the English or drowning at sea were very real possibilities for Ignacio and his companions during their escape from Jamaica.[70] But the repeated descriptions of that danger alongside expressing a desire to live, according to many of the testimonies, "among Roman Catholic Christians," has a formulaic quality undoubtedly shaped by the questions posed to the group. In fact, Governor Oregón had good reason to encourage those exact responses from the captives. In order to counter Castellón's claims that Simon Rodriguez had smuggled enslaved people into Cuba, thereby contravening the monopoly of the Grillo and Lomelín asiento and making the captives Castellón's property, Oregón turned to the precedent set by a remarkably similar case in Puerto Rico from four years earlier. That case involved the second escape from captivity of Gaspar de Espinosa, the Afro-descended translator who had worked for the governor of Puerto Rico during the 1650s, along with four other captives.

In 1664, Espinosa had been taken captive for a second time and sold into slavery to the French on St. Croix. During his captivity, he met a mariner from Tolú near Cartagena de Indias named Domingo Hernández. Described as a "pardo," or mixed-race man, Hernández had been taken captive at sea by English traffickers who sold him into slavery in St. Croix, despite his free status in Cartagena. In the maritime environs of St. Croix, holding mariners as captives proved difficult, and in the summer of 1664, Hernández, Espinosa, and three unnamed women of African descent stole a fishing boat and escaped to neighboring Puerto Rico. These were precisely the kinds of escapes that drove regional governors to demand treaties of rendition that crossed imperial borders, but fortunately for Espinosa and his companions, no such treaty existed between Puerto Rico and St. Croix. Rather than consider returning the group to slavery, the governor of Puerto Rico, Juan Pérez de Guzmán y Chagoyen, saw an opportunity in their arrival on the island.

While his predecessors had sold individuals who escaped slavery in the Lesser Antilles at public auction and pocketed the money for the Real Hacienda, Pérez de Guzmán had a different plan for Domingo Hernández and his companions. Espinosa retained social ties on the island, which meant that his free status was never in question, but since Hernández and the three women had been trafficked away from social connections and communities, their legal status was unclear in Puerto Rico. Pérez de Guzmán argued that the individuals who escaped slavery to Puerto Rico, like Hernández and the three women, could help "depopulate the Lesser Antilles, and repopulate this island, which is badly needed." As he explained, "the utility of selling them into slavery was very short" compared with the benefit of encouraging others to flee to Puerto Rico "in the service of our Holy Faith."[71] The Crown agreed and, on January 18, 1665, issued a royal cédula that declared Domingo Hernández and his companions free. By the 1680s, the logic behind this policy would develop into a more standard practice in which Spanish territories offered freedom to any enslaved person who escaped from slavery among Protestants on the condition that they sought baptism in the Catholic faith. In underpopulated regions of Spanish America, like Venezuela and Florida, this policy would have a transformative effect. Spanish authorities in those places encouraged self-liberated people of African descent to form free communities that served as bulwarks against Spain's enemies.[72]

For his part, Oregón modeled his response to the arrival of Ignacio Hernández and his companions in Havana off of the precedent set in Puerto Rico four years earlier. He ordered the removal of the captives from Castellón's authority and deposited everyone, except Juana de Quesada, into the custody of a member of the local cabildo, Pedro de Valdés Pino.[73] Oregón returned Juana, who was the only member of the group formerly enslaved in Cuba, to the man who claimed ownership over her where she faced punishment for running away and a return to slavery. For the remaining captives, Oregón argued that they deserved to be freed since, just like Domingo Hernández and his companions in Puerto Rico, they too had risked their lives in order to return to the land of Roman Catholics. For Oregón, this logic was sufficient to counter Castellón's claims to ownership over the group. The formulaic repetition of seeking to live among Roman Catholics in the testimonies of Ignacio Hernández and his companions undoubtedly reflects a mediation of their testimony to fit the conditions of freedom established by the royal cédula issued for Puerto Rico.

Despite Oregón's framing of the captives' status, many of the captives from Jamaica rejected the assumption that their captivity had made them slaves in the first place. Even as Madalena repeated the claim that she escaped Jamaica to live among Roman Catholics, she refused to recognize that her condition was ever that of a slave. The yearlong confinement by Havana's representative of the asiento underscored the racialized vulnerability experienced by Madalena, and she used her testimony to articulate her own understanding of freedom and unfreedom for herself and her daughter. But Madalena was not the only member of the group to express their own opinions about the nature of their status. Salvador Francisco de la Peña also testified to his free status before Havana officials, emphasizing that his mother, Catalina, had been free before he was born.[74] Salvador Francisco had not been free at birth—his father had freed him, his mother, and his siblings when he had been just a year old. Whether he truly did not remember the circumstances around his freedom or he feared articulating his enslaved past in this fraught moment is unclear. In his testimony, he emphasized only Catalina's free status at the moment of his birth to argue that he inherited her freedom and not her bondage. Salvador Francisco's articulation of his free status through genealogical details echoed Madalena's rejection of the logic that captivity by the English had made them slaves.

Some of the captives from Providencia argued that the martial context of their captivity in Jamaica made them prisoners of war rather than slaves. In articulating that position, individuals like Leonel Criollo emphasized their service to the Spanish Crown prior to their captivity and the treatment they received by the English in Jamaica. Leonel Criollo testified that he was "free and as such the said English treated him." He further elaborated that, in Jamaica, he "worked building the fortifications with the rest of the prisoners."[75] In other words, as a captive seized from a Spanish garrison and put to work building fortifications, Leonel Criollo argued that the English treated him like a prisoner of war rather than chattel. The extension of this argument, crucially, was that Leonel Criollo did not need Governor Oregón to grant him a freedom that he had never lost. Despite the certainty of his testimony, however, as a "negro mozo" (young Black boy), he understood the vulnerability of his status before Havana officials. This was a vulnerability that was doubtless underscored by the actual treatment Leonel Criollo and his companions received at the hands of their English captors.

The treatment that seventeenth-century prisoners of war received throughout the greater Caribbean was often contingent on factors such as the prisoner's race or status as well as the disposition of their captors. Spanish officials in the Caribbean, for example, tended to treat northern European prisoners of war as interlopers, especially in the decades before the Spanish Crown's recognition of the legitimacy of English colonies. From the earliest English forays into the Caribbean until the Treaty of Madrid in 1670, Spain considered the Caribbean a mare clausum and viewed English settlements as illegitimate. For the English soldiers and settlers on Providence Island who were taken captive during the 1641 Spanish attack, for example, this meant experiencing forced labor in Portobelo. According to the testimony of one English prisoner of war in Portobelo, thirty-three English prisoners labored on the city's fortifications "from five in the morning until seven at night," and "when weak with want of victuals and sleep they were knocked down and beaten with cudgells, and four or five died." Rather than describe their condition as akin to slavery, the Englishman testified that the Spanish supposedly treated them worse and forced them to work harder than enslaved Africans.[76] From an English perspective, their experiences contrasted sharply with the treatment normally afforded European prisoners of war.[77]

For some Spanish prisoners of war seized by the English, however, their racial background made them subject to actual, rather than just metaphorical, slavery. English colonists had a long history of treating racially stigmatized prisoners of war in the Americas as slaves, regardless of their prior status. The racialization of prisoners of war from Providencia, for example, began when Morgan's and Mansvelt's forces raided the island in 1666. Some Spanish soldiers were transported to Panama, where they testified about the loss of the Providencia to the English. But, as the experiences of Leonel Criollo and his companions make clear, phenotypically Black soldiers found themselves forcibly transported to Jamaica and forced to labor for the English colony. Unlike their Spanish counterparts, Leonel Criollo and his companions were not exchanged in Panama; instead, the English tallied them among the slaves and other goods taken off the island. Leonel Criollo and his companions likely understood the meaning behind their different treatment—the English viewed them as racialized and subject to coerced labor while their phenotypically white counterparts were not. Even though Leonel Criollo testified to being forced to work "with the rest of the prisoners," in fact, the captivity that he and his companions experienced was uniquely racialized by their English captors.[78]

Not all of the Spanish captives who labored on Port Royal's fortifications viewed their treatment as that of prisoners of war. Despite experiencing the same kind of labor coercion in Jamaica, Gregorio Rodriguez set himself apart from the captives from Providencia. After being taken captive from the Rio de la Hacha, Gregorio testified that his English captors transported him to Jamaica where he "worked at building the fortifications." But, unlike Leonel Criollo and the other men taken prisoner on Providencia, Gregorio argued that he worked "like a slave not a prisoner like the rest of them."[79] Although not stated explicitly in his testimony, Gregorio's captors likely sold him as a slave to a resident of Port Royal. If this was the case, Gregorio's new owner would have sent him to work on the fortifications, either to reap the wages Gregorio earned or because Jamaican colonial authorities ordered slave owners to relinquish a number of enslaved men to work on the fortifications.[80] Gregorio's testimony, in other words, reinforced the distinction between prisoners of war and slaves, even if it meant underscoring his own treatment as a slave by the English. Why Gregorio chose to highlight the distinction between his status among the English and that of the captives from Providencia is impossible to know, but one clue to understanding this choice might involve the social ties forged between the captives.

By the time he was called before Havana officials in 1668, Gregorio had lived and labored alongside the prisoners from Providencia for two years, and his testimony likely came in the context of the friendships they forged during that time together. If Gregorio used his testimony to add support to the argument that the captives from Providencia had never lost their freedom, he was not the only one. One woman, named Justa y Rufina after the third-century Sevillian martyrs, had been enslaved to a Spanish soldier in Providencia when the English attacked the island. She also testified to the free status of one of the captives whose family she had known before the English invasion. According to her testimony, Juan Catalan had been free on Providencia, as had his father, Fulano Catalan.[81] In recounting the genealogical details of Juan Catalan's status, Justa y Rufina's testimony echoes that of Salvador Francisco de la Peña, articulating the familial claims to freedom of Juan Catalan regardless of the captivity he experienced among the English. Like Gregorio Rodriguez, Justa y Rufina also testified that she chose to escape English Jamaica in order to live among Catholics and at great personal risk. But rather than simply repeat the conditions for freedom set out by Governor Oregón, both Gregorio Rodriguez and Justa y Rufina articulated their own sense of freedom and unfreedom. They used their testimonies to counter the argument that the captivity of some of their companions had ever made them slaves. Crucially, these testimonies—offered as asides in testimonies meant to explain their own backgrounds—undermined the racialized logic that any person of African descent escaping from captivity among the English was a slave whose freedom needed to be granted by Spanish officials.

Freedom Lost and Gained in Exchange for Baptism

The testimonies of Ignacio Hernández and his companions underscore the racialized vulnerability of Afro-descended captives in the greater Caribbean. Their experiences highlight a central ambiguity in the policy of freedom in exchange for baptism: as a result of widespread practices of captive-taking and human trafficking, some Afro-descended people escaping slavery among Protestants had previously been free subjects of the Spanish Crown. The captives from Jamaica made exactly this point when they rejected the logic that captivity had made them slaves. But the policy of liberation that Governor Oregón applied to their case undermined their previous statuses and threatened to legitimize captive-taking as a process of enslavement. For captives like Gregorio Rodriguez, whose wife relied on his income for survival in Rio de la Hacha, the precedent from Puerto Rico would not return him home. In that case, the governor of Puerto Rico assigned the escaped Afro-descended captives to productive roles in order to "repopulate the island," viewing Black bodies as useful for the project of imperial defense.[82] It was not slavery, but it was not freedom either.

Ignacio and his companions contested Oregón's framing of their status, but each member of the group nonetheless repeated the conditions required by the Havana governor: that they risked their lives to reside among Catholics. Understanding why they did so, and what was at stake, requires placing this moment in the context of changes to the transatlantic and intra-Caribbean slave trades in the 1660s. When the captives from Jamaica entered Havana in 1667, their arrival coincided with ongoing debates about the nature of the slave trade under the new asiento contract granted to Grillo and Lomelín. Analyzing the jurisdictional and economic sides of those debates clarifies both Nicolás Castellón's claims of ownership over the Jamaican captives and Oregón's efforts to counter those claims by using a similar case from Puerto Rico. Viewing this process through the lens of Ignacio and his companions underscores how the changes wrought to the intra-Caribbean and transatlantic slave trades would have important consequences for racially stigmatized captives seized and trafficked in the greater Caribbean as well.

For Ignacio and his companions, structural and jurisdictional aspects of the Grillo and Lomelín asiento would have profound impacts on their experiences in Havana. In order to prevent the privilege of purchasing enslaved African captives directly in the Americas from further enabling smuggling, Grillo and Lomelín were granted unprecedented jurisdictional authority over the slave trade in the form of resident judges called *jueces conservadores*. These judges had civil and criminal jurisdiction over the slave trade independent of the highest Spanish American courts, the authority of Spanish American viceroys, and even Spain's House of Trade. One of the duties of the *juez conservador* was investigating ships accused of smuggling African captives and pressing charges against captains caught engaging in the slave trade outside of the Grillo and Lomelín asiento.[83]

Among the *jueces conservadores* stationed throughout Spanish America was Castellón, the man who claimed custody over Ignacio and his companions when they arrived in Havana in 1667. Castellón doubtless attained his position due to his social prominence. He was born into an elite Cuban family and served as a member of the town council as well as lieutenant mayor of Havana.[84] Grillo and Lomelín sought to contract individuals like Castellón for positions as factors and judges, in part, because their local connections gave them on-the-ground knowledge about how the legal and illegal slave trade functioned. The arrival of a Cuban fisherman accompanied by people of African descent led Castellón to believe that the captives from Jamaica were being smuggled from the English island to Cuba, as he explained, "in contravention of the conditions . . . of the asiento."[85] In fact, Spanish subjects had experience making clandestine purchases of enslaved Africans in Jamaica and transporting them back to Cuba in the years since the English occupation of the neighboring island.[86] After all, it was those very intra-Caribbean and trans-imperial connections, which emerged during the years between the end of the Portuguese asiento and the 1660s, that convinced Grillo and Lomelín to structure their asiento through a trans-imperial, intra-Caribbean slave trade.[87] The success of the Grillo and Lomelín asiento depended on their representatives rechanneling the intra-Caribbean slave trade away from illicit exchanges and toward their own agents and factors in Spanish America. In the case of Ignacio and his companions, this involved Castellón claiming custody over the captives while investigating Simon Rodriguez on charges of smuggling.

Ignacio and his companions found themselves caught between two very different interpretations of their statuses. For his part, Castellón viewed the captives through their racial background and, therefore, as property of the

Grillo and Lomelín asiento. According to Castellón, Ignacio and his companions had "arrived without dispatches from factors of the asiento," implying that the arrival of any people of African descent into Cuba fell under the jurisdiction of the asiento. To underscore his argument, he reiterated the phrasing of the asiento contract, in which representatives of the asiento had authority over "todos los negros que se introdujieron y el valor de ellos [all of the Blacks that are introduced and the value of them]."[88] Ignacio and his companions, according to this logic, belonged to Castellón in the name of the asiento because they were "negros" who had been brought to Cuba. Although arguing for opposite results, this logic paralleled that used by Oregón to argue for the captives' liberation. For Oregón, Ignacio and his companions deserved freedom because they were "negros" who arrived in Cuba seeking to live among Catholics. Castellón and Oregón presented different arguments, but the fundamental assumptions remained the same. The growth of the intra-Caribbean slave trade and the expansive jurisdiction of the Grillo and Lomelín asiento tethered the status of people of African descent to slavery in moments of maritime mobility. The difference rested on whether that maritime mobility made Afro-descended people enslaved or free.

Apart from Juana, who returned to the condition of slavery in Cuba, the fate of Ignacio and his companions is unclear from the archival traces that remain. A remarkably similar case from two years later, however, might allow for a degree of speculation about their futures.[89] In 1669, nine people of African descent fled captivity and enslavement in Tortuga and arrived by sea at the port city of Santiago de Cuba on the island's eastern tip. In that case, the *juez conservador* ruled that two of the nine were slaves without masters and should be relinquished to the Grillo asiento factor. Two people in the group were formerly enslaved in Spanish America and the *juez conservador* ordered that they should be returned to those who claimed ownership over them, while the remaining five people were declared free, either because they had been born free before being taken captive or because they had escaped in order to be baptized. Six years later, however, the Council of the Indies overturned the *juez conservador*'s ruling about the two "masterless" Afro-descended captives and ordered them freed as well.[90]

If the case of Ignacio and his companions was adjudicated similarly, Ignacio, Justa y Rufina, and Cathalina would have all been initially returned to slavery and the rest of the group would have been freed. The decision to return Juana to her master indicates that Castellón might have ruled similarly for the others who had previously been enslaved in Spanish America.

For those declared free, the ambiguity of what "freedom" meant in this context remains unresolved. Was Gregorio allowed to return to his life selling "cachivaches" to support his wife, or did he enter into the service of populating and defending Havana? What about the captives from Providencia—an island society destroyed by an English invasion that scattered family members across the Caribbean? Did men like Salvador Francisco de la Peña have a say in where he went next, or was he enlisted in the militia and required to serve where needed? Did he ever see his mother, father, or sisters again? Neither the case from 1669 nor the documentation remaining from the case of Ignacio and his companions can answer those questions.

The encounter with Nicolás Castellón in Havana underscored the racialized vulnerability experienced by Ignacio and his companions as well as their responses to that vulnerability. As a result of the unprecedented jurisdiction of the Grillo and Lomelín asiento, the escapees from Jamaica became captives once again once they arrived in Cuba. And, although Governor Oregón interceded on their behalf, the process of collecting their testimonies illuminates the care and disposability inherent in racialized vulnerability.[91] During the process of adjudicating their status, one member of the group died in captivity in Havana, likely of the contagious disease that ravaged the port city when they arrived. Described as a "moreno criollo de Cartagena," or mixed-race person born in Cartagena, Leonisio Rodriguez had been free before being taken captive by the English but died in the custody of Castellón. In response to the death, the *juez conservador* of the asiento demanded that officials in Havana compensate him for the cost of the medical care administered to Leonisio during his fatal illness.[92]

Leonisio's death must be understood alongside the racialized logic that captivity by the English had created the potentiality of slavery for him and his companions in a way that left them unable to move about freely when they arrived in Cuba. This was true even for those members of the groups who had been legally free before their captivity. Read critically, however, the testimonies gathered by Governor Oregón reveal that Leonisio, Madalena, Ignacio, and their companions refuted that logic. Drawing from their understanding of vassalage, wartime captivity, and genealogies of freedom, the group from Jamaica shaped their testimonies to articulate their own understandings of freedom and unfreedom.

One detail that never came up during the discussion among Spanish Caribbean officials about the legal status of Ignacio, Madalena, or their companions was surprise over their shared experiences with captivity and human trafficking. All twelve people on that small boat had been taken captive throughout the greater Caribbean and Brazil before escaping from English Jamaica together. Yet their arrival in Cuba elicited no comment from Spanish officials on how they had become captives in the first place. Rather than exceptional, in other words, their experiences underscore the regularity of captivity and human trafficking in the seventeenth-century Caribbean. Nor were they the only ones whose experiences raised questions about their legal status but not the wider economy of captive-taking and human trafficking. Tomás Gutierrez's account of his own experiences of captivity and human trafficking also did not seem unbelievable or shocking to Spanish officials in Portobelo. Discussion of his experiences revolved around the timing of his captivity, not the fact of it.

That all of these experiences seemed so quotidian underscores one of the central arguments of this book, namely, that practices of captive-taking and human trafficking were widespread and common throughout the sixteenth- and seventeenth-century Caribbean world. Seeing the economy of captive-taking and human trafficking through the eyes of people like Madalena or Salvador Francisco de la Peña, crucially, forces a reassessment of the lived experiences of people of African descent in the greater Caribbean. If these experiences of forced dislocation were accepted without comment by Spanish Caribbean officials, then the threat of captivity and human trafficking must be seen as a component part of the communal experiences of people of African descent over this violent and tumultuous period. Traffickers curtailed pathways to freedom for people of African descent in Spain's Caribbean world throughout the sixteenth and seventeenth centuries. Transportation across imperial borders or away from family and communities of belonging, moreover, severed ties to social networks where one's legal status as free would have been common knowledge. Widespread experiences of this kind of racialized vulnerability have important implications for our understandings of race and slavery in the wider Atlantic world as well, the contours of which will be taken up in the conclusion.

Conclusion

Salvador Francisco de la Peña was only a year old in 1646 when his father petitioned for permission to purchase him, his sisters, and his mother out of slavery.[1] His father's desire to legally free his small family resonated with many of the Iberian soldiers tasked with manning the Spanish presidio on the recently reclaimed island of Providencia. Over the previous five years, many of the men stationed there had formed mixed-race families with the Afro-descended women seized from the English during the conquest of the island in 1641. Those women had experienced multiple moments of violent dislocation in the Caribbean, including at the hands of northern European traffickers who had taken them captive and sold them into slavery among the English on Providencia. By the time Salvador Francisco was born, women of African descent like his mother had formed affective and familial ties with Iberian men, securing a pathway to legal freedom for themselves and their children. Those pathways were cut short by Edward Mansvelt and Henry Morgan's forces during the 1666 raid, as captives like Salvador Francisco found themselves trafficked into slavery in Jamaica. Despite the efforts of his mother and father, the legal freedom bestowed on Salvador Francisco shortly after his birth did little to protect him from slavery once he was forcibly removed from his community and trafficked across imperial borders.

The experiences of Salvador Francisco de la Peña, his mother, and his sisters humanize and illuminate the broader implications of this book for Caribbean history and the history of race and slavery. To begin with, their lives are difficult to map onto a historiography that tends to treat Providencia within either an English or a Spanish context, but that rarely follows the experiences of individuals whose lives traversed the many times that the island switched hands. The multigenerational story of the Peña family only emerges by viewing the Caribbean as they experienced it—as an entangled space of

competing jurisdictions and polities shaped by violence and racialized vulnerability. And, just as their lives crossed imperial borders, unearthing their
family's experiences requires reading across imperial archives and historiographies. Only once we have done that work can we begin the think about the
implications of lives like theirs for the stories that we tell about race, slavery,
trade, and colonization in the sixteenth- and seventeenth-century Caribbean
and Atlantic world.

The life that Salvador Francisco's parents attempted to create for him in
the 1640s was deeply entangled with widespread practices of captive-taking
and human trafficking from the beginning. The relationship between Catalina Angola and Salvador de la Peña came as a result of imperial contestation over the island of Providencia. The Spanish decision to invade English
Providencia came in response to the raids conducted by northern European
traffickers, who had used captive-taking and human trafficking to make their
voyages since the second half of the sixteenth century. As raiding and trafficking transitioned to colonization for the English and French in the Caribbean, islands like Providencia remained central nodes for traffickers who
continued to sell captive women and men into slavery there and elsewhere.
By the 1630s, in fact, the activities of northern European traffickers created
enslaved majorities on Tortuga and Providencia. In retaliation for those violent maritime raids, Spanish officials launched a series of attacks on several
of the islands most frequently used by traffickers, including Providencia.
The decision by Spanish officials to plant a presidio after they dislodged the
English—a decision that put Catalina in Salvador de la Peña's household,
where she bore him three children—stemmed from a desire to curb the violent, regional economy in raiding and captive-taking that had created the
enslaved majority among the English on the island.

For her son, Salvador Francisco, the years between 1641 and 1666 were
spent growing up alongside his two sisters in a garrison settlement composed
of numerous Iberian and African families just like his. His young life changed
course dramatically following his captivity and sale into slavery in English
Jamaica. Salvador Francisco's life had been indelibly impacted by northern
European practices of slavery, from the circumstances that led to his birth to
his forced separation from his family as a young adult. But tracing his experiences, as well as those of his mother, highlights more than just the story of
a single family caught in overlapping moments of violence. Rather, Salvador Francisco's birth and his escape from slavery in English Jamaica allow
for a reinterpretation of a pivotal moment in the wider history of slavery

in the greater Caribbean, specifically the rise of racialized, chattel slavery in the English and French Caribbean. A brief history of how scholars have described northern Europeans' transition to chattel slavery in the Caribbean during the second half of the seventeenth century is necessary in order to understand how the experiences of the Peña family force a reassessment of some of the foundational assumptions embedded in that historiography.

Over the second half of the seventeenth century the labor force in the Caribbean colonies of England and France transitioned demographically from a majority of indentured servants to a majority of enslaved West and West Central Africans and their descendants. According to scholars, various factors account for the increase in the number of enslaved people laboring in the colonies of England and France around mid-century, including the rise of sugar plantation agriculture, the decline in the number of indentured servants arriving in the Caribbean, and increased efficiencies in the transatlantic slave trade. As early as the 1670s, many of the legal and institutional prerequisites of the slave-based plantation complex—such as racialized legal codes, massive investment in the transatlantic slave trade, and the use of state power to enforce slavery—were in place throughout the Atlantic world. Those innovations proved pivotal in the transition away from the informal slave trade conducted by northern European traffickers and toward a more formalized intra-Caribbean and transatlantic slave trade.

Central to that transition was the legal recognition throughout the Anglo-Atlantic of the concept of chattel slavery, which undergirded massive investment in the transatlantic slave trade by English merchants and the Crown. Prior to the 1660s, the informal sale of captives often involved payment in goods in open colonial markets. As Holly Brewer argues, this was fine for northern European traffickers whose overhead costs for obtaining captives from raiding were significantly lower than what would be required for merchant companies involved in trade in Atlantic Africa. Investment in the slave trade on a larger scale, however, required that buyers and sellers have access to contracts and legal recourse in the case of breached contracts. The growth of English involvement in the transatlantic slave trade through monopoly companies after 1660, in other words, depended on English law upholding the concept that people could be treated as if they were goods or chattel.[2]

Legally recognized chattel slavery facilitated the use of a wide variety of commercial mechanisms by merchants on both sides of the Atlantic and increased investment in the slave trade. The kinds of capital investment involved in something like the Royal African Company—with the concomitant costs of maintaining trade forts in Atlantic Africa and staffing a trade bureaucracy throughout the Atlantic world—required options for financing the sale of large numbers of enslaved women, men, and children in the Americas. Financing, in turn, required legally binding contracts for both buyer and seller. As the main driver in the creation of new English monopoly slave-trading companies, the Stuart monarchy used English common law courts in the 1660s and 1670s to craft legal decisions that embedded the notion that people could be property into English law.[3] The result was the appallingly rapid expansion of the transatlantic slave trade over the next century.

Ample scholarship has charted the demographic, legal, and social consequences of the rise of racialized chattel slavery in the Caribbean colonies of England and France over the second half of the seventeenth century and beyond.[4] In the process, racialized chattel slavery connected to the plantation complex has emerged as the paradigmatic form of coerced labor in much of the scholarship on race and slavery in the Atlantic world and beyond.[5] From this perspective, slavery as an institution took on importance in the Caribbean only when enslaved people became the predominant source of labor for European plantations owners engaged in the production of cash crops after the mid-seventeenth century. Prior to the transition to the plantation complex, English and French colonists had, in the words of one scholar, "little need or demand for slaves" in the Caribbean.[6] The assumption is that, prior to the plantation complex, race-based slavery was less important to the development of England's and France's Caribbean colonies because it was less demographically important. But slavery shaped the activities of northern Europeans in the Caribbean well before the plantation complex created either a "need" or a "demand" for enslaved people. The experiences of Salvador Francisco, his mother, or the many other captives who populate this book demand a more nuanced interpretation of the role of slavery in the English and French Caribbean before the ascendancy of sugar or the plantation complex.

Tracing the experiences of captives like Salvador Francisco provides a way of thinking about English, French, and Dutch participation in slave raiding, trafficking, and ownership well before the mid-seventeenth-century rise of plantation-based chattel slavery. Racialization was a component part of this process from the beginning. Northern European traffickers commodified a wide variety of captives over the sixteenth and seventeenth centuries. As this book has shown, the experiences of captives were also racialized in specific ways. Captives of European descent experienced forms of servitude rather than slavery, even if they sometimes decried their coerced labor at the hands of imperial competitors as an unacceptable form of bondage. Captives of African and Indigenous descent, by contrast, were sold into slavery, even if the institution of racialized, chattel slavery had not been clarified yet in English, French, or Dutch law. The Afro-descended women and men whom Salvador Francisco had known as a child on Providencia, for example, had been targeted by traffickers and sold into slavery among the English colonists on the island in the 1630s because of their racial background. The buying, selling, and holding of enslaved people among English and French colonists in the Caribbean predated the rise of the plantation complex and the attendant legal codes defining the institution. That sugar had not yet created "demand" among English or French colonists, in other words, did not prevent the captivity and sale into slavery of Catalina Angola and many others like her.

Practices of captive slavery that predated the plantation complex made people of African and Indigenous descent vulnerable to forced dislocation and unfreedom throughout the sixteenth and seventeenth centuries. Crucially, while that vulnerability was racialized from the very beginning, race did not automatically imply slavery in the mid-sixteenth and early seventeenth centuries, even if it implied the potentiality of being enslaved through captivity and human trafficking. The case of Pierre Bélain d'Esnambuc is instructive in this regard. Before he became the first royal governor in the French Caribbean, d'Esnambuc sailed in a multinational company of traffickers who engaged in raiding and captive-taking along the Spanish Main. When they sailed to western Hispaniola in 1620, they did so with the intention of selling the Afro-descended captives into slavery there.[7] Hispaniola attracted traffickers like d'Esnambuc, however, because they maintained trade relations with the Iberian, Indigenous, and African residents of the island's western half. The activities of northern European traffickers like d'Esnambuc, in other words, made a wide variety of people of African and Indigenous descent vulnerable to becoming potential subjects of slavery through captivity and human trafficking. But their amicable relations with people of African and Indigenous descent, especially the island's Maroon communities, indicate that they did not equate all racially stigmatized people with slavery. There is an important distinction here and one that, as this book has shown, eroded over the course of seventeenth century.

Pierre Bélain d'Esnambuc had a role to play in the erosion of cross-cultural alliances between traffickers and populations of Indigenous and African descent. Northern European colonization of various spaces in the Caribbean transformed those relationships, beginning with the Kalinago on St. Christopher. As England, France, and the Netherlands developed colonies in the Caribbean, northern European traffickers became less dependent on the safe anchorages provided by their former trade partners. New markets in English, French, and Dutch colonies incentivized increased raiding throughout the greater Caribbean, creating an increasingly predatory sea for a wide assortment of people, including Salvador Francisco's mother. Crucially, notions of the commodifiability of certain captives had not shifted from the late sixteenth to the mid-seventeenth century. Rather, it was northern European traffickers' reliance on alliances of cross-cultural trade that changed. As northern European traffickers were no longer dependent on amicable relations by the 1630s, in other words, trade partners of African and Indigenous descent became the subjects of raiding and captive-taking. Demand for captives who could be trafficked into slavery in the newly formed northern European colonies in the Caribbean drove this captive economy decades before the rise of the sugar plantation complex on those islands.

There is another way in which the experiences of captives and their captors over the sixteenth and seventeenth centuries recast origin stories central to Caribbean and Atlantic world historiography. One of those origin stories involves another act of maritime raiding and captive-taking that occurred a year before d'Esnambuc's encounter with Spanish galleons at the small island of Caymito in western Hispaniola. In 1619, traffickers aboard two ships, the *Treasurer* captained by Daniel Elfrith and the *White Lion* captained by John Colyn Jope, intercepted a Portuguese transatlantic slave ship on its way from Angola to Veracruz. After raiding the ship, Jope of the *White Lion* trafficked "20. and odd" Angolan captives from the Portuguese vessel to Point Comfort, Virginia.[8] Since those captive Angolans represented the first recorded sale of Africans into Virginia, 1619 has emerged as an important date for understanding the beginning of racialized slavery in North America. In other words, 1619 has served for scholars and the general public as a precursor to the institution of chattel slavery that would reshape Virginia and, by consequence, the history of race in the United States.[9]

Scholars have rightfully highlighted 1619 as a pivotal moment for the history of English North America, but too often that has meant treating the acts of Elfrith and Jope as exceptional.[10] It has meant, in other words, removing the act of captive-taking and human trafficking at the heart of why 1619 matters to North American history out of its sixteenth- and seventeenth-century Caribbean context. As this book has shown, there was nothing exceptional about the maritime raid on a Portuguese transatlantic slave ship in 1619, nor would those "20. and odd" Angolans be the last captives of African descent seized in the Caribbean and trafficked into slavery in North America. The experiences of the Peña family are instructive for thinking about the wider Caribbean history of raiding and captive-taking of which Virginia was a small part. Salvador Francisco's mother, Catalina, would have undoubtedly known people trafficked off Providencia and into slavery in Virginia in the 1630s. Over the next decades, they would encounter other captives from the Caribbean. During the English invasion of Jamaica, for example, English forces took captives of African descent, some of whom were trafficked into slavery in Virginia. The Caribbean legacies of 1619 underscore how the histories of race and slavery in North America and the Caribbean have been deeply entangled from the very beginning, despite the tendency to compartmentalize regional histories according to the arbitrary borders of modern nation-states.[11]

The experiences of the Peña family reveal the contours of this violent world as well as the responses of those people whose lives became entangled in practices of captive slavery. Their lives were in some ways exceptional, but only insofar as their multigenerational experiences of captivity and human trafficking across multiple imperial borders are legible in the archival traces left behind centuries later. For Salvador Francisco de la Peña, it is also a life left frustratingly ambiguous. The European men who left records about him cared less about his lived experiences and more about what he represented— an Afro-descended man caught in a Caribbean world that commodified Black bodies. That we can know so much about moments in his life but less about what happened after exposes in stark detail the possibilities and limits of colonial archives. Ambiguity, in this case, reflects power and was shaped by a racialized logic that, in Salvador's case, linked people of African descent with slavery.

Crucially, however, the archive is not completely silent. Within the structures of power that forced previously free people to defend themselves against being labeled slaves are the voices of a mother who articulated her claims to freedom and defended the birthright of her daughter, the son of a Spanish presidio captain and a liberated woman of African descent who grew up in a world where his freedom was common knowledge only to be trafficked into one that required him to rhetorically defend his status, and an Afro-descended fisherman who claimed volition in an English trafficking voyage in a bid to save himself from enslavement. Even if we can only trace moments in their lives, those moments reveal more than they conceal about a Caribbean world shaped by captivity, human trafficking, and slavery and the responses of people of African and Indigenous descent to the violence and instability of the world around them.

By focusing on what actually happened to people like Salvador Francisco de la Peña over this tumultuous century of Caribbean history, we are forced to confront a sixteenth- and seventeenth-century Caribbean world that is far more than a simple prelude to the eighteenth century. The 1650s and 1660s witnessed profound changes to inter-imperial relations and the intra-Caribbean and transatlantic slave trades—changes that would pave the way for the entrenchment of the sugar plantation complex and chattel slavery. At the same time, the practices of captive-taking and human trafficking that shaped colonization, trade, and slavery in earlier centuries do not have a clean ending. Imperial officials working for the interests of monopoly slave-trading companies continued in their efforts to curb raiding and human trafficking into the eighteenth century. Their efforts met with checkered success. As long as a market existed for captives, and as long as a system of labor exploitation linked people of African descent to slavery, traffickers continued to make their voyages in much the same way as they had over the previous century. Trafficking offers no clear end point, even as it shifted over time to meet market demands and respond to the varying levels of imperial oversight. Echoing the lives at the center of the previous chapters, this book must end with the ambiguity of a human practice of commodifying the Other that, in one form or another, persists in the present day.

NOTES

Preface

Epigraph: Epeli Hau'ofa, "Our Sea of Islands," *The Contemporary Pacific* 6, no. 1 (1994): 156–57. http://www.jstor.org/stable/23701593.

1. There is a rich and growing body of literature that has argued for the importance of studying the sixteenth- and seventeenth-century Caribbean on its own terms. See, for example: Alejandro de la Fuente (with the collaboration of César García del Pino and Bernardo Iglesias Delgado), *Havana and the Atlantic in the Sixteenth Century* (Chapel Hill: University of North Carolina Press, 2008); David Wheat, *Atlantic Africa and the Spanish Caribbean, 1570–1640* (Chapel Hill: University of North Carolina Press, 2016): esp. introduction; and Juan José Ponce Vázquez, *Islanders and Empire: Smuggling and Political Defiance in Hispaniola, 1580–1690* (Cambridge, UK: Cambridge University Press, 2020). Other scholars have argued for the importance of studying regions that did not become sites of sugar plantation agriculture. See Alberto Abello Vives and Ernesto Bassi Arévalo, "Un Caribe por fuera de la ruta de plantación," in *Un Caribe sin plantación*, ed. Alberto Abello Vives (San Andrés: Universidad Nacional de Colombia, 2006), 11–43; Jesse Cromwell, "More Than Slaves and Sugar: Recent Historiography of the Trans-imperial Caribbean and Its Sinew Populations," *History Compass* 12, no. 10 (2014): 770–83; Pablo F. Gómez, *The Experiential Caribbean: Creating Knowledge and Healing in the Early Modern Atlantic* (Chapel Hill: University of North Carolina Press, 2017); Ida Altman, *Life and Society in the Early Spanish Caribbean: The Greater Antilles, 1493–1550* (Baton Rouge: Louisiana State University Press, 2021).

2. Philip D. Curtin, *The Rise and Fall of the Plantation Complex* (Baltimore: Johns Hopkins University Press, 2012); Trevor Burnard and John Garrigus, *The Plantation Machine: Atlantic Capitalism in French Saint-Domingue and British Jamaica* (Philadelphia: University of Pennsylvania Press, 2016); Vincent Brown, *The Reaper's Garden: Death and Power in the World of Atlantic Slavery* (Cambridge: Harvard University Press, 2010); Trevor Burnard, *Mastery, Tyranny, and Desire: Thomas Thistlewood and His Slaves in the Anglo-Jamaican World* (Chapel Hill: University of North Carolina Press, 2004); Paul Cheney, *Cul de Sac: Patrimony, Capitalism, and Slavery in French Saint-Domingue* (Chicago: University of Chicago Press, 2017); Paul Butel, *Histoire des Antilles françaises: XVIIe–XXe siècle* (Paris: Perrin, 2007).

3. Eric Williams, *Capitalism and Slavery* (Chapel Hill: University of North Carolina Press, 1944).

4. Richard S. Dunn, *Sugar and Slaves: The Rise of the Planter Class in the English West Indies, 1624–1713* (Chapel Hill: University of North Carolina Press, 1972); Susan Dwyer Amussen, *Caribbean Exchanges: Slavery and the Transformation of English Society, 1640–1770* (Chapel Hill: University of North Carolina Press, 2007).

5. Much of the scholarship focuses on the debate surrounding how influential the Dutch in Brazil were in terms of bringing sugar-producing technology and practice to the Caribbean, especially to Barbados. See John J. McCusker and Russell R. Menard, "The Sugar Industry in the Seventeenth Century: A New Perspective on the Barbadian 'Sugar Revolution,'" in *Tropical Babylons: Sugar and the Making of the Atlantic World, 1450–1680*, ed. Stuart B. Schwartz (Chapel Hill: University of North Carolina Press, 2004). For a corrective to the discussion of the Dutch role in bringing sugar production to the Caribbean, see Russell R. Menard, *Sweet Negotiations: Sugar, Slavery, and Plantation Agriculture in Early Barbados* (Charlottesville: University of Virginia Press, 2006). Joseph C. Miller critiques the historiographical search for origins that is evident in histories that trace the rise of the sugar complex from the Mediterranean into the Caribbean: Miller, *The Problem of Slavery as History: A Global Approach* (New Haven, CT: Yale University Press, 2012). Robin Blackburn refers to this as the "idol of origins": Blackburn, *The Making of New World Slavery: From the Baroque to the Modern* (London: Verso, 1997), 33.

6. For scholarship on the legal origins of slave and servant law in the English Atlantic and questions of legal borrowing, see Jonathan A. Bush, "Free to Enslave: The Foundations of Colonial American Slave Law," *Yale Journal of Law & the Humanities* 5, no. 2 (1993): 417–70; Bradley J. Nicholson, "Legal Borrowing and the Origins of Slave Law in the British Colonies," *American Journal of Legal History* 38 (1994): 38–54; David Barry Gaspar, "'Rigid and Inclement': Origins of the Jamaican Slave Laws of the Seventeenth Century," in *The Many Legalities of Early America*, ed. Christopher L. Tomlins and Bruce H. Mann (Chapel Hill: University of North Carolina Press, 2001), 78–96; Vicki Crow Via, "A Comparison of Laws Importing and Regulating the Servants of Virginia and Jamaica in the Seventeenth Century," *Journal of Caribbean History* 38, no. 2 (2004): 310–33; Sally E. Hadden, "The Fragmented Laws of Slavery in the Colonial and Revolutionary Eras," in *The Cambridge History of Law in America: Volume I: Early America (1580–1815)*, ed. Michael Grossberg and Christopher Tomlins (New York: Cambridge University Press, 2008), 253–87; Christopher Tomlins, "Transplants and Timing: Passages in the Creation of an Anglo American Law of Slavery, Histories of Legal Transplantations," *Theoretical Inquiries in Law* 10 (2009): 389–421; Edward B. Rugemer, "The Development of Mastery and Race in the Comprehensive Slave Codes of the Greater Caribbean During the Seventeenth Century," *William and Mary Quarterly* 70, no. 3 (July 2013): 429–58.

7. For "slaving practices" I am building on Joseph C. Miller's call to historicize slavery as a process that unfolded through the dynamic and contingent choices of a variety of actors. See Miller, *The Problem of Slavery*, chapter 1.

Introduction

1. Philip P. Boucher, *France and the American Tropics to 1700: Tropics of Discontent?* (Baltimore: Johns Hopkins University Press, 2008), viii.

2. For the narrative of d'Esnambuc's arrival at St. Christopher and role as colonial governor, see Jean-Baptiste Du Tertre, *Histoire Générale des îles de Saint-Christophe, de la Guadeloupe, de la Martinique, et autres dans l'Amérique* (Paris: Chez Jacques L'Anglois, 1654), 5–6. For a discussion of the sources available for this history, see Doris L. Garraway, *The Libertine Colony: Creolization in the Early French Caribbean* (Durham, NC: Duke University Press, 2005), chap. 2.

3. The following account of d'Esnambuc's maritime career comes from the Archivo General de Indias (hereafter AGI), Santa Fé 38, r. 6, no. 166, "Carta de D. García Girón, Gobernador de Cartagena," January 30, 1621, unfoliated. For the printed account, see *Verdadera relacion del viage, y sucesso de los caravelones, galeoncetes de la guarda de Cartagena de las Indias, y su*

costa. Y la grandiose vitoria que antenido contra los cossarios piratas en aquel mar (Seville: por Bartolome Gomez de Pastrana, 1621).

4. AGI, Santa Fé 38, r. 6, no. 166, "Carta de D. García Girón," January 30, 1621; AGI, Santo Domingo 55, r. 5, no. 32, "Carta de Diego de Acuña, presidente de la Audiencia de Santo Domingo," October 12, 1625, fol. 2r; Jean-Pierre Moreau, *Les Petites Antilles de Christophe Colomb à Richelieu* (Paris: Éditions Karthala, 1992), 188–89; Gérard Lafleur, *Les Caraïbes des Petites Antilles* (Paris: Éditions Karthala, 1992), 22.

5. Corinne L. Hofman, Menno L. P. Hoogland, Arie Boomert, and John Angus Martin, "Colonial Encounters in the Southern Lesser Antilles: Indigenous Resistance, Material Transformations, and Diversity in an Ever-Globalizing World," in *Material Encounters and Indigenous Transformations in the Early Colonial Americas: Archaeological Case Studies*, ed. Corinne L. Hofman and Floris W. M. Keehnen (Leiden: Brill, 2019), 306.

6. Moreau, *Les Petits Antilles*; Hilary McD. Beckles, "Kalinago (Carib) Resistance to European Colonisation of the Caribbean," *Caribbean Quarterly* 38, nos. 2/3 (June-September 1992): 2; Lennox Honychurch, "Crossroads in the Caribbean: A Site of Encounter and Exchange on Dominica," *World Archaeology* 28, no. 3 (1997): 297; Laurence Verrand, *La Vie quotidienne des Indiens Caraïbes aux Petites Antilles (XVIIe Siècle)* (Paris: Éditions Karthala, 2001); Ernesto Mercado-Montero, "Indigenous Raiding, Captive Taking, and the Politics of Maritime Violence in the Long Sixteenth-Century Lesser Antilles," *Hispanic American Historical Review* 105, no. 1 (February 2025): 1–34.

7. "Carta del capitán Juan de Céspedes, gobernador de Puerto Rico, a S.M. informando sobre ataques de los caribes," San Juan, February 24, 1582, in *Cartas de gobernadores, vol. 2 (1580–1592): Historia Documental de Puerto Rico, Tomo XIX*, ed. Álvaro Huerga Teruelo (San Juan: Academia Puertorriqueña de la Historia, 2011), 112; "Carta del capitán Francisco de Bahamonde Lugo informa a S.M. de su viaje y llegada a la isla," San Juan, February 10, 1566, in Huerga, *Cartas de gobernadores, Vol. 1 (1550–1580): Historia Documental de Puerto Rico, Tomo XIX* (San Juan: Academia Puertorriqueña de la Historia, 2010), 185; Dutertre, *Histoire Générale des îsles*, 449; Fernando Santos-Granero, *Vital Enemies: Slavery, Predation, and the Amerindian Political Economy of Life* (Austin: University of Texas Press, 2009), 51–53; Neil L. Whitehead, *Lords of the Tiger Spirit: A History of the Caribs in Colonial Venezuela and Guyana, 1498–1820* (Providence, RI: Foris, 1988), 50; Louis Allaire, "Ethnohistory of the Caribs," in *The Oxford Handbook of Caribbean Archaeology*, ed. William F. Keegan, Corinne L. Hofman, and Reniel Rodríguez Ramos (New York: Oxford University Press, 2013), 102.

8. AGI, Santo Domingo 168, r. 3, no. 12, "Carta del gobernador Francisco Bahamonde de Lugo al rey," 1566, printed in Ricardo E. Alegría, ed., *Documentos históricos de Puerto Rico, 1546–1580 Vol. IV* (San Juan: Centro de Estudios Avanzados de Puerto Rico y el Caribe, 2009), 254.

9. For more on attempts to colonize Guiana, see Joyce Lorimer, *English and Irish Settlement on the River Amazon, 1550–1640* (London: Hakluyt Society, 1989); Sarah Barber, "Indigeneity and Authority in the Lesser Antilles: The Warners Revisited," in *The Torrid Zone: Caribbean Colonization and Cultural Interaction in the Long Seventeenth Century*, ed. L. H. Roper (Columbia: University of South Carolina Press, 2018), 47.

10. AGI, Santo Domingo 55, r. 5, no. 32, "Carta de Diego de Acuña, presidente de la Audiencia de Santo Domingo," August 1, 1625, fol. 3; Barber, "Indigeneity and Authority," 47; John Hilton, "Relation of the first settlement of Saint Christopher and Nevis, by John Hilton chief gunner and storekeeper . . ." in *Colonizing Expeditions to the West Indies and Guiana, 1623–1667*, ed. V. T. Harlow (London: Hakluyt Society, 1925), 1–3; John K. Thornton and Linda M.

Heywood, *Central Africans, Atlantic Creoles, and the Foundation of the Americas, 1585–1660* (New York: Cambridge University Press, 2007), 29; Lafleur, *Les Caraïbes des Petites Antilles*, 21; Du Tertre, *Histoire Générale des Antilles*, 5; Philip P. Boucher, *Cannibal Encounters: Europeans and Island Caribs, 1492–1763* (Baltimore: Johns Hopkins University Press, 1992), 41; Moreau, *Les Petites Antilles*, 135; Captain John Smith, *The True Travels, Adventures, and Observations of Captain John Smith* (London: Printed by I[ohn] H[aviland] for Thomas Slater, 1630), chap. 15; John Hilton, "Memoir," in Harlow, *Colonising Expeditions*, 2–17.

11. Moreau, *Les petites Antilles*, 196.

12. British Library, Egerton MS 2395, "Articles agreed upon by Capt. Warner, Mr Desnambucq, and Mr. Roisy to be maintained according to ye Commands they have from the Kings of France and England by virtue of their Commissions, 13 May 1627," and the Archive National d'Outre Mer, (hereafter ANOM), F3 52 Colonies; James A. Williamson, *The Caribbee Islands under the Proprietary Patents* (London: Oxford University Press, 1926), 27, 31; Barber, "Indigeneity and Authority," 195n2; L. H. Roper, *Advancing Empire: English Interests and Overseas Expansion, 1613–1688* (New York: Cambridge University Press, 2017), 33.

13. Deborah Cohen and Maura O'Connor, "Comparative History, Cross-National History, Transnational History—Definitions," in *Comparison and History: Europe in Cross-National Perspective*, ed. Deborah Cohen and Maura O'Connor (New York: Taylor & Francis, 2004), xiii–xiv; Michael Werner and Bénédicte Zimmerman, "Beyond Comparison: Histoire Croisée and the Challenge of Reflexivity," *History and Theory* 45, no. 1 (2006): 30–50.

14. Eliga H. Gould, "Entangled Histories, Entangled Worlds: The English-Speaking Atlantic as a Spanish Periphery," *American Historical Review* 112, no. 3 (June 2007): 765. This came from a larger forum titled "*AHR* Forum: Entangled Empires in the Atlantic World."

15. For models of this approach, see Christine Daniels and Michael V. Kennedy, eds., *Negotiated Empires: Centers and Peripheries in the Americas, 1500–1820* (New York: Routledge, 2002); Jorge Cañizares–Esguerra, ed., *Entangled Empires: The Anglo-Iberian Atlantic, 1500–1830* (Philadelphia: University of Pennsylvania Press, 2018). Older approaches discussed this in terms of comparative history. See J. H. Elliott, *Empires of the Atlantic World: Britain and Spain in America, 1492–1830* (New Haven, CT: Yale University Press, 2006); Jorge Cañizares-Esguerra, *Puritan Conquistadors: Iberianizing the Atlantic, 1550–1700* (Stanford, CA: Stanford University Press, 2006); Wim Klooster, *Revolutions in the Atlantic World: A Comparative History* (New York: New York University Press, 2009); Anthony Pagden, *Lords of All the World: Ideologies of Empire in Spain, Britain, and France, c. 1500– c. 1850* (New Haven, CT: Yale University Press, 1995); Paul W. Mapp, *The Elusive West and the Contest for Empire, 1713–1763* (Chapel Hill: University of North Carolina Press, 2011). Other than Pagden and Mapp, much of this work tends to prioritize comparisons between the English and Spanish at the expense of the French. For more on this critique, see John Robert McNeill, *Atlantic Empires of France and Spain: Louisbourg and Havana, 1700–1763* (Chapel Hill: University of North Carolina Press, 1985); Trevor Burnard, "Empire Matters? The Historiography of Imperialism in Early America, 1492–1830," *History of European Ideas* 33, no. 1 (2007): 87–107; Christopher Hodson and Brett Rushforth, "Absolutely Atlantic: Colonialism and the Early Modern French State in Recent Historiography," *History Compass* 8, no. 1 (January 2010): 101–17.

16. There is a rich historiography in which scholars adopt, either explicitly or implicitly, an entangled history approach to understand cross-cultural relations in the Atlantic world. See, for example, Eric Hinderaker, *Elusive Empires: Constructing Colonialism in the Ohio Valley*,

1673–1800 (New York: Cambridge University Press, 1997); Alida C. Metcalf, *Go-Betweens and the Colonization of Brazil, 1500–1600* (Austin: University of Texas Press, 2005); Thornton and Heywood, *Central Africans, Atlantic Creoles*; Amy Turner Bushnell, "Indigenous America and the Limits of the Atlantic World, 1493–1825," in *Atlantic History: A Critical Appraisal*, ed. Jack P. Green and Philip D. Morgan (Oxford: Oxford University Press, 2009), 191–221; Judith A. Carney and Richard Nicholas Rosomoff, *In the Shadow of Slavery: Africa's Botanical Legacy in the Atlantic World* (Berkeley: University of California Press, 2009). Borderlands historians also adopt this approach; see Juliana Barr, *Peace Came in the Form of a Woman: Indians and Spaniards in the Texas Borderlands* (Chapel Hill: University of North Carolina Press, 2007); Pekka Hämäläinen, *Comanche Empire* (New Haven, CT: Yale University Press, 2008); Kathleen Duval, *The Native Ground: Indians and Colonists in the Heart of the Continent* (Philadelphia: University of Pennsylvania Press, 2011); Michael Witgen, *An Infinity of Nations: How the Native World Shaped Early North America* (Philadelphia: University of Pennsylvania Press, 2013); Elizabeth N. Ellis, *The Great Power of Small Nations: Indigenous Diplomacy in the Gulf South* (Philadelphia: University of Pennsylvania Press, 2023).

17. Ralph Bauer and Marcy Norton, "Entangled Trajectories: Indigenous and European Histories," *Colonial Latin American Review* 26, no. 1 (April 2017): 3.

18. Andrew B. Fisher and Matthew D. O'Hara, eds., *Imperial Subjects: Race and Identity in Colonial Latin America* (Durham, NC: Duke University Press, 2009). Africans and their descendants also responded to enslavement by exploiting the entangled geopolitical world around them. See Elena A. Schneider, "A Narrative of Escape: Self Liberation by Sea and the Mental Worlds of the Enslaved," *Slavery & Abolition* 42, no. 3 (2021): 484–501.

19. Joseph C. Miller centers economic and social marginality as a driving force behind individual decisions to engage in and historical strategies of slaving. See Miller, *The Problem of Slavery as History*, chap. 1.

20. Rachel Sarah O'Toole, "Securing Subjecthood: Free and Enslaved Economies within the Spanish Pacific Slave Trade," in *From Galleons to the Highlands: Slave Trade Routes in the Spanish Americas*, ed. Alex Borucki, David Eltis, and David Wheat (Albuquerque: Diálogos Series of the University of New Mexico Press, 2020), 149–76; Wheat, *Atlantic Africa*; Gómez, *Experiential Caribbean*.

21. Marisa Vega Franco, *El tráfico de esclavos con américa (Asientos de Grillo y Lomelín, 1663–1674)* (Sevilla: Escuela de Estudios Hispano–Americanos de Sevilla, 1984); Alejandro García–Montón, *Genoese Entrepreneurship and the Asiento Slave Trade, 1650–1700* (New York: Routledge, 2021).

22. Saidiya Hartman, "Venus in Two Acts," *Small Axe* 12, no. 2 (June 2008): 11; Jenny Shaw, *Everyday Life in the Early English Caribbean: Irish, Africans, and the Construction of Difference* (Athens: University of Georgia Press, 2013).

23. Marisa J. Fuentes, *Dispossessed Lives: Enslaved Women, Violence, and the Archive* (Philadelphia: University of Pennsylvania Press, 2016). This work builds upon some of the theoretical work on archives and power from other imperial settings, such as Ann Laura Stoler, *Along the Archival Grain: Epistemic Anxieties and Colonial Common Sense* (Princeton, NJ: Princeton University Press, 2009). As historian Stephanie E. Smallwood has explained, archival silences do not always mean a lack of sources about enslaved people but an absence of anything that hints at the "interiority of their lives." See Smallwood, "The Politics of the Archive and History's Accountability to the Enslaved," *History of the Present* 6, no. 2 (Fall 2016): 123. The testimonies used

in this study do not provide glimpses of interiority, but they do allow for a discussion of lived experiences of enslaved and self-liberated people that do not exist in English, French, or Dutch colonial archives.

24. Sophie White, *Voices of the Enslaved: Love, Labor, and Longing in French Louisiana* (Chapel Hill: Published for the Omohundro Institute of Early American History and Culture by University of North Carolina Press, 2019). As White has shown, the French archives do contain ample testimonies to the enslaved experience but, just like for the Anglo-Atlantic, those sources come from the period after the 1650s. See Sophie White and Trevor Burnard, eds., *Hearing Enslaved Voices: African and Indian Slave Testimony in British and French America, 1700–1848* (New York: Routledge, 2021). See, also, Randy M. Browne, *The Driver's Story: Labor and Power in the World of Atlantic Slavery* (Philadelphia: University of Pennsylvania Press, 2024).

25. They also provide a unique window into histories of captivity, which tend to focus on the experiences of captivity or redemption from the perspective of a single empire rather than as an entangled process. See Linda Colley, *Captives* (New York: Random House, 2002).

26. This book draws heavily from *gobierno* and *indiferente general* in the Archivo General de Indias, specifically the letters sent from Spanish Caribbean governors and the reports that they compiled and dispatched to the Council of the Indies during moments when Spanish imperial officials planned attacks on English, French, or Dutch colonies or responded to acts of aggression by northern Europeans.

27. For more on gendered vulnerabilities, see Elise A. Mitchell, "Morbid Crossings: Surviving Smallpox, Maritime Quarantine, and the Gendered Geography of the Early Eighteenth-Century Intra-Caribbean Slave Trade," *William and Mary Quarterly* 79, no. 2 (April 2022): 192–93. See also Sowande' M. Mustakeem, *Slavery at Sea: Terror, Sex, and Sickness in the Middle Passage* (Urbana: University of Illinois Press, 2016); Michael A. Gomez, *Exchanging Our Country Marks: The Transformation of African Identities in the Colonial and Antebellum South* (Chapel Hill: University of North Carolina Press, 1998), 166–67.

28. Elsa Gelpí Baíz, *Siglo en blanco: Estudio de la Economía azucarera en Puerto Rico, Siglo XVI* (San Juan: Editorial de la Universidad de Puerto Rico, 2000); Jennifer Wolff, "Emaranhado: Puerto Rico y el comercio trasatlántico de esclavos, 1580–1630," in *Sometidos a esclavitud: los africanos y sus descendientes en el Caribe hispano*, ed. Consuelo Naranjo Orovio (Santa Marta: Editorial Unimagdalena, 2021); Marc Eagle, "The Audiencia of Santo Domingo in the Seventeenth Century" (PhD diss., Tulane University, 2005); María Cristina Navarrete Peláez, "De las 'malas entradas' y las estrategias del 'buen pasaje': el contrabando de esclavos neogranadino, 1550–1690," *História Crítica* 34 (July–December 2007); Lissette Acosta Corniel, "Negras, mulatas, y morenas en La Española del siglo XVI (1502–1606)," in *Esclavitud, mestizaje y abolicionismo en los mundos hispánicos*, ed. Aurelia Martin Casares (Granada: Universidad de Granada, 2015); Bethany Aram, "Caribbean Ginger and Atlantic Trade, 1570–1648," *Journal of Global History* 10, no. 3 (October 2015); Wheat, *Atlantic Africa*; Marc Eagle, "Tiempos contrarios: arribadas de barcos negreros en la Isla Española, siglo XVI," in *Los negocios de la esclavitud: Tratantes y mercados de esclavos en el Atlántico ibérico, siglos XV–XIX*, ed. Manuel Fernández Chaves and Rafael M. Pérez García (Sevilla: Universidad de Sevilla, 2019); Ponce Vázquez, *Islanders and Empire*; Marc Eagle, "Informal Entrepôts: Witness Testimony about Slave Ship *Arribadas* to Santo Domingo and San Juan in the 1620s," *Colonial Latin American Review* 32, no. 1 (2023): 11–33; Jennifer Wolff, "Liquid Geographies of Transatlantic Slavery: Caribbean Pathways of Forced Migration, 1580–1640," *Culture & History Digital Journal* 12, no. 2 (December 2023): 2–12.

29. Anne Pérotin-Dumon, "French, English and Dutch in the Lesser Antilles: From Privateering to Planting, c. 1550–c.1650," in *General History of the Caribbean: Volume 2: New Societies: The Caribbean in the Long Sixteenth Century*, ed. Pieter C. Emmer and German Carrera Damas (Hong Kong: UNESCO, 1999); Marcy Norton and Daviken Studnicki-Gizbert, "The Multinational Commodification of Tobacco, 1492–1650," in *The Atlantic World and Virginia, 1550–1624*, ed. Peter C. Mancall (Chapel Hill: University of North Carolina Press, 2007); Christian J. Koot, *Empire at the Periphery: British Colonists, Anglo-Dutch Trade, and the Development of the British Atlantic, 1621–1713* (New York: New York University Press, 2011); Linda M. Rupert, *Creolization and Contraband: Curaçao in the Early Modern Atlantic World* (Athens: University of Georgia Press, 2012); Kristen Block, *Ordinary Lives in the Early Caribbean: Religion, Colonial Competition, and the Politics of Profit* (Athens: University of Georgia Press, 2012); Ernesto Bassi, *An Aqueous Territory: Sailor Geographies and New Granada's Transimperial Greater Caribbean World* (Durham, NC: Duke University Press, 2016); Tessa Murphy, *The Creole Archipelago: Race and Borders in the Colonial Caribbean* (Philadelphia: University of Pennsylvania Press, 2021).

30. This builds on recent work such as Susanah Shaw Romney, *New Netherland Connections: Intimate Networks and Atlantic Ties in Seventeenth-Century America* (Chapel Hill: University of North Carolina Press, 2014), introduction; Roper, *Advancing Empire*.

31. Dunn, *Sugar and Slaves*, esp. chap. 6 and 7; Gabriel Debien, *Les esclaves aux Antilles françaises* (Guadeloupe: Société d'Histoire de la Guadeloupe, 1974); Winthrop D. Jordan, *White over Black: American Attitudes Toward the Negro, 1550–1812* (Chapel Hill: University of North Carolina Press, 1968); Curtin, *Rise and Fall of the Plantation Complex*; Ira Berlin, *Many Thousands Gone: The First Two Centuries of Slavery in North America* (Cambridge, MA: Harvard University Press, 1998); David Eltis, *The Rise of African Slavery in the Americas* (New York: Cambridge University Press, 2000); Menard, *Sweet Negotiations*; Amussen, *Caribbean Exchanges*; Rebecca Anne Goetz, "Rethinking the Unthinking Decision: Old Questions and New Problems in the History of Slavery and Race in the Colonial South," *Journal of Southern History* 25, no. 3 (August 2009): 599–612; John C. Coombs, "The Phases of Conversion: A New Chronology for the Rise of Slavery in Early Virginia," *William and Mary Quarterly* 68, no. 3 (July 2011): 332–60; Rugemer, "The Development of Mastery and Race in the Comprehensive Slave Codes of the Greater Caribbean," 429–58; Simon P. Newman, *A New World of Labor: The Development of Plantation Slavery in the British Atlantic* (Philadelphia: University of Pennsylvania Press, 2013); Michael Guasco, *Slaves and Englishmen: Human Bondage in the Early Modern Atlantic World* (Philadelphia: University of Pennsylvania Press, 2014).

32. Wim Klooster calls trade in this period "a peculiar mixture of trade, warfare, and colonization." See Klooster, *Illicit Riches: Dutch Trade in the Caribbean, 1648–1795* (Leiden: KITLV Press, 1998), 22; Pérotin-Dumon, "French, English and Dutch in the Lesser Antilles."

33. Gregory O'Malley, *Final Passages: The Intercolonial Slave Trade of British America, 1619–1807* (Chapel Hill: Published for the Omohundro Institute of Early American History and Culture by University of North Carolina Press, 2014), 86.

34. For more on how this financing worked, see Pérotin-Dumon, "French, English and Dutch in the Lesser Antilles," 115; Elizabeth Mancke, "Empire and State," in *The British Atlantic World, 1500–1800*, ed. David Armitage and Michael J. Braddick (New York: Palgrave Macmillan, 2002), 181.

35. "Traffic, n.," OED Online, December 2021.

36. Mark G. Hanna, "Well-Behaved Pirates Seldom Make History: A Reevaluation of the Golden Age of English Piracy," in *Governing the Sea in the Early Modern Era: Essays in Honor*

of Robert C. Ritchie, ed. Peter C. Mancall and Carole Shammas (San Marino, CA: Huntington Library, Art Collections, and Botanical Gardens, 2015), 134.

37. Philip De Souza, "Rome's Contribution to the Development of Piracy," *Memoirs of the American Academy in Rome: Supplementary Volumes* 6 (2008): 71–96.

38. Kevin McDonald, *Pirates, Merchants, Settlers, and Slaves: Colonial America and the Indo-Atlantic World* (Chicago: University of Chicago Press, 2015), 12–13; Kris E. Lane, *Pillaging the Empire: Piracy in the Americas, 1500–1750* (London: M. E. Sharpe, 1998), 4.

39. John Angus Martin, *Island Caribs and French Settlers in Grenada, 1498–1763* (St. George's, Grenada: Grenada National Museum Press, 2013); Carolyn Marie Arena, "Indian Slaves from Caribana: Trade and Labor in the Seventeenth-Century Caribbean" (PhD diss., Columbia University, 2017); Erin Woodruff Stone, *Captives of Conquest: Slavery in the Early Modern Spanish Caribbean* (Philadelphia: University of Pennsylvania Press, 2021); Murphy, *Creole Archipelago*; Mercado-Montero, "Indigenous Raiding, Captive Taking, and the Politics of Maritime Violence."

40. I draw on Jean M. O'Brien's work on how history can perpetuate a settler-colonial myth of Indigenous extinction. See O'Brien, *Firsting and Lasting: Writing Indians Out of Existence in New England* (Minneapolis: University of Minnesota Press, 2010). For an important counter to this myth in the Caribbean, see John Paul Paniagua, "Contesting Indigeneity in Colonial Cuba," *William and Mary Quarterly* 81, no. 3 (July 2024): 531–66.

41. In the Spanish Caribbean, the dramatic population decline of the Indigenous populations of the Greater Antilles led a Dominican friar named Bartolomé de las Casas to encourage the Spanish Crown to ban the enslavement of Indigenous people and instead encourage the forced transportation of enslaved Africans to the Caribbean. Esteban Mira Caballos, *El indio antillano: Repartimiento, encomienda y esclavitud (1492–1542)* (Sevilla: Múóz Moya Editor, 1997); Nancy E. van Deusen, *Global Indios: The Indigenous Struggle for Justice in Sixteenth-Century Spain* (Durham, NC: Duke University Press, 2015); Andrés Reséndez, *The Other Slavery: The Uncovered Story of Indian Enslavement in America* (Boston: Houghton Mifflin Harcourt, 2016), introduction and chap. 1; Stone, *Captives of Conquest*.

42. Ignacio Gallup-Díaz, *The Door of the Seas and the Key to the Universe: Indian Politics and Imperial Rivalry in Darién, 1640–1750* (New York: Columbia University Press, 2005); Murphy, "Kalinago Colonizers: Indigenous People and the Settlement of the Lesser Antilles," in Roper, *Torrid Zone*.

43. Frank Moya Pons, *History of the Caribbean* (Princeton, NJ: Markus Weiner, 2007), 50; Koot, *Empire at the Periphery*, 27; Dunn, *Sugar and Slaves*, 17.

44. Gabriel de Avilez Rocha, "Maroons in the *Montes*: Toward a Political Ecology of Marronage in the Sixteenth-Century Caribbean," in *Early Modern Black Diaspora Studies: A Critical Anthology*, ed. Cassander Smith, Miles P. Grier, and Nicholas Jones (London: Palgrave Macmillan, 2018); Robert C. Schwaller, "Contested Conquests: African Maroons and the Incomplete Conquest of Hispaniola, 1519–1620," *The Americas* 75, no. 4 (October 2018).

45. For more on the London-based merchants involved in the Providence Island Company, see Roper, *Advancing Empire*, 54–57; The National Archives [hereafter TNA], CO 124/2, "At a Court held for the Island of Providence at Warwick House," June 15, 1631, folio 22; Michel Christian Camus, *L'île de la Tortue au cœur de la Flibuste caraïbe* (Paris: Éditions L'Harmattan, 1997), 31–33; AGI, Santa Fé 223, "Consulta de Guerra," February 6, 1640, fols. 133r–134r.

46. Richard Pares, *War and Trade in the West Indies, 1739–1763* (London, 1963); Curtis Nettels, "England and the Spanish-American Trade, 1680–1715," *Journal of Modern History* 3,

no. 1 (March 1931): 1–32; Fabrício Pereira Prado, "Colônia do Sacramento: a situaço na fronteira platina no século XVIII," *Horizontes Antropológicos* 9, no. 1 (2003): 79–104; Lane, *Pillaging the Empire*; Héctor R. Feliciano Ramos, *El Contrabando inglés en el Caribe y el Golfo de México, 1748–1778* (Seville, 1990); Anne Perótin-Dumon, "The Pirate and the Emperor: Power and the Law on the Seas, 1450–1850," in *The Political Economy of Merchant Empires: State Power and World Trade, 1350–1750*, ed. James D. Tracy (Cambridge, UK: Cambridge University Press, 1997).

47. Alison Games, "Cohabitation, Suriname-Style: English Inhabitants in Dutch Suriname after 1667," *William and Mary Quarterly* 72, no. 2 (April 2015): 195–242.

48. AGI, Contaduría 1480, "Caja de Panamá, Testimonios de las Juntas de Real Hacienda," fols. 54–57v; AGI, Santa Fé 223, r. 3, "Carta de Salvador de la Peña, Capitán del Presidio de Santa Catalina," December 17, 1646, fol. 222v.

49. Jane Landers, *Black Society in Spanish Florida* (Urbana: University of Illinois Press, 1999), chap. 2; Linda M. Rupert, "Marronage, Manumission and Maritime Trade in the Early Modern Caribbean," *Slavery & Abolition* 30, no. 3 (2009): 361–82; Fernanda Bretones Lane, "Free to Bury Their Dead: Baptism and the Meanings of Freedom in the Eighteenth-Century Caribbean," *Slavery & Abolition* 42, no. 3 (2021): 449–65.

Chapter 1

1. Huerga, *Cartas de gobernadores: Vol. 2*, "Carta del Juan Melgarejo," February 3, 1582, p. 115; Huerga, *Cartas de gobernadores*, 2:125–27; Gelpí Baíz, *Siglo en Blanco*, 105.

2. Edouard Gosselin and Charles de Beaurepaire, eds., *Documents authentiques et inédits pour server à l'histoire de la marine* (Rouen: Impr. de H. Boissel, 1876), 158.

3. Sergio Manuel Rodríguez Lorenzo, *La Carrera de Indias: la ruta, los hombres, las mercancías* (Madrid: La Huerta Grande Robinson Librería Naútica, 2015).

4. Ponce Vázquez, *Islanders and Empire*, 42–43.

5. Gelpí Baíz, *Siglo en blanco*, 18–21; Navarrete Peláez, "De las 'malas entradas'"; Wolff, "*Emaranhado*"; Manuel F. Fernández Chaves, "Manuel Caldeira y la trata de esclavos en el Caribe, 1556–1562," in *Sometidos a esclavitud: los africanos y sus descendientes en el Caribe hispano*, ed. Consuelo Naranjo Orovio (Santa Marta: Editorial Unimagdalena, 2021); Eagle, "Tiempos contrarios"; Eagle, "Informal Entrepôts"; Wolff, "Liquid Geographies."

6. AGI, Santo Domingo 178B, "Memoriales de Alonso de Espinosa Centeno," fol. 32; Casey Schmitt, "Centering Spanish Jamaica: Regional Competition, Informal Trade, and the English Invasion, 1620–62," *William and Mary Quarterly* 76, no. 4 (October 2019): 12–14; Eagle, "Informal entrepôts," 27–28.

7. Eagle, "Informal entrepôts," 27.

8. Gelpí Baíz, *Siglo en blanco*, 209, 106. There was also competition over access to informal trade. David Wheat argues that city officials in Santo Domingo manipulated census numbers to direct the depopulations of Hispaniola between 1604 and 1606 toward the western half of the island in a bid to redirect valuable informal trade to Santo Domingo. See Wheat, *Atlantic Africa*, 112.

9. Epeli Hau'ofa, "Our Sea of Islands," *Contemporary Pacific* 6, no. 1 (Spring 1994): 153.

10. Murphy, *Creole Archipelago*, 4. Recent scholarship challenges the tendency to study the Caribbean through a single island or imperial system. See, for example, Bassi, *Aqueous Territory*.

11. For a wider discussion of this, see Ernesto Bassi, "Small Islands in a Geopolitically Unstable Caribbean World," *Oxford Research Encyclopedia: Latin American History* (March 2019).

12. Smith, *True Travels*, 52–53. Gérard Lafleur describes this as corsairs seeking "la bonne fortune." See Lafleur, *Les Caraïbes des Petites Antilles*, 26; Irene A. Wright, trans. and ed., *Further English Voyages to Spanish America, 1583–1594: Documents from the Archives of the Indies at Seville Illustrating English Voyages to the Caribbean, the Spanish Main, Florida, and Virginia* (London: Printed for the Hakluyt Society, 1951), xxv.

13. Gayle K. Brunelle, *The New World Merchants of Rouen, 1559–1630*, vol. 16 of Sixteenth Century Essays & Studies, ed. Charles G. Nauert Jr. (Kirksville, MO: Sixteenth Century Journal Publishers, 1999), 17; Kenneth R. Andrews, *The Spanish Caribbean: Trade and Plunder, 1530–1630* (New Haven, CT: Yale University Press, 1978), 182. According to Alejandro de la Fuente, "between 1580 and 1595, . . . hides were one of the most eagerly sought products by the French, English, and Dutch smugglers who traversed the waters of the Caribbean." See de la Fuente, *Havana and the Atlantic*, 21.

14. Paul Bréard, ed., *Documents rélatifs à la Marine normande et à ses armements aux XVIe et XVIIe siècles le Canada, l'Afrique, les Antilles, et les Indes* (Rouen: Société de l'histoire de Normandie, 1889), 149. P. E. H. Hair argues that designations such as Sierra Leone or the Isles de Pérou became stand-ins to simply signal a transatlantic voyage. See Hair, "A Note on French and Spanish Voyages to Sierra Leone 1550–1585," *History in Africa* 18 (1991): 138.

15. Fuente, *Havana*, 42. Hawkins is an example of seizing rather than purchasing.

16. Wheat, *Atlantic Africa*, 50–51.

17. Hair, "Note on French and Spanish Voyages," 137–8. For the decade between 1574 and 1584, Hair notes that nineteen voyages to Sierra Leone were recorded for Honfleur.

18. AGI, Santo Domingo 168, r. 3, no. 12, "Carta del gobernador Francisco Bahamonde de Lugo al rey," 1566, printed in Alegría, *Documentos históricos de Puerto Rico Vol. 4*, 254.

19. J. O. Ijoma, "Portuguese Activities in West Africa Before 1600: The Consequences," *Transafrican Journal of History* 11 (1982): 137–38; Marc Eagle and David Wheat, "The Early Iberian Slave Trade to the Spanish Caribbean, 1500–1580," in *From the Galleons to the Highlands*, 50–51.

20. Maria do Rosário Pimentel, "The Traffic of Slaves Between Continuities and Changes: From the Mediterranean to the Atlantic," in *Tradition and Innovation*, ed. Maria do Rosário Monteiro, Maria João Pereira Neto, and Mário Ming Kong (London: CRC Press, 2021), 422.

21. Wolff, "Liquid Geographies," 8.

22. Manuel Francisco Fernández Chaves, "El contrato de arrendamiento de 'los tratos de todos los ríos de Guinea y las islas de Buan' de 1574–1580: análisis y edición," in *Los negocios de la esclavitud: tratantes y mercados de esclavos en el Atlántico Ibérico, siglos XV–XVIII*, ed. Rafael M. Pérez García, Manuel Francisco Fernández Chaves, and José Luis Belmonte Postigo (Seville: Universidad de Sevilla, 2018), 105.

23. Alejandro Tapia y Rivera, *Biblioteca Historica de Puerto-Rico, que contiene varios documentos de los siglos XV, XVI, XVII y XVIII* (Puerto Rico: Imprenta de Marquez, 1854), 459.

24. Moreau, *Les Petites Antilles*, 38; Hofman et al., "Colonial Encounters," 364–66.

25. *A Summarie and True Discourse of Sir Frances Drakes West Indian Voyage* (London, 1589), 20.

26. Jean-Pierre Moreau, ed., *Un Flibustier Français dans la Mer des Antilles en 1618–1620: Manuscrit inédit du début du XVII siècle publié par Jean-Pierre Moreau* (Clamart: Editions J.-P. Moreau, 1987), 98. Kris E. Lane also discusses what he calls the "small arms" trade carried out between northern Europeans and "unconquered 'Cannibal Caribs'" in the opening decade of the seventeenth century. See Lane, *Pillaging the Empire*, 66.

27. AGI, Santo Domingo 155, no. 23, "El gobernador Luis Vallejo a Su Majestad," August 27, 1550, in Huerga, *Cartas de gobernadores*, 1:105. See also Andrews, *Spanish Caribbean*, 16.

28. Kenneth R. Andrews, ed., *English Privateering Voyages to the West Indies, 1588–1595: Documents Relating to English Voyages to the West Indies* (London: Published for the Hakluyt Society, 1959), 210.

29. Moreau, *Un Flibustier Français*, 98.

30. Gonzalo Fernández de Oviedo y Valdés, *Historia general y natural de las Indias, Islas y Tierra-Firme del Mar Océano* (Madrid: Imprenta de la Real Academia de la Historia, 1851), 270. See also Karen Ordahl Kupperman, *The Atlantic in World History* (New York: Oxford University Press, 2012), esp. chap. 4 for a description of the production of cassava bread as well as the crop's global impact.

31. Robert Harcourt, *A Relation of a Voyage to Guiana* (London: Hakluyt Society, 1928), 94.

32. Wim Klooster discusses one example where a Dutch captain named Commander Pieter Schouten sailed to St. Christopher in 1624 and "made the natives prepare cassava," indicating that occasionally coercion was involved in the production and trade of cassava. The other accounts reflect the relatively peaceful experiences like those of Drake. See Wim Klooster, *The Dutch Moment: War, Trade, and Settlement in the Seventeenth-Century Atlantic World* (Ithaca, NY: Cornell University Press, 2016), 134.

33. Quoted in Andrews, *Spanish Caribbean*, 75.

34. Bibiano Torres Ramírez, "Los primeros intentos de formación de la Armada de Barlovento," *Anuario de Historia de América Latina* 11 (1974): 33–51. Marc Eagle and David Wheat argue for the importance of sharing local knowledge about trade opportunities for the licensed sixteenth-century slave trade as well. See Eagle and Wheat, "Early Iberian Slave Trade," 57.

35. Nicolás de Cardona, *Descripciones geográficas e hidrográficas de muchas tierras y mares del norte y sur, en las Indias, en especial del descubrimiento del Reino de California* (Madrid: Turner libros, 1989), 10. Also cited in Jennifer Wolff, *Isla Atlántica Puerto Rico: Circuitos antillanos de contrabando y la formación del Mundo Atlántico, 1580–1636* (Madrid: Ediciones Dos Calles, 2022), 171.

36. AGI, Santo Domingo 168, r. 3, no. 12, "Carta del gobernador Francisco Bahamonde de Lugo al rey," 1566, printed in Alegría, *Documentos históricos de Puerto Rico*, 4:254.

37. Wolfgang Kaiser and Guillaume Calafat, "The Economy of Ransoming in the Early Modern Mediterranean," in *Religion and Trade: Cross-Cultural Exchanges in World History, 1000–1900*, ed. Francesca Trivellato, Leor Halevi, and Catia Atunes (New York: Oxford University Press, 2014), 110. See also Lauren Benton, *They Called It Peace: Worlds of Imperial Violence* (Princeton, NJ: Princeton University Press, 2024).

38. English traffickers attempted to raid two Portuguese transatlantic slave ships in 1592 while they watered at Dominica, causing them to sail to San Juan for protection. Jennifer Wolff points out that Portuguese slave ship captains also used claims that they had been attacked at sea to justify anchoring at ports outside of their licenses, so some caution and corroboration with other sources is required when reading accounts of maritime predation. See Wolff, *Isla Atlántica*, 120–21.

39. Andrews, *English Privateering Voyages*, 213–14.

40. Arturo Morales-Carrión, *Puerto Rico and the Non-Hispanic Caribbean: A Study in the Decline of Spanish Exclusivism* (Río Piedras: University of Puerto Rico Press, 1952), 22.

41. Wheat, *Atlantic Africa*, 68–69. In 1592, two different Portuguese transatlantic slave ship captains reported being chased by English ships near Dominica. See Wolff, *Isla Atlántica*, 120–21.

42. Andrews, *English Privateering Voyages*, 213–14.

43. Wolff, *Isla Atlántica*, 71.

44. Navarrete Peláez, "De las 'malas entradas,'" 164.

45. Wolff, *Isla Atlántica*, 28.

46. Jerónimo de Torres, "Relación sobre cosas de la Isla Española," May 29, 1577. Transcribed in E. Rodrigo Demorizi, *Relaciones Históricas de Santo Domingo, Vol. II* (Santo Domingo: Montalvo, 1945), 132.

47. Quoted in Manuel Arturo Peña Batlle, *La Isla de Tortuga: plaza de armas, refugio y seminario de los enemigos de España en Indias* (Madrid: Ediciones Cultural Hispanica, 1977), 46.

48. Torres, "Relación sobre cosas de la Isla Española," p. 135.

49. A vara is a unit of measurement equivalent to between 30 and 40 inches. Torres, "Relación sobre cosas de la Isla Española," 135.

50. "Una gran golosina." Torres, "Relación sobre cosas de la Isla Española," 131.

51. Gelpí Baíz, *Siglo en blanco*, 104. This builds on Jesse Cromwell's discussion of "inter-imperial foraging" for eighteenth-century Venezuela. See Jesse Cromwell, *The Smuggler's World: Illicit Trade and Atlantic Communities in Eighteenth-Century Venezuela* (Chapel Hill: Published for the Omohundro Institute of Early American History and Culture by University of North Carolina Press, 2018), 30.

52. Torres, "Relación sobre cosas de la Isla Española," 129–30; AGI, Santo Domingo 99, r. 15, no. 95, "Carta de Gabriel de Luján," Havana, December 16, 1583, unfoliated.

53. Baltasar López de Castro, "Memorial al Consejo de Indias," May 20, 1596. Reprinted in Demorizi, *Relaciones Históricas*, p. 169.

54. Violence, however, could go both ways. Ponce Vázquez discusses an example from 1569 in which a French ship exchanged hostages with trade partners in northwestern Hispaniola, only to have the Spanish attack them and ransom the captive French back to the ship's captain. Ponce Vázquez, *Islanders and Empire*, 63–64.

55. Ponce Vázquez, *Islanders and Empire*, 72.

56. "Carta del Arzobispo de Santo Domingo, Fray Nicólas Ramos, a Su Magestad," March 4, 1594. Reprinted in Demorizi, *Relaciones Históricas*, 145, 148.

57. For more on the use of rituals to facilitate trans-confessional trade, see Trivellato, "Introduction: The Historical and Comparative Study of Cross-Cultural Trade," in Trivellato et al., *Religion and Trade*, 13. For more on cross-cultural trade beyond boundaries of kinship, religion, or professional ties, see Cátia Atunes and Filipa Ribeiro da Silva, "Cross-cultural Entrepreneurship in the Atlantic: Africans, Dutch and Sephardic Jews in Western Africa, 1580–1674," *Itinerario* 35, no. 1 (2011): 49–76; Roquinaldo Ferreira, *Cross-Cultural Exchange in the Atlantic World: Angola and Brazil During the Era of the Slave Trade* (New York: Cambridge University Press, 2012).

58. AGI, Santo Domingo 175, "Información sobre la llegada del corsario francés Juan Bourdon a Coamo antes el gobernador Juan de Melgarejo," February 12, 1583, unfoliated; Gelpí Baíz, *Siglo en blanco*, 17, 104, 166.

59. Those goods might have also been intended for trade in Atlantic Africa before a return to the Caribbean. See Gosselin and Beaurepaire, *Documents authentiques et inédits*, 159.

60. Gosselin and Beaurepaire, *Documents authentiques et inédits*, 158.

61. Gosselin and Beaurepaire, *Documents authentiques et inédits*, 158. Sahures, or Sahurs, was also equipped out of Normandy for a voyage to "Terre-Neuve" with another ship named the *Renommée* in January 1574. In February and March 1575, Sahures was outfitted again

to sail to "Terre-Neuve" with two other ships, the *l'Etoile*, captained by Pierre Pinchemont, and the *Sansue*, captained by Guillaume Le Lièvre. It is unclear where Sahures encountered Hacquet, but it is tantalizing to think that Sahures was among the many captains who sailed under a commission to the Newfoundland fisheries and sailed south into the Caribbean to raid before a homeward voyage. See AGI, Contratación 169B, "Contra Gil Alberto, Juan Pulén, Fracisco y Juan Gumbelo, franceses presos que vinieron por Santo Domingo por piratas" unfoliated; TNA, CO 1/1, No. 54, "Petition of the Treasurer and Company, with the Scottish undertakers of the plantations in Newfoundland, to the King," March 16, 1621; and AGI, Contratacion, 169B, Numero 8: "Carta de don Diego Gómez de Sandoval al rey," August 1, 1618, unfoliated.

62. Aurelio Tió, *Nuevas fuentes para la historia de Puerto Rico: documentos inéditos o poco conocidos cuyos originales se encuentran en el Archivo General de Indias en la ciudad de Sevilla, España* (San Juan: Ediciones de la Universidad Interamericana de Puerto Rico, 1961), 515.

63. Gosselin and Beaurepaire, *Documents authentiques et inédits*, 159.

64. I have not yet found evidence of whether Hacquet made another voyage to West Africa or if the enslaved captives that he had on his ship in 1579 were seized during a raid.

65. Huerga, *Cartas de gobernadores*, 2:124.

66. This was true along the Spanish Main as well: "Pedro, Indian, précis of his deposition, Cartagena," February 16, 1587, in Andrews, *English Privateering Voyages*, 226.

67. AGI, Patronato 273, r. 6, "Auto del capitán y piloto Juan Rodriguez Puntallana," November 1653, fols. 142r–143r.

68. Wolff, *Isla Atlántica*, 191.

69. Alice V. M. Samson and Jago Cooper, "History on Mona Island: Long-term Human and Landscape Dynamics of an 'Uninhabited' Island," *New West Indian Guide* (January 2015): 43.

70. Wolff, *Isla Atlántica*, 191.

71. "Pleito contra los indios de la isla de Mona," in Alegría, Vol. 5, 448.

72. "Pleito contra los indios de la isla de Mona," in Alegría, Vol. 5, 496–98; Gelpí Baíz, *Siglo en blanco*, 105.

73. Wolff, *Isla Atlántica*, 191.

74. For more on the role of people of African descent in informal trade in Hispaniola, particularly women, see Acosta Corniel, "Negras, mulatas, y morenas," 214.

75. "Extract from Edmund Barker's narrative of the voyage of the *Penelope*, the *Merchant Royal*, and the *Edward* Bonaventure," Friday, May 24, 1594, in Andrews, *English Privateering Voyages*, 288.

76. Gosselin and Beaurepaire, *Documents authentiques et inédits*, 154.

77. Gelpí Baíz, *Siglo en blanco*, 104.

78. Andrews, *English Privateering Voyages*, 288.

79. Gosselin and Beaurepaire, *Documents authentiques et inédits*, 159.

80. For more on illicit trade in Hispaniola, see Marc Eagle, "The Audiencia of Santo Domingo in the Seventeenth Century" (PhD diss., Tulane University, 2005); Ponce Vázquez, *Islanders and Empire*.

81. Tapia, *Biblioteca Historica de Puerto-Rico*, 477.

82. "Testimonio de Pedro Osorio de Peralta," March 12, 1582, in Huerga, *Cartas de gobernadores*, 2:123–24. For more on *rescate*, see Molly A. Warsh, "Enslaved Pearl Divers in the Sixteenth Century Caribbean," *Slavery and Abolition* 31, no. 3 (2010): 346–47; Wheat, *Atlantic Africa*, 109–10.

83. AGI, Santo Domingo 155, r. 9, no. 65, "Carta de D. Juan de Céspedes, gobernador de Puerto Rico," September 20, 1580, unfoliated.

84. Kaiser and Calafat, "Economy of Ransoming," 110.

85. Mercado-Montero, "Indigenous Raiding,"; van Deusen, *Global Indios*; Stone, *Captives of Conquest*.

86. Irene A. Wright, "Rescates: With Special Reference to Cuba, 1599–1610," *Hispanic American Historical Review* 3, no. 3 (August 1920): 333–61.

87. AGI, Santo Domingo 168, r. 2, no. 37, "Carta de Diego de Carasa, gobernador de la isla de San Juan al rey," July 5, 1556, fol. 1v.

88. Wolff, *Isla Atlántica*, 175.

89. Gelpí Baíz, *Siglo en blanco*, 47–50. Feral cattle drove informal trade in other parts of the Spanish Caribbean as well. See Mercedes García Rodríguez, "Contrabando *versus* monopolio: las dos caras del comercio en la Cuba colonial," in *Entre lo legal, lo ilícito, y lo clandestino: Prácticas comerciales y navegación en el Gran Caribe, siglos XVII al XIX*, ed. Johanna von Grafenstein, Rafal Reichert, and Julio César Rodríguez Treviño (Mexico City: Instituto de Investigaciones, 2018), 164; Antonio Vázquez de Espinosa, *Compendio y descripción de las Indias Occidentales*, ed. Balbino Velasco Bayón (Madrid: Historia 16, 1992), 195; Ana Ozuna, "Rebellion and Anticolonial Struggle in Hispaniola: From Indigenous Agitators to African Rebels," *Africology: The Journal of Pan African Studies* 11, no. 7 (May 2018): 86.

90. Wolff, *Isla Atlántica*, 131.

91. "Carta del Juan Melgarejo," February 3, 1582, in Huerga, *Cartas de gobernadores, Vol. 2*, 115.

92. "Testimonio de Juan Sanchez Hortiz, San Germán," July 15, 1594, printed in Alegría, *Documentos históricos de Puerto Rico*, 5:526.

93. An arroba was about forty pounds. Huerga, *Cartas de gobernadores*, 2:125. According to reports, nearly four thousand cattle were slaughtered to produce hides to trade with Hacquet. See Huerga, *Cartas de gobernadores*, 2:127.

94. Gelpí Baíz, *Siglo en blanco*, 105. Salamanca purchased twelve *piezas*, which could have been twelve healthy adults or a higher number of Senegambian captives who were either young, old, or ill in some way. A *pieza de Indias* was a commercial term used to describe an enslaved African who was a healthy adult, wherein young, old, and ill African captives were measured in half *piezas*. See Wheat, *Atlantic Africa*, 110.

95. "Testimonio de Juan Sanchez Hortiz," in Alegría, *Documentos históricos de Puerto Rico*, 5:526.

96. According to testimony collected during the investigation into this affair, Méndez de los Ríos was accused of collecting the taxes owed by residents of San Germán for the enslaved Senegambians trafficked by Hacquet in cattle rather than specie. He then used those cattle to build his *hato*, or ranch, at Cabo Rojo. See Wolff, *Isla Atlántica*, 74.

97. "Testimonio de Alonso de Torres Maldonado, San Germán," July 19, 1594, in Alegría, *Documentos históricos de Puerto Rico*, 5:539.

98. These are what Michelle A. McKinley calls "thick relationships that factored into the calculus of liberty and bondage" in *Fractional Freedoms: Slavery, Intimacy, and Legal Mobilization in Colonial Lima, 1600–1700* (New York: Cambridge University Press, 2016), 13.

99. Gelpí Baíz, *Siglo en blanco*, 20–21.

100. Aram, "Caribbean Ginger and Atlantic Trade, 1570–1648," 410–30. Evidence points to some of the Senegambian captives trafficked by Hacquet laboring in the production of ginger

by 1586. See "El tesorero Juan de Vargas Zapata y el Contador Francisco Rodríguez a S.M., acusando al gobernador Diego Menéndez de Valdés y pidiendo que lo remuevan del puesto," San Juan, July 12, 1586, in Huerga, *Cartas de gobernadores*, 2:226.

101. "Carta del capitán Juan de Céspedes, gobernador de Puerto Rico, a S.M. informando sobre ataques de los caribes," San Juan, February 24, 1582 in Huerga, *Cartas de gobernadores, Vol. 2*, 112.

102. The process involved paramount chiefs inviting allies to plan an attack over several days of feasting, during which time elderly women recounted the insults committed by the enemy to encourage warriors to action. See Raymond Breton, *Relations de l'île de la Guadeloupe* (Basse-Terre: Société d'Histoire de la Guadeloupe, 1978), 76; Du Tertre, *Histoire Générale des îsles*, 443; Fernando Santos-Granero, *Vital Enemies: Slavery, Predation, and the Amerindian Political Economy of Life* (Austin: University of Texas Press, 2009), 51–53.

103. "Carta del capitán Francisco de Bahamonde Lugo informa a S.M. de su viaje y llegada a la isla," San Juan, February 10, 1566, in Huerga, *Cartas de gobernadores*, 1:185; Du Tertre, *Histoire Générale des îsles*, 449; Santos-Granero, *Vital Enemies*, 53. For Kalinago names mentioned here, see Breton, *Dictionaire François-Caraibe* (Auxerre: Giles Bouquet, 1666), 304.

104. "Carta del capitán Francisco de Bahamonde Lugo"; Santos-Granero, *Vital Enemies*, 50.

105. Breton, *Dictionaire caraibe-françois*, entry for acamátêti likia. Although Breton's dictionary came from a later period, and it is entirely possible that the term emerged over the course of the seventeenth century in response to continued European slave raids against Kalinago populations in the Lesser Antilles, I choose to retain this wording for an earlier century because it helps ground these practices in a Kalinago worldview.

106. Juan José Ponce Vázquez refers to contraband trade being "an intrinsic part of Hispaniola's culture" by the early seventeenth century. See Ponce Vázquez, *Islanders and Empire*, 59.

Chapter 2

1. Hofman et al., "Colonial Encounters," 306.

2. Norton and Studnicki-Gizbert, "Multinational Commodification of Tobacco," 262.

3. Breton, *Dictionnaire caraïbe-français*, 222; Whitehead, *Lords of the Tiger Spirit*, 65; Allaire, "Ethnohistory of the Caribs," 101. Evidence for this agreement came from a narrative provided by John Hilton in 1675. See Hilton, "Relation of the first settlement of Saint Christopher and Nevis," 1–3. See also Thornton and Heywood, *Central Africans*, 29. Tegreman would have been considered a "captain" among the Kalinago, who did not practice kingship in ways described by European observers. The European sources refer to the English being settled next to the "king's house," which likely meant the Kalinago's communal men's house, a large structure in the center of Kalinago villages. For more on authority in Kalinago society, see Martin, *Island Caribs*, 15.

4. AGI, Santo Domingo 55, r. 5, no. 32, "Carta de Diego de Acuña, presidente de la Audiencia de Santo Domingo," October 12, 1625, fol. 2r; Moreau, *Les Petites Antilles de Christophe Colomb à Richelieu*, 188–89; Lafleur, *Les Caraïbes des Petites Antilles*, 22.

5. For more on attempts to colonize Guiana, see Lorimer, *English and Irish Settlement on the River Amazon*; Sarah Barber, "Indigeneity and Authority in the Lesser Antilles," 47.

6. Moya Pons, *History of the Caribbean*, 50; Koot, *Empire at the Periphery*, 27; Dunn, *Sugar and Slaves*, 17.

7. Peter R. Galvin, *Patterns of Pillage: A Geography of Caribbean-based Piracy in Spanish America, 1536–1718* (New York: Peter Land, 1998), 84; Mark G. Hanna, *Pirate Nests and the Rise*

of the British Empire, 1570–1741 (Chapel Hill: Omohundro Institute of Early American History and Culture by the University of North Carolina Press, 2015), 75. Kris Lane gives the example of a Dutch fleet in 1623 under the command of Admiral Jacques l'Hermite in which careening was not performed faithfully and one of the ships was made unseaworthy. See Lane, *Pillaging the Empire*, 45. April Lee Hatfield describes another instance where Dutch mariners appealed to the Virginia General Court for release from service to their Dutch captain because their ship was "eaten with worms" and therefore too dangerous to sail. See Hatfield, *Atlantic Virginia: Intercolonial Relations in the Seventeenth Century* (Philadelphia: University of Pennsylvania Press, 2007), 80.

8. AGI, Santo Domingo 56, r. 6, no. 24, "Testimonio de autos sobre haber ordenado el presidente de la Audiencia de Santo Domingo, Nicolás de Velasco que declare un prisionero inglés que hizo en el puerto de Plata," March 18, 1646, unfoliated; Daniel Genkins, "Entangled Empires: Anglo-Spanish Competition in the Seventeenth-Century Caribbean" (PhD diss., Vanderbilt University, 2018), 24–25.

9. W. Frank Craven, "The Earl of Warwick, a Speculator in Piracy," *Hispanic American Historical Review* 10, no. 4 (November 1930): 460; Jean-Pierre Sainton, ed., *Histoire et Civilisation de la Caraïbe (Guadeloupe, Martinique, Petites Antilles): La construction des sociétés antillaises des origines au temps present: Structures et dynamiques: Tome 1: Les Temps des Genéses: des origines à 1685* (Paris: Éditions Maisonneuve et Larose, 2004), 196–203.

10. Norton and Studnicki-Gizbert, "Multinational Commodification of Tobacco," 264.

11. Whitehead, *Lords of the Tiger Spirit*, 84–85; Norton and Studnicki-Gizbert, "Multinational Commodification of Tobacco," 262–63.

12. K. R. Andrews, "The English in the Caribbean, 1560–1620," in *The Westward Enterprise: English Activity in Ireland, the Atlantic, and America, 1480–1650*, ed. K. R. Andrews, N. P. Canny, and P. E. H. Hair (Liverpool: Liverpool University Press, 1978), 109; Joyce Lorimer, "The English Contraband Tobacco Trade in Trinidad and Guiana, 1590–1617," in Andrews et al., *Westward Enterprise*, 124–50.

13. Norton and Studnicki-Gizbert, "Multinational Commodification of Tobacco," 270.

14. Lorimer, "English Contraband Tobacco Trade," 140.

15. K. R. Andrews, "Caribbean Rivalry and the Anglo-Spanish Peace of 1604," *History* 59, no. 195 (1974): 1–17.

16. Lorimer, "English Contraband Tobacco Trade," pp. 124–50.

17. Whitehead, *Lords of the Tiger Spirit*, 16; Cornelius Ch. Goslinga, *The Dutch in the Caribbean and the Wild Coast, 1580–1680* (Assen, Netherlands: Van Gorcum, 1990); Lorimer, *English and Irish Settlement*; Melissa N. Morris, "Virginia and the Amazonian Alternative," in *Virginia 1619: Slavery and Freedom in the Making of English America*, ed. Paul Musselwhite, Peter C. Mancall, and James Horn (Chapel Hill: Published for the Omohundro Institute of Early American History and Culture by the University of North Carolina Press, 2019); Carolyn Arena, "Indian Slaves from Guiana in Seventeenth-Century Barbados," *Ethnohistory* 64, no. 1 (January 2017): 65–90; Roper, *Advancing Empire*, 31.

18. Rev. C. Jesse, "An Houre Glasse of Indian Newes," *Caribbean Quarterly* 12, no. 1 (March 1966): 49–50.

19. For Dutch observations of similar commercial protocols in Guiana, see Jessica Vance Roitman, "Second Is Best: Dutch Colonization on the 'Wild Coast,'" in Roper, *Torrid Zone*, 70.

20. Huerga, *Cartas de gobernadores*, 1:140. For an excellent discussion of the informal trade in pearls and their circulation, see Molly Warsh, *American Baroque: Pearls and the Nature*

of Empire, 1492–1700 (Chapel Hill: Published for the Omohundro Institute of Early American History and Culture by the University of North Carolina Press, 2018), esp. 102–27.

21. Harcourt, *A Relation of a Voyage to Guiana*; John Smith, *The true travels and adventures of Captain John Smith into Europe, Asia, Africa and America: from Anno Dom. 1593 to 1629* Alex J. Philip, ed., (London: G. Routledge, 1905), 130–7.

22. Although exceptional in terms of leaving a testimony in the archives, the fact that Simón Martines was seized by traffickers off the coast of Cuba in the early seventeenth century was, in fact, quite ordinary. According to K. R. Andrews, "In 1618–19 pirates took nine of the frigates that plied the ports of eastern Cuba in a period of ten months." See Andrews, "The English in the Caribbean," 123.

23. AGI, Santo Domingo 55, r. 5, no. 32, "Carta de Diego de Acuña, presidente de la Audiencia de Santo Domingo," fol. 2.

24. AGI, Santo Domingo 55, r. 5, no. 32, "Carta de Diego de Acuña, presidente de la Audiencia de Santo Domingo," fol. 3.

25. Pérotin-Dumon, "French, English, and Dutch in the Lesser Antilles."

26. "Document No. 19, the Audiencia of Santo Domingo to the Crown, Santo Domingo, February 24, 1586," in Wright, *Further English Voyages to Spanish America*, 37.

27. British Library, Egerton MS 2395, "The State of the Leewards," January 13, 1675. See also Arena, "Indian Slaves from Caribana," 32. Not until 1632 would the island be claimed by the Compagnie des Îles de l'Amérique.

28. AGI, Indiferente General 1153, "Declaracion de un olandes remitido por el governador de Cartagena," unfoliated.

29. Murphy, *Creole Archipelago*, chap. 1, esp. 20–25.

30. AGI, Indiferente General 1153, "Declaracion de un olandes remitido por el governador de Cartagena."

31. AGI, Santo Domingo 55, r. 5, no. 32, "Carta de Diego de Acuña, presidente de la Audiencia de Santo Domingo," fol. 3.

32. Barber, "Indigeneity and Authority," 47.

33. Guasco, *Slaves and Englishmen*, 10, emphasis mine. Cécile Vidal makes a similar argument about viewing French New Orleans "from the perspective of its own epoch," rather than what came after. See Vidal, *Caribbean New Orleans: Empire, Race, and the Making of a Slave Society* (Chapel Hill: Published for the Omohundro Institute of Early American History and Culture by the University of North Carolina Press, 2019), 19.

34. Perhaps even more surprising is that Warner felt comfortable enough with the Kalinago of St. Christopher to land on the island initially with just two companions, staying there for a year before returning to England to seek investors and additional settlers. See Morris, "Virginia and the Amazonian Alternative," 280.

35. Hilton, "Relation of the first settlement of Saint Christopher and Nevis," 1–3; Thornton and Heywood, *Central Africans*, 29. This diverges slightly from the interpretation of Gérard Lafleur, who argues that conflict between the Kalinago and Europeans was often the result of a small group of Europeans being accepted as trade partners and violence erupting when more settlers arrived. I push this further by trying to understand why the Kalinago allowed Europeans to settle in the first place. See Lafleur, *Les Caraïbes des Petites Antilles*, 21.

36. See, for example, AGI, Indiferente General 1868, "Consultas originales de la Junta de Guerra y el Consejo de Indias," February 2, 1615, unfoliated; Moreau, *Un Flibustier Français*, 15.

37. Du Tertre, *Histoire Générale*, 5–6. Warner's colonial commission, granted in 1627, specifically declared the island as "not being in the Occupation or under the Government of any Christian prince or State." See BL, Egerton MS 2395, "Coppy extracted from the Originall of Sir Thomas Warners Commission for Govr of St. Xphers," September 29, 1629.

38. Anne Pérotin-Dumon describes the process whereby crews unloaded their ships, constructed tents, and set up forges and armories "for a sort of weapon manufacture and to produce iron bolts and nails needed for ship repair." This level of activity would have made the difference between permanent settlement and refitting hard to discern. See Pérotin-Dumon, "French, English, and Dutch in the Lesser Antilles," 120.

39. Yanna Yannakakis, *The Art of Being In-Between: Native Intermediaries, Indian Identity, and Local Rule in Colonial Oaxaca* (Durham, NC: Duke University Press, 2008), 13.

40. Richard Dunn describes "a paralyzing paucity of information about the first generation of English settlement in St. Christopher." See Dunn, *Sugar and Slaves*, 118.

41. For a good discussion of the archival messiness surrounding early chronology, see Barber, "Indigeneity and Authority in the Lesser Antilles."

42. Louis-Élie Moreau de Saint-Méry, *Loix et constitutions des colonies françoises de l'Amérique sous le Vent*, vol. 1 (Paris: A Paris chez l'Auteur, 1784–90), 20. This commission was dated October 31, 1626. For more on the adventurers, see Pierre Pluchon, *Histoire et la Colonisation Française: Tome premier: Le premier empire colonial: des origins à la Restauration* (Paris: Fayard, 1991), 75; Philip Boucher, "French Proprietary Colonies in the Greater Caribbean, 1620s–1670s," in *Constructing Early Modern Empires: Proprietary Ventures in the Atlantic World, 1500–1750*, ed. L. H. Roper and B. Van Ruymbeke (Boston: Brill, 2007), esp. 169.

43. Historians have variously placed the year of the English colonization as 1622, 1623, 1624, and 1626. See Amussen, *Caribbean Exchanges*, 25; Moya Pons, *History of the Caribbean*, 50; Carl Bridenbaugh and Roberta Bridenbaugh, *No Peace beyond the Line: The English in the Caribbean, 1624–1690* (New York: Oxford University Press, 1972), 31; Moreau, *Les Petits Antilles*, 187.

44. Martines testified that there were twenty-six Englishmen on the island. See AGI, Santo Domingo 55, r. 5, no. 32, "Carta de Diego de Acuña, presidente de la Audiencia de Santo Domingo."

45. See, for example, Karen Ordahl Kupperman, *Roanoke: The Abandoned Colony* (New York: Rowman & Littlefield, 1984); Roitman, "Second Is Best," 67–71.

46. Williamson, *Caribbee Islands*, 27, 31. According to Sarah Barber, the owner of Warner's ship, the *Gift of God*, was Ralph Merrifield, who had a letter of marque. See Barber, "Indigeneity and Authority," 195 n2. The arrival of these sixty enslaved Africans was the first recorded English slaving voyage to English colonies. See Roper, *Advancing Empire*, 33.

47. Sainton, *Histoire et Civilisation de la Caraïbe*, 211–15.

48. Boucher, *France and the American Tropics to 1700*, 60. His colleague, du Roissy, enjoyed a lengthy career in trafficking before signing onto d'Esnambuc's colonizing venture on St. Christopher.

49. Du Tertre, *Histoire Générale des Antilles*, 4.

50. Du Tertre, *Histoire Générale des Antilles*, 5; Boucher, *Cannibal Encounters*, 41; Moreau, *Les Petites Antilles*, 135; Smith, *True Travels*, chap. 15; Hilton, "Memoir," in Harlow, *Colonising Expeditions*, 2–17.

51. *Travels and Works of Captain John Smith*, ed. A. G. Bradley (Edinburgh, 1910), 2: 902.

52. AGI, Indiferente General 1153, "Declaracion del francés," unfoliated. In 1582, traffickers took a group of Kalinago captive and sold them in San Germán in Puerto Rico. The

community of San Germán was repeatedly sacked by the Kalinago until they had liberated the captives. See Huerga, *Cartas de gobernadores*, 2:115–19.

53. Murphy, *Creole Archipelago*, 26.

54. To describe these two types of interactions, I am drawing heavily from Daviken Studnicki-Gizbert, *A Nation upon the Ocean Sea: Portugal's Atlantic Diaspora and the Crisis of the Spanish Empire, 1492–1640* (New York: Oxford University Press, 2007), 180.

55. BL, Egerton MS 2395, "Articles agreed upon by Capt. Warner, Mr Desnambucq, and Mr. Roisy to be maintained according to ye Commands they have from the Kings of France and England by virtue of their Commissions, 13 May 1627"; Archives Nationales d'Outre Mer (hereafter ANOM), F3 52 Colonies.

56. Rochefort, *Histoire naturelle et morale des Iles Antilles de l'Amérique* (Rotterdam: Chez Arnould Leers, 1658), 270.

57. BL, Egerton MS 2395, folio 249.

58. TNA, CO 1/1, No. 13, "Commission to Jas. Earl of Carlisle to be Governor of the Carribee Islands," July 2, 1627, folio 42R; TNA, CO 1 /4, No. 17, "Warrant for the Earl of Carlisle or his assigns, and the owners of all tobacco brought from St. Christopher's, to have the sole profit thereof towards their charges and adventure," March 3(?), 1627. For more on the English commission, see Barber, "Indigeneity and Authority in the Lesser Antilles."

59. Moreau, *Loix et constitutions*, "Acte d'association des Seigneurs de la Compagnie des Isles de l'Amérique, du 31 Octubre 1626," 18; Boucher, "French Proprietary Colonies," 170.

60. AGI, Indiferente General 1153, "Declaracion del francés," unfoliated.

61. See Hatfield, *Atlantic Virginia*, 80.

62. BL, Egerton MS 2395, "Articles agreed upon by Capt. Warner, Mr Desnambucq, and Mr. Roisy." No archival traces of the court's operations exist, so it is impossible to know if the governors were successful in mitigating disputes fairly and transparently.

63. BL, Egerton MS 2395, "Articles agreed upon by Capt. Warner, Mr Desnambucq, and Mr. Roisy."

64. Geoffrey Plank, *Atlantic Wars: From the Fifteenth Century to the Age of Revolution* (New York: Oxford University Press, 2020), 203; Brindenbaugh and Brindenbaugh, *No Peace Beyond the Line*; Stephan Palmié, "Toward Sugar and Slavery," in *The Caribbean: A History of the Region and its People*, ed. Stephen Palmié and Francisco A. Scarano (Chicago: University of Chicago Press, 2011), 138.

65. For an account of the brief fighting in 1629, in which English settlers encroached on French territory, see Du Tertre, *Histoire Générale des Antilles*, 1:22.

66. See, for example, Margaret Ellen Newell, *Brethren by Nature: New England Indians, Colonists, and the Origins of American Slavery* (Ithaca, NY: Cornell University Press, 2015), esp. chap. 2.

67. See, for example, Gaspar, "Rigid and Inclement"; Rugemer, "Development of Mastery and Race"; Malick W. Ghachem, *The Old Regime and the Haitian Revolution* (New York: Cambridge University Press, 2012), chap. 1; Sue Peabody, "Slavery, Freedom, and the Law in the Atlantic World, 1420–1807," in *The Cambridge World History of Slavery*, vol. 3, *AD 1420–AD 1804*, eds. David Eltis and Stanley L. Engerman (Cambridge: Cambridge University Press, 2011), 594–630.

68. For a discussion of evolving French ideas about race and slavery alongside the establishment of colonies, see Éric Roulet, "Habitants, Nègres, et Sauvages: La naissance de la société coloniale des Petits Antilles françaises dans la première moitié du XVII siècle," in *La Fabrique*

de la race dans la Caraïbe de l'époque modern à nous jours, eds. Marine Cellier, Amina Damerdji, and Sylvain Lloret (Paris: Classiques Garnier, 2021), 91–110.

69. AGI, Indiferente General, 78, "Carta de Gobernador de Puerto Rico al Rey," February 12, 1632.

70. Richard S. Dunn, James Savage, and Laetitia Yeandle, eds., *The Journal of John Winthrop, 1630-1649* (Cambridge, MA: Belknap Press, 1996), 147; Newell, *Brethren by Nature,* 51–53.

71. Detailed censuses of the Lesser Antilles did not happen systematically until a 1678 census conducted by Governor William Stapleton. See Shaw, *Everyday Life in the Early English Caribbean,* esp. chap. 2; Natalie A. Zacek, *Settler Society in the English Leeward Islands* (Cambridge: Cambridge University Press, 2010), 46. An estimate for the French population comes from 1655. See Pierre Pelleprat, *Relation des P.P. de la Compagnie de Jésus dans les isles . . . de l'Amérique meridionale* (Paris, 1655), 54–55.

72. BL, Egerton MS 2395, "Articles agreed upon by Capt. Warner, Mr Desnambucq, and Mr. Roisy."

73. BL, Egerton MS 2395, "Articles of a Peace & Accord between the French and the English in the Charibbee Islands in the years 1637 and 1655," fol. 62. Again, similar articles appear in the colonial records of the Archives Nationales d'Outre Mer; however, due to the administrative disruption surrounding the purchase of the Compagnie des Isles de l'Amérique by the Knights of Malta in this period, which brought Philippe de Lonvilliers de Poincy to govern the island of St. Christopher, the treaty articles available in ANOM are a summary of where the laws stood in 1660 when de Poincy died. For this reason, I will again refer to the English copies available at the British Library. The French copies can be found at ANOM, F3 52, "L'Essentiel des Traités, Articles, Accords & Conventions faite entre les Frances et Anglois en l'Isle de St Christophe."

74. Captive sailors were frequently referred to as "perforst-men." See Henry Mainwaring, *The Life and Works of Sir Henry Mainwaring,* ed. W. G. Perrin (Navy Records Society, 1920), 2:22.

75. These maritime raids accelerated in the 1620s with the end of a twelve-year ceasefire between Spain and the Netherlands. The two European powers had been at war since 1566, but by 1608 financial exhaustion forced Spain's Philip III to agree to a truce. The collapse of that truce in 1621 spurred increased maritime violence in the Caribbean, culminating in 1628 with the dramatic seizure of the Spanish fleet by the Dutch ship captain Piet Hein. See Lane, *Pillaging the Empire,* chap. 3.

76. AGI, Indiferente General 78, leg. 2, November 1632.

77. AGI, Indiferente General 1153, "Carta de la Casa de la Contratación al Rey," December 6, 1629.

78. Smith, *True Travels,* 52–53.

79. For another case where a mariner claimed that his captain lied to the crew about his intentions when he left England, see AGI, Santa Fe 223, "Declaración de un marinero inglés," Cartagena, June 2, 1640, fol. 133r.

80. AGI, Indiferente General 2536, "Carta del Consejo de Indias al Rey," September 16, 1636.

81. Engel Sluiter, "Dutch-Spanish Rivalry in the Caribbean Area, 1594–1609," *Hispanic American Historical Review* 28, no. 2 (May 1948): 165–96; Kenneth Gordon Davies, *The North Atlantic World in the Seventeenth Century* (Minneapolis: University of Minnesota Press, 1974), 30.

82. AGI, Indiferente General 2536, "Carta del Consejo de Indias al Rey."

83. Klooster, *Dutch Moment*, 155.

84. AGI, Indiferente General 78, "Carta de Don Henrique Enriquez a la Junta de Guerra," December 12, 1632; Thomas G. Mathews, "The Spanish Domination of Saint Martin (1633–1648)," *Caribbean Studies* 9, no. 1 (April 1969): 5.

85. Guillaume Coppier, *Histoire et voyages des Indes Occidentales, et de plusieurs regions maritimes & estoignées* (Lyon: Por Jean Huguetan, 1645), 29.

86. The numbers are likely low estimates—they come from Spanish reports after a Spanish force attacked the island and took over the fort and, therefore, do not account for enslaved people who used the chaos of the attack to escape or for ship captains who fled the Spanish assault with captives onboard their ships. See Mathews, "The Spanish Domination," 10.

87. AGI, Indiferente General 1872, "Carta de don Luis de Valdes," St. Martin, August 22, 1636, unfoliated.

88. Trans-Atlantic Slave Trade Database, https://www.slavevoyages.org (accessed April 10, 2020).

89. Newell, *Brethren by Nature*, 24.

90. David Peterson de Vries, *Voyages from Holland to America, A.D. 1632 to 1644*, trans. Henry C. Murphy (New York: Kraus, 1971), 52.

91. AGI, Indiferente General 1872, "Carta de don Luis de Valdes," August 22, 1636.

92. Jean Baptiste Lepers, *La tragique histoire des flibustiers: histoire de Saint-Domingue et de l'ile de la Tortue, repaires flibustiers*, ed. Pierre-Bernard Berthelot (Paris: Les editions G. Crès, n.d.), 10.

93. AGI, Indiferente General 2536, "Testimonio del inglés," Puerto Rico, May 6, 1637, unfoliated.

94. AGI, Indiferente General 78, "Carta de Don Henrique Enriquez a la Junta de Guerra," December 12, 1632, unfoliated.

95. Mathews, "Spanish Domination of Saint Martin," 16.

96. AGI, Indiferente General 78, "Carta del Capitain General Enrique Enríquez de Sotomayor," December 12, 1632.

Chapter 3

1. AGI, Patronato 273, r. 5, "Autos sobre el desalojo de Tortuga," August 29, 1653, fol. 85v.

2. AGI, Patronato 273, r. 5, "Testimonio de Paul Aubert," May 5, 1652, fol. 82r.

3. Arne Bialuschewski, "Slaves of the Buccaneers: Mayas in Captivity in the Second Half of the Seventeenth Century," *Ethnohistory* 64, no. 1 (January 2017): 43; Luis Martínez-Fernández, "Far Beyond the Line: Corsairs, Privateers, Buccaneers, and Invading Settlers in Cuba and the Caribbean (1529–1670)," *Revista de Indias* 75, no. 263 (2015): 26. This is related to the buccaneers who came to prominence in the second half of the seventeenth century. See Lane, *Pillaging the Empire*, 97. While scholars describe the root word for "buccaneering," *boucan*, as a Taíno word, historian Arne Bialuschewski has recently argued that French sailors brought the word from their interactions with the Tupí-Guaraní peoples of Brazil. See Bialuschewski, *Raiders and Natives: Cross-Cultural Relations in the Age of Buccaneers* (Athens: University of Georgia Press, 2022), 8–9. The correlation between buccaneering and piracy was made famous by the account of Alexander Exquemelin, a former surgeon turned buccaneer in the second half of the seventeenth century and his famous depiction of buccaneering life. See A. O. Exquemelin, *The History of the Buccaneers of America* (Boston, 1856). See also Isaac Curtis, "Masterless People: Maroons, Pirates, and Commoners," in Palmié and Scarano, *The Caribbean*, esp. 153–54.

4. Alison Games, "'The Sanctuarye of Our Rebell Negroes': The Atlantic Context of Local Resistance on Providence Island, 1630-1641," *Slavery and Abolition* 19, no. 3 (December 1998): 1-21.

5. Ponce Vázquez, *Islanders and Empire*, 59; Mercedes García Rodríguez, "Contrabando *versus* monopolio: las dos caras del comercio en la Cuba colonial," in Grafenstein et al., *Entre lo legal, lo ilícito, y lo clandestino*, 164; Antonio Vázquez de Espinosa, *Compendio y descripción de las Indias Occidentales*, ed. De Balbino Velasco Bayón (Madrid: Historia 16, 1992), 195; Ana Ozuna, "Rebellion and Anti-colonial Struggle in Hispaniola: From Indigenous Agitators to African Rebels," *Africology: The Journal of Pan African Studies* 11, no. 7 (May 2018): 86.

6. Gabriel de Avilez Rocha, "Maroons in the *Montes*: Toward a Political Ecology of Marronage in the Sixteenth-Century Caribbean," in *Early Modern Black Diaspora Studies: A Critical Anthology*, ed. Cassander L. Smith, Nicholas R. Jones, and Miles P. Grier (London: Palgrave Macmillan, 2018), 15-35; Altman, *Life and Society in the Early Spanish Caribbean*, esp. chap. 2.

7. Quoted in Rocha, "Maroons in the *Montes*," 17. For more on this, see Stone, *Captives of Conquest*; Ponce Vázquez, *Islanders and Empire*, 35-37; Ozuna, "Rebellion and Anti-Colonial Struggle in Hispaniola"; Schwaller, "Contested Conquests." For more on Enrique, called Enriquillo by the Spanish, see Ida Altman, "The Revolt of Enriquillo and the Historiography of Early Spanish America," *The Americas* 63, no. 4 (April 2007): 587-614. Sylvaine A. Diouf writes about different typologies of Maroon communities, from "Hinterland Maroons" who maintained their distance from plantation societies to "Borderland Maroons" who occupied liminal spaces near plantation societies from which they derived social and material support. The Cabo de Tiburon occupied a middle ground between these two typologies through their commercial alliances with northern European traffickers: they maintained their distance from plantation societies but also had access to material support. See Diouf, *Slavery's Exiles: The Story of the American Maroons* (New York: New York University Press, 2014), 4-10.

8. Alliances between Spain's European competitors and self-liberated Africans and their descendants happened throughout the greater Caribbean, not just Hispaniola. A famous example of cross-cultural trade and alliance between Europeans and Maroons occurred in Panamá. See Marta Hidalgo Pérez, "El Atlántico como Puente entre tres mundos: esclavos, cimarrones, y corsarios en Tierra Firme en el siglo XVI," in *América y el mar*, ed. María del Mar Barrientos Márques and Alberto J. Gullón Abao (Cádiz, Spain: Editorial Universidad de Cádiz, 2019), 159-74; Jean-Pierre Tardieu, *Cimarrones de Panamá: La forja de una identidad afroamericana en el siglo XVI* (Madrid: Iberoamericana, 2009).

9. AGI, Santo Domingo 54, r. 2, no. 49, "Carta del governador Gómez de Sandoval al Rey," May 29, 1611, fol. 1v; Schwaller, "Contested Conquests," 635; Toby Green, *Fistful of Shells: West Africa from the Rise of the Slave Trade to the Age of Revolution* (Chicago: University of Chicago Press, 2019), 77.

10. In September 1606, for example, one of the Spanish patrols between La Yaguana and Bayaha captured nearly seventy Maroons. One month later, five different patrols seized over 150 African Maroons and executed thirty northern European traffickers.

11. AGI, Santo Domingo 54, r. 2, no. 49, "Carta del governador Gómez de Sandoval al Rey," fol. 2.

12. John K. Thornton, *A History of West Central Africa to 1850* (New York: Cambridge University Press, 2020), chap. 3.

13. Wheat, *Atlantic Africa*, 70-71.

14. Thornton, *A History of West Central Africa*, chap. 4; Linda M. Heywood, *Njinga of Angola: Africa's Warrior Queen* (Cambridge, MA: Harvard University Press, 2017).

15. Thornton and Heywood, *Central Africans*; Wheat, *Atlantic Africa*; Joseph H. M. Clark, *Veracruz and the Caribbean in the Seventeenth Century* (New York: Cambridge University Press, 2023), 124.

16. The scholarship on kinship ties aboard transatlantic slave ships is robust. See, for example, Stephanie Smallwood, *Saltwater Slavery: A Middle Passage from Africa to American Diaspora* (Cambridge, MA: Harvard University Press, 2009); Mustakeem, *Slavery at Sea*; Alex Borucki, *From Shipmates to Soldiers: Emerging Black Identities in the Río de la Plata* (Albuquerque: University of New Mexico Press, 2015); Clark, *Veracruz and the Caribbean*, 146. Jennifer L. Morgan has recently argued that the use of kinship terminology in the historiography, however, tethers Africans as outsiders in European hierarchical understandings of family versus kin. See Morgan, *Reckoning with Slavery: Gender, Kinship, and Capitalism in the Early Black Atlantic* (Durham: Duke University Press, 2021): 149–51.

17. For more on the trade to Spanish America, see Enriqueta Vila Vilar, *Hispanoamérica y el comercio de esclavos: los asientos portugueses* (Sevilla: Escuela de Estudios Hispanoamérica-nos, 1977).

18. Heywood and Thornton, *Central Africans*. The continual arrival of Central African captives in the early seventeenth century, after all, facilitated the creation and maintenance of what historians call an Atlantic Creole culture, which was shaped by Central Africans' exposure to European language, religion, and material culture through the Portuguese colony at Angola.

19. AGI, Santo Domingo 54, r. 2, no. 49, "Carta del governador Gómez de Sandoval al Rey," fol. 1v; Schwaller, "Contested Conquests," 635.

20. Green, *Fistful of Shells*, 93; Wheat, *Atlantic Africa*, 52.

21. For this broad definition, see David Eltis, *Rise of African Slavery*.

22. For more on the role of women in West Central Africa, see Heywood, *Njinga of Angola*; John K. Thornton, *Africa and Africans in the Making of the Atlantic World, 1400–1800* (New York: Cambridge University Press, 1992, reprint 1998), chap. 9 and 10.

23. There is no mention of what happened to the European captives.

24. AGI, Santo Domingo 52, r. 7, no. 100, "Carta de Antonio de Osorio al rey," December 31, 1607, fols. 3v–4r; Schwaller, "Contested Conquest," 634.

25. Wheat, *Atlantic Africa*, 112.

26. Marcy Norton, *Sacred Gifts, Profane Pleasures: A History of Tobacco and Chocolate in the Atlantic World* (Ithaca, NY: Cornell University Press, 2008), 153; Cromwell, *Smugglers' World*, 44. For more on the depopulation and subsequent interpretations of it, see Carlos Esteban Deive, *Tangomangos: Contrabando y Piratería en Santo Domingo, 1522–1606* (Santo Domingo: Fundación Cultural Dominicana, 1996); María Elena Muñoz, *La Política Internacional Europea y sus efectos en la Isla de Santo Domingo, siglos XVI–XIX* (Santo Domingo: Instituto Panamericano de Geografía e Historia, Sección Nacional Dominicana, 2008); Frank Moya Pons, *Manual de Historia Dominicana* (Santo Domingo: Caribbean Publishers, 2008); Ponce Vázquez, *Islanders and Empire*.

27. AGI, Santo Domingo 52, r. 7, no. 100, "Carta de Antonio de Osorio al rey," fol. 2v.

28. AGI, Santo Domingo 52, r. 7, no. 100, "Carta de Antonio de Osorio al rey," fol. 2v.

29. Michel Christian Camus, *L'île de la Tortue au cœur de la Flibuste caraïbe* (Paris: Éditions L'Harmattan, 1997), 27.

30. For example, demand in Europe for organic pigments like dragon's blood and orchil, which produced vibrant red and purple dyes, respectively, spurred the conquest of the Canary Islands and the enslavement of the Indigenous Guanche over the course of the fifteenth century. The trade in brazilwood, a flowering tree that produces a vibrant red or deep crimson dye, transformed the sixteenth-century political and social worlds of the Indigenous Tupi along the coast of Brazil after Pedro Álvarez Cabral returned from Brazil with a cargo of the dyewood in 1500. For more on this trade, see Amy Buono, "Crafts of Color: Tupi *Tapirage* in Early Colonial Brazil," in *The Materiality of Color: The Production, Circulation, and Application of Dyes and Pigments, 1400–1800*, ed. Andrea Feeser, Maureen Daly Goggin, and Beth Fowkes Tobin (Burlington, VT: Ashgate, 2012), 235–43; Bushnell, "Indigenous America," 198; Paula De Vos, "Apothecaries, Artists, and Artisans: Early Industrial Material Culture in the Biological Old Regime," *Journal of Interdisciplinary History* 45, no. 3 (Winter 2015): 277–336.

31. Amy J. Buono, "Representing the Tupinamba in the Brazilwood Trade in Sixteenth-Century Rouen," in *Cultural Exchanges Between Brazil and France*, ed. Regine R. Félix and Scott D. Juall (West Lafayette, IN: Purdue University Press, 2016), chap. 1; Alida C. Metcalf, *Go-betweens and the Colonization of Brazil, 1500–1660* (Austin: University of Texas Press, 2005), chap. 3.

32. The scientific name of the logwood tree is *Haematoxlyn campechianum*. It grows about fifty feet high and two feet thick. See Gilbert M. Joseph, "British Loggers and Spanish Governors: The Logwood Trade and Its Settlement in the Yucatan Peninsula: Part 1," *Caribbean Studies* 14, no. 2 (July 1974): 15.

33. Elena Phipps, "Global Colors: Dyes and the Dye Trade," in *Interwoven Globe: The Worldwide Textile Trade, 1500–1800*, ed. Amelia Peck (New Haven, CT: Yale University Press, 2013), 130.

34. Philip D. Morgan, "Virginia's Other Prototype: The Caribbean," in Mancall, *The Atlantic World and Virginia*, 349; Frédéric Mauro, *Le Portugal, le Brésil et l'Atlantique au XVIIe siècle, 1570–1670· Étude économique* (Paris, 1983); Phipps, "Global Colors," 130.

35. Rodrigo Alejandro De la O Torres, "La costa Yucateca y el fenómeno de la piratería: Confirmación y percepción del espacio, siglo XVI," *Anuario de Historia Regional y de las Fronteras* 24, no.1 (2019): 105–37.

36. Quoted from Othón Baños Ramírez, "Piratería forestall y economía-mundo: El caso de la Laguna (1558–1717)," *Relaciones* 132 (Autumn 2012): 80.

37. Baños Ramírez, "Piratería forestall y economía-mundo," 84.

38. Jorge Victoria Ojeda, "La piratería y su relación con los indígenas de las peninsula de Yucatán mito y práctica social," *Mesoamérica* 26 (December 1993): 211.

39. Michel Boccara, "El Way Kot: brujo águila," *Revista de la Universidad Autónoma de Yucatán* 155 and 160 (Mérida: 1985, 1987); Ojeda, "La piratería y su relación con los indígenas," 213–14.

40. Kenneth R. Andrews, *Elizabethan Privateering: English Privateering During the Spanish War, 1585–1603* (New York: Cambridge University Press, 1966); John C. Appleby, "Jacobean Piracy: English Maritime Depredation in Transition, 1603–1625," in *The Social History of English Seamen, 1485–1649*, ed. Cheryl A. Fury (Woodbridge, UK: Boydell, 2012); Hanna, *Pirate Nests*.

41. Peace could also mean execution in England: Walter Raleigh's violent interactions with the Spanish in South America led to his execution in 1618. See Roper, introduction to *Torrid Zone*.

42. AGI, Santo Domingo 53, r. 1, no. 5, "Cartas de Audiencia," 1609, unfoliated; Camus, *L'île de la Tortue*, 29.

43. An example of this kind of defense can be found here: AGI, Indiferente General 1870, "Carta del Gabriel de Echaves Osorio al Rey," November 29, 1629, unfoliated. The wider European debates over occupation and sovereignty have an extensive historiography. For an excellent discussion, see Lauren Benton, *A Search for Sovereignty: Law and Geography in European Empires, 1400–1900* (New York: Cambridge University Press, 2010).

44. AGI, Santo Domingo 53, r. 1, no. 5, "Cartas de Audiencia"; Camus, *L'île de la Tortue*, 29; AGI, Santa Fé 223, "Consulta de Guerra," July 20, 1635, fol. 1r. Interrogated sailors testified to Spanish officials about these dwelling places several decades later. See, for example, AGI, Patronato 273, r. 5, "Testimonio de Nicholas Stevens," September 1, 1653, fols. 88v–90v.

45. AGI, Santa Fé 38, r. 6, no. 166, "Carta de D. García Girón, Gobernador de Cartagena," January 30, 1621, unfoliated. For the printed account, see *Verdadera relacion del viage, y sucesso de los caravelones, galeoncetes de la guarda de Cartagena de las Indias, y su costa. Y la grandiose vitoria que antenido contra los cossarios piratas en aquel mar* (Sevilla: por Bartolome Gomez de Pastrana, 1621).

46. Camus, *L'île de la Tortue*, 29; AGI, Santa Fé 223, "Consulta de Guerra," February 6, 1640, fols. 133r–134r.

47. AGI, Indiferente General 78, no. 2, "Carta de Henrique Enriquez a la Junta de Guerra," December 12, 1632, unfoliated.

48. AGI, Indiferente General 1872, "Carta de Luis de Valdés," August 22, 1636, unfoliated.

49. AGI, Patronato 273, r. 5, "Testimonio de Paul Aubert," May 5, 1652, fol. 83r.

50. Carla Rahn Phillips, *Six Galleons for the King of Spain: Imperial Defense in the Early Seventeenth Century* (Baltimore: Johns Hopkins University Press, 1986), 184.

51. Du Tertre, *Histoire Générale des Antilles*, 1:22–25.

52. "Sir Wil. Killigrew to Sec. Dorchester," November 5, 1629, Calendar of State Papers, 102.

53. Moya Pons, *History of the Caribbean*, 51.

54. Hilton, "Memoir," in Harlow, *Colonising Expeditions*, 2–17; Paul Musselwhite, "'Plantation,' the Public Good, and the Rise of Capitalist Agriculture in the Early Seventeenth-Century Caribbean," *Early American Studies* 20, no. 4 (Fall 2022): 604, 614; Richard Sheridan, *Sugar and Slavery: An Economic History of the British West Indies, 1623–1775* (Baltimore: Johns Hopkins University Press, 1973), 86; Williamson, *Caribbee Islands*, 82.

55. Jean Baptiste Lepers, *La tragique histoire des flibustiers: histoire de Saint-Domingue et de l'île de la Tortue, repaires flibustiers*, ed. Pierre-Bernard Berthelot (Paris: Les editions G. Crès, n.d.), 74; Musselwhite, "'Plantation,' the Public Good, and the Rise of Capitalist Agriculture," 604.

56. Camus, *L'île de la Tortue*, 31.

57. TNA, CO 124/2, "Journal of the Governor & Company of Adventurers for the Plantation of the Island of Providence," May 19, 1631, fol. 18.

58. Unlike the Virginia Company, the Massachusetts Bay Company, or the colonial charter for Bermuda, the Providence Island Company was not exempt from paying customs to Charles I on all imports and exports to their island colonies. This, alongside the financial uncertainty of starting a new colony, left members of the Providence Island Company perpetually indebted. For more on this, see Karen Ordahl Kupperman, *Providence Island, 1630–1641: The Other Puritan Colony* (New York: Cambridge University Press, 1993), chap. 10.

59. TNA, CO 124/2, "At a Court Held for the Island of Providence at Warwick House," June 15, 1631, fol. 22.

60. Arthur Percival Newton, *The Colonising Activities of the English Puritans: The Last Phase of the Elizabethan Struggle with Spain* (New Haven, CT: Yale University Press, 1914), 108; Joseph, "British Loggers and Spanish Governors," 16.

61. Newton, *Colonising Activities*, 108–11; Kupperman, *Providence Island*, 310.

62. Camus, *L'île de la Tortue*, 33; Newton, *Colonising Activities*, 110.

63. TNA, CO 124/1, "Instructions to Capt. Newman of the Happie Return," 1636, fol. 94v–95; Linda M. Heywood and John K. Thornton, "'Canniball Negroes,' Atlantic Creoles, and the Identity of England's Charter Generation," *African Diaspora* 4 (2011): 82; Games, "The Sanctuarye of Our Rebell Negroes," 12.

64. TNA, CO 124/1, "Copy of a General Letter to Captain Hunt, 19 March 1636/7," fol. 110v; Dunn, et al., *The Journal of John Winthrop*, 260; TNA, CO 124/2, "Committee, 25 April 1638," fol. 336; Kupperman, *Providence Island*, 312; Games, "The Sanctuarye of Our Rebell Negroes," 13.

65. Heywood and Thornton, "Canniball Negroes," 82.

66. For more on the global dimensions of mid-seventeenth-century upheavals, see Geoffrey Parker, "Crisis and Catastrophe: The Global Crisis of the Seventeenth Century Reconsidered," *American Historical Review* 113, no. 4 (October 2008): 1053–79; Green, *Fistful of Shells*, 176.

67. Carlos Esteban Deive, *La Esclavitud del Negro en Santo Domingo (1492-1844)* (Santo Domingo: Museo del Hombre Dominicano, 1980), 129; Johannes Postma, *The Dutch in the Atlantic Slave Trade, 1600-1815* (New York: Cambridge University Press, 1990), 27.

68. AGI, Patronato 273, r. 6, "Autos sobre la resolución de conquistar la isla de Tortuga," 1653; Lane, *Pillaging the Empire*, 100; Clarence H. Haring, *Buccaneers in the West Indies in the Seventeenth Century* (London: Methuen, 1910), 68, 65, 82.

69. AGI, Patronato 273, r. 6, "Autos sobre la resolución de conquistar la isla de Tortuga," August 29, 1653, fol. 117v.

70. AGI, Indiferente General 1872, "Bernardo O'Brien del Carpio Relacion," April 18, 1636, unfoliated; Bialuschewski, *Raiders and Natives*, esp. chap. 2.

71. AGI, Patronato 273, r. 7, "Juan Francisco Montemayor y otros: recuperación Tortuga, etc.," March 16, 1654, unfoliated.

72. For more on the skills needed for sugar production, see Jordan B. Smith, "'The Native Produce of This Island': Processes of Invention in Early Barbados," *Early American Studies* 20, no. 4 (Fall 2022): 714–39.

73. AGI, Patronato 273, r. 7, "Juan Francisco Montemayor y otros: recuperación Tortuga, etc.," March 30, 1654, unfoliated.

74. The descriptions below come from his testimony: AGI, Patronato 273, r. 6, "Testimonio de Miguel Matamba," November 5, 1653, fols. 127v–128v.

75. Wheat, *Atlantic Africa*, 80–81.

76. Thornton, *History of West Central Africa*, 155; Heywood, *Njinga of Angola*, 126–30.

77. Wheat, *Atlantic Africa*, 95–97.

78. AGI, Patronato 273, r. 6, "Testimonio de Miguel Matamba," November 5, 1653, fols. 127v–128v.

79. The narrative of Bergara's experiences comes from AGI, Santo Domingo 55, r. 20, no. 126, "Testimonio de Josef de Bergara," Santo Domingo, May 19, 1640, fols. 5r–6v.

80. Other European captives seized and sold into indentured contracts would report that they had been assigned a term limit. See, for example, AGI, Escribanía 1033B, Legajo 28, pleito

del consejo n. 37, Consejo Año de 1668, "Autos hechos en la Havana por el Governador Francisco Davila Orexon, sobre haver llegado aquel Puerto, once negros huidos de poder de los Ingleses que los tenian por Esclavos en la Jamaica y dadoles Libertad," October 5, 1668, unfoliated.

81. According to historian Philip P. Boucher, the period between the death of Richelieu until Colbert took over overseas affairs can be described as "an era of *métropole* neglect" in which the colonies were largely left to their own devices. See Philip P. Boucher, *Les Nouvelles Frances: France in America, 1500–1815, An Imperial Perspective* (Providence: John Carter Brown Library, 1989), 32.

82. Dunn, et al., *Journal of John Winthrop*, 330, 573.

83. Dunn, et al., *Journal of John Winthrop*, 330, 573.

84. Bernard Grunberg, Benoît Roux, and Josiane Grunberg, eds., *Voyageurs anonymes aux Antilles* (Paris: L'Harmattan, 2018), 54–58.

85. AGI, Santo Domingo 55, r. 20, no. 126, "Testimony of Josef de Bergara," May 19, 1640, fol. 5v; BL Egerton MS 2597, "Chevalier de Poyncy, French Governor of St. Christopher's, to M. Warnard, Général des Isles de l'Americque," fol. 192; Melissa N. Morris, "Cultivating Colonies: Tobacco and the Upstart Empires, 1580–1640" (PhD diss., Columbia University, 2017), 187–89. Warner had dealt with multiple uprisings on St. Christopher over attempted bans on tobacco cultivation. See J. H. Bennett, "The English Caribbees in the Period of the Civil War, 1642–1646," *William and Mary Quarterly* 24, no. 3 (July 1967): 360–62.

86. Andrea Freeser, *Red, White, and Black Make Blue: Indigo in the Fabric of Colonial South Carolina Life* (Athens: University of Georgia Press, 2013), 83.

87. For more on how the English Civil War played out in the Anglo-Caribbean, see Bennett, "English Caribbees," 359–77.

88. AGI, Patronato 273, "Testimonio de Raimundo Burgos," September 15, 1653, fols. 123r–124v.

89. Moreau de Saint-Méry, *Loix et constitutions*, 1:37–38; Deive, *La Esclavitud del Negro en Santo Domingo*, 129.

90. AGI, Santo Domingo 55, r. 20, no. 126, "Testimonio de Domingo de Fonseca," May 18, 1640, fols. 2v–3r. For more on the etymology of *pechelingues*, see Engel Sluiter, "The Word Pechelingue: Its Derivation and Meaning," *Hispanic American Historical Review* 24, no. 4 (November 1944): 697.

91. AGI, Santo Domingo 55, r. 20, no. 126, "Testimonio de Domingo de Fonseca," fols. 3r–3v.

92. AGI, Santa Fé 223, "Testimonio de Francisco de Biafra," May 19, 1635, fol. 33r; Wheat, *Atlantic Africa*, conclusion.

93. Genkins, "Entangled Empires," 75–80. For a translation and discussion of this case and the archival document it comes from, see David Wheat, "A Spanish Caribbean Captivity Narrative: African Sailors and Puritan Slavers, 1635," in *Afro-Latino Voices: Documentary Narratives from the Early Modern Iberian Worlds*, ed. Kathryn J. McKnight and Leo Garofalo (Indianapolis: Hackett, 2009), 195–213.

94. Wheat, *Atlantic Africa*, chap. 1; Sandra E. Green, "Culture Zones in the Era of the Slave Trade: Yoruba Connection with the Anlo-Ewe," in *Identity in the Shadow of Slavery*, ed. Paul E. Lovejoy (London: Continuum, 2000), 87; Sherwin K. Bryant, *Rivers of Gold, Lives of Bondage: Governing Through Slavery in Colonial Quito* (Chapel Hill: University of North Carolina Press, 2014), 105–7; Linda Heywood, *Central Africans and Cultural Transformations in the American Diaspora* (New York: Cambridge University Press, 2002), i.

95. Wheat, *Atlantic Africa*, 257; Linda A. Newsom and Susie Minchin, *From Capture to Sale: The Portuguese Slave Trade to Spanish South America in the Early Seventeenth Century* (Leiden: Brill, 2007), 55.

96. AGI, Patronato Real 273, r. 6, "Autos sobre la resolución de conquistar la isla Tortuga, 1653," August 29, 1653, fol. 117v.

97. AGI, Patronato Real 273, r. 6, "Autos sobre la resolución de conquistar la isla Tortuga, 1653," fols. 116r–117v.

98. AGI, Patronato Real 273, r. 6, "Autos sobre la resolución de conquistar la isla Tortuga, 1653," fols. 118r–118v. For more on the banning, and continuance, of Indigenous slavery in Spanish America, see Reséndez, *Other Slavery*, chap. 5; Nancy E. van Deusen, "Why Indigenous Slavery Continued in Spanish America After the New Laws of 1542," *The Americas* 80, no. 3 (July 2023): 395–432.

Chapter 4

1. For clarity, I have chosen to use the modern names of these islands rather than switch between the seventeenth-century English names of Providence Island and Henrietta or the Spanish names of Santa Catalina and San Andrés, depending on which European power held which island. Games, "'The Sanctuarye of Our Rebell Negroes,'" 17.

2. AGI, Santa Fé 223, "Testimonio de Francisco de Biafra," May 19, 1635, fol. 32r–36v. For a detailed discussion of this case, see Wheat, *Atlantic Africa*, conclusion; Genkins, "Entangled Empires," 75–80. For a translation of this document and further analysis, see Wheat, "Spanish Caribbean Captivity Narrative."

3. For more on relationships between enslaved and free women of African descent and Spanish soldiers, see Wheat, *Atlantic Africa*, chap. 4. For more on thinking about the role of intimacy and care work in calculi of freedom and bondage, see Michelle A. McKinley, *Fractional Freedoms: Slavery, Intimacy, and Legal Mobilization in Colonial Lima, 1600–1700* (New York: Cambridge University Press, 2016).

4. Historian Jessica Marie Johnson has shown how warfare and competition for enslaved Africans often came on the heels of the violence of the Middle Passage, creating what she calls a "long Middle Passage" of continued dislocation. See Johnson, *Wicked Flesh: Black Women, Intimacy, and Freedom in the Atlantic World* (Philadelphia: University of Pennsylvania Press, 2020), 107.

5. For St. Christopher, the 1629 invasion is often treated as an early stage in the island's internal development. See Natalie A. Zacek, "Intimate Enemies: French and English Settlers and Commentators in Colonial St. Kitts," *Revista de Indias* 75, no. 263 (2015): 39–64; Matthew Mulcahy, *Hubs of Empire: The Southeastern Lowcountry and British Caribbean* (Baltimore: Johns Hopkins University Press, 2014), 33–34; Boucher, *France and the American Tropics*, 127. For Tortuga, see Lane, *Pillaging the Empire*, 100; Haring, *Buccaneers in the West Indies*, 68, 65, 82. For Providencia, see Kupperman, *Providence Island*.

6. For examples of this in the British historiography, see O'Malley, *Final Passages*; Kathleen S. Murphy, *Captivity's Collections: Science, Natural History, and the British Transatlantic Slave Trade* (Chapel Hill: University of North Carolina Press, 2023). The Portuguese slave trade also offered a different opportunity to earn a profit through the trade. See David Wheat, "Otros pasajes: Movilidades africanas y la polifuncionalidad de los navíos negreros en el Atlántico ibérico, siglos XVI–XVII," in *Sometidos a esclavitud: los africanos y sus descendients en el Caribe hispano*, ed. Consuelo Naranjo Orovio (Santa Marta: Editorial Unimagdalena, 2021), 89–116;

Eagle, "Informal Entrepôts," 27–28; Navarette Peláez, "De las 'malas entradas,'" 167; Wolff, *Isla Atlántica*, 131.

7. One example is a man named Diego Martín, a mixed-race man from Cuba who attained the rank of ship captain among the Dutch. See César García del Pino, *El Corso en Cuba. Siglo XVII* (Havana: Editorial de Ciencias Sociales, 2001), 31; Martínez-Fernández, "Far Beyond the Line," 24. See also Bialuschewski, "Slaves of the Buccaneers."

8. This builds on the work of Alvin O. Thompson, who has challenged the view that Maroon communities were heavily masculine or that women only joined those communities when taken captive by Maroon men. See Thompson, "Gender and Marronage in the Caribbean," *Journal of Caribbean History* 39, no. 2 (2005): 1–29.

9. AGI, Indiferente General 1153, "Declaración de Tomas Cordero," March 30, 1629, unfoliated.

10. AGI, Indiferente General 1153, "Declaración de Manuel Franco Camarino," 1629, unfoliated.

11. AGI, Indiferente General 1153, "Declaración de Manuel Franco Camarino," 1629, unfoliated.

12. AGI, Santo Domingo 55, r. 20, no. 126, "Testimonio de Josef de Bergara," Santo Domingo, May 19, 1640, fols. 5r–6v.

13. This, too, was a common strategy. See David Pieterszoon de Vries, *Voyages from Holland to America, A.D. 1632 to 1644*, trans. Henry C. Murphy (New York: Kraus, 1971), 52.

14. AGI, Indiferente General 1153, "Carta de la Casa de la Contratación al Rey," December 6, 1629, unfoliated.

15. Camarino claimed that the majority of the men capable of bearing arms on the island were "buenos soldados que avian asistido en Flandes en las guerras y en Italia." See AGI, Indiferente General 1153, "Carta de la Casa de la Contratación al Rey," 1629, unfoliated.

16. AGI, Indiferente General 1153, "Declaración de Tomas Cordero." March 30, 1629, unfoliated.

17. AGI, Indiferente General 2567, "Junta de Guerra," May 14, June 30, and August 13, 1629, unfoliated; Phillips, *Six Galleons for the King of Spain*, 181–82.

18. Phillips, *Six Galleons for the King of Spain*, 184–87.

19. "Sir Wil. Killigrew to Sec. Dorchester," November 5, 1629, CSP, 102.

20. Moya Pons, *History of the Caribbean*, 51.

21. It is likely that captives seized by the Spanish were sold into slavery elsewhere. Carla Gardina Pestana discusses the case of a man of African descent who offered to join the English Western Design forces in Hispaniola in 1655 who claimed to have been enslaved to Thomas Warner on St. Christopher before being taken captive by the Spanish. It is tempting to imagine that his captivity happened during the Spanish invasion of St. Christopher in 1629. See Carla Gardina Pestana, *The English Conquest of Jamaica: Oliver Cromwell's Bid for Empire* (Cambridge, MA: Harvard University Press, 2017), 77.

22. This framing builds on Allison Games's description of islands like Providencia as "multiracial, polyglot, and passionately contested new world societies." See Games, "The Sanctuarye of Our Rebell Negroes," 2.

23. AGI, Santo Domingo 101, r. 9, no. 142, "Carta de Juan Anuzquieta Quijano Gobernador de Cuba," May 12, 1635, unfoliated.

24. Johannes de Laet, *Historia ou Annaues dos Feitos da Companhia Privilegiada das Indias Occidentaes desde o seu começo até ao fim do anno de 1636*, trans. José Hygino Duarte Pereira

and Pedro Souto Maior (Rio de Janeiro: Officinas Graphicas da Bibliotheca Nacional, 1916), 621–37. Figures for the number of captives and their cost is on p. 637 and is also quoted in Linda M. Heywood and John K. Thornton, "Canniball Negroes," 81–82.

25. AGI, Patronato 273, r. 1, "Victoria de capitán Ruy Fernández de Fuenmayor: isla Tortuga," February 16, 1635, fol. 1v.

26. Heywood and Thornton, "Canniball Negroes," 82.

27. The sixteenth-century transatlantic slave trade involved experimentation on the part of Spain's House of Trade in granting licenses and contracts to a multinational variety of individuals. See Eagle and Wheat, "Early Iberian Slave Trade."

28. O'Malley, *Final Passages*, 8.

29. Newson and Minchin, *From Capture to Sale*, 160. For more on the role of Cartagena as a transshipment point for the intra-Caribbean slave trade, see Enriqueta Vila Vilar, "Cartagena de Indias en el siglo XVII: puerto negrero internacional," *Redescubriendo el Nuevo Mundo: Estudios americanistas en homenaje a Carmen Gómez*, ed. María Salud Elvás Iniesta and Sandra Olivero Guidobono (Seville: Universidad de Sevilla, 2011); Antonino Vidal Ortega, *Cartagena de Indias y la región histórica del Caribe, 1580–1640* (Sevilla: Universidad de Sevilla, 2002); Jorge Palacios Preciado, *La Trata de esclavos por Cartagena de Indias* (Tunja, Colombia: Universidad Pedagógica y Tecnológica de Colombia, Fondo Especial de Publicaciones, 1993).

30. Newson and Minchin, *From Capture to Sale*, 186.

31. AGI, Santa Fe 223, "Carta del Consulado de Lima," June 10, 1639, fol. 79r.

32. O'Malley, *Final Passages*, 8; David Wheat, "The First Great Waves: African Provenance Zones for the Transatlantic Slave Trade to Cartagena de Indias, 1570–1640," *Journal of African History* 52 (2011): 1–5; Newson and Minchin, *From Capture to Sale*, 147–86.

33. Morfa's life story is picaresque. See Kristen Block and Jenny Shaw, "Subjects Without an Empire: The Irish in the Early Modern Caribbean," *Past and Present* 210 (February 2011): 44–45.

34. AGI, Patronato 273, "Carta de Enríque Enríquez de Sotomayor," March 6, 1635, fol. 1r. For the five days, see AGI, Patronato 273, "Sobre haver desalojado el año de 1635 al enemigo que estava poblado y presidado en la isla de Tortuga," March 1635, fol. 17r.

35. de Vries, *Voyages from Holland to America*, 104.

36. Deive, *La Esclavitud del Negro en Santo Domingo*, 128.

37. TNA, CO 124/2, fols. 265–66; Games, "The Sanctuarye of Our Rebell Negroes," 12.

38. AGI, Patronato 273, r. 1, "Carta de los oficiales reales de Santo Domingo a Su Magestad," February 16, 1634, fol. 2r; AGI, Santo Domingo 870, l. 10, "Registro: Isla Española," Madrid, March 23, 1637, fol. 10v; Deive, *La Esclavitud del Negro en Santo Domingo*, 128.

39. AGI, Patronato 273, r. 1, "Victoria de capitán Ruy Fernández de Fuenmayor: isla Tortuga," February 12, 1634, fol. 3r.

40. AGI, Santo Domingo 870, l. 10, "Registro: Isla Española," fol. 10v.

41. Between 1620 and 1630, the price of an enslaved African in Cartagena was between 270 and 310 pesos, while that same individual would be purchased on average for 600 pesos in Lima. Newson and Minchin, *From Capture to Sale*, p. 160.

42. AGI, Santo Domingo 870, l. 10, "Registro: Isla Española," fol. 10v.

43. There is ample historiography on Daniel Elfrith, who sailed with commissions from the second Earl of Warwick, Robert Rich, and had ties to colonization in Bermuda. The classic article for this is W. Frank Craven, "The Earl of Warwick, a Speculator in Piracy," *Hispanic American Historical Review* 10, no. 4 (November 1930): 457–79. Elfrith has reemerged in recent historiography because of his role in the captivity and trafficking of "20 and odd" enslaved Africans

at Point Comfort, Virginia, in 1619. See, for example, Thornton and Heywood, *Central Africans,* 6–7, 27; Holly Brewer, "Not 'Beyond the Line': Reconsidering Law and Power and the Origins of Slavery in England's Empire in the Americas," *Early American Studies* 20, no. 4 (Fall 2022): 624.

44. For a good summary of the historiography of Providence Island, see Games, "The Sanctuarye of Our Rebell Negroes,'" 1–2. See also Newton, *Colonising Activities of the English Puritans*; Kupperman, *Providence Island.*

45. AGI, Santa Fé 223, "Informe del Capitan Toribio de Palacios y Sierra," May 26, 1666, fol. 522v.

46. According to the testimonies of an English mariner who defected from Providencia, he knew of two Dutch ships and one French ship, in addition to English vessels, that had received commission to raid Iberian shipping by the governor of Providencia. See AGI, Santa Fé 223, r. 2, "Carta de Cartagena," June 2, 1640, fol. 134r.

47. AGI, Santa Fé 223, "Relacion que hazen el capitan Gregorio de Castella y Mantilla y Juan de Somovilla Tejada … del viaje que hicieron a la isla de Santa Catalina," Cartagena, August 22, 1635, unfoliated.

48. Evidence that settlers on Providencia offered freedom in exchange for military service comes from the testimony of a French mariner who had been on the island when the Spanish attacked in 1635 and was subsequently taken captive in Jamaica. AGI, Santa Fé 223, "Copia de la carta que Francisco Díaz Pimienta escrivio a su Magestad dando quenta de haver recuperado de ingleses la isla de Santa Catalina," Cartagena, September 11, 1641, unfoliated.

49. AGI, Santa Fé 223, "Carta del gobernador de Tierra Firme Enrique Enríquez de Sotomayor," Portobelo, July 15, 1638, fol. 71v.

50. AGI, Santa Fé 223, "Carta de Cartagena," fol. 133r.

51. Games, "The Sanctuarye of Our Rebell Negroes," 11.

52. Genkins, "Entangled Empires," 115.

53. AGI, Santa Fé 223, "Carta de Cartagena," fol. 133r; Genkins, "Entangled Empires," 113.

54. AGI, Santa Fé 223, "Carta de Francisco Díaz Pimienta al Rey," September 11, 1641, unfoliated; Genkins, "Entangled Empires," 119.

55. Genkins, "Entangled Empires," 120.

56. For an extended discussion of the role of households in European "regimes of plunder," see Benton, *They Called It Peace,* chap. 3.

57. Spanish officials had argued for the need for a presidio on Providencia specifically because of what had happened on St. Christopher since the mid-1630s. See, for example, AGI, Panamá 19, r. 3, no. 37, "Carta de Enríque Enríquez de Sotomayor," July 18, 1636, fol. 1v.

58. AGI, Santa Fé 223, "Carta del general Francisco Díaz Pimienta y consulta de la Junta de Guerra," May 5, 1643, fol. 166r.

59. AGI, Contaduria 5101, "Carta de Francisco Díaz Pimienta," May 6, 1641, unfoliated.

60. TNA, CO 124/1, "Letter to Captain Hunt," March 19, 1636/7; Games, "The Sanctuarye of Our Rebell Negros," 12–13.

61. CO 124/2, "Committee," April 25, 1638, 336; Dunn, et al., *Winthrop's Journal,* 1:260; CO 124/2, April 25, 1638; CO 124/2, November 29, 1638, 346; Games, "The Sanctuarye of Our Rebell Negros," 12–13.

62. For more on the Hispanic names of enslaved Africans among the "charter generations" in Virginia, see Berlin, *Many Thousands Gone,* especially chap. 1; Hatfield, *Atlantic Virginia,* 138.

63. The total of 1,600 Africans comes from a report written over twenty years after the 1641 invasion by a Spanish officer named Captain Toribio de Palacios y Sierra. Although

Anglo-Atlantic scholars have cited this number as a reflection of the population of Africans and their descendants on Providencia at the moment of the invasion, the wording of the report seems to suggest that 1,600 was the total number of Africans taken captive over the course of the 1630s. Palacios wrote that the English "havian apresado" 1,600 Africans from transatlantic and intercolonial slave ships. The use of the Spanish pluperfect suggests that Palacios was describing habitual actions occurring in the past rather than a tally of the African population in 1641. AGI, Santa Fé 223, "Informe del Capitan Toribio de Palacios y Sierra," May 25, 1666, fol. 522v.

64. AGI, Santa Fé 223, "Informe del Capitan Toribio de Palacios y Sierra," fol. 522v.

65. Wheat, *Atlantic Africa*, 254–55. Other scholars have shown the various incentives that kept Afro-descended men enslaved in maritime industries. See Walter Hawthorne, "Gorge: An African Seaman and His Flights from 'Freedom' Back to 'Slavery' in the Early Nineteenth Century," *Slavery and Abolition* 31, no. 3 (2010): 411–28; Michael Jarvis, "Maritime Masters and Seafaring Slaves in Bermuda, 1680–1783," *William and Mary Quarterly* 59, no. 3 (July 2002): 585–622.

66. Sherwin K. Bryant refers to branding for identification as a form of "colonial race governance" in Spanish America. See Bryant, *Rivers of Gold, Lives of Bondage*, 45. For more on the use of brand marks and identification in freedom suits in Cartagena, see Chloe L. Ireton, "Black Africans' Freedom Litigation Suits to Define Just War and Just Slavery in the Early Spanish Empire," *Renaissance Quarterly* 73, no. 4 (Winter 2020): 1277–1319.

67. Marcus P. Nevius, "New Histories of Marronage in the Anglo-Atlantic World and Early North America," *History Compass* 18, no. 5 (May 2020): 1–14.

68. Games, "The Sanctuarye of Our Rebell Negros," 13–14.

69. AGI, Santa Fé 223, "Tres cartas de los oficiales reales de Tierra Firme y Decreto de la Junta de Guerra," May 4, 1645, fol. 196r.

70. AGI, Santa Fé 223, "Copia de un capítulo de carta del general Francisco Díaz Pimienta," December 28, 1643, fol. 196r.

71. For more on the term *esclavos del rey*, see María Elena Díaz, *The Virgin, the King, and the Royal Slaves of El Cobre* (Stanford, CA: Stanford University Press, 2000).

72. AGI, Santa Fé 223, "Carta de Jerónimo de Ojeda al Rey," January 3, 1648, fol. 256v.

73. AGI, Santa Fé 223, "Carta del gobernador de la isla Jerónimo de Ojeda," July 16, 1646, fol. 222r–222v.

74. AGI, Santa Fé 223, "Carta del gobernador de la isla Jerónimo de Ojeda," fol. 220v.

75. Saidiya V. Hartman describes the process of trying to uncover the intimate details of those encounters as a kind of blurring of the "uncertain line between witness and spectator." See Hartman, *Scenes of Subjection: Terror, Slavery, and Self-Making in Nineteenth-Century America* (Oxford: Oxford University Press, 1997), 4. Black feminist scholars have also argued that viewing all sexual relations of this kind as unilaterally rape is problematic because such an approach refuses to account for moments when Black women used intimate relations within the violence of slavery for their own ends. See Annette Gordon-Reed, *The Hemingses of Monticello: An American Family* (New York: W. W. Norton, 2008), introduction. For more on the necessity for care when detailing intimacy and violence in the archive, see Saidiya V. Hartman, "Venus in Two Acts," *Small Axe* 12, no. 2 (June 2008): 1–14; Marisa J. Fuentes, *Dispossessed Lives: Enslaved Women, Violence, and the Archive* (Philadelphia: University of Pennsylvania Press, 2016); Smallwood, "Politics of the Archive"; Marisa J. Fuentes, "Historical Care and the (Re)Writing of Sexual Violence in the Colonial Americas," *William and Mary Quarterly* 80, no. 4 (October 2023).

76. Scholars of sixteenth- and seventeenth-century Spanish America have shown the ways in which women of African descent used spaces of intimacy to create relationships of family, patronage, and obligation that they could wield for their own freedom or the freedom of their children. See Wheat, *Atlantic Africa*, chap. 4. Michelle McKinley argues that those same bonds often yielded "fractional freedoms" in the sense of continued obligations to a former enslaver. See McKinley, *Fractional Freedoms*, esp. introduction.

77. For more on the role of households in converting fortified outposts into colonies, see Benton, *They Called It Peace*, 63.

78. AGI, Santa Fé 223, r. 3, "Carta de Salvador de la Peña, Capitán del Presidio de Santa Catalina," December 17, 1646, fol. 222v.

79. AGI, Contaduría 1480, "Caja de Panamá, Testimonios de las Juntas de Real Hacienda," fols. 54–57v.

80. Lane, *Pillaging the Empire*, 92.

81. AGI, Patronato 273, r. 7, "Carta del fiscal don Francisco de Alarcon," March 16, 1654. For other assaults on neighboring Spanish ships, see AGI, Patronato 273, r. 6, "Carta de Juan Francisco de Montemayor Córdoba y Cuenca," November 3, 1653, fol. 133r. For reports on territorial raids conducted by sailors who called at Tortuga, see AGI, Patronato 273, r. 6, "Carta de los Vasallos desta ciudad de Baracoa," Cuba, 1653, fol. 161v.

82. For more on raids against Cuba, see César García del Pino, *El corso en Cuba, Siglo XVII* (Havana: Editorial de Ciencias Sociales, 2001); Irene A. Wright, "The Dutch and Cuba, 1609–1643," *Hispanic American Historical Review* 4, no. 4 (1921): 597–634.

83. AGI, Patronato 273, r. 6, "Carta de los Vasallos desta ciudad de Baracoa," Cuba, 1653, fol. 161v.

84. AGI, Santo Domingo 56, r. 4, no. 34, "Carta de Bitrián de Viamonte al rey," July 31, 1644, fol. 1r.

85. AGI, Patronato 273, "Testimonio de Francisco da Costa," August 29, 1653, fol. 84v.

86. AGI, Patronato 273, r. 6, "Testimonio de Miguel Matamba," November 5, 1653, fol. 128r; AGI, Patronato 273, r. 5, "Testimonios de Guillermo Armon, Paul Aubert, and Raimundo Burgos," May 5, 1652, and September 15, 1653, fols. 79v–123v.

87. AGI, Patronato 273, r. 7, "Juan Francisco Montemayor y otros: recuperación Tortuga, etc." March 30, 1654.

88. AGI, Patronato 273, "Carta de Montemayor," December 30, 1654, fol. 181v.

89. Eugenio Matibag, *Haitian-Dominican Counterpoint: Nation, State, and Race on Hispaniola* (New York: Palgrave Macmillan, 2003), 39; Camus, *L'île de la Tortue*, 43–44; Peter R. Gavin, *Patterns of Pillage: A Geography of Caribbean-based Piracy in Spanish America, 1536–1718* (New York: Peter Lang, 1999), 119.

90. AGI, Patronato 273, r. 7, "Consejo de Guerra," March 30, 1654, fol. 182v.

91. Eric Williams, *From Columbus to Castro: The History of the Caribbean* (New York: Vintage, 1970), 69.

Chapter 5

1. AGI, Escribanía de Camara 123A, "Residencias de Puerto Rico" no. 9, March 12, 1659–August 9, 1663, Madrid, "Causa principal sobre arribadas de navíos extranjeros y otras culpas fulminadas contra don José de Novoa y otros reos," fols. 741r–742v.

2. AGI, Santo Domingo 157, r. 2, no. 49, "Cartas de Juan Pérez de Guzmán, gobernador de Puerto Rico," August 31, 1664, unfoliated.

3. AGI, Escribanía de Camara 123A, "Causa principal sobre arribadas de navíos extranjeros," fols. 741r–742v; AGI, Escribania de Camara 1190, "Sentencia de José de Novoa y Moscoso, governador de Puerto Rico, 1665," unfoliated.

4. Vega Franco, *El tráfico de esclavos con américa*; García-Montón, *Genoese Entrepreneurship*.

5. Julie M. Svalastog, *Mastering the Worst of Trades: England's Early Africa Companies and Their Traders, 1618–1672* (Leiden: Brill, 2021), chap. 5; Klooster, *Dutch Moment*, 175–82; Mark Meuwese, *Brothers in Arms, Partners in Trade: Dutch-Indigenous Alliances in the Atlantic World, 1595–1674* (Leiden: Brill, 2012), 53, 315; K. G. Davies, *The Royal African Company* (London: Longmans, 1957), 38–42; George Frederick Zook, *The Company of Royal Adventurers Trading into Africa* (Lancaster, PA: New Era Printing, 1919), especially chap. 3 and 4.

6. For more on the global competition that sparked the second Anglo-Dutch War, see L. H. Roper, "Reorienting the 'Origins Debate': Anglo-American Trafficking in Enslaved People, c. 1615–1660," *Atlantic Studies* 20 (2022): 8; Alison Games, "Cohabitation, Suriname-Style: English Inhabitants in Dutch Suriname After 1667," *William and Mary Quarterly* 72, no. 2 (April 2015): 195–242; Gijs Rommelse, *The Second Anglo-Dutch War (1665–1667): International Raison d'État, Mercantilism and Maritime Strife* (Hilversum, Netherlands: Verloren, 2006). Historian Steven Pincus argues for the importance of ideological causes of the war among factions within Restoration politics that viewed the religious pluralism of the Dutch Republic as problematic. See Steven C. A. Pincus, "Popery, Trade and Universal Monarchy: The Ideological Context of the Outbreak of the Second Anglo-Dutch War," *English Historical Review* 107, no. 422 (January 1992): 1–29.

7. Menard, *Sweet Negotiations*; Dunn, *Sugar and Slaves*, esp. chap. 6 and 7.

8. R. Isabel Morales, *Happy Dreams of Liberty: An American Family in Slavery and Freedom* (New York: Oxford University Press, 2022), introduction.

9. Wolff, *Isla Atlántica*, 68–69; David M. Stark, "'There Is No City Here, but a Desert': The Contours of City Life in 1673 San Juan," *Journal of Caribbean History* 42, no. 2 (2008): 259.

10. Aram, "Caribbean Ginger and Atlantic Trade."

11. Wolff, *Isla Atlántica*, 32; Gelpí Baíz, *Siglo en Blanco*, 14, 20–21, 90. As early as 1586, the governor of Puerto Rico, Diego Menéndez de Valdés, was accused of engaging in illicit trade with northern European traffickers in order to obtain forty enslaved Africans whom he put to labor on his ginger plantation. See AGI, Indiferente General 1887, "El tesorero Juan de Vargas Zapata y el Contador Francisco Rodríguez a S.M., acusando al gobernadora Diego Menéndez de Valdés y pidiendo que lo remuevan del puesto," July 12, 1586, fol. 50v, also printed in Huerga, *Cartas de gobernadores*, 2:226.

12. Wheat, *Atlantic Africa*, 8–11, 16.

13. AGI, Escribanía de Camara 123A, "Causa principal sobre arribadas de navíos extranjeros," fols. 785v–786r, 876v.

14. AGI, Escribanía de Camara 123A, "Causa principal sobre arribadas de navíos extranjeros," fol. 954r.

15. AGI, Santo Domingo 157, r. 2, no. 49, "Cartas de D. Juan Pérez de Guzmán, gobernador de Puerto Rico," August 31, 1664, unfoliated. For more examples of how frequently fishing vessels were the targets of raids in this moment, see AGI, Santo Domingo 60, r. 2, no. 25, "Carta de Pedro de Carvajal y Cobos, presidente de la Audiencia de Santo Domingo," July 26, 1664, unfoliated.

16. AGI, Santo Domingo 157, r. 2, no. 42, "Carta de D. Juan Pérez de Gúzman, gobernador de Puerto Rico," May 31, 1663, unfoliated.

17. AGI, Santo Domingo 157, r. 2, no. 49, "Cartas de D. Juan Pérez de Guzmán, gobernador de Puerto Rico," August 31, 1664, fol. 1v.

18. For more on the Peace of Münster and Dutch-Spanish relations, see Ana Crespo Solana, "A Network-Based Merchant Empire: Dutch Trade in the Hispanic Atlantic (1680–1741)," in *Dutch Atlantic Connections, 1680–1800: Linking Empires, Bridging Borders*, ed. Gert Oostindie and Jessica V. Roitman (Leiden: Brill, 2014), 141; Jessica Vance Roitman, *The Same but Different? Intercultural Trade and the Sephardim, 1595–1640* (Leiden: Brill, 2011); Roper, *Advancing Empire*, 133.

19. AGI, Escribanía de Camara 123A, "Causa principal sobre arribadas de navíos extranjeros," fol. 785v.

20. AGI, Escribanía de Camara 123A, "Causa principal sobre arribadas de navíos extranjeros," fols. 741v–742r., 759v.

21. AGI, Escribanía de Camara 123A, "Causa principal sobre arribadas de navíos extranjeros," fol. 955r.

22. AGI, Escribanía de Camara 123A, "Causa principal sobre arribadas de navíos extranjeros," fol. 698r.

23. AGI, Escribanía de Camara 123A, "Causa principal sobre arribadas de navíos," fol. 643r.

24. For more on patronage and race in colonial Latin America, see Andrew B. Fisher and Matthew D. O'Hara, "Introduction: Racial Identities and Their Interpreters in Colonial Latin America," in *Imperial Subjects: Race and Identity in Colonial Latin America*, ed. Fisher and O'Hara (Durham, NC: Duke University Press, 2009), 1–39; R. Douglas Cope, *The Limits of Racial Domination: Plebeian Society in Colonial Mexico City, 1660–1720* (Madison: University of Wisconsin Press, 1994).

25. AGI, Escribanía de Camara 123A, "Causa principal sobre arribadas de navíos extranjeros," fol. 745v.

26. AGI, Santo Domingo 157, r. 1, no. 6, "Carta de José de Novoa, gobernador de Puerto Rico," November 11, 1658, unfoliated.

27. AGI, Escribanía de Camara 123A, "Causa principal sobre arribadas de navíos extranjeros," fol. 745v.

28. AGI, Escribanía de Camara 123A, "Causa principal sobre arribadas de navíos extranjeros," fol. 745v.

29. Wim Klooster, "Curaçao and the Caribbean Transit Trade," in *Riches from Atlantic Commerce: Dutch Transatlantic Trade and Shipping, 1585–1817* (Leiden: Brill, 2003), 204; Ana Crespo Solana, "Holanda en el Caribe desde la perspective comparada. Aportación al debate sobre los modelos de expansion en los siglos XVII y XVIII," *Catharum: Revista de Ciencias y Humanidades del Instituto de Estudios Hispánicos de Canarias* (2008): 39–48.

30. "Letter from Matthias Beck, December 24, 1655," in *New Netherland Documents*, vol. 17, *Curacao Papers, 1640–1665*, ed. and trans. Charles T. Gehring and ed. J. A. Schiltkamp (Interlaken, NY: Heart of the Lakes, 1987), 85.

31. "Letter from Matthias Beck, December 24, 1655," in *New Netherland Documents*, 85.

32. Heywood and Thornton, *Central Africans*, 259.

33. Postma, *The Dutch in the Atlantic Slave Trade*, 27.

34. "Letter from Matthias Beck, July 28, 1657," in *New Netherland Documents*, 105.

35. Postma, *The Dutch in the Atlantic Slave Trade*, 60, 111; Klooster, *Dutch Moment*, 182. For more on the nature of that trade in Atlantic Africa, see Romney, *New Netherland Connections*, esp. chap. 4.

36. *Voyages: The Trans-Atlantic Slave Trade Database*, Voyage ID no. 11362, accessed August 2023 (www.slavevoyages.org).

37. "Letter from Matthias Beck, June 11, 1657," in *New Netherland Documents*, 94–95; David Freeman, *A Silver River in a Silver World: Dutch Trade in the Río de la Plata, 1648–1678* (New York: Cambridge University Press, 2020), 6–7.

38. "Letter from Matthias Beck, June 11, 1657," in *New Netherland Documents*, 94.

39. "Letter from Matthias Beck, June 11, 1657," in *New Netherland Documents*, 94.

40. "Letter from Matthias Beck, July 28, 1657," in *New Netherland Documents*, 104.

41. "Letter from Matthias Beck, July 28, 1657," in *New Netherland Documents*, 104.

42. "Letter from Matthias Beck, July 28, 1657," in *New Netherland Documents*, 103.

43. AGI, Escribanía 963, "Sentencia de Jacobo Mandix por arribada a Portobelo," 1661, unfoliated.

44. *Voyages: The Trans-Atlantic Slave Trade Database*.

45. For more on Mathias, see Klooster, *Dutch Moment*, 175–76, 181.

46. F. Ribeiro Da Silva, *Dutch and Portuguese in Western Africa* (Leiden: Brill, 2011), 311–12.

47. *Voyages: The Trans-Atlantic Slave Trade Database*, Voyage ID no. 11363, accessed August 2023 (www.slavevoyages.org); Thornton, *Africa and Africans*, 122, 195. The rhetorical move to view deaths on a transatlantic slave-trading voyage as the death of a person rather than an aggregate number comes from Stephanie E. Smallwood, "Politics of the Archive."

48. In a letter to the Crown, Novoa claimed that Fon sold 109 enslaved Africans in Puerto Rico but claimed that he had been forced into San Juan for want of food, wood, and water and that Novoa allowed the sale of the enslaved Africans because "it had been so many years since [enslaved Africans] had entered the port" that "there was no one to cultivate the land." See AGI, Santo Domingo 157, r. 1, no. 6, "Carta de José de Novoa, gobernador de Puerto Rico," November 15, 1658, unfoliated.

49. Determining the ethnicity of the captives loaded on board the *St. Jan* is made difficult by the nature of trade between the Gold and Slave Coasts. Historians have long assumed that enslaved captives purchased by Europeans on the Slave Coast would have been speakers of, broadly, Gbe languages such as Ewe, Adja, or Fon, while captives purchased along the Gold Coast would have been speakers of Akan languages such as Fante or Twi. Historian Robin Law has argued that these distinctions are hard to draw because Gold Coast traders used ocean-going canoes to establish trade communities along the Slave Coast, what he calls a "Mina diaspora." See Law, "Ethnicities of Enslaved Africans in the Diaspora: on the Meanings of 'Mina' (Again)," *History in Africa* 32 (2005): 251.

50. "Letter from Matthias Beck, September 10, 1659," in *New Netherland Documents*, 128–33.

51. "Testimony of Jan Rijckartsen, Skipper of the *De Jonge*, November 25, 1659," in *New Netherland Documents*, 145. For more on the importance of studying nonlinear voyages of this nature, see Clark, *Veracruz and the Caribbean*.

52. "Letter from Matthias Beck, February 4, 1660," in *New Netherland Documents*, 158.

53. "Letter from Matthias Beck, August 23, 1659," in *New Netherland Documents*, 126.

54. "Letter from Matthias Beck, February 4, 1660," in *New Netherland Documents*, 158.

55. AGI, Escribanía de Camara 123A, "Causa principal sobre arribadas de navíos extranjeros," fol. 772v.

56. AGI, Escribanía de Camara 123A, "Causa principal sobre arribadas de navíos extranjeros," fols. 745r–755r.

57. AGI, Escribanía de Camara 123A, "Causa principal sobre arribadas de navíos extranjeros," fol. 698r.

58. Vernon W. Pickering, *Early History of the British Virgin Islands: From Columbus to Emancipation* (British Virgin Islands: Falcon, 1983), 33–37.

59. The practice of sailors carrying money or merchandise of their own or being entrusted with the funds of others in order to engage in trade may have been a common occurrence on Iberian ships. See David Wheat, "Tangomãos en Tenerife y Sierra Leona a mediados del siglo XVI," *Cliocanarias* 2 (2020): 545–69.

60. AGI, Escribanía de Camara 123A, "Causa principal sobre arribadas de navíos extranjeros," fol. 772v.

61. AGI, Escribanía de Camara 123A, "Causa principal sobre arribadas de navíos extranjeros," fol. 755r.

62. For an example of these orders, see AGI, Santo Domingo 1126, L. 1, "Carta del rey," October 25, 1656, Santo Domingo. For a discussion of efforts to amass supplies for the Spanish defense of Jamaica, see Schmitt, "Centering Spanish Jamaica"; Rafal Reichert, "La pérdida de la isla de Jamaica por la Corona Española y los intentos de recuperarla durante los años 1655–1660," *Ulúa: Revista de historia, sociedad y cultura* 7, no. 14 (July–December 2009): 9–33.

63. AGI, Escribania 1190, "Sentencia de José de Novoa y Moscoso." While *residencias*, or investigations into the conduct of outgoing Spanish officials, resulted in charges of smuggling for almost all of Puerto Rico's seventeenth-century governors, the fines levied against Novoa following his *pesquisa*, or special investigation, were particularly severe, as was his arrest. For more on this, see Angel López Canos, *Historia de Puerto Rico (1650-1700)* (Seville, 1975), 173–74.

64. Alex Borucki, David Eltis, and David Wheat, "Atlantic History and the Slave Trade to Spanish America," *American Historical Review* 120, no. 2 (April 2015): 449; García-Montón, *Genoese Entrepreneurship*, 101–3.

65. Vega Franco, *El trafico de esclavos con américa*, 8.

66. García-Montón, *Genoese Entrepreneurship*, 2.

67. García-Montón, *Genoese Entrepreneurship*, 108.

68. García-Montón, *Genoese Entrepreneurship*, 121.

69. Vega Franco, *El trafico de esclavos con américa*, 32.

70. AGI, Santo Domingo 157, r. 2, no. 42, "Carta de Juan Pérez de Gúzman, gobernador de Puerto Rico," May 31, 1663, fol. 1v.

71. John Coakley, "Jamaica's Private Seafarers: Politics and Violence in a Seventeenth-Century English Colony," in *The Golden Age of Piracy: The Rise, Fall, and Enduring Popularity of Pirates*, ed. David Head (Athens: University of Georgia Press, 2018), 35; C. H. Firth, "The Capture of Santiago, in Cuba, by Captain Myngs, 1662," *English Historical Review* 14, no. 55 (July 1899): 536–40. The Myngs raid was part of a deeper history of English attacks in Cuba. See Elena A. Schnieder, *The Occupation of Havana: War, Trade, and Slavery in the Atlantic World* (Chapel Hill: Published for the Omohundro Institute for Early American History and Culture by University of North Carolina Press, 2018), 32, chap. 1.

72. Reichart, "Le pérdida de la isla de Jamaica," 26; Hanna, *Pirate Nests*, 108.

73. Jamaican National Library, MS 1659, "Sir Christopher Myngs to Unknown, on Board the *Centurion* at Iago," July 19, 1663. The author thanks Andrew Rutledge for bringing this source to my attention.

74. Roper, *Advancing Empire*, 188.

75. Carla Gardina Pestana, "Early English Jamaica Without Pirates," *William and Mary Quarterly* 71, no. 3 (July 2014): 335.

76. Clarence Henry Haring, *Trade and Navigation Between Spain and the Indies in the Time of the Hapsburgs* (Cambridge, MA: Harvard University Press, 1918), 247–48; Michael Pawson and David Buisseret, *Port Royal, Jamaica* (Kingston, Jamaica: University of the West Indies Press, 2000), 28–29; Roper, *Advancing Empire*, 188.

77. TNA, CO 324/1, "Instructions for Thomas Windsor Lord Windsor Governor of Our Island of Jamaica in the West Indies," Whitehall, March 21, 1661/2, fols. 37–56; Pestana, "Early English Jamaica," 335.

78. R. G. Marsden, ed., *Documents Relating to Law and Custom of the Sea*, vol. 1, *A.D. 1205–1648* (Naval Records Society, 1915), 41. Windsor repeated this justification in a letter that he wrote to the governor of Santiago de Cuba after the invasion. See AGI, Santo Domingo 60, r.1, no. 1, "Carta de don Pedro de Carvajal y Cobos," February 15, 1663, unfoliated.

79. Koot, *Empire at the Periphery*.

80. Ville Kari, "Freebooters and Free Traders: English Colonial Prize Jurisdiction in the West Indies, 1655–1670," *Journal of the History of International Law* 21 (2019): 41–70; Helen Josephine Crump, *Colonial Admiralty Jurisdiction in the Seventeenth Century* (New York: Longmans, 1931), 98n11.

81. TNA, CO 1/18, no. 95, "Gov. Sir Thos. Modyford to his brother, Sir James," August 10, 1664, fol. 1r.

82. AGI, Santo Domingo 60, r. 2, no. 25, "Carta de Pedro de Carvajal y Cobos."

83. AGI, Santo Domingo 60, r. 2, no. 25, "Carta de Pedro de Carvajal y Cobos."

84. Nuala Zahedieh, "'A Frugal, Prudential and Hopeful Trade': Privateering in Jamaica, 1655–89," *Journal of Imperial and Commonwealth History* 2, no. 18 (1990): 148.

85. This is assuming that the captives would have been sold for the same price offered by the Royal Adventurers trading to Jamaica in 1664. See TNA, SP 29/67, no. 162, "Proposals for Re-Settlement of the Royal [African] Company," January 1663.

86. AGI, Indiferente General 2545, "Declaraciones hechas por los franceses,"; Roger C. Smith, *The Maritime Heritage of the Cayman Islands* (Gainesville: University of Florida Press, 2000), 60–61.

87. TNA, CO 1/25, fol. 65, 176–78; TNA CO 140/1, fols. 223–25, June 12, 1671; Michael Craton, *Founded upon the Seas: A History of the Cayman Islands and Their People* (Kingston, Jamaica: Ian Randle, 2003), 33.

88. TNA CO 140/1, fols. 223–25, June 12, 1671, quoted in Craton, *Founded upon the Seas*, 27.

89. TNA, CO 324/1, "A Brief Survey of Jamaica," [1664], fol. 149; Pestana, *English Conquest of Jamaica*, 166–68; Mary Draper, "Timbering and Turtling: The Maritime Hinterlands of Early Modern British Caribbean Cities," *Early American Studies* 15, no. 4 (Fall 2017): 769–800.

90. Michael J. Jarvis, *In the Eye of All Trade: Bermuda, Bermudians, and the Maritime Atlantic World, 1680–1783* (Chapel Hill: Published for the Omohundro Institute for Early American History and Culture by University of North Carolina Press, 2010), 234.

91. Lieutenant-General Sir J. H. Lefroy, ed., *Memorial of the Discovery and Early Settlement of the Bermudas or Somers Islands, 1511–1687*, vol. 2, *1650–1687* (London: Longmans, 1879), 220; Jarvis, *In the Eye of All Trade*, 490.

92. TNA, CO 1/17, no. 4, "Desires of the Royal Adventurers to Africa," February 26, 1662/3, fol. 1v.

93. AGI, Santo Domingo 157, r. 2, no. 49, "Carta de Juan Pérez de Guzmán, gobernador de Puerto Rico," August 31, 1664.

94. BL, Add. MSS 11411, fol. 31; BL, Egerton 2835, fol. 303, 171; C. S. S. Highham, *The Development of the Leeward Islands Under the Restoration, 1660–1688: A Study of the Foundations of the Old Colonial System* (Cambridge: Cambridge University Press, 1921), 18–19, 35; Leslie Theibert, *Making an English Caribbean, 1650–1688* (PhD diss., Yale University, 2013), 56.

95. AGI, Santo Domingo 157, r. 2, no. 36, "Carta de Juan Pérez de Guzmán, gobernador de Puerto Rico," May 31, 1663, fol. 1r.

96. AGI, Santo Domingo 157, r. 2, no. 51, "Carta de Juan Pérez de Guzmán, gobernador de Puerto Rico," August 31, 1664, unfoliated.

97. Vega Franco, *El trafico de esclavos con américa*, 127–30.

98. AGI, Santo Domingo 157, r. 2, no. 51, "Carta de Juan Pérez de Guzmán, gobernador de Puerto Rico," August 31, 1664, unfoliated.

99. The causes of the Second Anglo-Dutch War are debated among scholars, from arguments that focus of the political machinations of the Restoration Monarchy and, specifically, the anti-Dutch stance taken by James, Duke of York. See N. A. M. Rodger, *Command of the Ocean: A Naval History of Britain, 1649–1815* (New York: W. W. Norton, 2005). And older historiography places the causes of the war strictly on mercantile competition between the Dutch and English. See Charles Wilson, *Profit and Power: A Study of England the Dutch Wars* (New York: Longmans, Green, 1957). Steven C. A. Pincus, however, argues that the war sprang from religious and ideological controversies, in *Protestantism and Patriotism: Ideologies and the Making of English Foreign Policy, 1650–1668* (New York: Cambridge University Press, 2002). For a good overview of the debates, see Rommelse, *Second Anglo-Dutch War*, introduction.

100. TNA, CO 1/19 no. 127, "Governor Sir Thos. Modyford to Lord Archingdale [Sec. Lord Arglinton]," Jamaica, November 16, 1665.

101. TNA, CO 1/19, no. 130, "A true & perfect Narrative by Colonell Theodore Cary, declaring the proceedings in the late expedition from this Island of Jamaica against the Dutch, under the management of Lt. General Edward Morgan until his death, and afterward by Colonell Theodore Cary," Jamaica, November 1665; TNA, CO 1/19, no. 30, "Col. Theodore Cary to Sec. Lord Arlington," Jamaica, November 1665; TNA, CO 1/19, no. 127, "Modyford to Lord Arlington," Jamaica, November 16, 1665; Du Tertre, *Histoire Générale de Antilles* 3:245; Klooster, *Dutch Moment*, 104–9.

102. French colonists had complained, much like their English counterparts, that the newly created monopoly French slave-trading company, the Compagnie des Indes Occidentales, had not provided sufficient enslaved Africans. The declaration of war proved an opportune moment to seize African women, men, and children for their own plantations. See, for example, ANOM, C7 A1, folio 26, "Correspondence de Du Lion, gouverneur en la provence de la Guadeloupe," April 8, 1665; ANOM C8, "Correspondence de Prouville de Tracy," July 1, 1664; Klooster, *Dutch Moment*, 172; Boucher, *France and the American Tropics*, 155.

103. TNA, CO 153/1, no. 92, "A Narrative of Lord Willoughby's Proceedings," July 21, 1667; TNA, CO 1/29, no. 71, "An answer to the inquiries of his Majesty," December 9, 1671; TNA, CO 153/1, no. 63, "Report from Secretary Benjamin Worsley," February 1, 1673.

104. TNA, CO 153/1, no. 63, "Memorial for Secretary Benjamin Worsley to the Council for Trade and Plantations," February 1, 1673.

105. Casey Schmitt, "Warfare, Imperial Competition, and Serial Displacement in the Seventeenth-Century Caribbean," in *Beyond 1619: The Atlantic Origins of American Slavery*, ed.

Paul J. Polgar, Marc H. Lerner, and Jesse Cromwell (Philadelphia: University of Pennsylvania Press, 2023), 104–18.

Chapter 6

1. Europeans across the Atlantic world embraced the Roman legal concept of *partus sequitur ventrem* in which slavery descended through the maternal line. See Jennifer L. Morgan, "*Partus sequitur ventrem*: Law, Race, and Reproduction in Colonial Slavery," *Small Axe* 22, no. 1 (55): 1–17; Saidiya Hartman, "The Belly of the World: A Note on Black Women's Labors," *Souls: A Critical Journal of Black Politics, Culture, and Society* 18, no. 1 (2016): 166–73; Alejandro de la Fuente and Ariela J. Gross, *Becoming Free, Becoming Black: Race, Freedom, and Law in Cuba, Virginia, and Louisiana* (New York: Cambridge University Press, 2020); Guillaume Aubert, "'The Blood of France': Race and Purity of Blood in the French Atlantic World," *William and Mary Quarterly* 61, no. 3 (July 2004): 439–78. Historian Jessica Marie Johnson, however, cautions that manumission and manumitted women reveal how *partus* was imposed and constructed rather than hereditary or natural. See Johnson, *Wicked Flesh*, chap. 5.

2. AGI, Escribanía 1033B, L. 28, no. 37, Consejo Año de 1668, "Autos hechos en la Havana por el Governador Francisco Davila Orexon, sobre haver llegado aquel Puerto, once negros huidos de poder de los Ingleses que los tenian por Esclavos en la Jamaica y dadoles Libertad," October 5, 1668, unfoliated.

3. AGI, Escribanía 1033B, L. 28, no. 37, Consejo Año de 1668.

4. Jane Landers, *Black Society in Spanish Florida* (Urbana: University of Illinois Press, 1999), chap. 2; Rupert, "Marronage"; Linda Rupert, "'Seeking the Water of Baptism': Fugitive Slaves and Imperial Jurisdiction in the Early Modern Caribbean," in *Legal Pluralism and Empires, 1500–1850*, ed. Lauren Benton and Richard J. Ross (New York: Cambridge University Press, 2013), 199–231; George B. Mauvois, *Les marrons de la mer: Évasions d'esclaves de la Martinique vers les Îles de la Caraïbe (1833–1848)* (Paris, 2018); Fernanda Bretones Lane, "Free to Bury Their Dead: Baptism and the Meanings of Freedom in the Eighteenth-Century Caribbean," *Slavery & Abolition* 42, no. 3 (2021): 449–65.

5. Hatfield, *Boundaries of Belonging*, chap. 3.

6. Tatiana Seijas, *Asian Slaves in Colonial Mexico: From Chinos to Indians* (New York: Cambridge University Press, 2014), 103; García-Montón, *Genoese Entrepreneurship*.

7. Bernardo Vega, *La derrota de Penn y Venables en Santo Domingo, 1655* (Santo Domingo: Academia Dominicana de la Historia, 2013), esp. chap. 3.

8. Irene A. Wright, "The Spanish Resistance to the English Occupation of Jamaica, 1655–1660," *Transactions of the Royal Historical Society* 13 (December, 1930): 117–74.

9. Tracing the trajectory of the Porus captives required reading across imperial archives. Scholars of the Anglo-Atlantic have argued that the Porus Maroons "died out in the 1670s, fled to Cuba, or merged" with the Windward Maroons in eastern Jamaica. See Michael Craton, *Testing the Chains: Resistance to Slavery in the British West Indies* (Ithaca, NY: Cornell University Press, 1982), 74. Scholars of the Spanish Atlantic have noted the arrival of "slaves" to Portobelo without accounting for who those individuals were before their captivity. See Alejandro García-Montón, "The Rise of Portobelo and the Transformation of the Spanish American Slave Trade, 1640s–1730s: Transimperial Connections and Intra-American Shipping," *Hispanic American Historical Review* 99, no. 3 (2019): 415.

10. Wheat, *Atlantic Africa*; Gómez, *Experiential Caribbean*.

11. O'Toole, "Securing Subjecthood."

12. Block, *Ordinary Lives in the Early Caribbean.*

13. One of the mariners on board the *Blessing,* for example, described the Porus captives as "negros ladinos." AGI, Panamá 22, r. 6, no. 124A, "Declaración de Pedro Adaulfo," October 7, 1661, fol. 18r. For more on "ladinos" see Wheat, *Atlantic Africans,* chap. 6.

14. Wright, "Spanish Resistance," 127.

15. Francisco A. Scarano, "Imperial Decline, Colonial Adaptation: The Spanish Islands During the Long 17th Century," in *The Caribbean: A History of a Region and its People,* ed. Stephan Palmié and Francisco Scarano (Chicago: University of Chicago Press, 2011), 181; David M. Stark, *Slave Families and the Hato Economy in Puerto Rico* (Gainesville: University Press of Florida, 2017).

16. Antonio Vázquez de Espinosa, *Compendio y descripción de las Indias Occidentales,* Edición de Balbino Velasco Bayón (Madrid: História 16, 1992), 195.

17. It was also especially important to prevent the English from accessing foodstuffs, leading to hunger in the English camp. See Dunn, *Sugar and Slaves,* 152–53; Carla Gardina Pestana, "State Formation from the Vantage of Early English Jamaica: The Neglect of Edward Doyley," *Journal of British Studies* 56, no. 3 (July 2017): 493.

18. Wright, "Spanish Resistance," 130.

19. Block, *Ordinary Lives,* 138; Pestana, *English Conquest of Jamaica,* 184; Pestana, "The Jamaican Maroons and the Dangers of Categorical Thinking," *Commonplace* 17, no. 4 (Summer 2017), https://commonplace.online/article/vol-17-no-4-pestana/ [accessed September 2022].

20. Frank Cundall and Joseph L. Pietersz, *Jamaica Under the Spaniards: Abstracted from the Archives of Seville* (Kingston: Institute of Jamaica, 1919), 55, 62, 81.

21. For more on supplies and troops from New Spain, see Reichert, "La pérdida de la isla de Jamaica," 9–33.

22. AGI, Santo Domingo 1126, L. 1, "Carta del Rey," December 23, 1659, unfoliated.

23. See, for example, Ben Vinson III, *Bearing Arms for His Majesty: The Free-Colored Militia in Colonial Mexico* (Stanford, CA: Stanford University Press, 2001); Borucki, *From Shipmates to Soldiers,* 14.

24. O'Toole, "Securing Subjecthood," 166.

25. Block, *Ordinary Lives,* 134–35.

26. TNA, CO 1/15, no. 37, "Col. Edward D'Oyley, Governor of Jamaica, to his kinsman, Sec. Nicholas," Jamaica, March 1661.

27. Pestana provides an excellent description of the English patrol and the alliance agreed to by Lubolo. See Pestana, *English Conquest of Jamaica,* chap. 8, esp. 200–203.

28. AGI, Panama 22, r. 6, no. 124A, "Declaración de Thomas Alvarez," July 10, 1661, fol. 16r.

29. David Buisseret and S. A. G. Taylor, "Juan de Bolas and His Pelinco," *Caribbean Quarterly* 54, no. 4 (December, 2008): 96; Cundall and Pietersz, *Jamaica Under the Spaniards,* 81, 90; Mavis C. Campbell, *The Maroons of Jamaica, 1655–1796: A History of Resistance, Collaboration, and Betrayal* (Granby, Mass.: Bergin & Garvey Publishers, 1988), 20; AGI, Panama 22, r. 6, no. 124A, "Autos de Roberto Breton," July 10, 1661; AGI, Santo Domingo 178A, "Carta de Juan de Salamanca," June 28, 1660.

30. Campbell, *Maroons of Jamaica,* 25.

31. AGI, Panama 22, r. 6, nos. 124A, 124B, and 124C, "Autos de Roberto Breton," 1661.

32. AGI, Panama 22, r. 6, no. 124A, "Declaración de Fray Thomas Alvarez," October 6, 1661, fol. 15v.

33. AGI, Panama 22, r. 6, no. 124A, "Declaración de Joseph Vargas Machuca," July 6, 1661, fol. 11v.

34. AGI, Panama 22, r. 6, no. 124C, "Carta de Fernando de la Riva Agüero," July 10, 1661, fol. 1r.

35. Rafael Obando Andrade, *Africanos en los Confines del Imperio: Esclavitud, empoderamiento y lucha en la Honduras colonial (1525–1643)* (Madrid: Consejo Superior de Investigaciones científicas, 2020), 119.

36. García-Montón, "Rise of Portobelo," 414.

37. See, for example, Hanna, *Pirate Nests*, esp. chap. 3.

38. AGI, Panama 22, r. 6, no. 124A, "Autos de Roberto Breton," 1661, fols. 1v–32v.

39. According to Leo J. Garofalo, freedom papers for people of African descent in the seventeenth century were often issued as *cartas de libertad* for Afro-descended sea workers not necessarily as a means to prove the freedom of the holder of a *carta de libertad* but rather as a way for Spanish ship captains to prove that they weren't transporting and attempting to sell enslaved Africans without paying the *avería* or royal tax and a way for the Spanish Crown to control the movement of people within the empire. See Leo J. Garofalo, "The Shape of a Diaspora: The Movement of Afro-Iberians to Colonial Spanish America," in *Africans to Spanish America: Expanding the Diaspora* ed. Sherwin K. Bryant, Rachel Sarah O'Toole, and Ben Vinson (Chicago: University of Illinois Press, 2012), 36–38.

40. AGI, Panama 22, r. 6, no. 124A, "Declaración de Thomas Gutierrez," July 10, 1661, fol. 19v.

41. AGI, Panama 22, r. 6, no. 124B, "Autos de Roberto Breton," July 10, 1661, fol. 31r.

42. AGI, Panama 22, r. 6, no. 124A, "Carta de Fernando de la Riva Agüero," July 10, 1661, fol. 1v–2r.

43. AGI, Panama 22, r. 6, no. 124A–C; García-Montón, "The Rise of Portobelo," 414.

44. O'Malley, *Final Passages*, especially chap. 2 and 3.

45. AGI, Santo Domingo 178A.

46. AGI, Panama 22, r. 6, no. 124A, "Autos de Robert Breton," October 7, 1661, fol. 15v.

47. García-Montón, "Rise of Portobelo," 414.

48. AGI, Santo Domingo 178A, "Carta de Juan de Salamanca," Havana, June 28, 1660, unfoliated.

49. Pestana, *English Conquest of Jamaica*, 201.

50. BL, Add. MS 25120/74, "Coventry to Vaughn," June 8, 1676, unfoliated.

51. For more on European captivity in North Africa, see Nabil Matar, "The Barbary Corsairs, King Charles I, and the Civil War," *Seventeenth Century* 16, no. 2 (2001): 239–58; Robert C. Davis, *Christian Slaves, Muslim Masters: White Slavery in the Mediterranean, the Barbary Coast, and Italy, 1500–1800* (New York: Palgrave Macmillan, 2003); José Antonio Martínez Torres, *Prisioneros de los infieles: Vida y rescate de los cautivos cristianos en el Mediterráneo musulmán [siglos XVI–XVII]* (Barcelona: Ediciones Bellaterra, 2004).

52. TNA, CO 1/19, no. 127, "Governor Sir Thos. Modyford to Lord Archingdale [Sec. Lord Arlington]," Jamaica, November 16, 1665.

53. Daniel Nemser, *Infrastructures of Race: Concentration and Biopolitics in Colonial Mexico* (Austin: University of Texas Press, 2017), 5.

54. Michael Pawson and David Buisseret, *Port Royal, Jamaica* (Oxford: Clarendon, 1975), 98.

55. James Robertson, "Late Seventeenth-Century Spanish Town, Jamaica: Building an English City on Spanish Foundations," *Early American Studies* 6, no. 2 (Fall 2008): 377.

56. Robertson, "Late Seventeenth-Century Spanish Town," 377.

57. Cagway was renamed Port Royal in 1664. See Pestana, *English Conquest of Jamaica*, 221.

58. Robertson, "Late Seventeenth-Century Spanish Town," 365–67.

59. See, for example, Nuala Zahedieh, "'The Wickedest City in the World: Port Royal, Commercial Hub of the Seventeenth-Century Caribbean," in *Working Out Slavery, Pricing Freedom: Essays in Honour of Barry W. Higman*, ed. Verene Shepherd (Kingston, Jamaica, 2002), 3–20.

60. Hanna, *Pirate Nests*, 112–14.

61. AGI, Escribanía 1033B, L. 28, no. 37, Consejo Año de 1668.

62. AGI, Escribanía 1033B, L. 28, no. 37, Consejo Año de 1668.

63. AGI, Escribanía 1033B, L. 28, no. 37, Consejo Año de 1668.

64. AGI, Escribanía 1033B, L. 28, no. 37, Consejo Año de 1668.

65. Gunvor Simonsen and Rasmus Christensen, "Together in a Small Boat: Slavery's Fugitives in the Lesser Antilles," *William and Mary Quarterly* 80, no. 4 (October 2023), 611–46; James Dator, "Frank Travels: Space, Power and Slave Mobility in the British Leeward Islands, c. 1700–1730," *Slavery & Abolition* 36, no. 2 (2015): 335–59. Recently, scholars have shown that Africans and their descendants surmounted extensive maritime distances in their efforts to ameliorate their circumstances. See Elena A. Schneider, "A Narrative of Escape: Self Liberation by Sea and the Mental Worlds of the Enslaved," *Slavery & Abolition* 42, no. 3 (2021): 484–501; Kevin Dawson, "A Sea of Caribbean Islands: Maritime Maroons in the Greater Caribbean," *Slavery & Abolition* 42, no. 3 (2021): 428–48.

66. Pawson and Buisseret, *Port Royal*, 89.

67. Pawson and Buisseret, *Port Royal*, 51.

68. AGI, Escribanía 1033B, L. 28, no. 37, Consejo Año de 1668.

69. AGI, Escribanía 1033B, L. 28, no. 37, Consejo Año de 1668.

70. The 1664 Jamaican slave code granted slave owners practically unlimited leeway in the punishment of self-liberated slaves, legislating only against the "wanton" killing of enslaved Africans. See TNA, CO 139, "An Act for the better ordering and governing of Negro Slaves," fols. 66–69. For analysis of these laws, see Rugemer, "Development of Mastery and Race"; Stephanie Hunt-Kennedy, "'Had his nose cropt for being formerly runaway': Disability and the Bodies of Fugitive Slaves in the British Caribbean," *Slavery & Abolition* 41, no. 2 (2020): 212–33.

71. AGI, Santo Domingo 157, r. 2, no. 49, "Cartas de D. Juan Pérez de Guzmán, gobernador de Puerto Rico," August 31, 1664, fol. 1v.

72. See, for example, Landers, *Black Society in Spanish Florida*, esp. chap. 2; Rupert, "Seeking the Water of Baptism."

73. AGI, Escribanía 1033B, L. 28, no. 37, Consejo Año de 1668.

74. Donald Rowland, "Spanish Occupation of the Island of Old Providence, or Santa Catalina, 1641–1670," *Hispanic American Historical Review* 15, no. 3 (August, 1935): 300–305.

75. AGI, Escribanía 1033B, L. 28, no. 37, Consejo Año de 1668.

76. TNA CO 1/23, nos. 60, 60 I, "Deposition of Robt. Rawlinsone, Isaac Webber, and Richard Cree, before Sir Thos. Modyford, concerning the Spaniards dealings with the English upon Providence Island," Jamaica, October 5, 1668.

77. For an example of the kinds of prisoner of war negotiations that applied to Europe, see TNA, CO1/14, no. 1, "Agreement between the Marquis of Caracena, Lieut. Governor of Flanders, and General Monck, for the exchange of prisoners of war," Brussels, April 22/March 2, 1660.

78. O'Malley, *Final Passages*, 91.

79. AGI, Escribanía 1033B, L. 28, no. 37, Consejo Año de 1668.

80. Jamaican authorities sometimes demanded that slave owners in Jamaica send their enslaved men to work on the fortifications. At other times, colonial records refer to men being "hired," which undoubtedly included enslaved men whose wages went to their enslaver. See Pawson and Buisseret, *Port Royal*, 37–38.

81. AGI, Escribanía 1033B, L. 28, no. 37, Consejo Año de 1668.

82. AGI, Santo Domingo 157, r. 2, no. 49, "Cartas de D. Juan Pérez de Guzmán, gobernador de Puerto Rico," August 31, 1664-08-31, fol. 1v.

83. García-Montón, *Genoese Entrepreneurship*, 111–52.

84. For more on Castellón's family, see: Alexis Rives Pantoja, Juan Pose Quincosa, and Alex Rives Cecin, *De los cacicazgos a San Cristóbal de La Habana: Crítica a la leyenda Negra del exterminio indígena en Cuba* (Buenos Aires: Ashpa, 2015), 208–9.

85. AGI, Escribanía 1033B, L. 28, no. 37, Consejo Año de 1668.

86. AGI, Escribanía 1190, "Sentencia de la residencia de Pedro de Morales, gobernador que fue de Cuba," July 2, 1667, unfoliated; Schmitt, "Centering Spanish Jamaica," 697–726; Leví Marrero, *Cuba: Economía y Sociedad* vol. I (San Juan: Editorial San Juan, 1972), 132.

87. García-Montón, *Genoese Entrepreneurship*, 104.

88. AGI, Escribanía 1033B, L. 28, no. 37, Consejo Año de 1668.

89. Or, in the words of Saidiya Hartman, a use of the subjunctive to fashion "a narrative based upon archival research." See Hartman, "Venus in Two Acts," 11.

90. García-Montón, *Genoese Entrepreneurship*, 158.

91. Nemser, *Infrastructures of Race*, 15.

92. AGI, Escribanía 1033B, L. 28, no. 37, Consejo Año de 1668.

Conclusion

1. AGI, Contaduría 1480, "Carta de Capitán Salvador de la Peña visto en la Junta de Guerra," September 6, 1646, fols. 7v–8r.

2. Holly Brewer, "Creating a Common Law of Slavery for England and Its New World Empire," *Law and History Review* 39, no. 4 (November 2021): 765–834.

3. Brewer, "Creating a Common Law of Slavery."

4. This is too large of a historiography to cover in its entirety. For important works on connections between the rise of slavery, the plantation complex, and sugar in the English and French Caribbean, see Dunn, *Sugar and Slaves*; Gabriel Debien, *Les Esclaves aux Antilles françaises (XVIIe-XVIIIe siècles)* (Fort-de-France, Martinique: Société d'Histoire de la Martinique, 1974); Sidney Mintz, *Sweetness and Power: The Place of Sugar in Modern History* (New York: Penguin, 1985); Curtin, *Rise and Fall of the Plantation Complex*; Eltis, *Rise of African Slavery in the Americas*; B. W. Higman, "The Sugar Revolution," *Economic History Review* 53, no. 2 (2000): 213–36; Schwartz, *Tropical Babylons*; Menard, *Sweet Negotiations*; Trevor Burnard, *Planters, Merchants, and Slaves: Plantation Societies in British America, 1650–1820* (Chicago: University of Chicago Press, 2015); Martjin Van den Bel, "French Governors and Dutch Merchants: Comparing the First Sugar Plantations in the French West Indies and Barbados, 1638–1664," *Journal of Early American History* 12, nos. 2–3 (2022): 121–68; Nuala Zahedieh, "The Rise of 'King Sugar' and Enslaved Labor in Early English Jamaica," *Early American Studies* 20, no. 4 (2022): 619–39.

5. Joseph C. Miller has argued that even global histories of slavery tend to use the model of racialized, chattel slavery—specifically as it developed in the context of the nineteenth-century North American South—as a model against which other slaving practices are compared. See Miller, *Problem of Slavery as History*, chap. 1.

6. Phil Morgan, "Slavery in the British Caribbean," in *The Cambridge World History of Slavery*, vol. 3: *AD 1420–AD 1804* (Cambridge: Cambridge University Press, 2011), 379. For a similar argument in the French Caribbean, see Laurent Dubois, "Slavery in the French Caribbean, 1635–1804," in *Cambridge World History of Slavery*, 3:437.

7. AGI, Santa Fé 38, r. 6, no. 166, "Carta de D. García Girón, Gobernador de Cartagena," January 30, 1621, unfoliated,. For the printed account, see *Verdadera relacion del viage, y sucesso de los caravelones, galeoncetes de la guarda de Cartagena de las Indias, y su costa. Y la grandiose vitoria que antenido contra los cossarios piratas en aquel mar* (Seville: por Bartolome Gomez de Pastrana, 1621).

8. John Rolfe to Edwin Sandys, January 1619/20, in Susan Myra Kingsbury, ed., *The Records of the Virginia Company of London*, vol. 3 (Washington, D.C., 1933), 243; Engel Sluiter, "New Light on the '20. and Odd Negroes' Arriving in Virginia, August 1619," *William and Mary Quarterly* 54, no. 2 (April 1997): 395–98.

9. The year 1619 entered widespread public discourse as a result of a *New York Times Magazine* special issue about the legacies of race and slavery in US history. See Nikole Hannah-Jones, Caitlin Roper, Ilena Silverman, and Jake Silverstein, eds., "The 1619 Project," *New York Times Magazine*, August 18, 2019. The editors of the project expanded the magazine issue into a monograph that reiterated the arguments about seeing 1619 as a foundational date in American history. See *The 1619 Project: A New Origin Story* (New York: One World, 2021).

10. There are important exceptions to this, including John Thornton, "The African Experience of the '20. and Odd Negroes' Arriving in Virginia in 1619," *William and Mary Quarterly* 55, no. 3 (July 1998): 421–34; Philip D. Morgan, "Virginia Slavery in Atlantic Context, ca. 1550 to ca. 1650," in *Virginia 1619: Slavery and Freedom in the Making of English America*, ed. Paul Musselwhite, Peter D. Mancall, and James Horn (Chapel Hill: University of North Carolina Press, 2019); *Beyond 1619: The Atlantic Origins of America Slavery*, ed. Paul J. Polgar, Marc H. Lerner, and Jesse Cromwell (Philadelphia: University of Pennsylvania Press, 2023).

11. For a model of making these connections in the seventeenth century, see Linford D. Fisher, "'Dangerous Designes': The 1676 Barbados Act to Prohibit New England Indian Slave Importation," *William and Mary Quarterly* 71, no. 1 (January 2014): 99–124. Excellent scholarship on this issue exists for the eighteenth and nineteenth centuries, especially around the Haitian Revolution. See, for example, Brett Rushforth, *Bonds of Alliance: Indigenous and Atlantic Slaveries in New France* (Chapel Hill: University of North Carolina Press, 2012), esp. chap. 3; Ashli White, *Encountering Revolution: Haiti and the Making of the Early Republic* (Baltimore: Johns Hopkins University Press, 2010); James Alexander Dun, *Dangerous Neighbors: Making the Haitian Revolution in Early America* (Philadelphia: University of Pennsylvania Press, 2016); Brandon R. Byrd, *The Black Republic: African Americans and the Fate of Haiti* (Philadelphia: University of Pennsylvania Press, 2020).

INDEX

abandonment of captives, 30
acamátêti likia (Kalinago phrase for traffickers), 44, 227n105
Acosta Corniel, Lissette, 10
admiralty courts, 139, 163–64. *See also* international courts
Aguilera, Melchior de, 123–24
Aguira, Juan de, 147–50
Andrés, 77, 107
Anglo-Dutch War. *See* Second Anglo-Dutch War
Angola, Catalina, 17, 109–10, 129–31, 196, 205, 210
Angola, Francisco, 109
Angola, Geronimo, 105–6
Angola, Juan, 109
Angola, Ventura, 100
Angolan wave, 83–84
Antonio, 51–53
Aram, Bethany, 10, 42
Araña, Juan de, 129
Arará, Juan, 109
archival silences, 8, 210–11, 217–18n23
Archivo General de Indias (AGI), ix–xi, 7–9, 218n26
Arena, Carolyn, 14
Arguin, 26
Arguin captives, 26, 29, 40
Arisenendi, Nicolas de, 156
arribadas forzosas (forced arrivals), 31
Aruba, 146
asiento, Grillo and Lomelín: "Africanized" slavery and, 174; attempts to end informal trade and, 140; contours of, 17–19; end of Iberian Union and, 157–58; formalization of intra-Caribbean slave trade and, 17–18, 117, 153, 157–58; *jueces conservadores* and policing of, 200; monopoly companies and, 159; racialized vulnerability of

captives and, 186–87; response of English colonists to, 166; right to captives and, 173; sanctuary policy and, 18–19, 174, 199; status of arriving people of African descent and, 200–201; supply and transshipment in, 138–39; trafficking networks and, 138, 150, 153. *See also* Castellón y Sánchez Pereira, Nicolás
asiento, Portuguese, 7, 25–26, 117, 157, 200
Association Island. *See* Tortuga
Atlantic Creole culture, 235n18
Audiencia of Santo Domingo, 107

Bacalar, 89–91
Balanta, Martin, 109
Barbados, 64, 139, 146
Barbotière, Monsieur de, 37
Bauer, Ralph, 5
Beck, Matthias, 147–51, 152, 153
Bélain d'Esnambuc, Pierre: death of, 102; dyewood trade and, 92–93; making a voyage and, 12; racialization and, 208–9; St. Christopher and, 3–4, 16, 47, 57–58, 60, 75; trafficking networks and, 1–2, 5–6, 53, 60; treaty of St. Christopher and, 60–63
Bell, Philip, 105
Bergara, Josef de, 101–3
Biafra, Francisco, 105–6, 109–11, 121–22, 127
Biafra, Juan, 105–6
Blessing (ship), 166, 181, 184
Block, Kristen, 180
Boccara, Michael, 91
bodily markings, 127
Boll, Eric, 67–68
Bonaire, 146
Bontekoe (ship), 148
Bourdon, Jean, 34
Breton, Raymond, 44

ACKNOWLEDGMENTS

The book exists because of the tremendous generosity of friends, family, colleagues, and institutions. I am truly humbled by the number of smart people who graciously gave their time and energy to make this book better. With over a decade's worth of people to thank, I am sure that I have forgotten important interlocutors and friends and hope they know how much I appreciate them nonetheless. An initial thanks to the Hull Memorial Publication Fund of Cornell University, whose grant supported the publication of this book.

Nearly fifteen years ago, I had the enormous good fortune to begin an MA program in history at the University of Utah. My time at the U was transformative because of the support, mentorship, and enthusiasm of Rebecca Horn and Eric Hinderaker. Their doors were always open, and our long discussions about comparative history set me on a path that has culminated in this book. Nadja Durbach was a wonderful mentor and model as I thought about pursuing a PhD, and Wesley Sasaki-Uemura made sure that I was ready once I got there. My deepest thanks go to Eric, who encouraged me to apply to William and Mary to work with Brett Rushforth.

It is no exaggeration to say that this book would not exist without Brett. Over my years at William and Mary and since, Brett has been unflagging in his support of me and this book. His scholarly generosity had no bounds, as he was always willing to read countless drafts critically and carefully while pushing me to sharpen my arguments with good humor and care. Brett is a model of everything that I aspire to be as a scholar and a person, and I cannot thank him enough. Brett, you're the GOAT—thank you. I've also been lucky that this book found a home at the University of Pennsylvania Press with the incomparable Robert Lockhart, whose advice, edits, and support made this process so much easier and the book much better as a result. Thank you, Bob.

William and Mary was an incredible intellectual home for seven years, and I am so grateful to the scholars and friends who made that space so fulfilling. Paul Mapp helped guide my thinking and never failed to make time to discuss big ideas or read drafts. His good humor made the process a joy.

Unmatched in intellectual generosity or expertise is Guillaume Aubert, and I am extremely grateful to have received his mentorship and guidance at William and Mary. Fabricio Prado arrived at the perfect moment. His expertise in illicit economies and deep passion for transnational histories along with his willingness to read drafts and recommend readings made this work so much better. I met the brilliant Molly Warsh while she was a postdoctoral fellow in Williamsburg, and she has been a steadfast supporter ever since. I am so grateful to her for believing in me and this project over the years. Tom McSweeney and Fahad Bishara made me feel welcome in the legal history community and provided critical feedback at an opportune time. Richard Turits pushed me to think more critically about the so-what of my research. Other faculty at William and Mary made those seven years some of my happiest. The Dread Sovereign Frederick Corney kept the ship afloat with a perfect combination of wit and kindness, and I am grateful for all of his mentorship—big and small—over the years. Andrew Fisher stepped in at a critical moment to get me through the nineteenth century, and it is because of his guidance and good humor that comps was not my last stand. Cindy Hahamovitch and Scott Nelson were models of scholarly generosity and kindness. Leisa Meyer is a force unto herself, and I am grateful to have learned from her both in the classroom and out. I am especially grateful to everyone at the Omohundro Institute of Early American History and Culture. Christopher Grasso was a model educator who took the time on numerous occasions to discuss writing and argument, both of which I am better at because of him. Karin Wulf has been a tremendous influence on me as a scholar and I have valued her support and kindness over the years. The arrival of Joshua Piker toward the end of my time in graduate school enriched the scholarly community immeasurably—I am grateful for his support, keen editing, and mentoring. Nadine Zimmerli believed in this project before I did, and she has been a continued source of support and friendship. Thanks, too, to Nick Popper, whose sharp wit and friendship has made this process infinitely easier and more enjoyable. I was also lucky enough to receive informal mentoring from many of the postdoctoral fellows at the OI while I was a graduate student. Special thanks to Daniel Livesay, Carolyn Arena, Shauna Sweeney, Deborah Hamer, Alexander Dubé, Elena Schneider, and Allison Bigelow.

William and Mary was made intellectually and personally rich by all of the tremendous scholars and dear friends that I met there. I am grateful to Kristen Beales for all of the late-night discussions about research, Quakers, and sports. I couldn't ask for a better friend. I have long relied on Michaela

Kleber for her sharp wit, French expertise, and friendship—thank you. Caylin Carbonell's feedback and support during the writing process was invaluable. I was extremely lucky to enter graduate school with my cohort. Hannah Bailey is the most tremendous person, and I am so thankful for the pie deliveries, Prairie Home Companion trips, and so much more. Cara Elliott is one of the smartest people I know and capable of navigating Boston traffic on very little sleep. Beth (and Alan) Wood came into our cohort later, but their presence made it a family—from the pirate parties to the bouncy house, I am so grateful to those two for being the glue that kept us all together. Spencer Wells and Katie Snyder made this westerner feel more comfortable out east. I am grateful to Laura Ansley, Ian Tonat, Alex Finely, James Hill, Laurel Dean, Christopher Jones, Nathaniel Holly, Peter Olsen-Harbich, and Molly Perry for feedback and friendship over the years.

Numerous people have offered timely and sage feedback on my work, but Lauren Benton deserves special praise here. Despite not knowing me before I reached out, she agreed to participate in a manuscript workshop and read a version of my dissertation with close care and attention. Her brilliant insights on the role of captive-taking in the wider processes that my dissertation described served as the spark for this book, and I am extremely grateful for her support then and since. David Wheat has also been an unwavering ally in the process of working on the sixteenth- and seventeenth-century Caribbean from the very beginning. From helping me decipher paleography to serving as a critical and constructive outside reader on articles and this book, I am deeply indebted to David for his time and generosity. Gregory E. O'Malley also agreed to read this book manuscript and offered tremendously generous feedback at a critical moment. It was a great joy and privilege to receive feedback from him, whose work I found so foundational to my own.

Working in different languages and across archives was made much easier through the generosity of many people. Marc Eagle has always offered excellent advice and shared his work with me—it has been a joy to call him a friend. Kristen Block has been a generous and supportive mentor, interlocutor, and friend over the years. I have learned a tremendous amount from Juan José Ponce Vázquez and am grateful for his support, including his willingness to share key archival sources at critical moments. As a long-suffering Phillies fan, I am also grateful for his friendship. From his scholarship to his mentoring, Jesse Cromwell has been an ardent supporter of my work, and it is a joy to get to (finally) thank him in print. I value deeply Jack Bouchard's friendship as we both navigated the job market and book writing process and am grateful for all of his smart feedback. Thanks also to the archivists and librarians who supported this research, especially the archivists and staff at the Archivo General de Indias.

I have been lucky to call Cornell University home as I finished the book manuscript and am grateful to all of my colleagues here. Tamara Loos has been a chair par excellence and has gone above and beyond in ways big and small to help me finish this book. My mentors, Sandra Greene and Rachel Weil, have offered tremendous support over the past six years and I am grateful, especially, to Rachel for her willingness to read drafts and discuss ideas. The assistant professors' writing group has offered the kind of advice, feedback, and collegiality that make finishing a book so much easier. Thanks to Mara Yue Du, Cristina Florea, Mayer Juni, Ruth Lawlor, Nicholas Mulder, Kristin Roebuck, Rachel Sandwell, Paraska Tolan-Szkilnik, Camille Suarez, Michell Chresfield, and Justine Modica. Cornell and upstate New York have been particularly rich places to work, and I am grateful to the community of early Americanists here. Thanks to Jon Parmenter for his mentorship at Cornell and his willingness to read drafts of my work. Ernest Bassi has made Cornell an exciting place to work on the greater Caribbean, and I am grateful for his collegiality, intellectual generosity, and good humor. Pablo M. Sierra Silva has offered excellent feedback and support at critical moments. Tessa Murphy deserves more praise than I could fit in these acknowledgments. I don't know if she would have let me crash on the floor of her hotel room at the Association of Caribbean Historians' meeting in Curaçao if she knew what she was getting herself into, but I am so grateful to have her as an upstate New York colleague and for all of her support, keen insights, and mentorship over the years.

Numerous institutions have supported this work. The McNeil Center for Early American Studies provided me with a tremendous intellectual community to begin the process of rethinking and rewriting the dissertation. It was a joy and an honor to work alongside Daniel K. Richter, whose leadership of the McNeil and support of junior scholars was matched only by his good humor. Laura Keenan-Spero always lent an ear, and I am grateful to her for her support. Zara Anishanslin proved an impeccable mentor, and I am grateful to her for all of her advice and confidence-boosting when I went on the market. Jessica Choppin Roney deserves special thanks as a model of scholarly generosity who made Philadelphia a fun and productive place to be. Kathy Brown, Emma Hart, Christopher Heaney, M. Scott Heerman, Carolyn Eastman, Nancy O. Gallman, Michelle McDonald, and Roderick McDonald provided immensely useful feedback at critical moments and created a warm, productive scholarly community. Many predoctoral fellows offered feedback that sharpened my work, and their friendship provided good cheer over those two years. Elizabeth Ellis, Elise Mitchell, Lila Chambers, Timo McGregor, Sherri Cummings, and Peter Olson-Harbich deserve special thanks for their feedback and friendship.

I am grateful to several other institutions that provided me with space to work and a community of scholars. The John Carter Brown Library and the National Endowment for the Humanities afforded me a year away from teaching that proved indispensable for finishing this book. I am grateful to the wonderful scholarly community of the JCB, especially my fellow long-term fellows. Linford Fisher deserves special praise for his support of this project. Lin pushed me to think about change over time and offered important advice and feedback on my work during my time at the JCB. I am also grateful to him for creating a wonderful community in Providence. Carmen Alveal was a delightful companion and interlocutor. Thanks also to Michael Becker for his critical reading of my work and willingness to share sources and his time. Vikram Tamboli, Suzanne Litrel, Viviana Quintero Marquez, and Leo Garofalo provided essential feedback at various points. While a short-term fellow at the JCB, I also had the good fortune to meet Lauren MacDonald, whose feedback and friendship I value deeply. Thanks also to Randy Sparks for his mentorship in Providence and for buying two hungry graduate students dinner. While a W. M. Keck Foundation Fellow at the Huntington Library, I was fortunate enough to receive feedback and mentoring from a wonderful group of scholars. Roy Ritchie generously invited me over for dinner, and I am thankful to Molly Warsh, Mark Hanna, Dana Velasco Murillo, Alejandra Dubcovsky, Peter Mancall, Steve Pincus, Hayley Negrin, Daniel Livesay, and Carla Pestana for making my time in Pasadena so productive and enjoyable. Thanks also to Amanda Herbert at the Folger Institute for her support and mentorship.

Numerous conferences and working groups have read and commented on some of the work in this book. For their warm welcome and essential feedback, I am grateful to the students and faculty at New York University's Atlantic World Seminar, especially Nicole Eustace, Rebecca Goetz, and Susanah Romney. Augustus Mosse extended a generous invitation to Princeton University's Colonial and Revolutionary Americas Workshop, and Elizabeth Ellis and Michael Blaakman made me feel welcome and provided excellent feedback. Special thanks go to my Cornell colleagues Durba Ghosh and Robert Travers for their support both at Princeton and at Cornell. Durba deserves special praise for making me feel welcome in Ithaca over the course of our socially-distanced walks. Beginning a tenure-track job during a global pandemic was a challenge, but Durba made the transition so much easier. Providence College's Seminar on Early American History provided critical feedback on a particularly sticky chapter, and I am grateful to Adrian Weimer for the invitation. Thanks too to Owen Stanwood for his feedback and support. Junko Takeda, Brian Brege, and Karl Offen provided an excellent space to workshop Chapter 1 at Syracuse University's Early Modern Connected Histories Workshop, and I am grateful for their feedback, especially Karl's enthusiasm for this project and willingness to share sources with me. Thanks also to the graduate students at Brown University for their feedback during my Early American Graduate Seminar. I am deeply grateful to Christopher Jones (for many things, including being such an ardent supporter of my work and a dear friend) and Eric Herschthal for their invitation to the University of Utah's Rocky Mountain Seminar on Early American History and to the graduate students and faculty who offered important feedback. Holly Brewer deserves special thanks for her early and continued support of my work, and I am grateful for her invitation to participate in the Washington Area Early American Seminar, where I received invaluable feedback.

Many individuals have taken the time to offer me advice, mentorship, and feedback over the years. Erika Denise Edwards's belief in me and this project helped buoy me along during some particular difficult moments. Simon Newman has been both generous and astute in his willingness to read my work and provide feedback. April Lee Hatfield read the dissertation in its entirety and offered crucial feedback that allowed me to rewrite it. Thanks also to Rachel Herrmann for her support and good cheer. Randy Browne has been a constant supporter for which I am deeply grateful. For comments and advice over the years, I am also particularly grateful to Camilla Townsend, Nancy van Deusen, Margaret Newell, Alison Games, Rachel O'Toole, Tatiana Seijas, Katharine Gerbner, Matt Childs, Rob Taber, Ariela Gross, Marcus Rediker, Mary Hicks, Martha Few, Wim Klooster, Melissa Morris, Keith Richards, Michelle McKinley, Paul Polgar, Nuala Zahedieh, Daniel Nemser, Shavagne Scott, and Paul Musselwhite. To my early Caribbeanist working group—Jordan Smith, Ernesto Mercado-Montero, Tessa Murphy, Mary Draper, and Katherine Johnston—thank you all so much for your feedback and friendship. The excellent maps in this book were produced by John Wyatt Greenlee, and I am grateful to him for his patience working with me.

My family has been particularly supportive. A deep thanks to Margaret Shaw for always opening her home to Ben and me when we needed to get out west and for her support and kindness. I couldn't ask for a better mother-in-law. Thanks, too, to Brady Shaw for the adventures and to Mary Watt for her wit and humor. I miss Rod Shaw and Harmon Watt and wish they were both here so that I could thank them for welcoming me into such a wonderful family.

I am deeply grateful to my brother and his family. Thank you, Matt, for being the best big brother ever and for always asking when my book was going to be done. (It's done!) Now you can start asking about book two. Trinia Hunt has been immeasurably supportive over the years and opened her home to us with warmth and kindness—I'm lucky to have you as a sister. I have been working on this book as long as Hunter Schmitt has been around, and it has been such a joy to watch him grow into such a smart, confident, and capable young man. Thank you to Lauren Schmitt for all of her help picking thrift-store outfits and for her humor and kindness. Being an aunt to such wonderful kiddos has been such a joy and I love you both. I owe so much to my parents, Stephen and Carol. My dad always pushed me to do the best I could, and I am grateful that he was always there for me. My mother taught me to love books and to take joy in life. Thank you both.

In the end though, this book is dedicated to Ben Shaw, with whom I struck up a conversation twenty years ago that hasn't stopped since. What can I say about someone who is everything? Thank you, Ben, for bringing meaning, humor, and contentment to every single day—I wouldn't be here without you, and I am so grateful to get to share this life with you. Te quiero más cada día.